The Trojan Horse

To the people of Alberta

If liberty means anything at all, it means the right to tell people what they do not want to hear.

George Orwell

THE TROJAN HORSE

ALBERTA AND THE FUTURE OF CANADA

Trevor Harrison and Gordon Laxer

BLACK ROSE BOOKS

Montréal/New York
London

Black Rose Books No.Y229
Hardcover ISBN: 1-551640-35-X
Paperback ISBN: 1-551640-34-1
Library of Congress No. 95-79349

Canadian Cataloguing in Publication Data

Main entry under title:
The trojan horse: Alberta and the future of Canada
Includes bibliographical references.
ISBN: 1-551640-35-X (bound). —
ISBN 1-551640-34-1 (pbk.)

1. Alberta—Economic policy. 2. Alberta—Economic
conditions—1945- . 3. Canada—Economic policy— 1991- .
4. Canada—Economic conditions—1991- . I. Laxer, Gordon, 1944-
II. Harrison, Trevor, 1952- .

HC117.A5T76 1995 338.97123 C95-900717-2

Mailing Address

BLACK ROSE BOOKS
C.P. 1258
Succ. Place du Parc
Montréal, Québec
H2W 2R3 Canada

BLACK ROSE BOOKS
340 Nagel Drive
Cheektowaga, New York
14225 USA

A publication of the Institute of Policy Alternatives of Montréal (IPAM)

Printed in Canada

Contents

SECTORS

PEOPLE

Acknowledgments

This book would not have been possible without the efforts of many people. We first want to acknowledge the efforts of Larry Pratt, without whose initial participation and inspiration this project would not have been possible. Secondly, we wish to thank the authors for their co-operation and hard work in writing and rewriting their chapters. They generously accepted some of our comments and suggestions, and showed frequent good sense in ignoring many others.

We want further to express our appreciation to all those who attended an Authors Forum, held at the Stollery Centre at the University of Alberta, in January 1995. In order to protect the names of the innocent, we will not identify them here; but they know who they are and their comments and suggestions were an invaluable part of putting this book together.

Special thanks goes to Fran Russell of the Population Research Laboratory for her technical assistance; also to our ever-willing research assistant, Peter Puplampu; and Margaret McCutcheon who provided much needed help in "proofing" the manuscript.

We want also to acknowledge the efforts of our publisher, Dimitrios Roussopoulos, who took on the task of publishing this book with a sense of urgency; and Natalie Klym, Linda Barton, and Frances Slingerland, also of Black Rose Books, for their efforts in making this book a reality.

Finally, we want to thank Judith, Terri and our children for their sacrifices during the period when this book was being conceived and written. (A special thanks to Terri who went beyond the call of spousal allegiance in helping to proofread some of the chapters.) The book would not have been possible, and would mean much less, without them.

Any errors or omissions are, of course, the responsibility of the editors.

G. L. and T. W. H.

NOTES ON CONTRIBUTORS

Maude Barlow is chairperson of the Council of Canadians and a nationally-reknowned speaker and activist. She is author of *Parcel of Rogues* and *Take Back the Nation* (with Bruce Campbell), and co-author (with Heatherjane Robertson) of the best-selling book, *Class Warfare*.

David Cooper is CGA professor of accountancy at the University of Alberta, founding joint-editor of the academic journal, *Critical Perspectives on Accounting*, and author and co-editor of seven books and over forty articles.

Gurston Dacks is professor of political science at the University of Alberta. His teaching and research focus is on the politics of Alberta, the Yukon, and the Northwest Territories, as well as issues related to First Nations self-government.

Claude Denis is professor in sociology with Faculté St. Jean in Edmonton and adjunct professor of sociology at the University of Alberta. He is author of a soon to be published book on the NDP in Québec.

Sten Drugge is associate professor of economics at the University of Alberta. He specializes in regional economic analysis and macro-economic policy.

Fred C. Engelmann is a retired professor of political science at the University of Alberta. He is co-author of *Canadian Political Parties* and has written numerous articles on politics.

Joyce Green is a doctoral candidate in the Department of Political Science at the University of Alberta. She previously served as policy officer in the executive council office of the government of Yukon.

Trevor Harrison is a sessional instructor in both the Department of Sociology and the Department of Political Science at the University of Alberta. He is the author of *Of Passionate Intensity: Right-Wing Populism and the Reform Party of Canada*.

Joanne Helmer has been an editorial writer and columnist for the *Lethbridge Herald* for the past twelve years. She now writes news stories.

Gordon Laxer is a political economist and professor in the Department of Sociology at the University of Alberta. He is the author of *Open for Business. The Roots of Foreign Ownership in Canada*, which won the John Porter Award in 1992 as the best book written in Sociology and Anthropology in Canada.

Jim Marino is head of the Confederation of Alberta Faculties Association and Professor of English at the University of Alberta.

John McInnis is a former New Democratic member of the Alberta Legislative Assembly and Official Opposition Critic for Environment and Forestry. He is currently an executive member of the Alberta Environmental Network and a member of the Canadian Environmental Network task force on international forestry issues.

Melville L. McMillan is professor and chair of the Department of Economics at the University of Alberta. He specializes in public sector economics, and has served as a consultant to both government and international agencies.

George Melnyk is the former executive director of the Alberta Foundation for the Literary Arts, a former president of both the Alberta Publishers Association and the Writers Guild of Alberta, and a well-known nonfiction author, who is currently researching and writing the Literary History of Alberta.

Jonathan Murphy is the former executive director of the Edmonton Social Planning Council. He is current director of the Population Research Laboratory at the University of Alberta.

Dean Neu is an associate professor in the Faculty of Management at the University of Calgary and a member of the Alberta Institute of Chartered Accountants.

Simon Renouf is a well-known Edmonton lawyer, with an interest in health care policy issues over the past twenty years.

Heather-jane Robertson is director of professional development for the Canadian Teachers' Federation, an executive member of the Canadian Centre for Policy Alternatives, and co-author (with Maude Barlow) of the best-selling book, *Class Warfare.*

Gillian Steward is a prominent free-lance journalist and former editor of the *Calgary Herald.*

David Stewart is assistant professor of political science at the University of Alberta. He is currently involved in a study of leadership selection in Alberta.

Jeff Taylor is professor of labour studies at Athabasca University.

Linda Trimble is associate professor of political science at the University of Alberta. She is presently editing a book (with Jane Arscott of Dalhousie University), *In the Presence of Women: Representation in Canadian Government.*

Ian Urquhart is associate professor of political science at the University of Alberta and co-author (with Larry Pratt) of *The Last Great Forest.*

Allan A. Warrack is a business professor at the University of Alberta. He holds his doctorate from the University of Alberta and was former Alberta cabinet minister (1971-79) during the Lougheed administration.

Barry K. Wilson is Ottawa correspondent for the *Western Producer.* A long-time researcher in Western social, political, and agricultural affairs, he is currently working on a biography of Benedict Arnold.

CHRONOLOGY OF EVENTS, 1992-1995

1992

Sept. 9 — Don Getty announces his resignation as Tory leader and premier.

Nov. 28 — Nancy Betkowski beats Ralph Klein by one vote (16,393 to 16,392) in the first round of voting to pick Getty's successor.

Dec. 5 — Ralph Klein wins the Tory leadership over Betkowski, taking 46,245 votes to Betkowski's 31,722. Most of Klein's support comes from rural Alberta and Calgary.

1993

Mar. 29 — The government of Alberta provides a $50 million loan guarantee for Pacific Western Airlines (PWA).

Apr. 15 — Family and Social Services Minister Mike Cardinal announces a program in which 47,819 welfare clients (about 52 percent of all welfare recipients) will be put to work in the private sector, forest fire prevention, and clearing of land. Between March 1993 and August 1994, the number of adults on social assistance declines from about 122,000 to 68,000.

Apr. 30 — Under intense public pressure, Ralph Klein announces changes to MLA pensions. MLAs elected since 1989 get their pension contributions refunded. Those elected before 1989 still receive a pension but at a reduced rate. The pension plan for future MLAs is abolished.

May 6 — Treasurer Jim Dinning brings down a pre-election budget in which there are no tax increases or new taxes, but increases in health care premiums, job cuts in the public sector, and reductions in social assistance.

May 18 — A provincial election is called. Liberal leader Laurence Decore calls for "brutal cuts"; Ralph Klein counters with "major cuts"; New Democrat leader Ray Martin wants corporations to pay their share of taxes.

June 16 — Ralph Klein's Progressive Conservatives are elected, taking fifty-one of eighty-three seats, 44.3 percent of the popular vote. The Liberals win the remaining thirty-two seats, with 40 percent of the vote. The Opposition New Democrats are annihilated, winning no seats and only 11 percent of the vote, their worst performance since 1971.

Sept. 1 — Beatrice Foods gets a $2 million loan to build a cookie factory in Edmonton. The Alberta government and federal government contributed $1 million each.

Sept. 2 — Steve West announces the privatization of the Alberta Liquor Control Board's (ALCB) retail operations. Later, the government announces that it will also privatize the ALCB's wholesale operations.

Sept. 15 — A private members bill, Pr 4, "the Gimbel Foundation Act," is introduced in the legislature by Tory MLA Frank Bruseker. The bill would allow Dr. Howard Gimbel, a prominent eye surgeon already operating two private eye clinics in Alberta, to set up a "nonprofit" foundation which critics claim would open the flood-gates to private health services. Under criticism, the bill is later withdrawn, but with promises from the government that it will be brought back.

Sept. 18 — 2,000 Albertans march on the legislature to protest against cuts to social assistance.

Oct. 28 — Junior high and high school students stage demonstrations protesting against cuts in education in towns and cities throughout Alberta. In Edmonton, about 900 storm the legislature building and in Calgary 3,000 are involved.

1994

Feb. 5 — Ross Harvey succeeds Ray Martin as leader of the New Democrats.

Feb. 24 — Treasurer Jim Dinning brings down the budget. It contains no outright tax increases, but does raise individual health premiums from $30 to $32 per month, and family premiums from $60 to $64 per month, while seniors earning more than $18,200 per year also begin paying medical premiums. Also, it is announced that 1,800 more civil service jobs will be cut. The deficit, meanwhile, is held to $1.5 billion.

Feb. — The number of calls to the Edmonton Distress Line hits 3,248, an increase of 33 percent over the previous February. The number of calls related to suicide, family violence, financial concerns, and unemployment all rise significantly.

Apr. 19 — Following the murder by three young offenders of a young mother in her home, Ralph Klein and several other Tory MLAs call for the execution of anyone convicted of murder, including children as young as eight.

Sept. 1 — A study commissioned by the Canadian Centre for Policy Alternatives finds that privatization of the ALCB has led to higher liquor prices, decreased selection, reduced government revenues, and a rise in liquor-related offenses. The report concludes that the only positive result arising from privatization is increased availability.

Sept. 8 — 15,000 people turn out to a rally in support of keeping the Grey Nuns Hospital, a six-year old, full-time hospital in southeast Edmonton. It is the second giant rally to save the hospital. Health Minister Shirley McClellan says the rallies won't change her mind about turning the hospital into a community health centre.

Sept. 23 — Saying that Alberta's health care system had hit the "red line," Dr. Fred Moriarty, president of the Alberta Medical Association, calls for an eighteen-month moratorium in government cuts.

Oct. — Figures released by the ALCB show a net of $378.5 million dollars in 1993, the first (partial) year of privatization, down more than $26 million from the previous year.

Oct. 12 — Deputy Premier Ken Kowalski, the most powerful minister in the cabinet and the man whose support ensured Klein's election as leader in 1992, is dumped from the cabinet. He is promised a plum patronage job as head of the Energy Resources Conservation Board, but in the face of pressure from the oil patch and the public, Klein later rescinds the offer. Kowalski stays on as a backbencher and occasional government critic.

Nov. 8 — Under severe pressure from the Liberals and the public, the Tories withdraw controversial Bill 57, the Delegated Administration Act, which would have allowed cabinet ministers to hand over power for government programs to private corporations and agencies without legislative approval. The government uses closure, however, to push through Bill 41, the Government Organization Act, which allows ministers to create programs and services, and otherwise carry on business transactions with the private sector, likewise without legislative approval.

Nov. 12 — The Liberal Party elects a new leader, Grant Mitchell, to succeed Laurence Decore. His election is marred, however, by problems with the telephone balloting system. Second-place candidate Sine Chadi threatens at first to appeal the result, but later backs down.

Nov. 21 — Ralph Klein receives the Colin M. Brown Freedom Medal from the National Citizens' Coalition, a right wing pressure group based in Toronto, for his contribution to the principles of freedom of the market.

Dec. 12 — Ralph Klein is given high marks in *Barron's*, a weekly financial paper, for his ability to cut government spending and remain popular.

Dec. 15 — Minister of Transportation and Utilities Peter Trynchy is fired from cabinet for his poor judgment in using a government contractor to pave his driveway.

1995

Jan. 1 — The *New York Times* cites Ralph Klein's determination to cut the budget. Alberta, the paper continues, is now a model for other provinces and governments facing budget problems.

Jan. 5 — Ralph Klein receives another award, this time from the Fraser Institute, a Vancouver-based conservative think tank, for his efforts at balancing the budget.

Jan. 6 — Federal Health Minister Diane Marleau announces that she is going to get tough with provinces that allow extra billing. Ralph Klein says he will challenge Ottawa in court.

Jan 12 — In a feature article in the *Wall Street Journal*, Ralph Klein is credited for his impressive performance in slashing welfare rolls, cutting government, and taking on "special interest groups."

Jan. 19 — A two-year-old boy, Dalton Gregory Halfe-Arcand, dies in a taxicab while being transferred from Edmonton to St. Paul, a several-hour-drive north-east of Edmonton. The boy suffered from a rare form of Steven-Johnson Syndrome. Alberta Health calls for an investigation into his death, but Health Minister Shirley McClellan shrugs off suggestions that cuts in the provincial health budget prevented the boy from being transferred in an ambulance.

Feb. 7 — Ralph Klein kills controversial Bill 57, the Delegated Administration Act, which the government had threatened to reintroduce in the new session of the legislature.

Feb. 21 — Treasurer Jim Dinning presents a budget with $500 million in spending cuts, no tax increases, but (once more) increased medicare premiums. While admitting there is a budgetary surplus for 1994-95, Dinning sticks to further cuts arguing Alberta had "won the lottery" in oil royalties.

Feb. 23 — The *Wall Street Journal* once again features Ralph Klein. This time, he is dubbed "Canada's Reagan" and given high marks for his reform blitzkrieg which has touched every corner of government.

Mar. 13 — Statistics are released by the Edmonton Food Bank showing that people in Alberta are using food banks at nearly double the rate of people in the rest of the country.

Mar. 15 — An Angus Reid poll shows that 73 percent of Albertans strongly or moderately approve of Ralph Klein's performance and that, among decided voters, 68 percent would vote Tory if an election were held. But the poll also shows growing anxiety over health care and the spread of video lotteries.

Apr. 4 — Ralph Klein says he will push for changes in the Canada Health Act that, if enacted, "could be construed as a two-tiered system."

May — Figures released show that Alberta had the strongest growth rate in Canada in 1994, 5.7 percent compared with the Canadian average of 4.2 percent. At almost the same time, first quarter statistics for 1995 released by Industry Canada also show Alberta leading the country in business and personal bankruptcies, a 27 percent rise over the first quarter of the previous year. Bankruptcies are especially high in Edmonton, 49 percent above the previous year.

May — Following considerable rural upset over the closure of hospitals, several Tory MLAs begin to lobby to keep them open. Contrary to previous statements, Klein now says it is okay for MLAs to become involved in decisions about changes in health care policy.

June 8 — Provincial Tory leader Mike Harris rides Klein's formula for success to the premiership of Ontario.

June — An Angus Reid poll conducted between May 19 and May 25 is released. Forty-five percent of Albertans participating in the poll cite health care as the first or second most important issue in the province, up from 26 percent in February. The deficit falls to second place as an issue (25 percent), virtually tied with jobs/unemployment and education (both 24 percent).

June — Ralph Klein begins a twenty-two-day travel junket that takes him to London, Paris, Israel, and Egypt. In London he meets with high-ranking dignitaries and bond dealers to tell them of the Alberta "advantage" and his government's attack on the deficit. While there, he stays in a $400 per night hotel. As the trip wears on, however, Alberta business leaders who travel with Klein complain that he isn't meeting with them enough or helping enough in creating business opportunities for them.

June 13 — Bouyed by the comments of Ralph Klein and Health Minister Shirley McClellan, a group of doctors offers to buy or rent space in a hospital in Devon, just outside of Edmonton, to sell medical services to a wealthy international clientele.

June 17 — Transportation Minister Steve West announces the privatization of the design, construction, and maintenance of Alberta's main highways. The move, criticized by some as inefficient, costly, and even dangerous, is expected to result in the lay-off of 1,400 government workers.

June 23 — Treasurer Jim Dinning announces that an upsurge in oil revenues has produced a budget surplus of $958 million. He announces the extra money will not be reinvested in programs, however, but will go instead towards paying down the provincial debt.

July — Reports of chaos in the health system continue to rise. Physiotherapy is rationed in the Edmonton region. Meanwhile, non-elective surgery (some nonetheless serious in nature) is cancelled at the Royal Alexandra Hospital (one of the only two full-service hospitals in Edmonton) because of a severe nursing shortage and high patient load.

Chapter One

INTRODUCTION

Trevor Harrison and Gordon Laxer

> "Trojan Horse": Any person, process, or device which is intended to weaken, subvert, or destroy from within.[1]

A second wave of the new right is sweeping across Canada, obliterating Canadian traditions of using government as a positive force to correct the inequalities of the capitalist marketplace and providing public services for all. What happened to the "caring/sharing" — and peaceful — society that traditionally distinguished Canada from the United States? Having bypassed the full force of Margaret Thatcher's and Ronald Reagan's new right revolution in the 1980s, why is Canada in the forefront of the second wave of the new right in the mid-1990s?

Mike Harris won the 1995 Ontario election on a "get tough" platform involving a massive 30 percent cut in taxes and social services. Able-bodied welfare recipients will be forced onto workfare. Those who cannot make it in the tough job market of the 1990s, will be on their own. This sounded more like the dog-eat-dog ethos of Alabama than of Ontario.

But it isn't Ontario that is leading Canada down this path towards a new market-based morality. It's Ralph Klein's Alberta. Starting with the upsurge of Preston Manning's Reform Party in the late 1980s, Alberta-based parties have ridden the politics of middle-class anger and frustration at their declining living standards. Instead of blaming the rich and the corporations for fleeing their responsibilities to invest and pay taxes in Canada, they have lashed out at the poor, at various minorities, and at public sector workers as the causes of their tax woes and their financial insecurities. This kind of politics has been the stock and trade of U.S. Republicans since the 1960s, but major parties in Canada shied away from openly championing such un-Canadian traditions. Even Brian Mulroney, Canada's most pro-American prime minister ever, whose tenure witnessed the dismantling of one social program after another, felt he had to declare Canada's provision of social services "a sacred trust."

Not Ralph Klein, however. He has attacked the providers of social services — the teachers, nurses, civil servants and anyone else who works in the
public sector — as "special interests." For Klein, they are the parasites who
live off the hard-working folk, the taxpayers in the private sector. Even
worse are the recipients of social services, regularly admonished to be self-
reliant and self-disciplined. Mike Harris sat at the feet of Ralph Klein and
his alter ego, Rod Love, and learned how new right American politics could
win Ontario. The gun that started Harris' "common sense revolution" was
fired first by Ralph Klein in Alberta.

Lauded by the *Wall Street Journal, Barron's,* the *New York Times,* and
the *Globe and Mail,* awarded by both the Fraser Institute and the National
Citizens' Coalition, poster-boy for *Saturday Night* and *Maclean's* magazines, Ralph Klein — Canada's "original" Newt Gingrich — is big news.
"The province of Alberta is home to North America's most radical revolution in budget downsizing," gushes an admiring editorial writer for the
Wall Street Journal. "His reform blitzkrieg has touched — and cut — every
corner of government."[2] Alberta's great export used to be its oil; now, as
Ontario attests, it's Klein's model of how to remake government.

Why is the business community and its right-wing allies so enthralled
with the Klein government? What has been the real impact of the "Klein
revolution" upon Albertans? And what does it mean for Canadians elsewhere?

What Other Canadians Don't Know — But Should

Alberta's debt situation was never as bad as portrayed in the business
press. Contrary to the prevailing myth, Alberta is the sole place in Canada that does not have a real fiscal problem. Because of oil and gas revenues, Alberta is the only government with the capacity to easily wipe out
its deficits and its net debt. As Mel McMillan and Allan Warrack point
out in chapter ten, Albertans pay by far the lowest provincial taxes in
Canada. If Alberta had had a provincial sales tax or had simply raised its
existing provincial taxes to the average of the other Canadian provinces,
balanced budgets would have been as regular as the return of geese in
spring. There would have been no need for Klein's massive cuts to
health, education, and welfare.

But many — perhaps most — people are unaware of this. Barraged by
uncritical stories from the mainstream press, many of them unabashedly
propagandist, people outside of Alberta, upset with increasing taxes, declin-

ing services, and mounting public debts, may be forgiven for hoping that they too could have a premier like "good old Ralph."

Those outside of Alberta should not be fooled. Inside Ralph Klein's Alberta, another story is unfolding. Since Klein's remade Conservatives won the election in June 1993, politics and social policy have indeed been turned on their heads, but not in the beneficial manner portrayed in the corporate-controlled media.

Readers will discover in this book the dark underside of the Klein revolution: a crisis atmosphere that demands sacrifices from the have-nots but not from the comfortable; massive cuts to health, education, and welfare[3]; thousands of public employees laid off; young, well-educated Albertans leaving the province; normally decent people engaged in scapegoating and vigilantism; the sacrifice of long-term economic infrastructure for the fool's gold of "an Alberta advantage"; an economy dependent more than ever upon a few dwindling resources[4]; the rape of the environment under the guise of "sustainable development"; the spread of fear and intimidation.[5] Most of all, they will read about how a government which claims to listen to the people, has instead centralized power, curtailed civil democracy, and privatized public life. In the end, readers will learn that there are far fewer advantages to the so-called revolution than they have been told by a largely uncritical media.

This book provides a cogent analysis of the peculiar historical and political circumstances that allowed a government party to be taken over by right-wing populists, led by an opportunistic politician. It looks at the real meaning of the Klein government's policies: Not simply the elimination of the deficit/debt, but rather the large-scale social reengineering of a province's political culture to conform with the demands of moral conservatism and the neo-liberal agenda of the global corporations. The book examines why opposition to the Klein Tories, until now, has been largely muted, and the internal contradictions of the Klein government's policies that may yet create the basis for an effective opposition. Finally, in the absence of such an opposition, the book provides an unabashed forum for voices silenced and intimidated by the Klein juggernaut.

More broadly, however, the book also holds a warning for Canadians elsewhere regarding the real meaning of the Klein revolution.

The Klein Government, the "New" New Right, and Canada

The Klein government's policies, and their broader impact upon Canadian society, cannot properly be understood except in the context of "glo-

balization" and wider public debates over the role of government. Margaret
Thatcher and Ronald Reagan led the first new right revolt against active
governments guaranteeing full employment and universal social services.
Downsizing governments, tax breaks for the corporations and the rich, and
breaking unions were part of this first wave of new right enthusiasm for less
compassionate government.

Canada partly escaped the first wave. However, with the rise of Preston
Manning's Reform Party, whose core strength also resides in the province,
and Ralph Klein's reborn Conservatives, Alberta is in the forefront of the
second wave (see chapter seven). Newt Gingrich learned from Manning. "I
watched all his commercials. We developed the [contract with America]
platform from watching his campaign."[6]

No doubt the new right in the U.S. would also like to learn from Ralph
Klein. To be able to do unpopular things like reward one's wealthy friends,
destroy opponents, dismantle cherished social services, and yet see one's
popularity rise into the stratosphere is every new-right politician's dream.

But the Klein revolution has a deeper meaning for the rest of Canada.
For years, the American right-wing and its corporate allies have sought to
re-create Canada in their image, viewing Canada as the last bastion against
the monolithic "business-think" that otherwise dominates North American
politics. While Canadians willingly consume copious amounts of American
popular culture, few in the past were willing to trade the Canadian way of
life for that of their southern neighbours. Mass homelessness, poverty, two-
tiered health care, unsafe streets, racial conflict, and an economy dependent upon military expenditures are much tougher sells than Coca-Cola and
Madonna. Until recently, only the lunatic fringe of Canadian politics has
voiced support for the extreme right-wing ideas that underlie the pathology
of American life. With the Klein government, however, these ideas have at
last found a Trojan Horse for entering into Canadian public discourse and
policy, and thereby fundamentally changing the nature of Canada.

Of course, the Klein government's ideas have not been produced simply out of whole cloth; nor is Alberta alone in adopting some of the new
right's agenda. The new right's second wave, whether vocalized stridently in
the catch-phrases of Ralph Klein and his high-born Treasurer Jim Dinning,
or in the matter-of-fact justifications of Jean Chretien and Paul Martin, is a
response to the globalization of the transnational corporations and the
high tech financial speculators. The sovereignty of democratic states is being replaced by the discipline of the moneylenders and the global corporations. In this second wave, the deficit and debt are code words for
redefining the role of governments. In place of the ethic of serving the pub-

lic according to the democratic ethos of equality, community, and citizenship, governments in the second wave address consumers, stakeholders, and investors. The inequality and individual self-interest of the capitalist marketplace are now in; the collective good and compassion are out.

In particular, the events transpiring in Alberta are merely a piece in the growing global corporate takeover of individual states, governments, and the democratic process. Hence the Klein government's unfettered praise by the business press.

Today, many transnational corporations are larger and more powerful than countries. They are run and managed by elites who view themselves as an "international class." They owe no allegiance to the citizens who work in nearby offices and plants, who send their children to local schools, who run gas stations and cheer for local teams. This international class is above these things. And like fighter pilots, flying high over the ground below, it indiscriminately "bombs" small communities, cities, provinces, and states — the people — by way of shifting its capital around the globe at a moment's notice in search of big profits and little interference. It is easier to kill from a great height and call the devastating effects the inevitabilities of global competition. Like government and corporate officials in the three NAFTA amigos, the Klein government has thrown in its lot with these "high flyers." This book tells the story of a province coming unstuck in the late twentieth century under the aegis of globalization. In doing so, it may well hold up a mirror for other provinces and states to see their futures.

Alberta's Political Culture: Crisis and Quasi-Nationalism

This being said, Alberta is somewhat peculiar within Canada's political mosaic (see chapters four. nine. six, and twenty-one). In the early days of this century, populist notions were imported by American settlers. Later, a heavy dose of rugged individualism and laissez-faire ideology was added to the political mix by oil company executives from Oklahoma and Texas. Along the way, religious fundamentalism and more than a touch of paranoia also became part of Alberta's political culture. Finally, the instability of Alberta's resource-based economy paved the way for a series of political "crises" whose resolution has always involved, in one way or another, a rallying in support of Alberta's quasi-"national" government. The message is always the same. If we pull together we can defeat the "enemies" and return Alberta to prosperity and its natural state of grace.

Of course, the "enemies" have not always remained the same. In the late 1930s, "Bible Bill" Aberhart railed against the "fifty big shots," the Eastern bankers, industrialists, and railroaders — who were creating "poverty amidst plenty" in Alberta. Later, Ernest Manning (Preston's father) invoked the threat of "godless" communism to similar ends. By the 1970s and early 1980s, the enemies had changed. Under Peter Lougheed, external capitalists, in the guise of big U.S. oil, were now friends. The enemy instead was the federal Liberal government, supported by Central Canadian voters. They stole the oil boom. The hated National Energy Program became deeply embedded in Albertans' consciousness of why things went bust. They rallied around the flag.

Alberta premiers have always been the focal point in this rallying. Leadership cults and one-party politics have been the rule since 1935, blunting questions regarding the need for competing viewpoints. Since most Albertans have the same interests, the sustaining myth goes, why do we need competing parties? "We're all Albertans, right?" The status of mythical leader was bestowed in succession upon Aberhart, Manning, and Lougheed, but faltered under the hapless Don Getty (1985-1993). Best remembered by Albertans for being caught on the golf course when the collapse of the Principal Group of investment companies struck, Getty's loss of the leadership mystique seemed by late 1992 to signal the end of Tory reign.

How the Tories turned their fortunes around is told by David Stewart (chapter three). As in the past, the turn around can be attributed to the mythical leadership of one person — Ralph Klein — and his government's ability to once again use a "crisis" — this time, the debt and deficit — to rally Albertans.

Inside Alberta today, the atmosphere is like the beginning of the Second World War. Most Albertans are convinced that there is a major crisis, that everyone must sacrifice for the "war" effort. The Klein government's appeal for sacrifices in this time of crisis strikes a positive chord with the generous, community-spirited side of Albertans' natures. Volunteering for worthy causes is embedded in Alberta's culture. It harks back to pioneer days when everyone pitched in for a barn-raising for the new neighbours.

But Klein's message also appeals to the mean-spirited side. Following tradition, Alberta once again is seeking out "enemies." This time, however, in keeping with the lurch towards American right wing politics, the focus is on the "enemy within." In a perversion of traditional populist rhetoric, public servants, welfare recipients, even university students, and pensioners are now branded "special interests." It is their selfish demands, so the government claims, that have produced the enormous crisis of provincial debt and deficits. "Hard-working and responsible taxpayers won't give you a free lunch any more," so the line goes. "Get off your behinds and be self-reliant because you can't count on governments any more."

The Alberta media has played a role in the search for internal enemies. Rather than seeing their role as investigative and critical of government no matter what its political stripe, much of the media acts as a Pravda for the right. With the exceptions of the *Edmonton Journal*, the *Calgary Herald*, the CBC, and a few others, which provide balanced coverage, many reporters see their job as cheer-leader for the government.

Several chapters in this book examine the manner in which these sequential myths and folk-wisdoms have been constructed, manipulated, and disseminated to "average" Albertans — another mythical construction — in order to forge the consensus to fight the debt crisis that underlies the Klein government's support. But what exactly is the nature of Alberta's debt crisis? Indeed, why have Albertans believed their elites that there even is a crisis?

Killing the Debt Myth

Historically, Albertans have tended to be attracted to simple, straight forward explanations for the crises they faced. There is usually a kernel of truth to each but the explanation gets stretched beyond reason. Social Credit's "A plus B theorem" correctly identified the cause of the Depression. Economic capacity lay unused in capitalists' hands because Albertans and Canadians did not have the purchasing power to buy their goods. But many of Social Credit's solutions were off the wall. Likewise, the National Energy Program continues today, in rhetoric at least, as the demon that stole Alberta's future. Certainly it intruded unfairly into Alberta's oil and gas resources and imposed punitive taxes. But this did not explain why Texas and Louisiana were hit with the same devastating oil bust at the same time.

The recent debt and deficit is of the same vintage as these collective myths. This is not to say the debt and deficit are not problems, but they are not *the overwhelming crisis* that Klein and company make them out to be. The federal government faced a much higher debt in relative terms at the end of the Second World War but introduced the welfare state and reduced the debt at the same time. It did these things without imposing punitive taxes or creating a crisis atmosphere.

In Alberta, the Tories created the debt. Later, they also created, and benefitted from, the subsequent imagined crisis and its solutions. Like a perverse Phoenix, the Tories rose from the ashes on the wings of their own past incompetence!

Why did Albertans accept the crisis as defined by Klein? Before the great oil discovery at Leduc in 1947, Albertans were poor. They were raised on the frontier myths of self-reliance, rugged individualism, and low taxes. They were the only Canadians who did not gradually adjust to paying more taxes for enhanced health, education and social services through the 1960s and 1970s. With oil revenues gushing in at the equivalent of an 18 percent provincial sales tax before 1986, Albertans did not have to pay for the high level of services they got. It was a painless way to create a welfare state. When oil revenues were cut in half in 1986, the Conservative government did not level with the people and say "we finally need to raise provincial taxes towards levels all other Canadians are paying." Instead they pretended to balance the budget and quickly accumulated a large debt that exceeded by a narrow margin Alberta's large public assets (see chapter eleven).

Unbelievably, the Tories became even worse bunglers in subsequent years. As McMillan and Warrack show in chapter ten, the Conservative government of Don Getty reduced public spending on nonbusiness programs, bringing it down to the Canadian average by 1991. But Alberta's spending was kept higher than average by the large expenditures on "resource conservation and industrial development" or in simpler language, subsidies for business. At $706 per capita, these are almost three times as high as the average provincial expenditure across Canada ($265 per capita). At the same time, Conservative governments were very poor managers of public assets. They borrowed in New York with no hedge against currency fluctuations, costing Alberta hundreds of millions in increased spending.[7] They subsidized business and gave too generous wellhead tax holidays to the gas and oil industry (see chapter eleven by Dean Neu and David Cooper). There was a spending problem during the Tory years, but it was not spending on public services; rather, it was the amount squandered on risky investments, backing up Alberta's coddled corporate sector.

Having lost billions in spectacular business failures, the Conservatives, even if reborn as the Klein bunch, could hardly call on taxpayers to cough up more to confront the deficit and debt they created. Tax increases became a "no brainer" in Klein's Alberta. The debt provided the necessary crisis for the Klein Tories not only to remain in power but also to do what many in the party had wanted to do for years:[8] to fundamentally remake the size and role of government.

Don't Shoot the Taxman! Why Low Taxes Benefit Only the Well-to-do

Like much of North America, Albertans are caught up in a myth about taxes. As promoted by the Klein government and its corporate supporters, this myth has two components. The first is that "Alberta has a spending problem, not a revenue problem." Hence the justification for cuts in social programs and the elimination of thousands of public service jobs. This reasoning is faulty. Alberta's only spending problem is for business subsidies. When this spending is excluded, Alberta's per capita spending was below the national average before Klein took office.

The second myth is that low taxes provide the province with an "Alberta advantage." Lower taxes are not new. Alberta has had lower taxes than the other provinces since the 1960s, ample time to carry out an experiment about its powers to attract businesses to Alberta. If low taxes provided such an advantage, Alberta should have already diversified out of resource exporting dependency. It has not. Most of the industries that are in Alberta such as resources, tourism, and retail, must be here. After twenty-five years of the Alberta experiment of lower taxes, it has failed to attract much in the way of "foot loose" industries that do not need to be located here. Even were it correct, the Alberta advantage "experiment" is likely to go by the boards in any case, as Mike Harris' Ontario lowers provincial taxes towards Alberta levels. The point, however, is that the argument has been based on a false premise.

Sten Drugge's analysis (chapter twelve) shows that low taxes are a minimal factor in encouraging investment. Other things, such as a well-trained workforce, adequate infrastructure, and proximity to markets are more important. Moreover, in pursuing the "Alberta advantage," the province is in danger of losing "the Canadian advantage" of low-cost universal health care. The management consulting firm KPMG compared business costs in Canada and the United States and found that U.S. employers paid almost eight times as much for private medical premiums for their employees as Canadian employers paid for medical premiums under Canada's public health care system. This Canadian advantage has attracted American and Japanese auto investment to Ontario.[9]

Why were Albertans not persuaded that they could pay a little more in taxes to maintain the kind of services that would provide a real advantage for their children and society? We have noted Alberta's long history of services funded by resource revenues. But there are other reasons. First, it was never put to Albertans by established political leaders that the province had a choice in how to tackle the debt. Secondly, Albertans are just getting used to the GST, more hated in Alberta than elsewhere because the province has never had a provincial sales tax. Thirdly, Albertans' regional alienation makes them almost impervious to examples from other parts of Canada. They think taxes are too high elsewhere and that governments cannot be trusted with tax revenues: that they will blow it. By losing several billions in public money on the ventures of their business cronies, the Alberta Tories helped create widespread mistrust of government spending.

Contrary to another pervasive myth, there is no magic level of taxation that individuals are willing or not willing to pay. In general, people are upset over taxes when 1) they perceive that they are not receiving fair services for their dollar and that others are not paying their fair share; 2) there is not an accepted ethos of universal citizen rights to a broad range of public services; 3) they see some groups benefitting from programs that they themselves are not able to utilize; and 4) the taxes are visible (e.g., the GST). The marginal tax rate is highest in Sweden and amongst the lowest in the United States. Yet the Swedish parties advocating higher taxes to maintain generous social services won the 1994 election. On the other hand, in the United States voters endorsed Newt Gingrich's social services and tax cuts in 1994 Congressional elections. This proves Gosta Esping-Andersens contention that tax revolts are greatest where taxes are lowest.[10] By continuing to downgrade public services, and moving away from universality in program provision, the Klein government is pursuing policies that will further erode public support for taxes. Ironically, the big losers in this game of "driving down taxes" will be many of Klein's biggest supporters — those middle-income — "ordinary" Albertans.

Americanizing Canada from Within

Albertans and other Canadians may be attracted to the mania of debt reduction in order to preserve the public social services they cherish. If so they will be in for a rude shock. The Klein government is using the deficit and debt as an excuse for moving Alberta toward the American model of two tiers for health and education. The province is setting the stage in these areas for private elite systems for the well-to-do. Meanwhile, the public systems will be left impoverished, their services inferior.

Early signs of this Americanization can be readily seen. In 1994, provincial funding for kindergarten was halved to 200 hours per year, cutting $30 million from provincial expenditures (see chapter thirteen). Without offering a shred of evidence, Halvar Jonson, the minister of education, blithely intoned that "preparing children for formal learning can be attained with less time in the classroom." This nonsense is contradicted by early child-hood educators who stress that children who go unprepared into the school system "go into an antisocial stream right away. They become school drop-outs and they feed into teenage delinquency and crime."[11] Under pressure from angry parents, Jonson admitted that kindergarten had benefits for dis-advantaged children and in an act of generosity increased provincial fund-ing in 1995 from 200 hours to 240 hours, 60 percent of the level before the cuts.

Alberta now has a patchwork of kindergarten practices. In Edmonton, school boards took precious money from already slimmed-down school pro-grams and put it into kindergartens. They remain free at the full 400 hours. Calgary opted to set up a two tiered system. Parents who can afford the full program will have to pay up to $466 to start their youngsters in September while those who don't have the means will start their children in the free program in February. But many parents in rural areas do not have the op-tion to pay for extra hours.

In the grades one to twelve also, Alberta is moving towards a two-tiered system through the rhetoric of "schools of choice." Charter schools, an-other fad imported from the United States designed to protect the educa-tional standards of the well-to-do, will be allowed. They are public schools autonomous of school boards and their aim is usually to set up a homoge-neous group of students. As John Mason, an advocate of charter schools in Alberta put it "We're not interested in having academically challenged kids. And we're not going to have behaviour problems. We're taking the cream of the crop."[12] In 1994 Alberta's tax reform commission recommended a voucher system to allow parents to spend their money in either public or private schools. If charter schools and private schools proliferate in Alberta and skim off the best students from well-to-do parents, the remaining pub-lic schools will eventually become repositories for children of the middle in-come, the poor, and the challenged. Equality of opportunity will be lost.

Health care is undergoing drastic reorganization and massive cuts at the same time, causing the greatest anxiety amongst Albertans[13] a subject taken up by Simon Renouf in chapter fifteen. Amidst the upheavals of hos-pital closings and nursing layoffs, an American-style two-tiered system of health care also appears to be emerging. In years past, the Conservatives over-built hospitals, placing many in rural Tory ridings. Since 1994, they have begun closing them or greatly reducing beds, citing the need to cut costs. Community care has been the buzz-word. In the spring of 1995, how-ever, under pressure from doctors and corporate supporters, the Klein gov-ernment reversed itself, saying that perhaps "redundant" hospitals should

be sold off to private operators to conduct "unnecessary" medical procedures. Suddenly the hospitals, closed six months before, have a purpose
again.

A hospital in Cardston near the Montana border is taking American
patients as private patients. To avoid charges of giving special treatment to
rich foreigners while making the poor natives at home wait for inferior services, Klein promises to let rich Albertans use private health services too. "Albertans ... simply want to say 'look, I want to get into this hospital
quicker'."[14] Meanwhile, Klein presses the federal government to define
what is meant by essential services under medicare and let patients pick up
the rest.

By January 1995, there were about fifteen private health clinics in Alberta relying on double dipping. Alone amongst the provinces, Alberta allowed them to charge patients a "facility fee" and for clinic doctors to claim
standard medicare fees from the province. In another development, a proposal is in the works for eye surgeon Howard Gimbel of Calgary to set up a
private research hospital. In response to inquiries from investors to buy
shut-down hospitals and run them as businesses, Klein responded, "Give us
a proposal, we're willing to listen to anything reasonable."[15] At the same
time medicare premiums are shooting up and will cost $860 per year by
1997 for families earning $30,000 or $40,000.

A lucrative private sector in health care requires an inferior public
health sector. Otherwise there would be no incentive for the well-to-do to
pay extra for private services. Alberta appears to be going down the same
road travelled by Margaret Thatcher's Britain in the 1980s, towards the
creation of a private health care system for the rich and a lower quality one
for the rest.

The Other Faces in the Revolution

Much of the media coverage of the Klein revolution has focused on
Klein himself or his ministers. Occasionally, a particularly dramatic story
will draw people's attention to some of those impacted by the changes. This
book looks, in a broader manner, at some of the groups most affected by
the revolution.

As Gurston Dacks, Joyce Green, and Linda Trimble show in chapter
eighteen, the Klein revolution has been particularly hard on women. As in
other Western countries in the past few decades, Alberta women overcame
dependency on men to a great extent by depending on the State. As nurses,
social workers, teachers, and other workers in the public sector, the prov-

ince provided employment opportunities for many Alberta women to stand on their own feet. At the same time the State provided public health, education, and daycare and elder care services that enabled many Alberta women to escape from some of the traditional unpaid work they had previously been expected to do at home. As Alberta throws off its socially supportive roles, many women may be forced back into dependency on men. Women have disproportionately lost their jobs or seen their salaries and benefits cut. Moreover, they also have been asked to pick up much of the slack through increased "volunteer" work now that the government has cut back on programs such as kindergarten, health care, and seniors' programs.

It is not a good idea to be poor in Alberta. The province has the second lowest minimum wage and one of the lowest rates of unionization. If you don't have a job and rely on social support payments, you have been hit particularly hard by the Klein revolution. As Jonathan Murphy relates in chapter twenty, the number of adults on assistance in Alberta declined, from 122,000 in March 1993, to 68,000 in August 1994. Those who remained on assistance saw their benefits cut. With vocal encouragement from the Klein government, many former recipients were driven from the province.

It also is not a good idea to be old. Fred Engelmann (chapter nineteen) shows that only 9 percent of Alberta seniors earn over $40,000. More than half earn individual incomes of less than $15,000. But the Klein government has not refrained from attacking the living standards of senior citizens, traditionally a bedrock of Tory supporters. Amongst the many reductions in provincial support, many seniors will now pay full health care premiums, lose property tax reductions and pay greater amounts for long-term care or lodge programs. Perhaps the government feels that Alberta's seniors should have foreseen the Klein revolution coming when they were young because few have the opportunity now to make up for lost provincial support.

The Changing Role of Government

Some think that with all the downsizing and privatization of government that the Klein revolution is about reducing government. This is not so. The Klein regime has centralized power, imposed its brand of moral discipline, and turned over much governance to private businessmen, who usually have close ties to government. It's not so much about reducing governing as abrogating democracy.

Despite the rhetoric about turning responsibility over to the community, Klein wiped out the tax and many of the spending powers of local, democratically-elected school boards. The province abolished more than half the school boards and now appoints school superintendents. Much like Margaret Thatcher's revolution, the Klein government does not want local democratic bodies standing in the way of its revolution for the well-to-do and the corporations.

Tapping into Calvinist religious culture, the Klein regimen calls on Albertans to learn self-discipline. Learning to get along with less and moral slimming analogies tap into Albertans' guilt about the fat and morally degenerate years of the oil boom. Claude Denis (chapter seven) shows how the individual is called upon to be responsible when taking a pay cut or receiving a lower level of services. Communities and individuals are called upon to provide the caring services withdrawn by the province.

Lowering expectations is part of the new right agenda of the transnational corporations. For them, unions are too strong. Regulations to make corporations responsible to communities regarding technological change, closures, the environment, and pay equity keep the corporations in place and reduce their profits. To get away from these conditions they started to flee from the developed countries and set up shop in the third world. But that was not always the best answer. The political and financial instability in Mexico is a case in point. It would be much better for transnationals to create third-world like conditions in the advanced countries. Why not start a bidding war amongst countries and provinces to see which can best create such conditions?

The Klein revolution is about joining the global race to the bottom. Middle-class Albertans must learn to lower their expectations. Then super salesman Klein can traipse to Asia or Texas to "sell" Alberta to the transnational corporations. Come to Alberta, so the pitch goes. We have "the lowest tax regime of any province in the country" he tells his business audience as they sup on sumptuous meals paid for by Alberta taxpayers. No doubt in private he also tells them about other "Alberta advantages": weak unions, minimal environmental regulations, low corporate taxes, and a work force cajoled to labour for minimum wages and reduced benefits.

Alternatives to the Klein Revolution

Neighbouring Saskatchewan has done things differently. In February 1995, Roy Romanow's New Democratic government brought in the prov-

caused entirely by Tory govmt

ince's first balanced budget in thirteen years, a year ahead of schedule. When they had taken office in October, 1991, Romanow's government faced a $14 billion debt and an $850 million annual operating deficit. The province had a weaker economic base than Alberta, yet Saskatchewan was able to eliminate its deficit without massive cuts in jobs and public services. How did Saskatchewan do it?

Like Alberta, Saskatchewan received an unexpected revenue windfall from oil and gas, potash, gambling, and increased consumer spending following a bumper wheat crop in 1994. Unlike Alberta, however, Saskatchewan opted both for fiscal restraints, planned reorganization in some services, notably health, and tax increases, including a deficit-reduction flat tax, a rise in provincial sales taxes from 7 to 9 percent, and a five cent per litre tax on gasoline.

There are important differences in the way Saskatchewan and Alberta chose to deal with their debt problems. We do not necessarily agree with everything the Romanow government has done. The point is that there are more ways to kill the debt-beast than that provided by the Alberta model — a model that we believe is fundamentally flawed in its long-term implications.

The best way to end Alberta's and Canada's deficit and debt problems is to create long-term jobs in sustainable industries at good rates of pay. The OECD measures the "output gap," the difference between what an economy produces and what it could produce with full employment. In 1992 Canada had an output gap of over 10 percent. This was the largest any OECD country had experienced in thirty years. The U.S. rate was just under 2 percent.[16] With an unemployment rate of 8.3 percent to 9.7 percent compared to Canada's 10.4 percent to 11.3 percent between 1991 and 1994, Alberta's output gap is only a little lower than Canada's as a whole.[17]

Klein does not worry about the output gap or the unemployed. He thinks like the corporations. The more unemployed there are, the more they will scare the rest who are working into accepting poorer wages and working conditions.

But Albertans worry. In a poll in June 1995, they listed unemployment as the number two issue along with the deficit and education.[18] High unemployment in Alberta and Canada hurts most people. The unemployed pay few taxes and necessitate increased social spending. Along with too high interest rates, this is the root cause of the deficits and the declining level of social services.

The Klein strategy is to run budgetary surpluses through cutting thousands of public sector employees and to hell with the consequences. This is

wishful, short-term thinking. Public infrastructure from highways and public transit to education, libraries, and health care are essential for economic
growth. An efficient infrastructure and highly educated human capital,
rather than low taxes, attract industry to come and to stay. Alberta is investing too little in public infrastructure now and this will come back to haunt
Albertans in the future. Bob Saari, who manages the Alberta branch of the
Canadian Manufacturers Association, warns that "the Alberta government
... must be very careful to ensure that it does not go past an efficient infrastructure in its cutting."[19]

Klein's hope is that the "Alberta advantage" of low corporate taxes will
take up the slack of public-sector layoffs. In Klein's first two years, Alberta
was lucky and rode a mini oil boom which led to job creation and higher
than expected government revenues. In his 1995 budget speech, Alberta's
Treasurer Jim Dinning, admitted, "We got lucky. We won the lottery."[20] But
he did not expect it to last. Neither do we. Letting giant transnationals in
the oil and forestry industries pay low taxes and royalties will not produce
the needed investment and work. The tax giveaways of the past decade
show this. These foreign corporations earn higher profits at taxpayers' expense and then invest them elsewhere. For example, Imperial Oil earned
profits of $359 million in 1994 and instead of investing it in more explora-
tion in Alberta, sent 70 percent of these profits across the border to its
Exxon owners. Although flush with profits, Imperial continued to slash employment in Canada, dropping its work force to 8,200 in 1995 from 14,700
in 1990.[21]

Instead of relying on foreign transnationals to invest and create jobs
here we need governments to develop investment strategies involving local
companies and social capital funds such as Manitoba's Crocus Fund, which
would have location commitment to Alberta and Canada. Instead of laying
off thousands of public servants and dangerously eroding the level of education, health, and social services, Alberta needs to develop a strategy of
greater investment in real output, in both the private and the public sectors.

In time, we believe the flaws of "Kleinism" will become apparent to
others, including Albertans. The hold of charismatic leaders on their devoted followers is a fragile thing. It can appear to be impregnable one moment and come crashing down the next. It's difficult to predict when and
under what conditions that might happen.

In the spring of 1995, Ralph Klein's popularity was higher than it had
ever been. But behind his rosy facade, the tough medicine was beginning to
be felt by those outside the public sector. Signs of health care chaos and declines in education were starting to appear. Anxiety was in the air and re-

flected by polls which showed health care as the number one concern, over-shadowing deficits and debt by a two to one margin.[22] Will concern about the nature of changes in these sectors begin to erode Ralph Klein's popularity? Only time will tell. In the meantime, there are lessons in the Alberta experience for Canadians elsewhere.

Conclusion

In her portrait of Ralph Klein (chapter two), Gillian Steward quotes the Czech novelist Milan Kundera: "[T]he struggle of man against power is the struggle of memory against forgetting."[23] Of course, the Klein revolution is about forgetting. Forget that the Tories have been in power since 1971, or that they created the debt. In the mode of classical revolutionaries, "Kleinism" portrays itself as unfettered by past experience in its efforts to carve out a new Utopia.

What might memory teach us if we stopped long enough to listen? First, little of the Klein revolution is new; in fact, we have been through a lot of this before. Deregulation, freeing markets, reducing government. These phrases underpinned many of the great financial boondoggles of the past two hundred years. Was the recent collapse of the Baring's Bank the result of too much regulation? For that matter, did the collapse of Alberta's own Principal Group of investment companies in 1986 come from too much regulation?

But there are other lessons to be learned from the Klein revolution. One is that the nice face of liberal democracy goes easily askew when economic times grow hard. A companion lesson is that an economy dominated by a few resource sectors, and lacking a tradition of opposition and debate, is an easy mark for populist demagogues. It is not seniors, students, teachers, and the poor who are "special interests" ruining it for other Albertans. It is the real special interests: the corporations and the well-to-do that Klein represents who are taking their spoils from the majority. Under the cloak of the debt scare, they are refusing to carry their share of responsibilities.

Alberta needs a new social contract, one that builds a spirit of community based on a sharing of economic opportunities for all. This is our home. It needs nurturing for the long term. Quality educational and health services are essential for building community and long-term economic prospects.

Importing American politics of judging everything by pure capitalist morality will lead to an American-style polarized society and unlivable cities.

It will also erode any reason for Canada to remain independent of the United States.

Democracy is a recent and fragile thing. It is sustained only through the vigilance, critical thinking, and participation of ordinary citizens. Economic and political elites do not really want to share power. Albertans are now paying the price for years of failing to learn this lesson. Unless Canadians elsewhere understand what is really happening in Alberta, they may discover too late that the Klein "gift" of low taxes and "instant" debt gratification is actually a Trojan Horse bearing genuine dangers for a sovereign and democratic Canada.

Notes

1. *The Living Webster: Encyclopedic Dictionary of the English Language* (New York: Delair Publishing Company, Inc., 1981), 1058.
2. The *Wall Street Journal,* 23 February 1995, A12.
3. The number of people using foodbanks in Alberta today is twice the national average. The number of users of the Edmonton foodbank alone rose from 10,302 in January 1993, just after Ralph Klein came to power, to 17,909 in January 1995 (*Edmonton Journal,* 15 March 1995, B1).
4. While Alberta's economy was tops in Canada in 1994 (*Edmonton Journal,* 16 May 1995, A1), this growth was fuelled by oil and natural gas exports. Alberta's domestic economy is doing considerably worse. During the first quarter of 1995, Alberta also led the nation in personal and business bankruptcies (*Edmonton Journal,* 3 May 1995, D7).
5. See S. Das' column in the *Edmonton Journal,* 15 May 1995, A6; also, the Afterward in this book detailing the intimidation experienced by some writers of this book.
6. *Edmonton Journal,* 15 March 1995, A3.
7. *Financial Post,* 20 January 1995, 14.
8. See the discussion of the plans put forward by Elaine McCoy, a candidate for Conservative leader who ran against Klein to succeed Getty in 1992, in M. Lisac, *The Klein Revolution* (Edmonton: NeWest Press, 1995), 68-9.
9. *Globe and Mail,* 16 May 1995, B8.
10. G. Esping-Andersen, *The Three Worlds of Welfare Capitalism* (Princeton, N. J.: Princeton University Press, 1990), 177.
11. Comments of Fraser Mustard, head of the Canadian Institute for Advanced Research, cited in the *Edmonton Journal,* 17 February, 1995, A3.
12. Cited in chapter thirteen.

13. An Angus Reid poll in March 1995 found that almost three times as many Albertans said the Klein revolution had a "negative impact" (56 percent) as said it had a "positive impact" (20 percent). *Edmonton Journal,* 19 March 1995, C3.
14. *Edmonton Journal,* 5 April 1995, A1.
15. *Edmonton Journal,* 10 March 1994, A7
16. Linda McQuaig, *Shooting The Hippo* (Toronto: Viking, 1995), 68-9.
17. Statistics Canada, *Labour Force Annual Averages 1989-1994* (Ottawa: Statistics Canada, 1995). U.S. unemployment hovered between 6.6 percent and 7.4 percent from 1991 to 1993. U.S. Bureau of Census, Statistical Abstract of the United States, Washington 1994.
18. The Angus Reid Group, *Alberta's Public Issues Agenda,* 8 June 1995, 4. Respondents were asked "what is the most important issue facing Alberta today? And what in your opinion is the second most important issue? 45 percent said health care; 25 percent the deficit; 24 percent jobs; 24 percent education.
19. *Edmonton Journal,* 15 February 1995, C7.
20. CBC Television Edmonton, 21 February 1995.
21. *Edmonton Journal,* 22 April 1995, A8.
22. The Angus Reid Group, *Alberta's Public Issues Agenda.*
23. M. Kundera, *The Book of Laughter and Forgetting.* Translated by M. H. Heim (Markham, Ontario: Penguin, 1986), 3.

POLITICS

Chapter Two

KLEIN THE CHAMELEON

Gillian Steward

> The struggle of man against power is the struggle of memory
> against forgetting.
> > Czech novelist Milan Kundera.[1]

When Ralph Klein was nineteen years old, he enroled in the Calgary Business College to learn bookkeeping, business math, economics, and law. Klein was a high school drop out, married, and soon to be a father. He had lived in Calgary all his life, grown up in Tuxedo, a blue collar neighbourhood in the city's northeast. In many ways he was an ordinary young man, moulded by a city on the range that was famous for its annual Stampede, but not much else.

It wasn't long, however, before the young Klein caught the attention of Elsie Tighe, the principal of Calgary Business College. She was so impressed by Klein, that as soon as he finished his two-year course she invited him to apprentice as a teacher. Klein accepted her offer, became a teacher, and was named principal when Ms. Tighe retired. He was only twenty-two. "Klein had a level head and the ability to meet face to face with people," Ms. Tighe said in an interview when Klein was elected mayor of Calgary fifteen years later.

No Ordinary Man

Klein wasn't principal for long. The school closed six months after his appointment. But his ability to absorb what he needed to know and reflect it back like a mirror came so naturally, that shortly after the business college closed, he was appointed Public Relations Director for the Alberta and Northwest Territories division of the Red Cross, even though he had no previous experience or training for such a position. From there he went on to do the same kind of work for the Calgary United Way.

Part of Klein's job was mixing with various media personalities and convincing them to run his press releases, or put in a good word for the United Way, during their radio disc jockey banter. But for someone as able as Klein, the world of well-meaning, but often boring, charitable agencies couldn't hold his attention for long. In 1969, he used his media contacts to land a reporter's job with CFCN Radio. Again, he had no experience or training for this position. Usually reporters went on to work in public relations, not the other way around. Not Klein, however. Before long, he had moved over to CFCN Television.

The image of Ralph Klein as "ordinary" is deeply embedded in the minds of Albertans, and is one of his greatest assets. Almost everyone refers to him as Ralph rather than Klein, or The Premier. He revels in the role of the ordinary man who has managed to capture one of the highest political offices in the land and has his eye on an even higher one. But how many people are offered a teaching job right after finishing a course? Become a college principal at twenty-two? How many "ordinary" people have had a career like Ralph Klein's?

Ralph Klein has never been ordinary. He doesn't have the veneer that often comes with a university degree. But he has a keen intelligence that allows him to instantly assess and react to his surroundings; a combination of intuition, emotion, and adrenalin that helps everyone from guerilla fighters to salesmen survive and thrive. Ralph Klein also has an innate ability to speak and communicate that people find instantly engaging, as Ms. Tighe noted when he was one of her students. Even now, after twenty-five years in the public limelight, there is emotional energy in his voice, and he uses his face and the rest of his body to punctuate the message. When he speaks, there is a lot more than just words coming out of his mouth.

And Klein has a knack for impressing people who can help him get what he wants. At the Calgary Business College, he impressed the principal so much he replaced her when she retired. When he was mayor he won the approval of Juan Antonio Samaranch, the regal head of the International Olympic Committee (IOC). Because of their close relationship, Klein was able to maintain an upper hand during much of the planning and execution of the 1988 Winter Games in Calgary. When the games were over Samaranch made Klein a member of the Olympic Order, the IOC's highest honour. Klein also successfully wooed Premier Don Getty. In the late 1980s he started publicly complimenting him, even though most Albertans thought their premier was an embarrassment. Getty's support helped Klein win a Conservative nomination. Getty quickly appointed him to cabinet after he became an MLA.

The First Few Years of Fame

Ralph Klein could easily have been a successful insurance salesman, real estate agent, or stock broker. But it's doubtful he would have become such a successful politician, if he hadn't been a television reporter during the 1970s. For eleven years he honed his television communication skills and in the process became a minor celebrity.

Klein the TV reporter, like Klein the premier, knew that he couldn't afford to be boring if he wanted to keep his job. He could afford to make mistakes, he could be offensive, even rude. He could be a hero, he could make a fool of himself, but he could not be boring. To survive in TV, he had to make people pay attention, and keep paying attention. This notion coincided well with Klein's natural curiosity and sense of adventure. He was different from most television reporters because he actively sought out the quirky and the unfashionable. He liked reporting on the seamier side of life as it unfolded in biker gangs and massage parlours. And the bikers and masseuses seemed to like, and trust, him. But he could also hold his own with city aldermen and commissioners, too. He was so good at chatting up people, that he could be late for city hall press conferences and still leave with more information than the reporters who had been on time. Once he even climbed into an air duct so he could eavesdrop on a closed meeting and report the proceedings.

A good television reporter has to condense even the most complex information into simple, short statements voiced with appropriate emphasis and emotion. Additional information is conveyed with filmed events or interviews. They must be trimmed and shaped too, so the message is clear and direct because viewers don't get a chance to flip back if they don't understand something, like they can with newspapers or magazines.

In the archives of the Glenbow Museum, there is film footage of Ralph Klein reporting from Toronto in 1979. He had been sent there to find out if easterners really did hate westerners. After a number of cursory interviews with Torontonians strolling about the streets, he went and stood under the CN Tower to report his ambiguous conclusion, one that I found impossible to understand, no matter how many times I replayed the film. What was important, however, is that he sounded sincere, as though he really cared about Canadian unity. He successfully created a message through image and emotion alone.

Klein was also adept at creating news when there wasn't any. In 1979 he lived on the Blackfoot Reserve, east of Calgary, for three weeks to better understand native issues. The subsequent television reports featured interviews with various Blackfoot talking about racism, poverty, alcoholism, and day-to-day life. This wasn't exactly news, especially in light of the issues raised, sit-ins and armed stand-offs carried out in the 1970s by radical native groups such as the American Indian Movement (AIM). But reporting from a house on the reserve, or a tavern in Cluny in his folksy, unpretentious style, Klein left the impression that the Blackfoot had just been discovered by him, and while they had their problems, they were ordinary people like the rest of us. He didn't give much credence to any of the radical native politics of the time in his coverage of native issues. Rather, he focused on chiefs and band administrators who preferred to work within the hierarchical, colonial system established by the government and the Department of Indian Affairs. Instead of challenging the system and those who were part of it, as AIM and others had done, Klein featured those who had done well by it because they knew how to play the game.

Klein took up another crusade in 1979, one that would eventually take him into politics. Calgary was growing as fast as a young adolescent, pumped with new money from rising oil and gas prices. Multi-million dollar building projects were the order of the day. One such project — the Civic Centre — would have seen all of east Calgary and its old shops, run down apartment buildings, and hotels razed to the ground and replaced by a covered mega-mall and municipal complex.

Klein took up the cause of the pensioners, poor people and small businesses who lived and worked in the area. When the 1980 municipal elections rolled around, he announced that he was running for mayor. The announcement took almost everyone he knew by surprise. He didn't have any big money behind him. He didn't even have a platform other than a desire to get Calgary back into the hands of ordinary people and away from the developers and business types who controlled city hall. Klein would later say that he decided to leave TV journalism for politics because he had become "biased" in favour of citizens fighting against city hall's plans for a new civic centre. He said he wasn't being objective anymore, but reporting his "thoughts" on the issue. Since he made these remarks after he was elected, it's hard to know if Klein used his power as a television reporter to project himself into politics or if he used his public prominence to cast doubt on the integrity of the media.

Klein's quixotic campaign attracted Rod Love, a head waiter at a popular restaurant and a self-described political junkie. He became the campaign manager and chief strategist, something Klein badly needed. For while Klein was a natural performer, and loved the adulation his performances brought him, he was not a good organizer. When he was in television,

camera crews and news editors helped him look good. Now Rod Love
would perform the same function. When the campaign was over, Klein had
beaten the incumbent mayor, Ross Alger, and well known lawyer Peter Pe-
trasuk, with a campaign budget of about $25,000. He was thirty-seven years
old, had no experience in politics, and was now the mayor of Canada's fast-
est growing city. Klein appointed Rod Love as his executive assistant. A
short time later Love married the mayor's personal secretary.

Booming Along with Ralph

When Klein first moved into city hall, Calgary's business community
had nothing but disdain for him. They saw him as an interloper, a crude,
rude TV reporter who knew nothing about the complexities of business or
politics. Klein portrayed himself as a champion of ordinary Calgarians: the
people who hung out in the St. Louis Tavern just behind city hall; the people who were upset about potholes and road paving; people like his old
neighbours in Tuxedo Park. Remarkably, although he had been a television
reporter for eleven years, he still had that "ordinary" air about him. He was
pudgy. He lived in a house in the middle-middle-class area of Lakeview, that
was neither grand, nor shabby. A house like the houses that most people in
Calgary lived in. His wife Colleen (he had remarried while he was a TV reporter) was an accounting clerk at a supermarket.

Klein's commitment to the ordinary citizen was soon tested, and he
didn't do very well. The issue was the Saddledome and where it should be
built. The powerful Stampede Board wanted it located on the Stampede
Grounds so it could be a lucrative part of their empire. The neighbouring
residents of Victoria Park were not enthusiastic about this proposal. Victoria
Park was a poor community, and the Stampede would have to expropriate
part of it to accommodate the Saddledome. Residents feared property values would dive, and the neighbourhood would be driven even closer to ex-
tinction. At first Klein fought for a different location, but he eventually
backed the Stampede Board and its allies, the city commissioners, and
opted for the Victoria Park location. The little people of Victoria Park had
lost the battle. But Klein was well aware that most people in Calgary were
eager for a hockey rink that could house an NHL franchise and also could
be used as bait to lure the Winter Olympics.

To fully understand Ralph Klein's success as mayor (he ran three times,
and in the last election garnered 93 percent of the vote), it is important to
remember what was happening in Calgary in the 1980s. The city was at the
height of the biggest boom ever when Klein was elected. People and money

were flowing into Calgary as fast as water off a glacier in spring. A group of local businessmen and civic boosters had already organized a bid for the Winter Olympics. And only a year into Klein's term, the IOC awarded Calgary the 1988 Games. When the price of oil plummeted in the mid-1980s and oil companies started laying off employees, public and private funding of Olympic administration and facilities stalled the effects of the recession for several years.

Downtown Calgary was almost entirely rebuilt during Klein's reign as mayor, much of it with taxpayers' money. Before Klein there was no Saddledome, new city hall, civic plaza, performing arts centre, the flashy downtown Bankers Hall shopping centre. During his tenure, China Town was expanded and refurbished; Prince's Island was groomed into a major downtown attraction; Light Rail Transit was extended into the northeast and northwest of the city. Olympic facilities for ski-jumping, bobsledding, luge, and speed-skating were built. For several years the Winter Games focused Calgarians' energy and attention, and brought the city international recognition.

The 1980s were a heady, exciting time for many Calgarians. And in his inimitable way, Ralph Klein absorbed that optimism and beamed it back to people like a beacon. He publicly promoted huge building projects, even though he had swept into office opposing one. In the early 1980s, some citizens opposed plans for Bankers Hall Shopping Centre because it would cast a permanent shadow on streets and shoppers below. But Klein said: "Sunlight shouldn't get in the way of commerce." The power brokers he had scorned as a TV reporter became some of his best allies. One of his most important confidants was Brian Scott, a powerful and charismatic lawyer who represented many of the large developers. Klein also relied heavily on George Cornish, the chief city commissioner.

When preparations for the Olympics began heating up Klein allied himself with Juan Antonio Samaranch, the head of the International Olympic Committee, and the antithesis of the ordinary man. The mayor caught Samaranch's attention, and loyalty, after he flew some of his Blackfoot friends to Montréal to initiate Samaranch as an honourary chief during a brief stopover. But when the Lubicon Band of northern Alberta called for a boycott of the Olympics to bring attention to their poverty and outstanding land claim, Klein quickly denounced them. And a few weeks before the Olympics got underway, he flew to Europe, again accompanied by his friends from the Blackfoot Reserve, to persuade people that not all Indians in Canada were hard done by.

Massaging the Media

While Klein hobnobbed with the rich and powerful, he cleverly maintained his public image of the ordinary man. He was careful not to isolate himself at city hall or Chamber of Commerce meetings. His TV experience had given him an entrée into many sectors of Calgary society. He knew that most people weren't particularly interested in city council meetings. Calgarians wouldn't judge him on his performance there. He would be judged by his performance on TV and his personal contact with Calgarians. So he skipped a lot of council meetings and became a highly visible public relations man. He could be seen at everything from Chinese New Year celebrations to the stock car races. In 1985, he drove a Camaro superstock around three circuits at the opening of the Race City Speedway. And then when he tried to get out of the car, got stuck in the window. Needless to say, the crowd loved it. At the official opening of a swimming pool, he dove in, spare tire and all. When twenty-two mayors from across Canada were in Calgary for a conference, he took them all to the grotty St. Louis for a beer.

Of course, many of these antics were duly recorded by the media in photographs, films, and stories. For the media, Klein was a godsend. He was always good for a quotable quote on any issue, an unusual pose, two minutes of lively film ... and leaks. Many of the reporters, photographers, cameramen, and cartoonists who covered him also drank with him. But there was a lot more than just boozy, male camaraderie going on. The journalists got information and tips from Klein. Sometimes he, or Rod Love, would even let them read confidential documents, as long as they didn't reveal the source. When Klein left the mayor's chair for a chair at the provincial cabinet table, the local media lost one of their best sources of news. Klein was good for guaranteed reaction to any issue, quotable quotes, leaks to the media, and a sense of humour, wrote Don Martin, city hall columnist for the *Calgary Herald*.[2]

Klein's ability to manipulate the media, particularly front-line reporters and columnists, stemmed from his own experiences in TV journalism. He knew they would be willing to overlook all kinds of flaws, as long as there was the promise of important leaks and tips. He was so adept at this sort of manipulation that he even managed to turn his mistakes and shortcomings into good TV material, adding to the notion that he had nothing to hide; that with Ralph Klein, what you see is what you get.

One of the most interesting examples occurred shortly after he was elected mayor. During a televised interview, a CFCN reporter asked Klein about rumours that he had associated with prostitutes and drug dealers before he became mayor. Klein replied in a matter-of-fact manner that as a reporter he had to associate with such people because that's the way he did investigative stories. Without so much as a blink of the eye he turned what could have been a devastating interview into an opportunity to tell people about all the fascinating things he had done as a reporter.

In another televised interview, a reporter asked him about an impaired driving charge. Again, Klein waded right into the allegation, admitted it was true and talked about what he learned from the experience. He concluded by saying "those are the licks you have to take" if you are going to drink and drive. When rumours started circulating that he had ordered two policemen to drive him home because he was too drunk to drive, he told a television reporter that the policemen had "offered" to drive him home because they wanted to take him on a tour of the city's high crime areas.

Klein became so adept at turning controversy into acclaim he even managed to create a mythology about himself beyond Calgary. The "eastern creeps and bums" affair is a prime example. During a routine speech to the New Comers Club, at the height of the boom, Klein said easterners who wanted to come to Calgary to commit petty crime, or rob banks, weren't welcome. He called them "bums and creeps."[3] Only one reporter was at the luncheon, but when the story appeared on the front page of the *Calgary Herald*, media across the country latched onto it. In headlines and newscasts from Victoria to St. John's, Klein was portrayed as a paranoid, rude, redneck Albertan. Again, Klein jumped right into the controversy, relishing all the attention. He didn't back away from print or electronic interviews. Instead, he went on a tour of eastern Canada to explain his remarks, and reassure easterners that he and other Calgarians weren't really bigots or rednecks. He got even more coverage. And most of it was beamed back to Calgary. He may not have thoroughly convinced easterners of his position, but by the time the affair had cooled down, Ralph was still a hero to most Calgarians. He had said publicly what many people were talking about over coffee or beer.

It's doubtful Klein could have successfully shuffled all his competing images without the wily and workaholic Rod Love. Klein knew how to make the most of the moment. But Love, who sports a large handlebar mustache, knows how to make the most of the future. He is a plotter, a strategist who thrives on the power to control people and events. During Klein's term as mayor, Love spent much of his time on the phone cajoling, or browbeating, reporters and columnists into doing favourable stories about his boss, or unfavourable stories about Klein's enemies. He also kept Klein on a short leash. He made sure he didn't forget his important appointments, and didn't do or say anything too outrageous. Love was on holidays when Klein made his infamous "bums and creeps" speech, but usually he was never too far from Klein's side. Even today, he stands just behind Klein during media scrums, and screens most of the requests for interviews and meetings with the premier. And Love still berates editors and reporters over the phone if he doesn't like their spin on a Klein story. He is the shadow side of Klein's easy charm. The spike on the sole of the hush puppy. He needs Ralph Klein as much as Klein needs him. Love has taken a run at public office twice but failed miserably each time. He sought a federal PC nomination in southeast Calgary when Klein was mayor but was defeated by Lee Richardson. When Klein was environment minister he ran for the Tories in a by-election in Calgary Buffalo and finished third.

The Big Gamble Pays Off

In 1989, when the glory days of the Olympics were well behind him, Ralph Klein decided he needed another challenge. Being mayor had become too easy. "You find yourself saying the same things to the same groups, the same way. There comes a time when one looks forward to new challenges and new opportunities to do things for people," he said during an interview.

He announced he was running for the Tory nomination in Calgary Elbow, which included some of Calgary's wealthiest neighbourhoods. This was a bit of a turnabout for Klein. Only a short time before he had been touted as the man to harvest southern Alberta for the Liberals, who gained momentum every time Premier Don Getty made a gaffe. But like a chameleon, Klein had changed his party colours many times. He openly admitted he had held Social Credit, Liberal, and Tory party cards. He backed Ron Ghitter when he ran for the leadership of the Tory party after Peter Lougheed retired. He attended a rally for Prime Minister Brian Mulroney in the days when Mulroney was still popular enough to appear at public rallies. He expressed interest in the provincial Liberals until Laurence Decore, the former mayor of Edmonton, was elected leader. He was eventually attracted to the Tories, he told a reporter, by Premier Don Getty's "sensitivity to people" not the party's "right-wing, free enterprise" philosophy.[4]

Klein won handily the nomination. But the election didn't come so easily. He won by only 900 votes. Many voters in Mount Royal and Elbow Park didn't like Klein's boorish ways, or the way he had inserted himself into their party. Other voters were less than inspired by the thought of another term for Don Getty. But a win is a win, and before long Getty invited Klein to join the cabinet as environment minister.

There was a lot of speculation in the media about how the free-wheeling Klein would adapt to the discipline of the party and cabinet system. For his part, Klein continued to publicly support Premier Getty, even though he was highly unpopular with many party members, and Albertans in general. Klein also promised that his department would be more open to environmentalists, and expressed the hope that he could use his skills as a communicator and mediator to create a consensus between them and the business community.

At the outset, environmentalists were enthusiastic about Klein's appointment. And he did do a number of things to make the ministry more open and accessible. But by the time Klein decided to run for the leadership of the party in 1992, environmentalists felt betrayed. The business community, however, made few public complaints. Klein had once again moved up another rung on the ladder of his ambition by promising to work with the marginalized, but in fact doing the exact opposite.

Klein kept a relatively low profile during his years as environment minister. He wasn't the flamboyant bon vivant he had been as mayor. He was much sterner. At a press conference he lost his temper and gave an environmentalist the middle finger salute. When he decided to run for the Tory leadership he allied himself with the sobersides of the party's rural right wing. He eventually rode into the premier's office on a wave of conservative angst over deficits and debt, big government, and elitist politicians. The Reform Party had prepared the way for him. But the Reform Party didn't have a provincial wing. Once again Klein had taken advantage of the changing tides and rolled into office.

He also managed to secure his power base in Calgary with the help of some powerful moneybags in the business community. Key to his campaign team were: Art Smith, businessman, backroom political fixer, and former Tory MP; Bruce Green, lawyer and lobbyist for the real estate development industry; and Al Bell, long connected to the construction and development industry. Peter Lougheed, the other Calgary premier, had been able to count on the movers and shakers in the oil industry for support. Klein had never been an integral part of that corporate culture, so he turned to the support he had established during his term as mayor. When he became premier his campaign team became his kitchen cabinet.

A new image of Ralph Klein had been crafted, and it was very different from the old image. When he was the mayor he was the jolly, fun loving ambassador of city hall — the kind of mayor that made people feel good about

being a Calgarian. His free-wheeling, casual, simple style of speaking and be-
having, was a reflection of how many Calgarians wanted to see themselves and
their city. It fit perfectly with the expansionistic, heady times of the 1980s.

Conclusion

Klein's new image fits perfectly with the flip side of those free-wheeling,
free-spending days. Now Ralph Klein is the tough soldier, the guy who won't
blink, even when faced with the toughest of challenges. He is the macho
hacker and slasher, who has to do painful things to people, for their own
good, and the good of Alberta. Instead of spending public money to tart up
city hall, or build hockey arenas, Klein is closing hospitals and making parents pay for kindergarten. It's hard to believe that when Klein left the
mayor's chair in Calgary, the city had a debt of $1.6 billion; only Montréal
owed more money than Calgary. It's hard to believe that the Ralph Klein
who now appears to abhor any kind of spending by government, once said
that spending public money during a recession was the best way to put people to work, and keep businesses from going bankrupt. "I think those were
brilliant decisions," he told a reporter just before he left for Edmonton.

When the interviewer asked him if he shouldn't have made some effort
as mayor to retire the debt faster, Klein replied: "It's like a mortgage on a
house. You pay it off over a reasonable time and don't try to incur any new
debt that's unnecessary." And then he added, "The civic debt just doesn't
worry me. It's not something new."

I don't know exactly when Klein became a born-again fiscal conservative. But he certainly learned his lines well. To watch him on TV, it's hard to
imagine that he has ever been anything but a deficit and debt slasher. His
ability to conceive and project an image on television that suits the times,
and the minds of voters, undoubtedly is his most important asset. Former
U.S. President Ronald Reagan was able to accomplish the same feat. And to
this day, he remains popular with the American people, even though his
term in office was marked with scandal, corruption, and a decline in the
standard of living for most Americans.

But Klein isn't just a puppet. He, and Rod Love, still have an uncanny
instinct for survival (or extremely good pollsters) because they are not
afraid to take radical action to maintain power. Before the last provincial
election Klein convinced most of his caucus they could do without a pension plan. It was a risky move, but without it, there was a good chance
Ralph's Team would have lost the election. Klein also recognized that the
spending habits of Ken Kowalski and Peter Trynchy were tarnishing him

and his government. So he dumped them from cabinet even though their support had been instrumental in the leadership campaign and the subsequent election. Klein has no qualms about turning on people who helped him achieve his goals, and allying himself with new power brokers.

And like Ronald Reagan, Klein is the just the right person to deliver the neo-conservative cant. He can preach the dogma of big business in a simple, folksy manner that appeals to people who feel powerless and marginalized. If an "ordinary guy" like Ralph Klein believes in cutting and privatizing health care and education, then it can't be all bad. Only an "ordinary guy" like Ralph Klein could brag about cutting people off welfare, and get away with it.

Most politicians can't stretch the canopy of credibility that thinly; their image would shred to tatters. But most politicians haven't learned to use television as well as Ralph Klein has. Television is a minute by minute medium that caters to the present. Viewers can't reread a newscast. They can't catalogue newspaper clippings and easily compare past and present. Most newscasts don't have time to present the history of an issue; they only have time for what happened today. Television is of the moment, just like Ralph Klein, and each moment is singular: it has no relationship to the moment before or the moment after. Television has no memory, and induces short memories in viewers. It is extremely useful for politicians like Ralph Klein. He doesn't have to have a clear ideology or cumbersome party apparatus to maintain power. Instead, he determines what ideology is important: what ideology will keep him in power. Television is all about projecting images, rather than specific thoughts or ideas. Context is secondary, if of any significance at all. That's why Ralph Klein has been able to present a myriad of images during his years in public life, and yet still be regarded by many Albertans as an "ordinary" man who is in touch with the people, and governs on their behalf.

Notes

1. M. Kundera, *The Book of Laughter and Forgetting*. Translated by M. H. Heim (Markham, Ontario: Penguin, 1986), 3.
2. D. Martin, column in the *Calgary Herald*, 22 March 1989, A3.
3. *Calgary Herald*, 7 January 1982, A1.
4. *Calgary Herald*, 15 January 1982, A5.

Chapter Three

KLEIN'S MAKEOVER OF THE ALBERTA CONSERVATIVES

David Stewart

> I'm going to be Laurence Decore's worst nightmare.
> Ralph Klein, December 1, 1992.[1]

On June 15, 1993, a cheering throng of Alberta Conservatives celebrated their seventh consecutive majority government as Premier Ralph Klein joyously welcomed them to the "miracle on the prairie." The miracle was the perpetuation in government of a party mired at 18 percent in the public opinion polls only months before the election.[2] Unquestionably, the agent of the miracle was Ralph Klein.

Miraculous victories were not the norm for Conservatives in Alberta. Since first seizing office in 1971, the party had won every provincial election. In the early 1990s, however, its grip on power seemed to be slipping. Part of the problem faced by the Conservatives was the stewardship of Klein's predecessor, Don Getty. Getty became leader of the party in 1985 but was unable to fully assume the mantle of Peter Lougheed. Unfortunately for Getty, his tenure as leader coincided with a dramatic downturn in the Alberta economy. His government stopped adding to the Heritage Fund and began running deficit budgets. Moreover, Getty's somewhat "hands off" style of management proved unpopular with Albertans. Indeed, in the 1989 election, Getty was defeated in his Edmonton riding and was forced to run in a by-election in a "safe" Conservative rural riding. Getty's decision in September 1992 to step down offered the party a chance of escaping his unpopularity: of going to the electorate with the claim that the party had changed and that things would be done differently under a new leader.

Conventional political wisdom suggests that a change of leaders provides governing parties with a tempting means of transforming themselves

in the eyes of the electorate. New leaders proclaim their innocence of unpopular decisions or mistakes made by the party in the recent past and argue that they constitute real change. Generally, such claims are
unsuccessful and most of these new leaders — like John Turner and Kim
Campbell — quickly lead their parties onto the opposition benches. Only a
minority are successful in retaining power for their party. Ralph Klein is
perhaps the most notable recent addition to that minority. This chapter explores Klein's "makeover" of the Conservative party, in particular the threat
posed by the Liberal party, the opportunity afforded by a new leadership selection process, some of Klein's pre-election actions as premier, and his performance in the 1993 election.

The Emergence of an Opposition Threat

The need for a makeover of the Conservative party must be understood in the context of the emergence of a strong opposition party in Alberta. Entering the 1993 election the New Democrats formed the official
opposition but their legislative strength was misleading. The New Democrats were not a genuine threat to Conservative hopes of reelection. Rather,
the threat came from the reborn Liberal party which actually attracted
more votes than the New Democrats in the 1989 election.

This was not the case during the Lougheed years. The provincial Liberals suffered from association with their federal counterparts, an association
which did not disappear despite a severing of links between the two levels in
1977. Lougheed was successful in fighting elections against the federal Liberals and tarring the provincial Liberals with the federal Liberal brush. In
his famous words "a Liberal is a Liberal is a Liberal." The election of a federal Conservative government in 1984 removed some of the federal stigma
from the provincial Liberals. In October of 1988, in a move which further
transformed their image, the Liberal party elected former Edmonton
mayor Laurence Decore as their leader.

Decore's ascension to the leadership of the Liberal party was momen-
tous because of his mayoral record of administrative competence and fiscal
responsibility. This was an area of considerable government vulnerability.
Attacks on the Conservative record in running up the deficit as well as its
management skills in dealing with such problems as the Gainers strike, the
Principal collapse, and the NovAtel loan guarantees had much resonance
with voters. Under Decore, the Liberal party emphasized the fiscal and
management shortcomings of the Conservatives. The 1993 election campaign saw Decore travel around Alberta with a deficit clock which rang up

Alberta's ever increasing debt. This prop was aimed at demonstrating the Conservative's lack of fiscal responsibility.

The changed circumstances of the Liberal party could also be seen in their financing. In 1989, the year of the last election, the Liberals could not compete financially with their main rivals. The Liberal party raised only $1.4 million while the Conservatives almost tripled that figure with $3.7 million. In 1993, however, the Liberals crept closer to the Tories, trailing the governing Conservatives by less than $600,000 ($3,151,599 to $3,717,794).[3] In 1993, the Conservative dynasty faced a better financed and organized Liberal party which offered as their candidate for premier an individual with an established record of managerial skills and fiscal responsibility. Having thus positioned themselves as a party which could offer Albertans "safe" change, the Liberals were poised to confront the government on a vulnerable flank.

In 1971, Peter Lougheed led the Conservatives to power in part by convincing Albertans that they had nothing to fear from electing a Conservative government and that by doing so they could "replace the complacency and ineptitude which he argued had crept into the Social Credit."[4] In 1993, Decore and the Liberals could essentially use the same words to indict the Conservatives. The election promised to be the most competitive the province had seen in some time.

The attractiveness of the Liberal message on the debt and deficit was enhanced by the popularity of the federal Reform Party (see chapter four). Under Preston Manning, the right-wing, populist Reform Party was similarly attacking the federal Conservatives in Alberta on the issue of deficits and debts. But this was not the only common ground between the Liberals and Reform. The two parties also were of like mind with respect to parliamentary reform. Both advocated more use of free votes and the institution of recall to rid constituencies of unpopular and unresponsive MLAs. In keeping with what seemed to be the temper of the time in Preston Manning's Alberta, the Liberal party also moved to offer a more comfortable home for "social" conservatives. A number of Liberal candidates made clear their opposition to the protection of gay rights, and Decore declared his opposition to abortion clinics in the province. In spite of their repositioning and popular message, as they approached the next election, the Liberals suffered from a problem common to opposition parties facing an incumbent and unpopular leader: the tendency to assume the next election would be about that leader and his or her record in government.

Parties in government, however, are not simply the passive victims of changes in the political winds. They can both tack their sails and choose new captains. Alberta's Conservatives did both. The Conservative party which chose Klein as leader was different from the Conservative party which had existed two years earlier.

The old Conservative party was closely associated with the federal Conservative party, an association of limited benefit given the unpopularity of Brian Mulroney's government and the concomitant popularity of Preston Manning's Reform Party in Alberta. Reform attacked the federal Conservatives for not adequately addressing the deficit "problem" and for not being open or responsive to the concerns of the grass roots. Similar attacks could have been launched as effectively on the provincial Conservatives and in the context of Alberta politics might well have made Reform the government.

Reform, however, declined to enter provincial politics. On the same weekend in 1991 in which Reform reaffirmed their commitment to avoid provincial politics, the Alberta Conservatives decided to weaken their connections with the federal Tories. No longer would the party's constitution commit them to promoting "the interests and principles" of the federal Tories and provincial members would no longer be "required" to "work" for federal Tory candidates. Such changes obviously would make it easier for Albertans who supported the federal Reformers to remain at home in the provincial Conservatives. Albertans whose first loyalty was to Reform no longer needed to worry that their support for the provincial Conservatives militated against the interests of their first love.

The Direct Election Opportunity

In addition to this distancing, the provincial Conservatives decided to change their leadership selection method from the traditional convention and delegate system to a direct vote by all members. They hoped this would allow individuals to develop a more direct stake in the party, revitalizing it through an infusion of new members, and otherwise providing the party with a more "populist" image. Getty's decision to step down provided the party with an opportunity to utilize this new method.

The direct vote certainly attracted new members to the party. Most of those who voted in the party's 1992 leadership election joined the party for the first time that year. Moreover, only a tiny minority of the 1992 voters had ever held an elected office within the party or even engaged in campaign work in 1989.[5] Unlike delegates to previous Conservative conventions, most of the 1989 voters were not members of the federal Conservatives. Only 35 percent of the second ballot voters in 1992 were members of any federal political party and of that group just 57 percent were federal Tories. Fully 38 percent of the voters who held a federal membership were Reformers. The relatively high proportion of Reformers who participated in the selection of a provincial Tory leader is particularly striking when one notes that in April of 1992 there were 45,488 Reform Party members in Alberta.[6] Using the 78,251 second ballot voters as a base, roughly one-quarter of Reform's membership voted in the Tory leadership race. The decision of the provincial PCs to reduce their ties with the feds was thus an astute strategic move that kept open a provincial home for thousands of Reformers.

To understand the Conservative recovery, it is important to look closely at the leadership selection process that made Klein premier. The 1992 Conservative leadership election marked the first use of the universal ballot to select a leader in Alberta. The rules adopted for this selection process were minimal. In order to participate one needed only to be a Canadian citizen, sixteen years of age or older, with a six month residence in Alberta. And of course, one had to purchase a $5 Conservative membership for 1992. There were no deadlines or cut off points for obtaining a membership. Indeed memberships were available at the polls on the day of both ballots.[7] As with traditional leadership conventions, an absolute majority was necessary for victory. If no candidate secured a victory on the first ballot, a second ballot would be held a week later with the choice limited to the three leading vote getters. To avoid a further ballot, a preferential ballot would be used the second week.

This "premier primary" was a huge success. In a round table on leadership selection, Conservative MLA and current speaker of the legislature Stan Schumacher maintained that "the adoption of a direct election format has had a dramatic and rejuvenating effect on the PC party ... [and] created genuine excitement and prominent media coverage."[8] The process involved thousands of Albertans with more than 52,000 voting on the first ballot and more than 78,000 people turning out for the second vote. The race attracted three times as many candidates as the previous leadership convention but generated no where near the same amount of negative media and public attention.[9] Six members of the Getty Cabinet sought the leadership as did one former member of Peter Lougheed's cabinet and two individuals who had never before sought elected office as Tories.[10] The campaign was neither exciting nor riven with intense policy debates. The highlights were the all-candidate forums held in regional centres across Alberta. As one would expect with nine candidates, the two to three hour forums, featuring opening and closing remarks by each candidate, allowed for limited policy debate. Klein, the environment minister, was perceived as the front runner, a status engendered or enhanced by endorsements from a majority of the Tory caucus.

The leadership race provided an early indication that Conservatives were trying to distance themselves from Getty and push his government's record into the background. As the *Calgary Herald* explained, "Candidates have charged the party fell out of touch with Albertans during Getty's leadership."[11] The *Edmonton Journal* indicated that Getty did not seem to mind this: "Getty said he isn't holding any grudges despite Betkowski's promise of a new politics and Klein's railing against the status quo."[12]

The first ballot results took most observers by surprise. Confounding expectations, Health Minister Nancy Betkowski, on the basis of overwhelming support in her home town of Edmonton, finished one vote ahead of Klein. As the second ballot results would show, the neck-and-neck first round results obscured somewhat the strength of Klein's candidacy as he ran first in forty-five of the eighty-three constituencies. Clearer, however, was the lead of the two front runners over the other seven candidates who attracted less than 40 percent of the vote and who carried just fourteen ridings. Indeed, the gap between the front runners and third place Rick Orman was sufficiently large to induce Orman to forgo his right to contest the second ballot. While rules required the inclusion of his name on the ballot, he in fact did not campaign and urged his supporters to support Betkowski. Orman was joined in his support of Betkowski by five of the other six candidates, contributing to the impression that Betkowski was headed for a relatively easy second ballot victory. One of the other candidates, Culture Minister Doug Main went so far as to claim that Ralph had "zero growth potential."[13] Mr. Main possessed an uncanny ability for underestimating and annoying Ralph Klein. Earlier in the leadership campaign he said in reference to Klein, "We can't win this province back, we can't be the government — with a smoking, drinking, paving, glad-handing premier."[14]

The week between the ballots was not marked by substantive policy debate. Betkowksi and Klein both continued to present themselves as the agents of change but the major sources of attention were the endorsements of Betkowski by the other candidates, her unwillingness to debate Klein on TV, and suggestions from Klein's caucus supporters that Betkowski could not win an election for the party. Some even suggested that Betkowski's gender would hinder her ability to serve as an effective premier. As Lloydminster MLA Doug Cherry put it, "You know women, they get moody."[15]

The Klein camp also used the week to stress that he rather than Betkowski represented real change. In Klein's words, "I've only been there three and a half years. Nancy has been around since the beginning ... She is really the Tory establishment."[16] In addition, Klein suggested that he would be more likely to keep the Conservatives in power, and that for this reason the supporters of opposition parties were trying to get Betkowski elected. As he put it, "I don't know if the Liberals are voting for Nancy because they like her. I think the Liberals who are voting for her think that I'm going to be Laurence Decore's worst nightmare."[17]

The second ballot demonstrated Klein's ability to mobilize support, highlighting especially his popularity in the critical areas of Calgary and rural Alberta. Betkowski outpolled Klein in the opposition stronghold of Edmonton but Klein carried almost every other riding in the province. Betkowski retained most of her first ballot voters but was hurt by the decisions of many supporters of the minor candidates to sit out the second ballot. Her biggest problem, however, was that Albertans came out of the woodwork to vote for Ralph Klein and against her.[18] More than 80 percent of the individuals who voted only on the second ballot backed Klein, turning what was projected to be a close race into a one-sided victory. Six months later, a number of highly placed Conservatives would partially attribute their election victory to the successful leadership election and its ability to energize the party and generate new members.

Klein's leadership campaign reveals something of both his style and the audience most receptive to his message. Unlike his major opponents, Klein's campaign did not rely heavily on detailed position papers or specific proposals for the first "200 days" of his government. Instead, he appealed to voters who wanted a simple, more grass roots oriented style of governing. Klein attracted voters who wanted the common people to have a more direct voice in government. Voters who believed that "we need a government that gets the job done without red tape," that "problems could be solved by bringing them back to the grassroots," who trusted the "simple down to earth thinking of ordinary people rather than the theories of intellectuals," and who wanted referenda on all constitutional amendments, opted overwhelmingly for Klein.

The nature of Klein's appeal is further demonstrated by the background of his supporters. Klein voters were disproportionately male, unlikely to have completed a university degree, and more likely to report a low income level. While 60 percent of Betkowski voters held post secondary degrees, Klein's staunchest backers were those who had not completed high school. The likelihood of a Betkowski vote also increased with income. While farmers, ranchers, and voters who held clerical jobs or were hourly employed were Klein's strongest supporters, students, health care workers, administrators, and other professionals generally preferred Betkowski.

Klein's victory over Betkowski also is instructive in terms of understanding the degree of change in the Conservative party. Opening up the party to individuals who did not support the federal Conservatives proved significant. Federal Reformers were an important part of the Klein support coalition with 75 percent of them opting for him over Betkowski. Her highest levels of support came from the voters who were also federal Tory members. In spite of this, it appears that the choice of Klein was one which was not aimed at broadening the Conservative appeal. Rather, it was a choice more likely to solidify Conservative support in areas where they had been victorious in 1989. Looking at the 1992 results on a riding by riding basis illustrates this point. Betkowski did substantially better than Klein in ridings not held by the Conservatives, but Klein was the clear choice in Tory controlled ridings.

A New Government?

As premier, Klein attempted to demonstrate that his government was not a replica of Getty's and that real change had taken place. Klein's ability to avoid association with the Getty regime was aided by a rather extraordinary lack of support from Getty's cabinet. While he was supported by most MLAs, the same was not true of the provincial cabinet. Klein was backed by only a minority of the group which worked most closely with him. This lack of cabinet support provided Klein with much room for manoeuvring following his victory since he owed few debts to his fellow cabinet ministers. None of the cabinet members who contested the leadership were part of the Klein cabinet. Klein's cabinet was top heavy with his campaign supporters, most of whom, for whatever reasons, had not played prominent roles under Getty.

The legislature looked quite different after Klein took over. Of the sixteen Conservatives who occupied the front bench with Getty, only seven remained to flank Klein. The turnover in cabinet was nothing short of phenomenal. Getty's cabinet was relatively large at twenty-six, Klein — in a popular move which provided an initial indication that his government would be different from Getty's — reduced it to seventeen. In spite of this reduction, however, he also managed to promote seven back benchers, with the result that more than half of those who served in Getty's cabinet did not serve under Klein.

Many of the important decisions governments make are not made by the plenary cabinet but by cabinet committees. Under Getty the most important committees were Priorities, Finance and Coordination, and Treasury Board. Lending credence to Klein's attempts to escape the image of Getty's government is his absence from those committees. The Priorities, Finance and Coordination (PFC) committee is also notable for the relative paucity of Klein supporters: Of the eleven members of this Inner Cabinet only three supported Klein in his quest for the leadership. Klein's new committee system had at its forefront an Agenda and Priorities (A and P) Committee. The membership of A and P was dramatically different from that of Getty's PFC. None of the eight PFC members who failed to support Klein's leadership bid were appointed to A and P. Indeed, none of these eight PFC members were appointed to cabinet at all! Most of the cabinet ministers who were not reappointed by Klein were individuals who held positions of significant authority in the Getty administration. At the level of personnel, the Klein cabinet and inner cabinet looked substantially different.

Klein found other ways to distance himself from his predecessor. In a somewhat controversial decision, Getty decided that his new office would not be in the legislature but instead on the 27th floor of the Manulife Building in downtown Edmonton — a much more luxurious and expensive location. Klein quickly made clear that the government of Alberta was not going to pay for these new digs. As well, Getty suggested that as an elder statesman he would not attend legislative sittings. In response to public criticism of this decision, Klein indicated that Getty's salary should be reduced for nonattendance. These measures to distinguish himself from Getty flew in the face of Klein's victory statement that he had become a Conservative because of Mr. Getty and the effusive thanks he bestowed on Getty in his victory address. This somewhat ruthless attack on the former premier displayed a sensitivity to popular opinion and helped further the perception that a new government was in office.

But the most significant change Klein was able to institute as he filled out Getty's mandate was ending the MLA pension scheme. At the time, Alberta MLAs possessed a very lucrative pension scheme, a fact that (in the context of public furor over government "waste") made them vulnerable to a Liberal election attack. Indeed, the Liberals planned to highlight these and other legislative perks in their campaign. Shortly before the election was called, however, Klein moved on the pension front. Instead of reforming the pension scheme he abolished it. No MLA elected in 1989 or after would qualify for a public pension. By making the cut-off point 1989 Klein ensured that he himself would not benefit but the many former cabinet ministers who had decided not to run again would retain rather generous benefits.

The impact of this decision should not be underestimated. First, it was extremely helpful in reinforcing Klein's populist image. Albertans thought the scheme was too lucrative; Klein listened and took action. Secondly, the Liberal plan to draw attention to pensions and perks was largely derailed by the elimination of pensions. Thirdly, the perception was reinforced that a Klein-led government was different from Getty's, not only in style and personnel but also, to some degree, in substance. Fourthly, criticism of the federal pension scheme and perks was to be a key element of the Reform Party's 1993 federal campaign. By acting to cancel such measures at the provincial level, Klein kept the provincial Tories singing from the same page of the hymn book as the federal Reformers.

Klein's makeover of the Conservative party continued in the 1993 provincial election.[19] As Doug Main hinted in his comments about Klein becoming a "paving" premier, leadership candidate Klein had not seemed overly concerned with debts and deficits. But as premier, Klein made it clear that his government was committed to balancing the budget and was ready to make the massive spending cuts necessary for such an achievement. The emphasis on balancing the budget and making the required spending cuts once more firmly tied the provincial Conservatives to the most popular federal party in the province: Reform. Reform's message on this issue was virtually indistinguishable from that of the provincial Conservatives: that it also was indistinguishable from the provincial Liberals seemed increasingly irrelevant as the campaign wore on. Rather, the message hammered home the difference between Klein Tories and Getty Tories. While Getty Tories might irresponsibly run up a deficit and a debt, Klein Tories not only disagreed with these actions, they were prepared to reverse course and clean up the mess. The Klein Conservatives seemed as much in competition with the Getty Conservatives as they were with Decore and the Liberals. That competition was one Klein and his team would easily win.

The Conservative resurgence is illustrated by fundraising and spending during the campaign period. As noted earlier, the Liberals had become more competitive in terms of financing. However, once the 1993 campaign was officially launched the Conservatives were able to outspend the Liberals by a two to one margin and money flowed much more freely into the Conservative party's coffers. Seventy-seven percent of the 1993 money donated by corporations to the Conservatives came during the campaign. The corresponding figure for the Liberals was 63 percent. Obviously, as the election outcome became clearer, corporate money was returning to the Conservatives.

The premier's attack on the deficit undoubtedly made his party more attractive to corporate donors and this combined with his abolition of MLA pensions did much to neutralize the Liberal campaign. Klein's teflon-like ability to escape blame for the Getty era hammered the final nail into the Liberal coffin. With issues neutralized, the 1993 election was free to turn on image and personality. In this new battle of Alberta, Decore and his debt clock would prove no match for Ralph Klein and his "He Listens, He Cares" campaign. The Liberals had attempted to outflank the Conservatives on the right and fight an election on the government's fiscal record. Under Klein the Conservatives were able to counteract the flanking manoeuvre and fight the election on terrain more favourable to them.

Conclusion

A year before the election it seemed that Albertans were going to witness something seen only rarely in the province: A change of regimes. Arguably, the province witnessed such a change, but not one which brought a new party into power. Reform and the Liberals helped construct a political climate in which deficits and debts were the most important issues, essentially forcing the Conservatives to respond by changing leaders, repudiating responsibility for the deficit, and promising to eliminate it quickly. They were elected on an issue from the Reform agenda with a leader who was the choice of most Reformers who voted in the December 5, 1992, "premier primary." Under Ralph Klein's leadership, the Conservative party presented itself as the agent of change and made sufficient cosmetic and substantive changes to make that presentation convincing to the electorate. Klein proved an immense asset to the party. The popular ex-mayor of Calgary campaigned as if he wanted to be the next mayor of Alberta and his folksy style and common touch proved much more attractive to Albertans than the austere image projected by Decore. Since the Depression, the only political change Albertans have accepted has been "safe change." In 1993 the safest change seemed to be the reelection of the Conservative government albeit disguised as Ralph's Team.

Klein's victory in the 1992 and 1993 elections should be seen as exemplifying a transformation of the Conservative party. Superficially, but meaningfully, the transformation in the eyes of voters need not have gone much beyond Klein's physical replacement of Getty. Victory in general elections is often dependent on getting voters to have the right question in mind as they cast their ballots. For the Conservatives in 1993 it was crucial that the question voters asked themselves was not "do I want to reelect a Conservative government?" but rather, "do I want to elect 'Ralph' and his team?" The fact that a yes to the latter was also a yes to the former was unimportant. Voters did not hold Klein responsible for the actions of the Getty government *even though Klein was part of "Don's Team" in the 1989 election and had thereafter loyally served in Getty's Cabinet.* The Conservative campaign message in 1993 was that Klein brought real change and was not accountable for previous Tory problems. This was a message that the opposition Liberals seemed unable to contradict and one for which they seemed curiously unprepared. Klein may indeed have been Laurence Decore's worst nightmare. The opposition leader's nocturnal ordeals were about to spread to other Albertans.

Notes

1. *Edmonton Journal,* 1 December 1992, A5.
2. See the *Alberta Report,* 28 June 1993, 6.
3. These figures are taken from the 13th and 17th Annual Reports of the Chief Electoral Officer of Alberta.
4. D. Elton and A. Goddard "The Conservative Takeover, 1971." In C. Caldarola, ed., *Society and Politics in Alberta* (Toronto: Methuen, 1979), 52.
5. The data on participants in the 1992 Conservative leadership election comes from a survey I conducted of second ballot voters in that election.
6. T. Flanagan "A Comparative Profile of the Reform Party of Canada." Paper presented to the Annual Meeting of the Canadian Political Science Association, Charlottetown, 1992.
7. This rule distinguished the Alberta Conservative process from virtually every other universal ballot held in Canada. Most of them possessed some sort of cut off point after which one was not eligible to vote for the leader. In some cases the cut off points were about the mid-way point of the contest.
8. Stan Schumacher in "Reforming the Leadership Convention Process, Round-table Discussion on Leadership Selection," *Canadian Parliamentary Review,* Volume 16, No. 3 (1993), 8.
9. For a discussion of the 1985 convention see K. Archer and Hunziker, "Leadership selection in Alberta: The 1985 Progressive Conservative Leadership Convention." In R. K. Carty, L. Erickson, and D. Blake, *Leaders and Parties in Canadian Politics* (Toronto: Harcourt Brace Jovanovich, 1992).
10. The candidates were, in order of first ballot finish: Health Minister Nancy Betkowski, Environment Minister Ralph Klein, Energy Minister Rick Orman, Culture Minister Doug Main, Social Services Minister John Oldring, Lloyd Quantz, Reuben Nelson, Labour Minister Elaine McCoy and former Education Minister David King.
11. *Calgary Herald,* 2 December 1992, A1.
12. *Edmonton Journal,* 5 December 1992, A5.

13. *Edmonton Journal,* 1 December 1992, A5.
14. *Edmonton Journal,* 6 December 1992, A6. Despite being one of only two Edmonton MLAs in the Conservative caucus, Main was not invited to enter Klein's cabinet.
15. Mr. Cherry tried to clarify his comments claiming that he was only joking. In his clarification he explained, "you know what the female race is like. Some days aren't as good for them as others — same as men" (quoted in the *Edmonton Journal,* 4 December 1992, A7).
16. *Edmonton Journal,* 1 December 1992, A5.
17. Ibid.
18. Those who voted only on the second ballot were extremely hostile to Betkowski. Not only did less than one-fifth of them vote for her, but more than one-quarter ranked her ninth out of nine candidates.
19. Most of the candidates who ran as Conservatives in the 1993 election had not been candidates in 1989. Although Klein was not directly responsible for this, he was the prime beneficiary since it helped substantiate his claim that a new government was in place.

Chapter Four

THE REFORM-ATION OF ALBERTA POLITICS[1]

Trevor Harrison

The Reform Party is strange ... in that they've pretty well picked up on everything that we have stood for in this province.

Don Getty, 1990.[2]

The Klein revolution frequently is seen as a response to political pressures exerted upon it by supporters of the federal Reform Party. In consequence, the Tories are viewed as something of a Reform clone. I want to challenge this dominant narrative in several ways. In particular, I want to suggest that Reform's initial rise was in part a response to an internal crisis of Alberta politics, specifically within the ruling Tory party, and that only later did Reform's federal presence lead to the restructuring of Alberta politics. Despite an obvious ideological compatibility, I want to further suggest that the future relationship between Reform and the Klein Conservatives may be less than compatible.

Reform and the Provincial Tories: The Dominant Narrative

Dominant explanations attribute the rise of the Reform Party federally to largely external factors, specifically anger vented at the Mulroney government. These explanations go something like this. In 1984, the Mulroney Conservatives were elected with the massive support of Western voters. In office, however, they disappointed these supporters. Increasingly alienated from the party they had long supported, right-wing Tory voters in the West began to look for a new political vehicle. In 1987, the Reform Party arose to fill this need.

Thereafter, as Reform grew in support, the federal Tories declined. In turn, anger in Alberta with the federal Tories began also to eat into support for the provincial Tories. Finally, in order to garner the Reform vote provincially, the provincial Tories broke with their federal counterparts and became, all but in name, a provincial wing of the Reform Party.

This narrative is largely correct, as far as it goes. But it also submerges some important questions. Are Reformers and Klein supporters necessarily synonymous? More fundamentally, perhaps, what was the influence of Alberta's internal politics upon the rise of Reform? These are questions that frame this chapter.

Do Reformers Support the Klein Conservatives? (And Vice Versa?)

Every year, around February, the Population Research Laboratory at the University of Alberta in Edmonton conducts a massive survey of about 1,250 Albertans. Among the political questions always asked are people's federal and provincial voting preferences. The 1994 survey found that over 55 percent of provincial Conservative support came from people who supported Reform, 18 percent from federal Tories. Similarly, 50 percent of Reform's federal support came from provincial Conservatives. In short, the assumption of a high correlation between federal Reformers and provincial Tories is somewhat correct. Nonetheless, this relationship is far from perfect. For example, 34 percent of federal Reform supporters said they would vote for a provincial Reform Party — if one existed. Clearly, many Reformers do not see Ralph Klein as having remade the provincial Tories in the exact image of Reform. In the recent past, moreover, this overlap of Tory and Reform support was even less evident.

An Angus Reid poll, conducted in 1990, showed that, among decided voters, the Reform Party would get 43 percent support if it ran provincially, compared with 20 percent for the Liberals, 19 percent for the New Democrats, and only 18 percent for the Tories.[3] Another Angus Reid poll, in February of 1991, showed the Reform Party gaining 48 percent of the vote if it ran provincially in Alberta, compared with the Tories' 12 percent.[4]

Why was support for the ruling Conservatives so low during these years? How did the party reverse its fortunes only a couple of years later? And what was Reform's influence on this turnaround? To answer these questions, one has to go back a few years to a time when Ralph Klein was still mayor of Calgary and Reform was just a glint in Preston Manning's eye.

Setting the Stage: the Lougheed Years

In February 1982, Peter Lougheed's Tories had already been in power for eleven years. His government had presided over numerous changes to the province during that period. Alberta was now largely urbanized and secular. Like its premier, Alberta struck a confidant, even cocky, figure upon the national stage.

These changes had been accompanied by a profound transformation in the role of government. Partly as a result of the great oil wealth that had flowed to Alberta during the 1970s, partly as a result of deep changes to Canadian confederation during this same period that had significantly devolved power to all the provinces, the Alberta government now played a much larger role in the lives of its electorate.

This new role was most evidenced by an expansion of provincial government service. Throughout the 1970s, Albertans increasingly demanded new services, to which the Lougheed government obliged and more. Hospitals, court houses, liquor stores, and other assorted buildings, arose everywhere as testimony to the largesse and munificence of the Tory government. Next to the oil field sector, the real winners during the Lougheed years were construction companies and sellers of red brick.

It was the heyday of province-building. As elsewhere in the West, the Alberta government began also to intervene more in the economy. Megaprojects were the primary economic vehicle of choice, but other opportunities soon arose. Eventually, Alberta even bought its own airline, Pacific Western Airlines, whose initials some wryly said meant "Peter Wanted an Airline."

One area, however, where the Tories were less intrusive than the previous Social Credit administration of Ernest Manning was in moral and social matters. The Socreds had tended to view themselves as protectors of public morality. By contrast, the dominant members of the Lougheed cabinet, if somewhat patrician, were mostly small "l" liberals. Laissez-faire may have been preached in economic matters; it was practised somewhat more fully on moral questions.

The first decade of Tory rule was a kind of golden age for Alberta. By early 1982, however, Lougheed's luck had begun to run out. During the previous two years he had been involved in a bitter conflict with the federal Liberals over the National Energy Program (NEP) and patriation of the Constitution. The parties had finally resolved these disputes, the first with the signing of an oil pricing agreement in September 1981, the second with an agreement, *sans* Québec, in November of the same year, to patriate the Constitution. Then, suddenly, the price of oil declined. The country, including Alberta, entered a recession that lasted throughout the remainder of 1981 and 1982.

Albertans have never forgiven the Liberals for the NEP and the subsequent recession. Even today, the NEP remains a kind of mythic demon that came out of the east, blocking out Alberta's day in the sun. Talk to any Alberta Reformer long enough and you will find the NEP like a Jungian archetype haunting his or her psychological alleyways.

The recession, however, also opened further cracks that had already begun to appear in provincial Tory support. Since 1979, a number of fringe parties had arisen on the Tory's right flank. Most of these parties were virulently anti-French, anti-Québec, anti-immigrant, anti-metric, and pro-laissez-faire — except, of course, if it meant ending wheat boards or other subsidies of which they approved. The most notable of these parties, Elmer Knutson's Confederation of Regions party (CoR) and Doug Christie's Western Canada Concept (WCC), were also separatist.

At first, the anger that fuelled these parties was directed almost solely at Canadian federalism and the Trudeau Liberals, particularly in the immediate aftermath of the 1980 federal election. However, the recession of 1981-82 displaced at least some of this discontent onto Lougheed's government as well. Perhaps more importantly, discontent with the Tories began also to spread beyond the extreme right fringe to other, more moderate elements in the province. Two not incompatible groups, in particular, became increasingly discontented. The first were social and moral conservatives, uneasy with changes to Alberta's normative order; the second were economic conservatives equally uneasy with the gap between Lougheed's free enterprise rhetoric and the reality of his interventionist policies. Faith in the Lougheed Tories began to waver.

In February 1982, Gordon Kesler, a thirty-five-year-old oil scout and rodeo rider, running for Western Canada Concept, won a by-election in Olds-Didsbury. Kesler's fifteen minutes of fame were not substantively important. Later that year, Lougheed's party took seventy-five of seventy-nine seats (62 percent of the vote) in, once again, winning office. In retrospect, however, Kesler's victory was a kind of warning shot sent by Alberta's right wing across the bow of the good ship Tory. While still largely inchoate and small in 1982, these discontented elements were nonetheless the vanguard of the political transformations that would soon follow.

In 1985, Lougheed announced he was quitting as leader. Despite growing unease with some of his administration's policies, the man that some called King Peter remained admired and respected by most Albertans. The throne was now empty. Who would succeed him?

Getty No Lougheed

In the 1950s, Peter Lougheed was a punt returner for the Edmonton Eskimos. Among other members of that star-studded team was a tall, handsome young quarterback named Don Getty. In later years, the two remained good friends, business partners, and, following the 1971 election, also political colleagues. Getty became energy minister. Then, in the mid-1970s, he quit politics to form his own business. Now, in 1985, the Tories handed him the leadership ball.

Unfortunately for Getty, the playing field was no longer tilting in Alberta's favour. The Lougheed Conservatives had been elected in 1971 on a platform of diversifying Alberta's economy. Although they made some progress in this regard, Alberta remained then — as now — heavily dependent upon a few staple industries, particularly oil and gas. As a result, no Western Canadian province experienced more economic volatility than Alberta during the 1980s.[5] When Getty took over, the provincial economy was about to suffer its second major recession of the decade.

In the midst of the recession of 1985-86, the Getty government adopted the full range of fiscal measures available to them: raising taxes, cutting expenditures, and running a deficit. Albertans, still coming down from the heady 1970s, sought out someone to blame for the change in circumstances. And while, as in the past, much fell upon the federal Liberals and central Canada, inevitably some of the blame also alighted on the provincial Tories and the new premier.

A leader's image is rarely a work in progress. More often it is something that becomes fixed, all at once, by some event or circumstance. For many Albertans, Don Getty's image was formed one June day in 1987 when the Principal Group collapsed. Reporters, wanting to interview him, were told by Getty's press secretary that he was "working out of the office." Getty's "office" — captured by a media photographer — turned out to be a golf course.

For many Albertans, the picture taken that day of Getty standing, mouth open, clutching a golf club, forever defined his image: a quiet, even detached figure, out for a Sunday stroll. Where Lougheed was a workaholic who viewed politics as a vocation, Getty seemed to view it as a hobby, something to do in between holidays in Palm Springs. Albertans had come to depend upon Lougheed to defend their interests; they were not sure they could count on Getty for the same. Within a short time, Albertans concluded that Getty was no Lougheed.

The first sign that Albertans were not pleased with the new-look Al-

berta Tories came in the 1986 provincial election. It was contested by a record ten political parties, many of them on the discontented right, and
twenty independent candidates. Although Getty's Tories again won, taking
sixty-one of eighty-three seats, their percentage of votes dropped to just
over 51 percent, while both the New Democrats and Liberals made substantial gains. Perhaps more ominous for the Tories, the percentage of eligible
voters casting ballots dropped to just over 47 percent, down from 66 percent the previous election.

By 1986, many Westerners also were increasingly frustrated with Brian
Mulroney's federal Tories. Only in Getty's Alberta, and to a slightly lesser degree in Bill Vander Zalm's British Columbia, however, did this frustration result in the idea of forming an alternative federal party. Throughout the fall of
that year, small but influential groups of discontented conservatives met in
various towns and cities in the two most westerly provinces. In the spring of
1987, they held an assembly in Vancouver and agreed to form a party. Later
that fall, a convention attended largely by Albertans was held in Winnipeg, at
which the Reform Party was founded. Preston Manning, the son of Alberta's
former Socred premier, was chosen leader. The rest, as they say, is history.

A year later, the Reform Party contested its first federal election,
eventually won by Brian Mulroney's Conservatives because of a polariza-
tion of votes around free trade. But Reform's performance was credible.
Running in only seventy-two Western ridings, Reform garnered 275,767
votes, 8.5 percent of all votes cast in those ridings. The party showed particularly strongly in Alberta where it obtained over 15 percent of all votes
cast, most of them in the south, including Calgary, and rural areas — all
key areas of provincial Tory support. One explanation for this overlap of
support seems obvious: Lacking a strong provincial government, conservative Albertans increasingly were turning to a federal alternative to protect their interests.

Had Ralph Klein — or even Peter Lougheed — been Alberta premier
in 1986-87, would the Reform Party have gotten off the ground? It is an in-
triguing question. Perhaps not. Certainly, its success would have been
blunted. In any case, after 1988, Reform and the provincial Tories were on
an inevitable collision course over who would capture the hearts and minds
of Albertans.

Getty and Meech Lake

In March 1989, Getty surprised everyone, including it seemed himself,
by announcing a snap election, then proceeding to run a lacklustre and

bumbling campaign. The Tories won anyway, taking fifty-nine of eighty-three seats, mainly because most Albertans saw no real alternative. The Liberals under new leader Laurence Decore were unknown, and lacked organization outside of Edmonton; the NDP, led by Ray Martin, were too "socialist." Nonetheless, the Tory percentage of vote once more declined, this time to just over 44 percent, as voter turnout rebounded to 54 percent. Getty himself was defeated, only returning to the legislature after capturing a "safe" rural seat in a Stettler by-election.

Political scientist Allan Tupper has said that the election was notable by "the absence of an explicitly 'right-wing' party," which he attributes to Albertans coming to entrust their faith in the three established parties.[6] I suggest, however, that a better explanation for this absence is that, by 1989, right-wing voters in the province had found a new champion in the Reform Party.

By early 1990, Reform was steadily gaining in federal support. But its members were also contemplating seriously whether the party should enter provincial politics. Nowhere was this considered more seriously than in Alberta where a committee, jokingly referred to as the "Task Force to Scare the Hell out of Don Getty," was formed to study the question.[7] Getty increasingly found himself under pressure from those within the Tory party who wanted the party to refashion itself in the image of Reform. This pressure came from a number of prominent Tories who simultaneously held Reform Party memberships, among them former Tory MLAs Stephen Stiles and Walter Szwender, and (then) current MLA's Marvin Moore, Ray Speaker, and Doug Main, the latter having been elected to the provincial legislature only after failing to gain a seat running for Reform in the 1988 federal election.[8]

Increasingly, Albertans in general also wanted a provincial Reform Party. As we have seen, in the spring of 1990, an Angus Reid poll indicated that the Reform Party would get 43 percent support if it ran provincially, almost certainly enough to form a majority government. Another poll, conducted by The Dunvegan Group during this same period, showed that 48 percent of Albertans wanted Reform to become active in provincial politics. Responding to these results, Getty said: "The Reform Party is strange … in that they've pretty well picked up on everything that we have stood for in this province except for one and that is Meech Lake."[9] It was, however, a notable exception.

The political circumstances surrounding the Accord are well known. In April 1987, Brian Mulroney met with the premiers at Meech Lake, just outside of Ottawa, to discuss constitutional changes that would allow

Québec to put its name on Canada's constitution "with dignity" and, not coincidentally, also repay Tory political debts owed to Québec nationalists for their support in 1984. To the surprise of everyone, the first ministers arrived at a constitutional agreement that granted Québec much of what it wanted. Subsequently, each of the premiers formally signed the agreement. All that remained for the Accord to become final was its formal ratification by the House of Commons and all ten provincial legislatures within three years.

Almost immediately, however, opposition arose to the Accord. The Accord's critics came from a wide spectrum of Canadian society: women's groups, Native Canadians, people from every part of the country and every political stripe; and, yes, outright bigots. As opposition mounted, the premiers who had signed the Accord found themselves in a no-win situation. On the one hand, they were duty bound to defend a document to which they had agreed; anything else would make them appear weak, vacillating, and untrustworthy. On the other hand, their continued defense of the Accord increasingly cost them credibility with their electorates. In the end, Meech Lake shipwrecked the careers of almost every politician who had been a signatory to the document.

Getty, whose support of the Accord seems to have been based on a genuine desire to address Québec's constitutional isolation, was placed in perhaps the worst situation. For, over the next three years, no organization was more responsible for mobilizing public opposition to the Accord, and gained so much politically from doing so, than the Reform Party whose base of support was strongest in Alberta.

The infamous last-second meeting in Ottawa in 1990, called by Mulroney to save the Accord, only added to Getty's political problems. It was bad enough in many people's eyes that he seemed to go along with the manipulative efforts of Mulroney, a man despised by many Canadians. In this, Getty appeared to be merely a naive dupe. But pity turned to outrage when stories later revealed that Getty at one point had physically blocked Newfoundland premier, Clyde Wells, a hero to many in English-speaking Canada for his opposition to the Accord, from leaving the closed-door meeting.[10]

Eventually, of course, the results of the week-long meeting went for naught. The Accord collapsed under the combined weight of time, public disapproval, and the Mulroney government's cynical machinations. The unravelling of Canada's political system accelerated. The political impact of the Meech Lake fiasco was felt no more dramatically, however, than in Alberta.

The Tories Move Right

After the Accord's failure, Getty's Tories were in political freefall. They were clearly out of step with many Albertans. The party itself was increasingly rent by internal divisions, particularly between its Reform faction and those who retained close ties with the federal Tories.

Getty had long attempted to blunt Reform's challenge. In response to Reform's growing insistence upon senate reform, in 1989 he had held an election to select Alberta's candidate to fill a vacant Senate seat. As we have seen, Getty also went so far as to suggest that there were no genuine differences between his party and Reform, a tactic he employed even more in the year following the collapse of the Meech Lake Accord. Getty's attempts at garnering support-by-association failed, however, to placate the anger of Reform-minded Albertans.

At the party's convention in April 1991, the Alberta Tories took several steps to try to staunch the bleeding. The most dramatic of these steps saw them sever formal ties to the federal party. The decision was especially applauded by prominent cabinet minister Ken Kowalski, a third of whose riding executive reportedly held Reform memberships.[11] But the convention also saw other important changes, most notably Getty's sudden adoption of the Reform Party's tough stand towards Québec and the constitutional negotiations that, with the failure of the Meech Lake Accord, were soon to begin anew. "Here in Alberta we have been generous — not just to Québec but to all of Canada," he said. "But if all we get for our generosity is people turning their backs on us, then the generosity will diminish." As for the threat of Québec's separation, Getty had a warning. "We don't like the idea of a huge gaping hole in the middle. But if the hole is created in the map of Canada, we too will remember. '*Je me souviens*' has its own equivalents in English."[12] Getty's stance was widely applauded by the Tory delegates.

Like a ship breached by high seas, Alberta's Tories began to list ever more violently to the right. Constitutional hearings held throughout the province in 1991 saw Alberta Tories parrot Reform in opposing such things as the Charter of Rights and Freedoms, official bilingualism, and multiculturalism, while favouring increased provincial rights and the establishment of a Triple-E Senate. When this failed to improve their electoral chances, Getty and some of his colleagues moved even further to the right. In early 1992, Getty made a desperate bid to recapture the field taken by Reform with a strident attack on official bilingualism and multiculturalism.[13] The Tory's rightward shift began to pay dividends. An Angus Reid poll conducted in January 1992, showed the Tories with a slim lead over the NDP and the Liberals. But Getty's approval rating continued to trail that of the other party leaders.[14] He had to go. The only question was "when?"

The answer was not long in coming. In September 1992, Getty tendered his resignation, just as the referendum on the Charlottetown Accord got under way. He was tired, hoping no doubt that passage of the Accord would place a crown upon his otherwise uneventful political career. It was not to be. The Charlottetown Accord, dubbed by many Son of Meech, was resoundingly defeated.

Several people quickly announced their intention to seek the Tory leadership. The decision, however, soon narrowed down to two candidates: Long-time cabinet minister Nancy Betkowski and Environment Minister Ralph Klein. Betkowski, whose profile had been raised several months earlier when she publicly disagreed with Getty's comments on doing away with bilingualism and multiculturalism, appealed to moderate Albertans, particularly in Edmonton. Klein's strength lay in Calgary, where he had once been mayor, and rural Alberta, areas coincident with Reform Party support.

In a radical experiment in direct democracy, borrowed from Reform, every member of the Tory party was allowed to vote in selecting the new leader. After the first round of voting in late November, Betkowski and Klein were separated by one vote, far ahead of the other contenders. The vote was a shock to the solid Reform bloc within the Tory party who feared that it was going to be captured by what they viewed as Betkowski's "red" Tory contingent. With only a week before second round voting, Klein's powerful rural supporters, led by Ken Kowalski, pulled out all the stops to recruit new party members to vote for Klein. It paid off. When the votes were counted the next week, 26,000 more votes had been cast than the week previous, and Klein had taken the bulk of them.

Klein's victory was certainly personal. But it also was a victory for Reform's constituency within the party. As political scientist David Stewart notes in chapter three, 38 percent of those casting votes in the second round held federal Reform Party memberships. Looked at another way, fully one-quarter of all the Reform Party members in the province voted in the Tory leadership race. While we cannot know for sure their voting preference, it seems reasonably certain that the bulk of these Reformers supported Klein.

The leadership convention signalled, among other things, an end to the broadly inclusive politics of Peter Lougheed. There was no longer room in the Alberta Tories for compromise. A lot of Albertans wanted a leaner, meaner approach to politics, and Klein promised to give it to them. A few months later, the Klein-led Tories scored a stunning victory over the lacklustre Liberals and hapless New Democrats. Alberta politics had been "Reformed."

Reform and the Tories, Today and in the Future

The Reform Party and the Klein Conservatives are twin spawn of the same political culture. As such, they reflect many of the same beliefs and values. Both are "neoconservative": heavily pro-free market/pro-business on economic matters, traditionally conservative on such things as law and order and morality. Both are influenced and supported by the elite of Canada's right-wing organizations, the Fraser Institute and the National Citizens' Coalition.[15] Both parties are neopopulist, or right-populist, building their support upon a defense of the illusory general interest of "the people" against various "special interest" groups. Both parties also tend to draw their political strength from people of similar demographic backgrounds: older, male, middle and upper middle income earners. But Reform and the Klein Tories are not identical.

Take leadership, for example. On the one hand, the success of both parties is very much a credit to their leaders, both of whom exhibit populist styles, perhaps Klein even more than Manning. Certainly, Klein can match Manning homily for homily any day. On the other hand, they could not be more different. Where Manning is shy and devoutly religious, Klein is a garrulous backslapper and unapologetic imbiber. Manning is very much a hands-on leader, setting policy and devising strategy. By contrast, Klein relies heavily upon those under him, often seemingly uninterested and uninformed regarding day to day government operations. Manning's approach to politics is largely ideological; Klein's is (charitably) pragmatic, (less charitably) opportunistic.

These leadership differences are reflected in the nature of the two parties. The Reform Party is less a political party, more an ideological movement aimed at rolling back small "l" liberalism and the welfare state. This cannot be said of the Klein Tories. They are simply a political party. Although the Tories underwent a major facelift when Klein took over, the party's core power-brokers — Dinning, West, Day — have been around for some time. The oft-repeated mantra of a "Klein revolution" obscures the fundamental continuity that actually underlies much of the Klein government's policies. There has been much less change within the provincial Tories than meets the eye.

This continuity is reflected in the continued support of big business for the Klein government. No less than previous Tory governments, the Klein government remains heavily in thrall to what might be termed Alberta's "oil-igarchy." By contrast, although Reform's policies are certainly strongly influenced by a pro-business, pro-market ideology, big business contributions to Reform still make up only a small portion of Reform's finances. Big business is not yet sure that Reform is really a big player, and may also be concerned with some of Reform's more populist rhetoric, particularly its stated commitment to end business subsidies. Big business has no such concerns with the Klein Tories. They know that the Klein Tories know who butters their bread.

Despite these differences, it is fair to suggest that Reform and the Klein Tories are something like political Siamese twins, with all the opportunities, dependencies, and encumbrances that entails. Clearly, the Klein government's political success or failure will influence Reform's chances in the next federal election. But the situation also is much more complicated than one might at first think. Indeed, in at least two ways the success of Klein's Tories may well spell disaster for Reform.

First, there is no assurance that the Klein Tories will throw its support behind the federal Reformers. In fact, the opposite seems more likely to be the case. Klein's government is, after all, still a Tory government. And, since September 1994, Klein has made a series of speeches and held several meetings with Jean Charest, the popular interim leader who is trying to rebuild federal Tory fortunes.

Understandably, these actions have angered Reform. "He's looking for trouble," warned Reform MP Ray Speaker, a former Alberta Socred and Tory cabinet minister. "Nobody is asking him to intervene in federal politics. So why is he doing it?" Klein's response was as simple as it was disingenuous. "I'm a Conservative and I'll do what I can to bolster the fortunes of the Conservative party both provincially and nationally."[16]

Why is Ralph Klein doing it? In part, Klein's cozying up to the federal Tories is a calculated move to keep open his political options. Reform support has steadily declined since the 1993 federal election, leaving a possible opening for the federal Tories to rebound. Klein is thus hedging his bets. But also, if Klein harbours federal leadership ambitions, as has been rumoured, only the Tories would provide him with such an opportunity. It is no secret that a Charest-Klein marriage — perhaps with Mike Harris as best man? — is viewed by many Tories as the ticket for rebuilding the Mulroney alliance between Québec and English-speaking Canada, particularly the West.

But the Klein government's success also poses a second problem for Reform. With the federal budget of February 1995, Chretien's Liberals took a significant step in decentralizing of power to the provinces — a move supported by Reform. As this occurs, however, Ottawa will play a decreasing role in Canadians' lives. The major responsibility left to federal governments will be that of cleaning the statues of prime ministers past of pigeon droppings at least once a year. By contrast, the power of provincial governments will increase. The tendency of Albertans to turn to their provincial government to protect their interests will be strengthened by the reality that the legislature is where real power resides. Federal political parties, including Reform, will be increasingly redundant. The separatist and quasi-separatist impulses that since the 1970s have underlain much of Alberta politics will have had their way.

Conclusion

I have argued here that the Reform Party first rose, in part, in response to a crisis in Alberta politics and that, only later, did Reform's influence result in the kind of political changes that brought about the Klein revolution. I have further argued that, despite many similarities between Reform and the Klein Tories, they are not exactly identical and, indeed, because of strategic political reasons may well be on a collision course. If this is the case, Albertans may see in the future increasing tension between these two political Siamese twins.

Notes

1. The author wishes to thank Gordon Laxer, David Stewart, and the participants at the Author's Forum for their helpful comments.
2. *Edmonton Journal,* 13 March 1990, A1.
3. *Edmonton Journal,* 13 March 1990, A1.
4. *Edmonton Journal,* 5 March 1991, A8.
5. See chapter three, "The Rise of Reform." In T. Harrison's *Of Passionate Intensity: Right-Wing Populism and the Reform Party of Canada* (Toronto: University of Toronto Press, 1995).
6. A. Tupper, "Alberta Politics: The Collapse of Consensus." In H. G. Thorburn, ed., *Party Politics in Canada,* 6th Edition (Scarborough, Ontario: Prentice-Hall Canada, 1991).
7. D. Braid and S. Sharpe, *Breakup: Why the West Feels Left Out of Canada* (Toronto: Key Porter Books, 1990), 32.
8. *Edmonton Journal,* 29 October 1989, A7.
9. *Edmonton Journal,* 13 March 1990, A1.
10. A. Cohen, *A Deal Undone* (Toronto: Douglas and McIntyre, 1990).

11. *Edmonton Journal,* 7 April 1991, A3; and 8 April 1991, A1.

12. *Edmonton Journal,* 7 April 1991, A1.

13. *Edmonton Journal,* 18 January 1992, A1.

14. *Edmonton Journal,* 17 January 1992, A1.

15. Both organizations have publicly honoured Ralph Klein for his approach to deficit fighting. See the *Edmonton Journal,* 18 October 1994, A6; and 7 January 1995, A3.

16. See *Edmonton Journal,* 22 September 1994, A3; 24 September 1994, A3; and 11 May 1995, A3.

Chapter Five

CULTIVATING THE TORY ELECTORAL BASE: RURAL POLITICS IN RALPH KLEIN'S ALBERTA

Barry K. Wilson

> In this province, if you voice any objection to government policy, it is like you disappear. You are ignored.
> Barb Bonneau, president, Rural Dignity of Canada.[1]

In its 1995 budget, the Klein government finally made it clear that rural Alberta will be expected to pick up a greater share of the burden of provincial deficit cutting. During the previous two years, for reasons of politics, ideology, and Tory common sense, the burden fell heaviest on the cities (especially Liberal Edmonton) and on the civil service. In rural Alberta, however, the rod was spared. Hospitals were largely untouched and farm programs, while tinkered with, were not gutted.

There was a reason for this. Rural Alberta, as it has been for more than two decades, is a Tory power base. Rural voters, over-represented in the legislature — three-quarters of Alberta's population is urban, but half the legislative seats are rural[2] — faithfully returned Conservative MLAs even as city voters began to have their doubts. When former Tory leader and Premier Don Getty lost his Edmonton seat in the 1989 election, he fled to the safety and certainty of rural Stettler, where grateful and politically-astute voters gave the premier 71 percent of their votes in a by-election, and then watched the provincial money roll in. Rural Alberta has been good to the Tories. The Tories have returned the favour.

The new year signalled the beginning of a change, however. It was announced that hospitals will be closed, much to the consternation of a few rural residents who complained of being "betrayed" by the government that they so fervently elected only two years before.[3] Meanwhile, schools also will be consolidated, with longer bus rides for some kids; farm program spending will plummet; and transfers to rural municipalities will be cut. Food banks, a major growth industry in urban life in Alberta for over ten years, have even made an appearance in some small towns.[4]

On top of this, from Ottawa came word that the annual $560 million Western Grain Transportation Act subsidy, long a target for Alberta government complaints, will be ended this year. The certain result: Higher shipping costs for the province's grain farmers and much more pressure on the rural roads that will have to accommodate more grain trucking as rail lines are abandoned.

Yet for all those signs of danger ahead, there has been little rural outcry. Larry Goodhope, for one, is not about to utter a negative word about the Klein government's policies for rural Alberta. As executive director of the Alberta Association of Municipal Districts and Counties, he has to continue working with the province on behalf of the rural governments that pay his salary. "It would be difficult for us to criticize the government for cutting spending and trying to balance its books," he said weeks after the budget. "For years, it has been standing policy for the association to urge the government to do just that. We can hardly complain when they do what we asked."[5]

It is a cautious acquiescence to cuts that Barb Bonneau finds frustrating. From the vantage point of her farm home northeast of Edmonton, she has anxiously watched the Klein government chip away at the services that have helped sustain rural Alberta over the years. "The thing is, it is coming at us from all sides, federal and provincial," says Bonneau, president of the national rural advocacy group Rural Dignity of Canada:

> There is no doubt the budget-cutting and deregulation leaves rural and isolated areas more cut off from services. Lots of things are happening. The trouble is, it's hard to see if there is anyone in charge with a plan, or is it different people cutting in their own areas without an idea of the overall effect? It's like unravelling the whole damn sweater.[6]

Rural Acquiescence

Yet for all her criticism, this veteran of rural Alberta politics also ruefully admits what she sees as another fact of life: the Klein government remains popular in rural Alberta. In the 1993 election, Liberals and Conservatives split the urban seats — Tories dominating in Calgary; Liberals sweeping Edmonton. In the countryside, Conservatives took more than four seats for every Liberal win. As it has been for a quarter century, rural Alberta provides the governing Conservatives with a solid base of support.[7] "I'm sure most rural voters still think they are on Ralph's team," says Bonneau. "In this country, if you paint a country fence post blue, it would get elected as a Tory."

Peace River farmer Art Macklin concedes the point, albeit with an edge to his voice. He is past president of the National Farmers Union (NFU) and anything but a fan of Conservative policies on farm supports, rural service cuts, or agricultural products' marketing. Yet Macklin also sees little evidence that Tory support in the countryside is eroding. "That doesn't mean the policies are correct, or that we just have to accept them without fighting back."[8]

Be that as it may, there is precious little evidence that Macklin could collect much of a following in an all-out assault on Klein policies. While it is most vocal of critics, the NFU does not have broad support. In a province with tens of thousands of farmers (the number varies wildly, depending on the definition), NFU membership numbers in the hundreds. The vast majority of Alberta farmers simply have not responded to the left-wing, confrontational politics of the NFU, preferring to straddle the centre of the road that has moved ever-further right in Alberta. Typical of the farm lobby across Canada, Alberta farm groups would rather compromise to "keep their place at the table" of government consultations than engage in the no-compromise, guerrilla-theatre tactics that the NFU has favoured over the years.

The other logical centre of critical analysis and power — the Alberta Wheat Pool with its thousands of members, local committees, elevators across the province, and a democratic structure that selects spokesmen who can legitimately claim to speak for farmers who have voted — has all but taken itself out of the public political debate. Beginning in late 1993, Pool delegates decided to keep a low profile after a bruising political fight with the government over barley marketing policy that cost the Pool business. In the future, the co-operative, farmer-owned grain company will lobby quietly in Edmonton for its interests, but will not send its leaders onto political platforms to fight more general political battles, even though it disagrees with many government positions on grain marketing and farm policy. The financial bottom line will not allow it. Farmers who disagree with the Pool and who agree with the government have shown they are willing to take their grain delivery business elsewhere. In the business climate of the 1990s, the Pool has decided financial returns are more important than the defence of political or ideological positions. It no longer chooses to throw its political weight around in Alberta.[9]

As a result, there are no real centres of opposition in rural Alberta, save a smattering of Liberal MLAs and the occasional vocal critic like Bonneau or Macklin. In part, this reflects a reality that even critics concede: most rural Albertans, conservative in their outlook, consider themselves well represented by the views of their Conservative governors. Years of political co-existence, coupled with the patronage, service, and propaganda efforts of a strong rural Tory caucus in Edmonton, have forged a strong link between the governed and the governing party.

But there is more to it than that. There is a political manipulation side to this story as well. In part because of government planning, the provincial farm lobby has been neutralized as a source of independent, critical analysis of government positions. Most farm spokesmen are either supportive or silent.

Rural Tory Planning[10]

It is a piece of good political fortune that Alberta Conservatives have worked hard to arrange. Over the past twenty-five years, through careful use of the powers of access, influence, and public dollars, the Alberta government has helped create the farm lobby it wants. It is a lobby that argues in favour of reduced government support and regulation, more market freedom, and greater access to American markets. It also believes in a weakening of long-standing national grain policies that favour central desk selling and "equal opportunity" grain marketing that Alberta governments have opposed as an impediment to entrepreneurial grain farmers, as well as the province's livestock and processing sector.

Now, when the Alberta agriculture department organizes province-wide consultations with farmers, it tends to receive advice that it wants to hear. The absence of a critical mass of organized farm and rural opposition has given the Alberta government an almost free hand to create farm policy, legitimized by an extensive consultation process that reinforces government claims that it is speaking for farmers.

It is neither an accident nor a particular reflection of Ralph Klein's revolution. It is a process of government/farm lobby symbiosis that Klein inherited and has used to good effect.

It began in 1971. Peter Lougheed led the Progressive Conservatives to their first provincial election victory that year, riding the crest of an urban revolt against the old-fashioned ideas of the rural-based Social Credit Party. The Lougheed government, elected with a largely urban base, had some big dreams for Alberta — economic diversification, provincial power, and increased benefit for the province from its constitutional ownership of natural resources.

It was an agenda with some profound implications for rural and agricultural Alberta. The new Tory government saw federal policies as the enemy, discriminating against Alberta's brand of mixed and entrepreneurial agriculture. There were a number of specific complaints. The farm economy of the province was a mix of grain and livestock, yet the major federal policies encouraged an export grain industry. The Canadian Wheat Board also was a target. It was appointed by Ottawa, emphasized export of raw grain, had a monopoly over those exports, and pooled revenues from sales. These rules meant that individual farmers with a good product and a flair for marketing had no chance to cash in on their special advantage. To make matters worse, the seventy-four-year-old Crowsnest Pass grain subsidy (the Crow rate) subsidized the export of raw grain. The provincial cattle industry, as well as grain processors, argued the export subsidy penalized them by artificially raising the price of grain they had to buy in competition with stocks destined for subsidized export.

The Canadian Wheat Board became an enemy and Lougheed ended up demanding (unsuccessfully) that the provinces should have the right to appoint Board commissioners. The Crow rate also became a target and while Alberta argued for its demise, the government subsidized the province's cattle industry to offset what it said were the negative effects of the Crow on Alberta's cattlemen.

Agriculture out of Step

Agriculture was one of the industries least in tune with the Lougheed vision of a diversified, provincially-dominated economy. What was worse, the most powerful farm lobby — the Alberta Wheat Pool — supported the Wheat Board's subsidizing and centralizing policies that the Alberta government found so distasteful. Unifarm, the province's umbrella farm group formed in 1969 and recognized as the "voice of agriculture" by the Social Credit government, was highly influenced by the Pool, its largest member.

The Conservatives set out to find a farm constituency to support their farm policy blasphemies that challenged the reigning theology of export-oriented grain subsidies and federally-controlled grain marketing. Deputy Premier and Agriculture Minister Hugh Horner was given the job. He immediately began to encourage the province's cattle producers to voice their opinions, giving them an audience and the legitimacy of government sympathy. And he created the Alberta Grain Commission (AGC) with a mandate to advise the government on appropriate grain policies. The commission was headed first by John Channon, a federal civil servant unhappy with federal grain policies. It promoted diversification, provincial power, erosion of the powers of the Canadian Wheat Board, and changes to the Crow rate.

Most important, the AGC provided the government with an alternate voice to the Alberta Wheat Pool. "In 1971, the Conservatives came in with the idea of diversifying the economy," Channon recalled years later. "Agriculture was one of its targets but the Pool was dominant and it seemed to be opposed to many of the government ideas." Doug Radke, deputy agriculture minister in 1995 and a veteran of the provincial civil service, offers a similar take on history. "My guess is the judgment was made there wasn't sufficient debate [possible] because no one was capable of competing with the Alberta Pool and its resources."

The government set out to fix that with the Grain Commission, which still exists as a key advisor to the government. Over the years, it has been a mix of bureaucrats and government-chosen farmers with guaranteed access to the ear of the minister. For some rural farm leaders, it has proven to be a training ground to move on to Conservative politics. For some smaller farm groups with views aligned with the government's, it has proven to be an avenue of influence.

On the advice of the Grain Commission, the government went one step further. It began in the 1970s to fund small commodity groups like the Palliser Wheat Growers Association (now the Western Canadian Wheat Growers' Association) and the Western Barley Growers Association that were being formed to promote an entrepreneurial, anti-Wheat Board view for wheat and barley producers. Although the groups attracted only a few hundred paying members, they became highly influential as advocates of low-subsidy, open-market policies. Ironically, the government has spent hundreds of thousands of Alberta taxpayer dollars to fund groups arguing against government intervention in their industry.

Later, the government expanded the effort by approving legislation making it possible for commodity leaders to apply for a mandatory "check-off" which forces all producers of the commodity to send money into a commission set up for research and promotion, including promotion of political views. Those who object can apply for a refund, but few go to the trouble. Meanwhile, the check-off has provided millions of dollars for research and political campaigning against the Wheat Board, in favour of unrestricted access to the American market (access is now controlled by the Wheat Board), and against government regulation. Barley, canola, and soft white wheat producers have taken advantage of the check-off legislation.

A Ripe Farm Climate

All of this has helped create a political climate in the farm community that is ripe for deregulation, opposed to many federal intervention policies, and anxious to see less government. It has left the Alberta Wheat Pool largely out in the cold, at odds with its government and with much farm opinion, and paying the commercial price when it tries to exert political influence. Pool officials believe that hundreds of thousands of dollars of business went to other grain companies after it adopted such controversial policies as opposing an open market to the United States for barley sales.

Nick Taylor, former Liberal party leader and a veteran rural MLA, says the power of the Pool to influence the provincial debate has declined sharply under successive Conservative governments. Pool president Alex Graham agrees:

> If you suggest the Pool has a lot of influence, I disagree. In Alberta, I don't think we have had a strong, significant impact. We get respect, but I don't think Alberta Pool has been successful in having a strong impact in terms of policy-setting.

For Tim Harvie, chairman of the Alberta Barley Commission, this is simple common sense. "I think the right wing reflects the soul and the sentiment of Alberta. The fact that the right wing outlasted the left wing simply reflects the reality of the province."

Despite the bravado, the evidence suggests government has been something more than a neutral bystander. Through deft use of the power of money and access, the Tories helped determine which ideology would prevail.

Pseudo -Consultation and Washer Democracy

In recent years, Alberta Agriculture has organized the most extensive farmer consultation exercises in its history. On three separate occasions, and in three different ways, the province's farmers were asked to offer direction on the future of agriculture, a business plan for the department, and an appropriate farm income safety net program. The answers were remarkably close to opinions the department had floated beforehand. Agri-

culture must become more entrepreneurial and market-driven. The department should become more focused and less intrusive. As much as possible,
governments should get out of the income support business and allow the
market to rule.

The results have allowed the government to preach retrenchment while
claiming to speak for average farmers. Once again, despite government protests to the contrary, critics suggest the government has organized farm opinion and the consultation process to produce the answers it wants to hear.

The opinions have been drawn in a number of ways. Randomly-chosen
focus groups have been organized, public meetings held, forms filled out.
In some cases, farmers at meetings were asked to put dots on a sheet to
show which policy options they favoured — a form of "dotocracy" that left
those who opposed the public majority feeling isolated and less likely to
swim against the stream.

The most interesting result, however, came when farmers at government-
organized focus groups were asked whether they favoured improved government income support programs, or whether they favoured removing
"impediments" that keep farmers from earning their living from the marketplace. Before each meeting, a spokesman for a coalition of farm groups offered a summation of options that leaned against any solution involving more
government. A discussion paper on which the preparatory talk was based offered a definition of "self-reliance," for example, that involved farmers exer-
cising their financial, production, and marketing skills "without the
hindrance of collectivist restraints." Discussion followed and then at the end
of the meeting, farmers were asked to throw a washer into one of two pots at
the door — the "safety nets" pot or the "self-sufficiency" pot. Government officials said they were surprised that 75 percent favoured self-sufficiency. It has
become the basis for an Alberta government claim that farmers want government out of their lives, as long as "impediments" like Canadian Wheat Board
controls on grain marketing and subsidy distortions also are ended.

But one farm leader who went to a focus group later marvelled that
"the response wasn't a hundred percent. The way it was set up, who
wouldn't vote for self-sufficiency?" He asked not to be identified because of
the need to continue working with the Alberta government.

Conclusion

However it developed or was created, the existing state of grace between rural Alberta and the Klein government appears to be the genuine
article. Hardly a peep has been heard from rural lobby groups as the gov-

ernment has campaigned for grain freight rate subsidy reform, a weakening of Canadian Wheat Board powers, and diminished safety net levels.

The depth of support for those policies is about to be tested. Many of the political goals are being realized. Both Edmonton and Ottawa have announced cuts to farm income-support spending, beginning this year. Effective August 1, 1995, the almost century-old Crow rate ended and the grain transportation system began deregulation. The provincial government announced it is stepping up efforts to force Ottawa to end the Wheat Board's monopoly on sales into the U.S., possibly including a provincial plebiscite in late 1995 on the issue.

Combined with the announced closure of at least five rural hospitals in the next few years and the implementation of the other cuts promised in the 1995 budget, rural Alberta is poised to witness a change in the way it does business and receives services — changes that have been in the making for years, encouraged by those who claim to speak for rural Alberta; changes that will significantly impact rural life.

Barb Bonneau, for one, is not convinced that Albertans will like what they see:

> I think the attitude now around here is that if you fail, it is your own fault, you were not efficient. That is what these changes are based on, everybody for themselves. If people here discover this isn't really to their liking once they get it and things don't work out, they may well turn on the people that gave it to them. Alberta governments have disappeared before, you know.

Notes

1. Interview with Barb Bonneau, 18 March 1995.
2. See M. Lisac's column in the Edmonton Journal, 29 April 1995, A8. In the same article, Lisac also notes that of the current fifty-three Tory MLAs, twelve are farmers.
3. *Edmonton Journal*, 1 April 1995, A7.
4. *Edmonton Journal*, 16 March 1995, A5.
5. Interview with Larry Goodhope, 16 March 1995.
6. Interview with Barb Bonneau, 18 March 1995.
7. For details of the 1993 election results, see the *Canadian Parliamentary Guide* (Toronto: InfoGlobe, spring 1994).
8. Interview with Art Macklin, 15 March 1995.
9. The *Western Producer*, 8 December 1994.
10. The analysis that follows of the Alberta government's efforts to influence and direct farm opinion is based on interviews conducted in November 1994 for a *Western Producer* special report which appeared 5 January 1995.

Chapter Six

REDEFINING NORMAL: LIFE IN THE NEW ALBERTA

Joanne Helmer

> Normal doesn't live in Alberta anymore.
>
> Alberta Treasurer Jim Dinning, 1994.[1]

Truer words were never spoken. Premier Ralph Klein's Conservatives have adopted an unusual approach to government. The new philosophy is: if it ain't broke, break it.

Yet its massive restructuring of the public sector has swept through Alberta with a minimum of opposition. Compared to the B.C. public's reaction in the 1980s to former premier Bill Vanderzalm's privatization spree, Klein and Company have had it easy.

Why is that? Do Albertans all agree with the Thatcherite revolution they are experiencing? Do they all speak with one voice, as former premier Peter Lougheed always claimed?

Hardly. When 15,000 people march to protect the Grey Nuns Hospital in Edmonton, when 160,000 sign petitions during the first sitting of the legislature in 1994[2], when almost 20,000 Southern Albertans sign a petition to save a Calgary hospital, when a seniors' group discovers from its own survey that less than 2 percent of its members approve of the government's approach, substantial grassroots opposition to the Klein agenda does exist. In Alberta, where conservative governments have been placed next to God for generations of voters, where the election of a few New Democrats and participation in an annual walk for peace are considered radical actions, that level of public protest is phenomenal.

But it is an inconsistent, fragmented, and leaderless opposition. Weeks go by when Albertans seem to have fallen asleep again. Even union leaders with the resources and structure to organize are afraid to step out on a limb, for fear of finding no one behind them, including their own members.

"My members are still Albertans," says Carol Anne Dean, president of the Alberta Union of Provincial Employees, as an explanation for the union's timidity. "We lived in a comfort zone for a long time and the members tend to think what happened in New Zealand or the U.S. can't happen here. They live in denial." Surprisingly, she doesn't argue with the criticism of Dr. Yonaten Reshef, human resources professor at the University of Alberta, who told the *Globe and Mail* that Alberta labour blew an historic opportunity to rally the people.[3] "We didn't have our act together," Dean admits.

As a result, if it can be said that Ralph Klein started an old-fashioned prairie fire in the summer of 1993, it's also true his opponents have generally failed to get their water bombers off the ground two years later. Many of the reasons for this malaise are unique to Alberta.

Alberta is Different

Alberta is different from other provinces. Albertans' historic endorsement of American-style individualism, their post-war animosity toward organized labour and opposition political parties, the fiscal and social conservatism that nurtures the federal Reform Party, and their general dislike of politics, all work against the creation of a strong opposition movement.

Alberta's economic and social connection to the U.S. has always been at least as strong as its east-west connections to the rest of Canada. Physically, its southern links were manifested in events like the fervent Independence Day celebrations in Fort Macleod that lasted well into this century. The town of Magrath still flies an American flag along with the Alberta and Canadian flags.

The enormous amount of money flowing into the Heritage Trust Fund in the early 1970s helped fuel Albertans' sense of independence and arrogance. One Southern Alberta Liberal has long been convinced Albertans supported the Canada-U.S. Free Trade Agreement so strongly in 1988 because they would prefer to deal with Americans than Eastern Canadians. Although that sentiment was apparent all through the province's history, John Boras believes the bitter oil price wars between Alberta and Ottawa during the Lougheed era strengthened it.

Carol Anne Dean provides another clue to understanding Albertans. "We might be Canadian, but part of Alberta's political culture is to look to our own advantage."

The sense of community in Alberta is different. When Saskatchewan Premier Roy Romanow told author and *Globe and Mail* columnist Robert

Mason Lee that he respects the co-operative Canadian way, his comments rang true. Romanow said:

> Our history, even from the Depression years, is to pull together as a community in the face of challenges, whether climatic or fiscal. Our tradition in a crisis has been to rally around the community, the farm, and the province.[4]

But when Alberta's former premier Don Getty expressed similar sentiments after the price of oil fell through the floor in the 1980s, everybody recognized it as cynical politicking. Albertans don't co-operate. They compete.

Strangely, Albertans did not adopt the whole package of individualism from across the border. One of the crucial aspects of the American democratic spirit is missing: the distrust of authority. Albertans grant a rare degree of trust to their elected officials. They are even less comfortable challenging authority than most Canadians. A haze seems to separate the governors form the governed, as if election automatically confers extraordinary wisdom and intelligence. Albertans prefer to take their politicians on faith.

It is not overstating the case to suggest that a near-Victorian sense of propriety limits the Alberta public's imagination when it comes to politics. Voters rarely acknowledge the possibility of duplicity or incompetence in their politicians. They shield their eyes even when a Principal Group blows up.

They would rather pretend than fight. People were so sick of politicians when Ralph came along, says former Tory cabinet minister John Gogo, that they believed him when he said he's one of us. Gogo says the public sees Klein as "nonpolitical."

Albertans are more afraid of their neighbour's reaction to a protest than the government's, suggests retired provincial court judge Martin Hoyt. Valerie Poulin agrees. She's the Lethbridge woman who raised over 19,000 signatures in Southern Alberta almost single-handedly in less than two months to save the Calgary Children's Hospital. An Ontario emigrant, Poulin discovered Albertans will sign a petition but don't want to do anything their neighbours might consider silly. "They don't want to get involved," she says. "They won't rock the boat."

An Action Canada and Common Front organizer says she is constantly restraining instincts honed elsewhere. "People tell me my ideas for protest are not appropriate here," says Lethbridge professor of sociology, Ronnie Leah.

Conformity and deference play right into the hands of a politician like Ralph Klein.

Klein's Strategy

In a brilliantly executed public relations strategy — credited by some to Klein's executive assistant Rod Love — Klein and Company turned all of these peculiar Alberta characteristics to their political advantage. Then they added two more ingredients, a drop-dead attitude and the roller-coaster speed for implementing changes recommended by New Zealand's architect of privatization, Sir Roger Douglas.[5] Albertans witnessed the drop-dead attitude early on in two impulsive acts.

In 1993, when Klein finally understood the public's anger over the golden pensions for retiring MLAs, he cancelled the entire MLA pension plan. He didn't debate the idea, or examine it for flaws, or consider alternatives. He just dropped the guillotine (see chapter three).

Later, after he campaigned for reelection and discovered the depth of Albertans' revulsion with the Getty government's loose industrial strategy, Klein and his inner circle came upon an even bolder idea: Why not cancel government, too?

But even in Alberta it's not as easy to gain applause for the second blunt attack as for the first. Eliminating government is more complicated than dumping a pension plan. Further, the Conservatives couldn't spare the time for a lengthy public debate, even if they were so inclined. They were in a hurry. They had promised to eliminate the province's deficit in their first term. So they took their plan through the back door. As late as November 1994, after the introduction of Bill 57 that would allow the cabinet to wash its hands of all public services, the premier still refused to describe his social and political restructuring as a revolution (see chapter eight).

This understatement allows many Albertans to abstain from involvement. Gogo believes a huge chunk of the public is still stuck in the Lougheed era. He and many others interviewed for this chapter say most Albertans have yet to feel the impact of Klein's restructuring on their own lives. What they don't feel personally, they can still deny.

Recently, there has been a move to have the Bull Trout named an official emblem of Alberta. The ostrich might be a better choice.

A Moving Target

The speed with which the Tory's strategy has been implemented also helps confuse the public and slow the formation of an opposition. Alberta is experiencing a peacetime blitzkrieg. The Klein government has adopted Sir Roger Douglas' advice that reform must always take place faster than the interest groups ability to mobilize. Opponents can't fire at a moving target, he said. The strategy works as well in politics as it does in war.

Linda Karpowitz, president of the Alberta Federation of Labour and co-chair of the Common Front, points out that by the time opposition organizes to respond to a proposed change, the decision is already implemented. Sheryl McInnes, also of the Common Front, says the restructuring is so fast and widespread that people are not sure whether to worry about their grandma, their own job, or the cuts to kindergarten. They don't know where to begin or how to stop the momentum. They feel powerless.

Neil Reimer, leader of the Alberta Council on Aging, an umbrella organization representing 450 seniors' groups, says "There are quantum changes so vast I would defy anybody, even Klein, to write down a full list." It takes about an hour just to explain changes to seniors' programs. With the amendment of the Seniors Benefit Act, which allows the government to alter programs without going to the legislature, the government has made changes Reimer doesn't know about.

The Klein Flu

Many Albertans are literally sickened by the potential for social deterioration as a result of the government's agenda. The usual winter virus was called the Klein flu in 1994. It has left many Albertans demoralized and in disarray.

The Conservatives borrowed from the hugely successful Reform Party script that says nurses, doctors, teachers, seniors, the poor, women, — indeed, any group that tries to encourage debate about anything except a single-minded devotion to the bottom line of public spending — is only protecting its own interests, and so can be ignored. The result is to silence many of the people most knowledgeable about the internal workings of public institutions, and to control the debate about services.

The first to be attacked were social allowance recipients, the unemployed, and the working poor. Perhaps that's to be expected. Social programs and the vulnerable people who rely on them are easy targets anywhere in North America, maybe more so in Alberta. Carol Anne Dean figures Albertans place tenth in Canada on the compassion/caring meter.

"Few of these people have the energy needed to fight back," says Marjorie Benz, director of the Edmonton Food Bank. "In late 1993 these people were angry. Now they passively accept the idea their kids won't eat and the rent won't be paid." Meanwhile, Albertans are turning to food banks at a rate twice the national average. In January 1993, 10,302 people used the Edmonton food bank; in January 1994, 14,582; in January 1995, 17,909.[6]

The passivity of the public's response to cuts just whetted the Tories' appetite. Former University of Lethbridge president John Woods says while the government is balancing the books and getting at the group widely seen as lazy, welfare parasites, it's also going after a group the public believes is privileged and pampered. According to Woods, the Klein government is settling a number of scores:

> His ministers don't like universities or the arts. They don't like fancy people, privileged doctors, or uppity nurses. Albertans are conservative, sensible and practical. Simplicity is a civic and personal virtue. They're not interested in fanciness.

Klein's government appeals to these values.

Woods' theory finds support elsewhere. David Taras and Allan Tupper suggest Klein's populism feeds and exacerbates a politics of resentment whose target is well-educated, public-sector workers. They contend that, at least for some, his government represents the triumph of the world of street smarts and hard knocks over the world of books and abstractions.[7]

Sheryl McInnes, of the Common Front, adds:

> There's a deep layer of anti-intellectualism out there. People say they don't need to be educated to know what's going on. We see it in the government's idea that nurses don't need a degree, that they only need six weeks experience in a hospital ward.

McInnes is referring to a committee of Conservative MLAs attempting to de-professionalize the professions. She fears "we'll have an educated population in the future but Albertans will make good little (foot) soldiers for the corporations."

In this new atmosphere, it's no wonder that when the little guy named Klein went after the fat cats with their high salaries and high-falutin ideas, a lot of Albertans cheered. Gogo agrees. The common folks eat it up when he goes after the special interest groups, he says.

Special Interests

But what is a "special interest group"? In Klein's Alberta, it's everybody outside of the loop.

Any opposition to the government's agenda is made to sound self-serving, says the president of the University of Calgary faculty association. Helen Holmes says:

> The white paper on advanced education uses code words like responsibility and accountability and learner-centred education. To this government, responsibility means user pay. The user pay edict will result in higher tuition, which will hurt the middle classes more, since they are the primary beneficiaries.

But because the discussion is wrapped in Klein's comfort words, the implication is unclear to much of the public. It's tough in a public forum to argue against responsibility or accountability, Holmes says.

> We can't say we don't want to be accountable, but what does it mean? It's really a series of secret performance indicators. The government wants us to spend all kinds of time and energy measuring their idea of effectiveness, but it won't measure what we consider to be important. When we argue against these words, we are easily misunderstood by the public. But the issues we dispute easily in a public forum are not under discussion.

Nurses face the same problem, says Heather Smith, president of the United Nurses of Alberta. Nurses are dismissed as self-serving by the premier when they challenge the substitution of skilled people with unskilled, or the increased hiring of private duty nurses in hospitals by patients' families. "We're trying to get nurses to understand that today they're providers, tomorrow they're consumers. They need to speak up, at least among their families and communities."

While it's difficult for them to go public, the deteriorating situation in hospitals is certainly on their minds. Smith tells of a pact formed among a group of retired nurses to provide care for one another if one of them is forced to enter hospital. They promised to take turns sitting at the bedside, to make sure someone was available to speak up for the patient. Five years ago they wouldn't have had to make such a pact.

This is a group which defied the government as recently as 1988 with an illegal strike (see chapter twenty). But they've been worn down. Nurses lost 3,000 jobs in 1994. Smith says as full-time nurses are laid off and re-hired as part-timers, with no benefits and no job security, they become a more pliable work force. They're subjected to "terrorism in the work place," she says. Still, Smith suggests that nurses might find the courage to speak up if hospital administrators and trustees would, but the latter two groups have been too busy protecting their own interests or hoping for jobs with the new regional health authorities.

Even if that accusation is not true in all instances, the government benefits by the division in the community. But it is true in some cases, as one trustee inadvertently suggested to me. He says the first loyalty of the re-gional boards is to the government that appointed them, not to the local public. "In one stroke, the government wiped out a forum for democratic participation," he says. "What's happening in Alberta violates the principle of a third level of government that responds directly to local concerns." Will he speak up? No. There's no doubt in his mind he would be off the board if he waved a red flag and he figures he can be more useful on the board than off (see chapter nine).

Even many academics who might have complained about the lack of an orderly plan to downsize public services were spooked by a well-chosen bully tactic. If the Klein government can seize the assets of one professional association, as it did at the Banff Centre, it can do so twice or three times.

Ironically, although they've been among the government's most loyal supporters, seniors also are seen as a special interest group. Dismayed lead-ers like Neil Reimer state:

> We're a layer of society. Seniors are put on an unjustified guilt
> trip if they try to fight for what they have. To a twenty-year-old, a
> fifty-five-year-old is a senior and that generation born after 1930
> is better off than most. But people over sixty-five years old were
> teens during the depression. They didn't get started building fi-
> nancial security until the 1950s. The average income of a senior
> woman is $11,000 and that's not ripping off the system.

But who's listening?

Bullies and Backlash

There is more than just scapegoating going on in Alberta, however. John Woods also believes Premier Klein is fuelling a backlash against liberalism, although the debate is not transacted in the open as it is in the United States:

> People ask questions about the way we've been doing things in the past twenty-five years and the received opinion is that society is not improving. We're less decent, less moral people than we would like to be. And the source of public policies are the universities, the intellectual elite; not the simple, hardworking unprivileged sector which has to struggle hard.

Did Klein start this revisionist view or simply join a revolution already in the making? *Edmonton Journal* columnist Mark Lisac spends some time examining that question in his book, *The Klein Revolution*.[8] He is puzzled that a fellow he believes to be decent and intelligent can shuffle his way to the top of a radical social transformation. Lisac is reluctant to use a harsh word like fascism to describe the antidemocratic spirit apparent in the new processes imposed on Albertans, even though by his own definition the word fits, right down to the use of scapegoating, the denigration of rational debate, and the defence of a dominant group's social and political position.

Perhaps, in the end, it doesn't matter whether Klein started the trend. Maybe, as Father Daniel Berrigan said of J. Edgar Hoover, if Hoover had not been available to the America of this century, American genius would have created someone like him. Berrigan surmised that Hoover sensed the direction of America's crusade of the day, legitimizing and bestowing upon it the sacrosanct name of law and order.[9] Maybe Klein did the same, recognizing there was a backlash against tolerance and liberalism in Alberta. Perhaps Klein is just the inevitable consequence of two decades of Conservative excess and expediency.

This doesn't absolve him, however. Political leaders set the tone of their period, for good or ill. Klein has recognized the political value of intemperance, and has played on the public's fears. In reacting, and allowing his cabinet to react, to complicated social issues with the harshest, simplest solutions — like declaring that young offenders should hang — he has actively discouraged intelligent, informed public debate.

Examples of similar tactics abound: Dianne Mirosh's suggestion that English-speaking immigrants are superior; Klein's own proposal that foreign students should pay the full cost of advanced education, as if Alberta gains nothing from their presence here. As with so many other things the Klein government has borrowed from America, it seems also to have borrowed the right wing's renewed focus on race, immigration, and ethnic diversity.[10] If, as others have suggested, the success of such political tactics depends on the public's gullibility and fear, Albertans were ripe by the time the Klein government came along. The commissioner of the Alberta Human Rights Commission, Jack O'Neil, publicly worried in late 1994 about a growing intolerance toward immigrants and homosexuals, and the number of people taking a perverted pride in wearing the label, "redneck."

The redneck phenomenon hit Alberta in the spring of 1994. Soon, a Medicine Hat man was selling bumper stickers proclaiming pride in the term. An Edmonton man played with the idea of a Northern Redneck Association. Its impact even reached into the legislature, where Cypress-Medicine Hat MLA Lorne Taylor adopted the label. The new atmosphere put the prudish, politically correct — those people who take all the fun out of life by demanding civility and mutual respect in public discourse — on the defensive.[11]

Ted Byfield, founder and editor of the right-wing *Alberta Report*, cheered the new attitude.[12] He defended the former president of the Quebec Manufacturers Association, Richard Le Hir, who said modern society had nothing to learn from native culture. Like so many redneck views that claim to be born of "common sense," Byfield's opinion, and Le Hir's, demonstrate wilful ignorance. A quick trip to any good public library would educate both. But that would open a debate they don't want. Who knows where it might lead?

Byfield's attitude is similar to that of Advanced Education Minister Jack Ady who insisted he and I could not discuss the future of universities in Alberta because we were not on the same wavelength. I had been impertinent enough to ask who would teach the thousands of new advanced education students he predicted for the next few years if reduced government funding continued to reduce faculty members. It seemed a rational question. Ady's aggressive response to the question was intended to intimidate and silence, not illuminate.

Power is intoxicating. It strengthens old bullies, unleashes those in hiding, and often creates new ones.

The Common Front

Nobody in Alberta missed Klein's response to the initial protest rallies. At best, he ignored them. Jim Marino, director of the Confederation of Alberta Faculty Associations, says public protest sometimes played into the government's hands. When the Alberta Teachers Association took out full page ads to complain about education restructuring, it gave Klein and Steve West an excellent opportunity for public posturing. "It fulfilled their prophecy, that 'we'll hurt them until they scream,'" Marino says. When protesters had little or no effect on policy, the organized groups quickly came to believe the government would not be moved. The ineffectiveness deepened existing divisions. With barely concealed irritation, Neil Reimer complains that even people who should know better have viewed the restructuring from their own corner of the world. "They hold one protest and throw in the sponge."

As a result, the only province-wide opposition movement, called the Common Front, did not materialize publicly until October 1994. Its survival is not guaranteed even now, originating as it does from a combination of the Action Canada Network and organized labour. Neither of those groups have been embraced by Albertans in the past. While the Common Front began with some seed money, it entered 1995 with no budget and no paid staff in its provincial office. Out of necessity, it has depended for its energy on committed people who are already exhausted by battles in their own workplace. The Front's plan to nurture independent local groups in every community is also based in practical need as much as philosophy.

A smaller Edmonton group started in August 1993. Albertans for Social Action brought together social service agencies and published an alternative budget at the end of 1994 calling for deficit elimination in six years rather than in three, and a 4 percent cut to public spending rather than 20 percent. But it's practically unknown outside Edmonton and has little influence inside the city. Organizers sound grateful when a few church congregations in the wealthier parts of the city will listen to them.

The Common Front is enjoying some success. Many small towns, as well as the cities, have core groups trying to counter the two prevailing moods of hopelessness and jubilation. But while the organization's birth was heralded by supporters as an important first step in the formation of a strong opposition, it generated so little public attention that when former Liberal leader Laurence Decore was asked about it at the end of 1994, he responded: "What's that?" Even one of its founders, Trudy Richardson, of the United Nurses of Alberta, says she thought the Common Front would have achieved more by the end of 1994 than it did. "I thought people would be angry by now. They're still scared."

Members of the group harbour a real fear that the Klein agenda is so seductive it's unbeatable in the short term. Even more, they fear that the corporate model of development in general, currently gripping Alberta and other parts of Canada, is too strong to be quickly overturned. "Every government, whether Tory or Liberal or New Democratic, will be forced to knuckle under to the corporate agenda to one degree or another," predicts Anne McGrath, Oxfam worker and Common Front leader in Calgary.

To which Ross Harvey, the cynical New Democrat leader asks: "What do you expect when capitalism has just won the Third World War?" Even Mark Lisac's view of the revolution ends bleakly, talking with people who survived the Great Depression. A sugar-coated globalism where the vines curl around your neck, is the way he describes Klein's plan.

With Klein and others of his persuasion having stolen the future, at least in the short-term, many Common Front members believe their best hope in the next few years is to educate more voters to understand policy alternatives and their right to participate in formulating public policy: to teach Albertans that democracy means more than casting a ballot every four or five years.

But as John Maynard Keynes once said, "We're all dead in the long run." Is there nothing else that can be done now?

What Will it Take?

Professor Reshef says unions have been too polite in Alberta, too conservative in the face of the attack. "The bottom line is if you play by the rules of the game [against Klein], you lose." But the majority of Albertans are not ready for a counter-revolution. In fact, many are still waiting to see, first, if they'll personally gain from a low-tax regime.

John Gogo doesn't believe the average Albertan will quickly challenge the Klein agenda, even though he agrees it's moving too fast and cutting too wide a swath. Only when middle-aged people are forced to look after a serverly ill and aging parent, because there's no other place for them to go, will they realize what's happened, he predicts. Only when they're forced to pay $40 every time they need an eye exam, will they start asking questions. Only one other possibility will move the public quicker, he says. "If large numbers of people are cut off the welfare rolls and forced to the streets, Albertans won't stand for widespread homelessness."

Linda Karpowitz has similar expectations. She looks at the newspapers flooded with horror stories about the impact of the Klein program on individuals and says, "Soon, people will catch on that the problems are even greater than what gets into the media."

But what constitutes widespread homelessness? At the end of February 1995, CBC reported 2,000 homeless on the streets of Calgary. Other stories told of hundreds of homeless in Red Deer. But there's no public march on the legislature.

Some of those working directly with the lowest income groups are not optimistic. "Before this started, I couldn't believe people could be so desperate," says Marjorie Benz.

> Sixteen months ago, I thought the churches or the community would see the level of destitution and put pressure on the government to ease up. I couldn't cope if I didn't believe that when Albertans have a better understanding, they won't allow it to continue. But I see that education process taking longer now.

Members of the Common Front are overwhelmed by the unfamiliar in a province where normal has become abnormal. Even the usual process of revolution has been turned upside down: in Alberta the government ignites change while the public is frozen.

But Klein has altered course at times, or at least left that impression. Among other things, he dropped the idea of a water tax, apparently under pressure from his rural, farm supporters. He also revoked his appointment of former Deputy Premier Ken Kowalski to the Energy Resources Conservation Board, this time under pressure from both the public and the Tory's important supporters in the oil and gas industry. And, in the spring session of the legislature in 1995, the government arbitrarily threw more money into the pot for kindergarten. At the very least, it suggests this government can be made to blink sometimes. Could other cracks appear in the Klein monolith?

Several possibilities exist. Gogo says Klein has turned everything upside down in the legislature. Caucus members summon the ministers. Are some MLAs becoming upset with the changes? How about calls from their constituents? Are some Tory MLAs' phone lines burning up with calls from conservative voters worried about their health care system or whether their children will be able to afford to go to university in this province? How many Albertans are growing disenchanted with Klein's personal behaviour and libertarian social policies on gambling and alcohol? (Southam national columnist Catherine Ford says organizations all over the province have had early morning meetings cancelled because the premier didn't show up.[13]) Is there, as Joan Crockatt, *Edmonton Journal* political reporter suggests, the possibility that a new social conservatism might follow the fiscal conservatism we've already seen.[14] Would that divide the Tory camp?

Conclusion

Calgary author George Melnyk says it's inevitable the core of Conservative support will grow dissatisfied when they realize there's no great glory in paying off a debt. They're used to christening grand new building projects. That same core might be angered if they're forced to skip a trip to Arizona next winter.

When a group as conservative as the Lethbridge Police Association flatly rejects the city's attempt to pass along the government's 5 percent wage cut, it suggests something is brewing quietly in the ranks.

Or, at least that the fire might consume itself and life can get back to normal.

Notes

1 Quoted in M. Lisac's column in the *Edmonton Journal,* 22 September 1994, A14. Where not otherwise credited, all direct quotes from individuals are the result of personal communication with the author.

2 Clerk's office, Legislative Assembly of Alberta.

3 *Globe and Mail,* 2 November 1994, A13.

4 *Globe and Mail,* 18 February 1995, D2.

5 R. Douglas, *Unfinished Business* (Auckland: Random House, 1993).

6 *Edmonton Journal,* 15 March 1995, B1.

7 D. Taras and A. Tupper, "Politics and deficits: Alberta's challenge to the Canadian political agenda." In D. M. Brown and J. Hebert, eds., *Canada! The State of the Federation* (Kingston: Institute of Intergovernmental Relations, Queen's University, 1994).

8 M. Lisac, *The Klein Revolution* (Edmonton: NeWest Press, 1995).

9 D. Berrigan, *America is Hard to Find* (Garden City, New York: Doubleday and Co., 1972).

10 B. Ehrenreich, "The challenge to the left." In Paul Berman, ed., *Debating P.C.: The Controversy Over Political Correctness on College Campuses* (New York: Dell, 1992).

11 *Alberta Report,* 22 August 1994, 44.

12 Ibid.

13 *Calgary Herald,* 18 February 1995, A6.

14 Access Television, 17 February 1995.

IDEOLOGY

Chapter Seven

The New Normal: Capitalist Discipline in Alberta in the 1990s[1]

Claude Denis

> This is the new normal.
>> Alberta Treasurer Jim Dinning, August 1993.[2]

A good many people seem to think that governments have lost all power at the hands of global economic forces. Markets lead, policy must follow — so they say. Some even argue that sovereignty is a concept whose time has gone.[3] They forget, or don't want to know, that State power is directed not only at resisting or filtering external forces but also toward governing a State's own citizens. It would be good, also, to keep in mind that governments and markets typically function as partners much more than as adversaries. In any case, one of the fundamental vocations of government in modern societies is disciplining populations in the context of a transnational capitalist economy. Thinking about this provides an important key to understanding what the Klein government's restructuring is all about.

The Alberta government is only one of several currently taking dead aim at its deficit. Saskatchewan was actually first at balancing its budget, in February 1995; and Federal Finance Minister Paul Martin Jr.'s 1995-96 budget projected as much as a 35 percent reduction to Ottawa's deficit over two years. Each of these three governments, however, is doing things its own way, with different mixtures of tax increases and expenditure cutbacks (see Graph 7.1). While both Regina and Ottawa are raising taxes and making a point of saying so,[4] the Alberta government is adamant in claiming that it is not raising taxes at all — although it will admit to raising all manner of user fees. Overwhelmingly, it is argued, Alberta's balanced budget will be achieved through smaller — not richer — government. In the process, the role of government in society will be transformed. Here lies the originality of Ralph Klein's restructuring program.

Graph 7.1
Tax and Cut Combinations of Three Governments

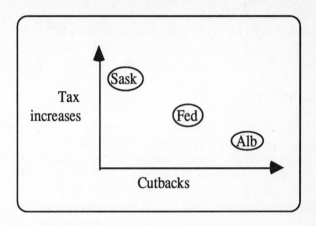

While they work on reducing their deficits, the federal and Saskatchewan governments do not claim to be trying to transform society. Rather,
they defend their actions by saying that they are doing what is necessary to
preserve as much as possible of Canadians' way of life. This is why Paul Martin Jr., for example, feels the need to reassure Canadians that "national
standards" remain important for Ottawa, despite changes in the system of
transfer payments to provinces that will reduce the federal government's influence on how the money is spent, severely diminishing its role in the life
of the federation.[5] In contrast, the Klein government's ambition is to transform society. Contrary to then-Deputy Premier Ken Kowalski's claim that:
"Our approach will be to basically have a very, very limited amount of legislation and that will be the wave of the future,"[6] the Klein government has
been very busy. Compared to the Getty years, for example, the first three
legislative sessions[7] of the Klein government had proportionately more sitting days and adopted as many bills.

What is it in Conservative Alberta that is in such dire need of transformation that a Conservative government would launch the kind of restructuring that is being called a "revolution"?[8] In order to answer this question,
I will need to take a few steps back and look at some *cultural preconditions* of
a capitalist economy and at a couple of developments in the world economy
over the last few decades.

Capitalist Discipline and the Welfare State

Some sociologists argue that one of the State's key tasks in its partnership with capitalism is that of *moral regulation*,[9] which is to say the process by which certain codes for everyday living are naturalized and justified, while others are marginalized. Culturally specific ways of being and thinking are thus made to seem natural; this automatically makes alternatives appear unnatural. It is through such moral regulation that a population will *accept* being disciplined, for it will come to think of a particular discipline as natural, normal. This is important because for a capitalist economy to work, people must be disciplined in very particular ways, as workforce and as members of families — both of which are strongly gender-structured.

Let me, by way of example, draw your attention to your wristwatch.[10] For the past two to three hundred years in Western societies, we have been ruled by the clock in a unique way. The rule of timepieces started with big, public clocks in the towers of city halls all over Europe, and gradually found its way through miniaturization to just about everyone's body, first with pocket watches and then with wristwatches. Not to mention the presence of clocks all over our homes, beginning with alarm clocks which do their best to ensure that we get up at the time we are supposed to — so as not to be late for work, so as to get the children to school on time for the morning bell, etc. This development accompanied the growth of manufacture and then industrial capitalism; the punch clock near the entrance to the shop floor marking the importance of a time-disciplined workforce for the factory owner's ability to make a profit. This relationship to time, peculiar to modern societies, is a cultural trait. And it is within this culture that the capitalist economy operates, depending for its growth on the timeliness of women and men.

However, in the last fifty years or so, some things have happened that have undermined this operation. I need to highlight two for the purposes of this chapter's argument. First, the development of the welfare State has modified the civic and economic culture of Western societies in such a way that for whole sectors of the population, the self-discipline consistent with optimal profit-making has become less of a compelling value. Social safety nets that were generous compared to what existed before brought with them a heightened sense of security, and a sense that people were owed that security by the State. Secondly, this was accompanied by the development of the consumer society, higher living standards for a mushrooming middle class, and — again — the expectation that people were owed this always increasing prosperity.[11] It seemed for a while that, under conditions of democracy, the State was being disciplined by the citizenry: we expected security and prosperity, and the State was to deliver.

If nothing else, a second development made this expectation unsustainable: starting in the mid-1960s the international economy entered a crisis of profitability. The deep recessions associated with the years 1973, 1981, and 1989 are symptoms of this gathering crisis. Part of the difficulty was that the prosperity of the post-World War II decades was tied-up with increasing production costs and in particular high labour costs, both directly as paid in wages and indirectly in contributions to the financing of welfare-State programs. As long as corporations remained easily profitable, such high costs were — albeit grudgingly perhaps — accepted. This ended in the late 1970s, Margaret Thatcher's and Ronald Reagan's rise to power being the political expression of business' return to a narrow conception of the bottom line: profits would return by slashing labour costs.

Both these trends contributed mightily to the digging of ever deeper government deficits. The welfare State has been, by definition, a big spender; and lowered profitability resulted in a protracted economic slowdown that has reduced government revenues at the same time that it increased their unemployment-related outlays. Government debt, in turn, has created upward pressure on interest rates, which among other things makes it more expensive for business to borrow and more generally contribute to slowing economic activity. This is one important reason why government debt is disliked by business interests — despite the fact that *lending* to government is a quite profitable business. In this context, from the standpoint of international capital, two things need to be done, both of them politically difficult to handle.

First, government deficits must be drastically reduced, if not eliminated, through an attack on the welfare State. Tax increases are to be kept at a minimum. Again, from the point of view of capital, such a policy orientation is easy to understand: wealthy people gain little from being protected by welfare-State programs, and have the most to lose from tax increases. Paul Martin Jr. appears to be on his way to taking care of this first task. So, of course, is Jim Dinning.

Secondly, in order for comfortable overall profitability to return, the populations of North America and Western Europe must accept increasingly numerous and painful sacrifices. Men and women must be disciplined anew, for a post-welfare-State economy: labour costs must come down, the workforce must be compliant, families must take over welfare and care services that are dumped by the government and cannot be run at a profit by the private sector. And, for all these sacrifices to be borne over a long period, people have to be convinced that they are justified — that they are, in fact, the normal way to live. Hence Jim Dinning's remonstrance to his fellow cabinet ministers shortly after the election, when several of them appeared to be on their way to spending more than what was allowed by the targets set for their departments: "This is the new normal."[12] This is a now oft-repeated theme of the Klein government (see chapter five): that the old kind of normal doesn't live in Alberta anymore.

Albertans, then, must be weaned from the culture of the welfare State. One might say that, rugged individualists that they are, Albertans never bought into that culture. The fact, however, is that it *has* become embedded into Alberta's social fabric — even if it did fit somewhat uneasily with the province's established political culture. So Albertans must forget what they were used to, and they must acquire a new sense of what is normal.

Anywhere else in Canada, a government that undertook this kind of program would run into very stiff opposition. The peculiarity of Alberta in this respect is that those elements of the welfare State that were developed directly by the provincial government (e.g., the proliferation of small rural hospitals) were not connected to a corresponding State-oriented ideology, and were not financed with taxpayers' money, but rather with oil royalties.[13] This made the Alberta welfare State unusually vulnerable to attacks couched in the self-reliance discourse that remained the dominant political language in the province. And so, even hospitals in small rural centres — the heart of one of the pillars of Tory support — are now being hit by Jim Dinning's axe.[14]

In any case, the originality of the Klein restructuring is that, through its strenuously argued attack on welfare-State budgets and government structures, it is attempting to accomplish the second task ordained by capital: to create the kind of conditions required for the return of easy profitability. It cannot be said that either Martin or Janice Mackinnon, the Saskatchewan treasurer, are pursuing quite this same goal.

A Shallow Sense of Values

At first glance, Ralph Klein and Preston Manning, the Reform Party leader, would appear to promote identical transformations in the role of government and to claim the support of the same political constituencies. It does not take long, however, to notice important differences in the political values embodied by both men (see chapter four). While a dominant feature of Manning's image and appeal is his religiosity, Klein's image is that of the fun-loving ordinary guy who never saw a drink he didn't like and who values his freedom above all else.[15] This difference goes beyond the personal image of party leaders. It goes a long way, in fact, toward explaining policy decisions by the Klein government such as the privatization of liquor sales and the introduction of large numbers of video lottery terminals (VLTs) — two kinds of issues (drinking and gambling) which have traditionally met with strong moral disapproval from conservative Christians.

In contemporary political debates, a distinction is often made between neoconservatism, which puts considerable emphasis on tradition, religion and family values, and neoliberalism, which is more exclusively concerned with the freedom of markets and individuals from government interference and with economic "efficiency." While Manning's Reform Party clearly displays a strong neoconservative component, Klein's government is much more characterized by the neoliberal outlook.[16]

Without going into great detail about this here, it is useful to note that a conservative electorate such as Alberta's can respond positively to the kind of values embodied by both Klein and Manning. If Manning can be seen as resembling an evangelical preacher, Klein is the cowboy, or the oil industry's roughneck. These characters belong very much in the same landscape of Alberta's rural conservatism, along with the fact that the preacher and the cowboy-roughneck do not always see eye to eye. There are days when your average person will think the preacher a little too grim, and others when the cowboy is judged a little too rowdy.

The Klein government may yet come to grief, in fact, over the VLTs, the proliferation of which is opposed by a good majority of Albertans.[17] The Klein government would thus be pushed more toward the neoconservative end of the right-wing spectrum, and away from neoliberalism. In any case, insofar as Alberta conservatism is concerned, it seems appropriate to borrow the current advertising slogan of an Edmonton TV station to characterize both Klein and Manning: "They're ours."

There is something new in this ability of right-wing politicians such as Ralph Klein to make strong disciplinary appeals without having to call upon religious values. Indeed, this is one reason why it cannot be said that Alberta under Klein is *going back* to a world of tradition. One may ask, at this point: what *are* the Klein government's values? For the neoliberalism which dominates its outlook, economic freedom and efficiency are the controlling values. It is hard not to consider such values rather shallow, especially when compared with the moral urgency that stems from religious motivation or from progressive humanism. It also is hard to imagine these neoliberal values having a lasting electoral appeal: we may expect that, in the medium term, the profile of such issues as "family values" will increase, at the expense of some of the more cold-blooded focus on efficiency.

Moral Regulation and the Media

Through moral regulation, a civic/economic culture is made, with governments as key participants. This making, however, is enormously dependent upon the mass media, for it is through the media that most people learn of most government activity. Indeed, except for the civil servants and other public sector workers whose daily lives are being transformed by government restructuring, the main contact most Albertans have with the Klein revolution is indirect, as they watch the news and read the paper. As the impact of the cuts becomes more keenly felt, direct contact will increase, probably in parallel with gradually waning media interest. By then, however, the work of cultural transformation will be largely done.

This is why the research that led to this chapter involved a content analysis of one year's output of two media outlets, each important in its own way: the *Edmonton Journal* and *Alberta Report*. Among other distinguishing features, the daily *Journal*, which is part of the pan-Canadian Southam chain, has liberal leanings and is widely seen as critical of the Klein revolution; while *Alberta Report*, the Western-based news magazine, has a very upfront, very conservative outlook. One may reasonably expect coverage to diverge. As we will see, however, the difference will not be simply a matter of supporting or decrying government practice — although this may be in part a function of the criteria we used to select articles from the *Journal* and *Alberta Report*.

In content analysis, items from a given source are systematically evaluated and selected according to a set of criteria appropriate to a specific research project. In this case, articles were selected if their title or opening paragraph dealt with provincial government initiatives and/or statements, for the period dating from the election of the Klein government in June 1993 to the end of the second session of the 23rd legislature in June 1994. A record of each media source's version of government practice was thereby gathered. We ignored articles generated by and focused on opposition to government action, so as to maintain the focus on what the government *wanted to* communicate.

The focus on government-generated stories accounts in part for the low level of overt criticism found in both sources — but especially in the *Edmonton Journal*, of course. This is not an accidental result, nor does it signal a defect of the method. On the contrary, the key here is that, no matter what their political leanings may be, large daily newspapers (and network news broadcasts) that claim to offer balanced news coverage supply their readers with vast amounts of information originating from governments. The political outlooks of reporters and editors will influence the writing and placement of news reports, but government messages *will be* transmitted. In magazines such as *Alberta Report*, which do not claim to be nonpartisan, the selection of stories will in the same sense play a still greater role, even before the expressed opinions of writers are considered. In this respect, the political leanings of a mainstream newspaper will often count for little next to the sheer amount of their coverage of recognized social actors. Moreover, no social actor gets anywhere near the amount of coverage afforded governments. For this reason we may talk of a partnership of State and media in the process of moral regulation.

Three hundred and five articles from the *Edmonton Journal* and seventy nine from *Alberta Report* were selected. A full 36 percent of the *Journal* articles appeared on the front page. A large number of prominent reports are involved, then, signalling sustained media coverage of intense government activity and informational output. Lest this seems a trivial thing to note, let me repeat that few social actors are able to argue their cases on the front page of a major daily paper even a few times a year, let alone more than a hundred times.

Once articles were selected, three types of information were sought: what area(s) of government activity was or were involved (Municipal Affairs, Education, Environment, etc.), what was the government saying or doing (creating regional authorities, eliminating jobs in a particular department, promising no tax increases, etc.), and what language was used by government spokespersons to explain, justify, defend that particular activity (renovating the house, being business-like, being responsible, etc.). The goal was to get a clear picture of what the government was saying it was doing, and how it made sense of it all.

Ralph's Regimen

Analysis of the coverage of government activity in the *Edmonton Journal* and in *Alberta Report* shows that the disciplinary practice of the Klein government has two categories of targets and two messages. The targets are, on the one hand, the population in general and, on the other hand, "deviants" — the latter being set up as a counter-example which good Albertans ought not to follow. The government's first message aims at putting into place a business culture to replace the welfare-State culture. Through a continuous use of business metaphors, Albertans are to be convinced that their province is, indeed, a business, and that every social concern comes down to either the profit motive or at least an overriding concern for cost-effectiveness — no matter the occasional incoherence in the metaphors. Thus, we are told both that the government is committed to "getting out of the business of business,"[18] and that it is incorporating "a more business-like approach to managing its finances"[19]; which is why every government department is developing "business plans." In the same spirit, the minister responsible for advanced education declared that the goal of a university education is to "train somebody with a marketable skill."[20]

The second message is that Albertans have been irresponsible, both individually and collectively, and that they must now become responsible. They must learn self-discipline. Thus, the *individual* is called upon to be responsible when he or she is to take a pay cut; when he or she faces either higher user fees or lower-quality government service; when, upon seeing payments from the government reduced or eliminated, he or she is admonished to get a job; when faced with providing services to family members that used to be the purview of paid professionals. Also, the government claims to be making *communities* responsible by regionalizing the administration of the Health and Education systems.

The campaign for self-discipline actually started, very smartly, with a focus on the government itself: the MLAs' pension plan was eliminated just before the election, and a pay cut to MLAs and cabinet ministers quickly followed. In short order, the premier and his minister then set themselves up as examples for the civil service: "The savings are important, but equally important is the message that we will not ask the public sector to do what we will not do ourselves."[21] At this point, the government asked the civil service, and then other public sector workers (nurses, teachers, etc.), to take voluntary pay cuts — making it clear that if workers said no, potentially deeper cuts would be legislated anyway. The government thus created a situation where self-discipline was forced upon the public sector as a lesser evil.

Beyond targeting the public service, cutbacks and restructuring in the two most talked about sectors, health and education, also are aimed at the population as a whole — with the notable exemption of those able and eager to buy better educational and health services. A third area of general high-impact deep changes, which has however received less attention, is the Municipal Affairs sector. In these sectors, the disciplinary drive goes forward through regionalization of administration, following a centralization of decision-making on the size of budgets: communities and regional authorities are handed the responsibility of choosing where to cut deepest. Thus, in Education, at the same time that they lost financial autonomy, school boards have been handed more responsibility: "It's up to the individual school boards to ... find new and better and more cost-effective ways of doing things."[22] In the same spirit, government expects "increased involvement from parents, the community and business"; lack of resources notwithstanding, this is touted as "greater grassroots control."[23] Regionalizing of Health Care is presented in similar ways: it "will ensure that the local needs are addressed at the source."[24]

Self-discipline, indeed, is the order of the day. And for women, doubly so: they are losing their civil service jobs more than men and they are expected to take charge, for free in their families, of activities that until now were thought of as "social services" (see chapter eighteen). As a matter of fact, the disciplining impulse is sharpest with respect to cuts in the Family and Social Services department, as the government claims to be in the process of creating social services that will help people to help themselves.[25] The bottom line in this field, noted the premier, is that "government doesn't and indeed, cannot have all the answers, all the money, all the compassion."[26] Not a hint of generosity here: government would only commit itself "to helping those who need help the most."[27] To get a good sense of how restrictive this policy is, one need only consider the "Reshaping Child Welfare" plan, under which abusive parents were to re-assume more responsibility for their children: the minister, Mike Cardinal, argued that "government can never be a good parent ... only parents of those children can be good parents."[28] Even for the few who qualify for government help, explained Cardinal, "the goal is not to make welfare unbearable. ... But it has to be uncomfortable enough that people will try to find an alternative way of living."[29]

Government stringency in Family and Social Services is extreme, as is its rhetoric, which results in users of the social welfare system being portrayed as quasi-deviants, an un-Albertan group that should be seen by all Albertans as an example to not follow. The Klein revolution's discourse on social welfare has often taken a harsh tone reminiscent of its statements about such issues as crime and, especially the Young Offenders Act and the death penalty — both areas outside a provincial government's jurisdiction. Indeed, in mid-1993, upon hearing that crime statistics were down in Edmonton, Mike Cardinal remarked that the removal from welfare rolls of "single employables" had forced young men to get jobs, which cut into their leisure time and thereby kept them from committing crimes.[30]

In advocating the reinstatement of the death penalty, Ralph Klein himself suggested that a provincial referendum might take place. And, as he decided to create a "task force on youth crime," he noted: "Albertans' and Canadians' concerns about issues of youth crime and punishment are bigger than a jurisdiction question."[31] The same goes for the Charter of Rights and Freedoms, which government members such as Steve West, Diane Mirosh, and then-Deputy Premier Ken Kowalski have blamed for contributing to the increase in youth crime. Said Kowalski: "Essentially, what the Charter has done is changed the perception in the democracy from the right of a majority ... to the right of a minority identified as one (individual)."[32] Similar claims are being made about multiculturalism and "community development." Government programs dealing with multiculturalism have been drastically cut; the Human Rights Commission has been threatened with elimination several times[33]; and storms of controversy have surrounded a Court of Queen's Bench decision to extend human rights protection to gays and lesbians — with government members deploring the decision and considering the possibility of legislation to reverse it.[34]

It is on this nexus of issues (law and order, human rights) that the government's cultural crusade is most visible. In this sense, it is only superficially strange that the disciplining message of the Alberta government is expressed most clearly in areas outside its jurisdiction (including, in the winter and spring of 1995, gun control legislation): they provide the Alberta government its best opportunities to voice stern views on the laxity of moral standards in contemporary Canadian society. This also is where the crux of *Alberta Report*'s own cultural politics is most visible. Thus, in our content analysis, we found that 11 percent of its coverage of the government was focused on the Multiculturalism and Community Development Department, where "political correctness," "special rights," and "special interest groups" were lambasted. By contrast, only 5 percent of the *Edmonton Journal*'s coverage dealt with this Department.

It ought to be clear, then, that what the Klein Tories find objectionable is much more than budget deficits: it is the kind of society that Alberta/Canada has become. Deficit cutting, in this perspective, is a means to a para-economic end: a deep cultural transformation. Who but highly determined governments could take on such a task *and* have some hope of succeeding? How could the march of globalization go on without such cultural taskmasters?

Conclusion

What general lessons can be learned from this disciplining of Alberta? Most obviously, we must conclude that it is not because governments shrink that they become less important, less central to society. Among other things, only a government can produce the kind of cultural transformation that the Klein revolution is accomplishing. More generally, it is only through the State that populations can be morally regulated to the extent and in the ways that capitalism requires: if one considers capitalism as not only an economic system, but as a system that has developed historically as a combination of political, economic, and cultural forces, then it can be seen that certain cultural changes can endanger the ability of capitalism to maintain itself. To the extent that the combination of welfare State and consumer society have weakened the self-discipline of populations, capitalist reproduction has been undermined. And this is where the "Klein revolution" comes in, with its attempt at re-disciplining Albertans. Only shortsightedness, then, could bring one to claim that the demise of the welfare State is synonymous with the fading away of the State as such. Even if all welfare activities were removed from State practice, much would remain of what makes our societies State-centred.

Also, it turns out that it still matters what political party wins elections. As the federal government and Alberta's and Saskatchewan's provincial governments are showing, there is a considerable difference in the way governments of various political stripes interpret their mandates from the population. Even a *conservative* NDP government such as Saskatchewan's orchestrates its restructuring by trying to continue *providing* at least as much as it is *disciplining*.[35] And while the providing impulse has entirely left the Alberta Tories, Ottawa's Liberals are once again hanging somewhere in between. The political trends in other provinces parallel this continuing left/right spectrum. But we ought also to keep in mind that the whole spectrum has drifted rightward — as the recent Ontario election attests — as the debt obsession has become all but universal in Canada.

Finally, we should note that the Klein revolution is not taking Alberta back to the old days before oil, when — we are told — Albertans were true individualists and government was small. The business-oriented civic culture that is developing in Alberta has a distinctly post-welfare-State character: it is not as if the last fifty years had never happened. One result of this is that the considerable distrust of business interests, which was aimed at Central Canada, has been almost entirely replaced by a distrust in the government. In the NovAtel and Principal Group scandals, for instance, very little public anger has been expended toward the businessmen involved, whereas the Getty government was practically destroyed by the controversy. Indeed, although this chapter has been little concerned with the political sources of the "Klein revolution," it seems clear that it was born at least in part out of the opportunistic combination of (a) a deeply unpopular government that needed to reinvent itself if it was to have any hope of winning the coming election, (b) a discredited economic diversification policy that cost Alberta taxpayers billions of dollars in failed business ventures, and (c) the global new right ideology that extols the freeing of markets and maligns government activism in all but a few disciplining spheres of society.

In this respect, the degree to which Alberta is now thoroughly possessed of a business language is a direct outcome of the omnipresence of the mass media in our lives, and of the media's vocation as a loudspeaker for society's dominant interests. Finally, Alberta is emphatically *not returning* to the self-reliance of old: social networks involving extended families and churches have been enormously reduced over the last half-century, and they are not being replaced as the government leaves the field of care. The Klein revolution is not a restoration, a return to an old order: Alberta is being disciplined for a new age of capitalism. Looking back is going to be no help in finding out where it is taking us.

Notes

1. The research from which this chapter developed was funded by a Summer Research Grant from the Faculté Saint-Jean, University of Alberta, which allowed me to benefit from the excellent work of two research assistants, Chantale Breton and Hanae Kiyooka. Trevor Harrison and Gordon Laxer were generous, patient, and helpful editors. I also want to thank Danyèle Lacombe, whose reporting for CHFA, Radio-Canada's radio station in Alberta, alerted me to specific gender effects of the government's restructuring. She also read my typescript and made helpful comments.
2. *Alberta Report*, 23 August 1993, 6.
3. See for instance M. Mandel, "Sovereignty and the New Constitutionalism." In D. Drache and R. Perin, eds., *Negotiating with a Sovereign Quebec* (Toronto: Lorimer, 1992), 215-229.
4. This is not to say that Ottawa and Regina are working from the same guidebook: Paul Martin Jr. is more willing than Janice Mackinnon, his Saskatchewan counterpart, to cut deeply in government expenses, and less willing to raise taxes. As will be shown below, however, their approaches share a number of traits when compared with the Alberta formula.

5. On this issue, see for instance D. Farquharson's column in the *Edmonton Journal*, 5 March 1995, A8.

6. *Edmonton Journal*, 31 August 1993, A5.

7. The fourth session of the 22nd Legislature and the first two of the 23rd.

8. See M. Lisac, *The Klein Revolution* (Edmonton: NeWest Press, 1995).

9. See in particular P. Corrigan and D. Sayer, *The Great Arch. English State Formation as Cultural Revolution* (London: Routledge, 1985).

10. I am borrowing this example somewhat freely from a number of writers, both in the English and French-speaking worlds. My specific source is Jacques Attali, *Histoires du temps* (Paris: Éditions du Seuil, 1982).

11. All this, of course, notwithstanding the maintenance in poverty of part of the population of every Western country and an increase in the distance separating rich northern countries and the poor south.

12. *Alberta Report*, 23 August 1993, 6.

13. See M. Lisac's column in the *Edmonton Journal*, 25 May 1995, A12. From the early 1970s to the mid-1980s, Peter Lougheed's Conservatives had a State-oriented ideology when it came to promoting the diversification of Alberta's economy. What was involved here was a government-business alliance, with government as senior partner and financier; it was very far from the kind of social-democratic ideology that has provided the welfare State with its best justifications.

14. Although cuts were relatively slow in reaching these health care facilities, the winter and spring 1995 saw the beginning of the end for large numbers of small hospitals, as regional health authorities grappled with their reduced budgets. See, for instance, in the space of only a week, the cuts and protests in the regions east and west of Edmonton: both R. Pedersen's and D. Thomas's articles in the *Edmonton Journal*, 20 May 1995, A5; and K. Powell's story in the *Edmonton Journal*, 21 May 1995, A8. At this writing, the Westview Regional Health Authority has just backed off its plan to close most acute care hospital beds in the region, following a demonstration by 800 people at a public meeting; see R. Pedersen's article in the *Edmonton Journal*, 25 May 1995, A1.

15. On Klein, see Lisac, *The Klein Revolution*; on Manning, see M. Dobbin, *Preston Manning and the Reform Party* (Toronto: Lorimer, 1991); and T. Harrison, *Of Passionate Intensity: Right-Wing Populism and the Reform Party of Canada* (Toronto: University of Toronto, 1995).

16. It should be noted, however, that a neoconservative strand exists on the Conservative backbench and in the person of government leader Stockwell Day, and that opposition from this group has so far been muted.

17. See the opinion poll published in the *Edmonton Journal*, 19 March 1995, C3.

18. *Alberta Hansard*, 28 March 1994, 892.

19. *Alberta Report*, 27 September 1993, 14.

20. *Edmonton Journal*, 14 March 1994, A7.

21. *Alberta Report*, 4 October 1993, 23.

22. *Edmonton Journal*, 6 May 1994, B4.

23. *Alberta Report*, 14 February 1994, 6-11. See also, in this collection, Robertson and Barlow, chapter thirteen.

24. *Edmonton Journal*, 3 February 1994, A7.
25. *Edmonton Journal*, 16 June 1993, A1.
26. *Edmonton Journal*, 29 September 1993, A1.
27. *Edmonton Journal*, 13 January 1994, A8.
28. *Alberta Report*, 22 November 1993, 13.
29. *Alberta Report*, 31 January 1994, 10.
30. The much less glamorous reality is that the drop in crime statistics resulted not from an actual decrease in criminality, but rather from a change in police procedures for registering complaints. See the editorial in the *Edmonton Journal*, 8 March 1994, A6.
31. *Edmonton Journal*, 20 April 1994, A5; and 29 April 1994, A1.
32. *Edmonton Journal*, 22 April 1994, A1.
33. On this issue, see the editorial in the *Edmonton Journal*, 11 September 1994, A10.
34. On April 12, 1994, Justice Anne Russell ruled that Alberta human rights law was in contradiction with the Canadian Charter of Rights and Freedoms, and was therefore unconstitutional. The government ended up appealing the decision and, at this writing (May 1995), the case is before the Alberta Court of Appeals. See C. Lord's article in the *Edmonton Journal*, 11 May 1995, B1.
35. Of course, in order to provide, a government will need relatively high taxes. The contradiction is only superficial: in order to provide, one needs revenues. The point of the providing government, of course, is that it largely redistributes wealth through its services to the population.

Chapter Eight

THE PRIVATIZATION OF PUBLIC LIFE[1]

Gordon Laxer

> The whole purpose of the exercise [privatization of the Alberta Liquor Control Board] was to get the government out of the business of being in business.
>
> Ralph Klein, March 1994[2]

In Klein's Alberta, people are no longer portrayed as citizens and wage-earners in a democratic community. They are now primarily consumers, investors, and stakeholders, acting as individuals in the private marketplace. The public sphere is discredited. It is viewed as bloated, inefficient, and staffed by public employees holding on to their vested interests. Users of public services, from welfare recipients to university students, are viewed as living off the taxes of hard-working people in the private sector. By contrast, the marketplace is portrayed as the purveyor of all that is good. It's efficient, competitive, and teaches people tough love: how to be self-reliant. The marketplace removes the "privileges" of "special interest groups" who (it is implied) are parasitically living off those who are "doers" in the private sector.

Such are the ideological assumptions of the Klein government. These assumptions underlie an attempt to reverse the 1960s and 1970s expansion of what constituted the public sphere. Feminists said in the early 1970s, "the personal is political" and reinterpreted issues like child care, abortion, and the care of the elderly, formerly seen to be private matters, as public issues. Now Klein and the new right are trying once more to privatize public life by drastically narrowing the area of the political. Indeed, in privatizing or proposing to privatize such things as registries, jails, environmental protection services, as well as some court services, the Klein government seems to be implying that there are no core areas of government public sector delivery. Little-noticed in this move from a societal model of citizen-participant to that of market-player, is that the democratic ethics of equality and the collective good are replaced by the capitalist ethics of inequality and private greed. Are we returning to eighteenth century private government delivered by friends of the monarch?

Fifteen years after Margaret Thatcher and Ronald Reagan launched their now widely discredited revolutions[3] to privatize as much of the public sphere as possible, King Ralph and company have undertaken the most extensive privatization of public life in any province in Canada.[4]

On September 2, 1993, Steve West, then municipal affairs minister and the most ardent exponent of privatization in Klein's cabinet, announced that the government would sell all Alberta Liquor Control Board (ALCB) stores. It came like a bolt out of the blue. Two days earlier he had assured the union representing ALCB employees that their jobs were safe. Privatization was apparently not planned and the government kept changing its mind. One day the large supermarket chains could sell alcoholic beverages within their stores. "Anybody can apply for a licence. We're under a free market system," said West on January 31, 1994.[5] The next day Ralph Klein declared, "I've said there would be no alcohol sold in grocery stores." The ALCB warehouse in St. Albert was originally not going to be sold, then it was to be sold. Finally it was leased.

The way the ALCB was sold is characteristic of the Klein government's actions on privatization. Make your decisions in haste based on ideology and carry them out quickly before opposition can build. In the fall of 1994, the government went a step further by introducing Bills 41 and 57 which would enable it even to privatize without legislation (see chapter nine).

What have they privatized, why have they done it, and what are the consequences? These questions are addressed in this chapter.

Why Privatize?

Before Margaret Thatcher, few had ever heard of privatization. It was generally accepted in the Western world that there was a legitimate role for public institutions to carry out functions that private business did badly or not at all. Pure market capitalism, it was thought, did not provide for the needs of those outside or poorly placed in the labour market. The old, the sick, the unemployed, the young, and the poor all needed to be helped by the public sector. As well, in Canada, where foreign ownership has been higher than in any other advanced country, public enterprise was a traditional way of increasing domestic control of economic life. Public enterprise was also used to diversify the economy away from raw resource exports — to go beyond the role of "hewers of wood and drawers of water." This public enterprise tradition included Alberta, where Social Credit set up the provincially-owned Treasury Branches, a savings bank network established to remove the monopoly control of eastern, "outsider" banks. In 1939, Social Credit set up a provincial marketing board with the power to engage in, amongst other things, "manufacturing, distributing, merchandising, or natural products" [sic]. The marketing board alarmed business interests, but never achieved anything.[6]

An alternative to crown corporations was initiated by Social Credit in the creation of Alberta Gas Trunk Line (1954), in which the government owned a minority share. Lougheed's Tories continued the model of quasi-State enterprise by setting up the Alberta Energy Company (1973) to develop nonconventional oil reserves.[7] His government also acquired Pacific Western Airlines (1975).

The Klein revolution is about overthrowing these Canadian and Albertan traditions of positive government. Why the sudden craze for privatization in Alberta? Partly, it's in the "air."

Far from acting rationally, corporations often get caught up in fads. For example, Michael Hammer and James Champy's *Reengineering the Corporation*[8] sold two million copies and encouraged businesses to radically rethink their processes of doing business. Many companies interpreted reengineering as massive "downsizing" and the elimination of middle management layers. After eight years of downsizing in which well over one million executives and workers lost their jobs in the United States, Champy admitted to second thoughts in 1995. University of Wisconsin business professor Kenneth De Meuse found that companies that downsized had lower profits in the five years after downsizing compared to those that did not.[9]

Privatization is another such fad. At the urging of business representatives, governments are plunging in without studying beforehand whether in fact privatization will be more efficient or achieve public policy goals. Not long ago, it was conventional wisdom that expanding or "creeping" socialism was inevitably triumphing everywhere. Now, new-right liberals preaching the virtues of free markets have captured the future by convincing people that global competition is forcing governments to become leaner and less intrusive everywhere. "It's inevitable," "We have no choice," they say.

Privatization. Everyone's doing it. It's being done by Republicans in the United States, the ideological soul mates of Klein's Conservatives. It has already been done in New Zealand.

The chief architect of New Zealand's radical program of dismantling the welfare State, while implementing a plan of massive privatizations, was

Sir Roger Douglas, then finance minister in the Labour government. Today, leader of a fledgling political party that seeks to privatize everything if elected, he travels the world selling his book, *Unfinished Business*[10], and his ideas. Douglas addressed the cabinet in Edmonton, where it was reported that half liked and half disliked what they heard. Klein's very words seem to come from the New Zealander. In his book, Roger Douglas sets out ten principles for the reform of government. His eighth principle "don't blink" has been repeated many times by Klein. The second and third principles: "implement reforms in quantum leaps," and "it's almost impossible to go too fast," have been taken to heart.

Other outside intellectual influences include U.S. authors David Osborne and Ted Gaebler, whose book *Reinventing Government*[11] is reportedly a sort of bible for cabinet ministers. Osborne and Gaebler advocate streamlining governments and making them more responsive to users. But these and other outside voices are more justifications and models for directions the Klein government already wants to go in than the cause of the government's break from Social Credit and Lougheed traditions. This is not a government of deep thinkers. Cabinet ministers did not read these and other authors and suddenly see the light. There were Alberta reasons for the about-face.

Like the Reform Party, the nerve centre of the Klein government is Calgary, the most conservative big city in Canada. While other parts of Canada underwent a major boom in the mid-to-late-1980s, Calgary and Alberta's oil industry were painfully coming off the great speculative oil boom of the late 1970s and early 1980s. With world oil prices falling from $40 U.S. per barrel to a low of $9 per barrel in March 1986, the oil patch faced massive debts. Dreams of $100 per barrel oil futures, that everyone connected to the industry believed, led many oil companies into debt, with the willing complicity of the banks. When the dream faded, the industry, whose Canadian headquarters are located in Calgary, spent the rest of the decade reducing costs and climbing out of debt. They did this by massive layoffs, streamlining operations, contracting out, and curbing excesses. By the early 1990s, the oil industry had substantially reduced the price at which it could make a profit. Many in the oil patch and in like-minded political circles in Calgary were asking, "why can't we do the same with government?"

More decisive to the privatization push, were the spectacular failures of the Lougheed government's grand efforts at diversification. When he was elected in 1971 to replace the long-serving Social Credit regime, Lougheed pointed out the dangers of relying on nonrenewable resources such as oil. "We have perhaps ten years left to diversify Alberta's economy," he said. Using booming oil revenues to set the foundation for a nonresource-based economy, the Lougheed government supported diversification into financial services, cellular telephones, magnesium smelting, food processing, and other sectors. Don Getty's tenure (1985-1992) came just when world oil prices crashed and his regime was the unfortunate inheritor of these ventures gone bad.

Despite the infusion of government monies, Alberta's financial sector was the first to fall. The failures of the Canadian Commercial Bank, the Northland Bank, the provincial takeover of North West Trust and Heritage Savings and Trust, and the really big one — the collapse of the Principal Group — demonstrated the failure of Alberta's "dirigiste" policies.[12] Then came the failures of NovAtel, Magcan, Gainers, and many other smaller companies that had been backed by provincial loan guarantees. The government lost over \$2 billion[13] and Albertans turned against an activist public role in the economy. The stage was set for the ideologues and crass opportunists.

It is not the Tories alone, however, who believe in the virtues of privatization. The Opposition Liberals, who under Laurence Decore's leadership tried to do a right-wing end run around Klein (see chapter three), usually start off legislature debates by applauding the government's latest privatization venture.[14] "We agree with what you are doing, but criticize you for how you are doing it," they say. Public discussion is about means, not ends.

The means are corrupt. They are variations of the same old patronage that had ministers in bed with their business pals. But privatization opened up vast new areas where the Conservative regime could create "entrepreneurs" who did not operate in a free market but were dependent on government licences and contracts. It is a new world of political patrons and clients reaching into every community. Mark Lisac invents a new term, "the red market" to contrast with the "black market." In the red market, the lines between public and private interests are blurred. Private firms have a monopoly in selling government information. Government awards contracts and licences without calling tenders. Rural MLAs are powerful people who are good to know. They can get you into large new areas of privatized services.[15]

Steve West, who in October 1994 moved from Municipal Affairs to Transportation, is the most ardent champion of the privatization of everything. In debate on a well-thought-out Opposition bill to study costs and benefits before privatizing, West declared: "There isn't a government operation, a government business, a Crown corporation that is as efficient as the private sector, and indeed they're 20 to 40 percent less efficient."[16]

Where did the minister get the efficiency figure of twenty-to-forty percent? Obviously not from a government study. He or his advisors must have been reading Madsen Pirie, president of the Adam Smith Institute in London, and a leading author of Thatcher's privatization initiatives. These are the exact figures Madsen cites, but likewise does not substantiate, in his book, *Privatisation*.[17]

West must not have been reading his Osborne and Gaebler carefully, though. They caution that:

> Privatisation is one arrow in government's quiver. But just as obviously, privatisation is not *the* solution. Those who advocate it on ideological grounds — because they believe business is always superior to government — are selling the American people snake oil.[18]

What is Privatization?

The term is used so loosely it covers a multitude of sins. Under Margaret Thatcher it was mainly about selling crown monopolies and turning them into private monopolies such as British Gas and British Telecom. One of the touted benefits of selling the crown jewels is to reduce government debt. But this is just an accounting trick. Through privatization, a public asset that was never listed as such appears in the credit column.

Pirie lists twenty-one methods of privatizing. They include: 1) selling the whole crown corporation by public share issue; 2) selling or giving it to the workforce; 3) contracting out the service to private business; 4) charging for the service; 5) repealing monopolies to let competition grow; 6) use of vouchers; and 7) State withdrawal from the activity.[19] Alberta has ignored Pirie's first two methods and relied mainly on numbers 3, 4, and 7. The latter is very inefficient, but upholds the ideology of competition.

Privatization of Public Registries

In the fall of 1993, Alberta privatized the delivery of most registry services. This was important not only for itself but because it pioneered a new form of privatization that removed ministerial responsibility and legislature scrutiny from the operation of government. Steve West, then minister of municipal affairs, who was privatizing Alberta's liquor stores at the same time, set up Alberta Registries in a semi-autonomous body that was later to be called a "designated administrative authority" (DAO). A year later,

DAOs became the basis for the controversial Bill 57 (see chapter nine). Alberta Registries contracts private agents to sell public registry services on a fee-for-service basis. These include motor vehicle registration, driver licensing, searches associated with motor vehicles and with drivers, land titles transactions, personal property encumbrances, business corporation information, and certain vital statistics information. It was all done without legislative approval.[20]

Privatized registries were made popular through the brilliant red-tape cutting idea of "one-window" shopping. Instead of chasing from one ministry to another to figure out which office to go to, and experiencing long waits in bureaucratic offices, the public can now get all registry services from a single agent. Hours of operation are more convenient and locations more accessible. It is not clear, however, why privatization was necessary to make these sensible changes. Why could Alberta Registries not have delivered one-window shopping, better hours and better locations, and nonbureaucratic service directly, using public servants?

Alberta sets a base fee for each transaction. Private agents markup prices to users. For the majority of services the markup is limited to a fixed maximum, four dollars (for example) for vehicle registration. But for nine transactions such as stolen or lost vehicle plates, the province receives nothing and the agents are allowed unlimited markups. In another twenty-four registrations such as the oral driving test, the province also receives nothing and agent fees are capped (eg., $20). For twenty-six services such as birth, marriage licences, death certificates, and land title searches, the government receives a set amount, but agents' charges are not limited. In small towns, where there is little or no competition, some outrageous markups have been charged.[21] Government revenues are about the same after privatization compared to before,[22] but the public is paying more for the services.

There are concerns with private-sector delivery of registry services. How well are the agents screened and trained? Will some shady characters who have a sinister interest in people's names and addresses get into the business? In 1994, thieves broke into three private registry offices in Calgary and stole documents and document-making equipment. One of the agents suggested that the robberies were made to fabricate driver's licences.[23] Will the agents sell, or fail to protect, personal information? After five-days training as driving examiners, instead of the previous six-months to one-year training, will agents be sufficiently skilled to determine driving competence? Will the profit motive be an incentive for agents to grant drivers licences too readily?

The ALCB Fiasco

Unlike privatization of public registries by administrative fiat, a bill was introduced and passed in November 1993 to sell off public liquor stores. But the bill was almost an afterthought. Privatization had been under way for two months.

Why did the government sell an asset which generated over $400 million in revenues annually and was so efficient the retail markup was only 6 percent above the wholesale price? The purpose seemed to be purely ideological. Klein told the legislature: "The whole purpose of the exercise" [privatization of the ALCB] was to "get the government out of the business of being in business."[24]

Nevertheless Steve West, the minister in charge, expected concrete benefits. He predicted that privatization would lead to a "leaner, more efficient" system and that selection and convenience would be enhanced. Privatization would not lead to more alcohol abuse, he claimed. The government expected to get a windfall of $88 million by selling public assets and to maintain revenues from alcohol sales.

Have government expectations been met? In December 1994, a delayed and misleading government report tried to put the best face on the fiasco.[25] But in reality the minister's predictions failed on most fronts, as shown by a Centre for Policy Alternatives study.[26] Statistics Canada confirmed that prices were on average 6 percent above those of the public system a year earlier. An advertising flyer from a private store in Edmonton tempted customers with "1993 ALCB prices" and "save up to 20 percent." To meet criticisms of high prices, Alberta gradually lowered provincial taxes starting in August 1994. Since privatization, annual provincial revenues from alcohol sales have declined by at least $30 million and could suffer even more.

Why were prices higher and revenues lower? Contrary to West's claims, the public system was more efficient. The ALCB enjoyed "economies of scale," buying in bulk and distributing efficiently. Private owners marked up products from 12 percent to 36 percent, not 6 percent, above the wholesale price but did not make high profits.

Selection at most individual stores was down substantially. The government report claimed there were 35 percent more products in the province than previously. True but misleading. Who was going to drive all over Alberta to pick up all the brands they used to get at any ALCB store?

Greater convenience was the one area in which the government achieved its goal. There were more stores, about 600 in May 1995, and

longer hours. The greater number of outlets will only last if Alberta continues to exclude supermarket chains from selling booze in their main stores.

The government has not told the public what happened since privatization. Has alcohol use increased as it did in Iowa? Has it risen amongst mi-
nors and the already intoxicated, now that private retailers have a vested
interest in selling as much as possible? Has alcohol-related crime risen? The
province has not informed us. The Calgary Police reported a 61 percent
rise in crimes at liquor stores in the first half of 1994 over the comparable
period in 1993.

Did the province receive a bonanza by selling assets? No. In a hurry to
dismantle the old system, because private owners could not compete with
the ALCB, the properties were dumped on the market. At most Alberta will
receive half the $136.6 million it cost to acquire them.

The government bragged that "more than 3,000 jobs have been created" by privatizing the ALCB. These were not full-time job equivalences
and it ignores the more than 1,500 full-time public-sector job equivalents
lost at much better wages. Perhaps that was the point: to reduce moderate
wages to levels barely above the minimum wage.

Privatizing the ALCB has not been widely viewed as a failure. An An-
gus-Reid poll conducted in April 1994 showed that while Albertans were
critical of prices and selection, 55 percent approved of privatization.[27] They
are romanced by the *idea* of private ownership even while disliking the *reality*. Some seemed to get vindictive pleasure in reducing union wages. These
reactions are typical of American Republicans and sets Albertans apart from
other Canadians.

Why did the government allow only a small-business competitive system
to replace the ALCB? It was the most inefficient method, making it easy for
critics to point out the superiority of the public system. Two alternatives
were readily available. The Thatcherite route of selling the whole system to
a single operator to maximize asset sales and realize scale efficiencies was
apparently rejected outright. A second way was to let supermarkets take
over most beer and wine sales in their grocery stores and leave the rest to
specialty shops. The supermarkets lobbied hard for this and they could
have kept prices down. Klein's government changed its mind in public
about the supermarket option several times and may still in the end allow it,
as Iowa did after two years of a Mom and Pop system.

Why didn't the Klein government follow the more sensible ways? Ideology. They were cutting the size of the public service and the ALCB workers
served as a convenient symbol of bloated government. Klein's right populists courted the image of favouring small business.

Privatizing Other Services

Registries and the ALCB were the earliest privatizations but not necessarily the most important in the long run. Alberta is heading down the road towards American-style, two-tiered health care, a subject discussed by Simon Renouf (see chapter fifteen). How far it will travel down that road was unclear in early 1995. Mike Cardinal, the social services minister, laid out a process for the regionalization of services to neglected children and announced that 1,300 provincial workers involved in the delivery of these services will be laid off (see chapter twenty-one). Responsibility for foster care, school counselling and help for youths who commit crimes will likely be given over to such private agencies as McMann (for-profit) and Catholic Social Services (non-profit). Charter schools, discussed by Robertson and Barlow in chapter thirteen), may be the first step towards privatizing education.

Private bailiffs may be used to carry out seizures, despite opposition from the Alberta Law Reform Institute, which has stated, "A public official ... who owes his or her first duty to the court and not to the creditor, [should] carry out the seizure."[28] Living up to its reputation as Texas North, Alberta may privatize at least one provincial jail. "You are warehousing people," explained Ken Rostad, the justice minister. Wackenhut and the Corrections Corporation of America claim they can cut operating costs by up to 15 percent. Critics wonder how sensible it is to create a private jailing industry whose economic interests lie in raising the number of prisoners and whose profits would be hurt by rehabilitation.

Every provincial department is engaged in privatization ventures of one sort or another. The scope and nature of such privatizations is shown in Figure 8.1.

What Wasn't Privatized and Why

Sometimes it seems that Klein's government favours privatizing everything. This is not so. They are reluctant to touch some areas because of political self interest.

The second largest bank in Alberta, the Treasury Branch, is the major sacred cow. The Opposition Liberals have been gunning to sell off the Treasury Branches, using the neoliberal argument that they compete unfairly with private-sector lending institutions. Provincial Treasurer Jim Dinning rejected Liberal demands and also the recommendations of his Financial Review Commission to review and possibly sell the Treasury Branches (and four smaller provincial financial institutions). Dinning's rea-

Figure 8.1
Some Highlights of Privatization Plans for Alberta

Agriculture, Food and Rural Development
• Increase private-sector delivery of info, technology, and services
• Private veterinary labs to develop animal health quality
• Transfer responsibility for pest monitoring to private sector

Economic Development and Tourism
• Alberta Research Council to "nurture" technology-based activities and spin
  them off to private companies

Energy
• Private sector to carry out energy audits, education, information

Environmental Protection
• Deregulate, privatize, outsource, and partnership where possible

Family and Social Services
• Services to Neglected Children to be privatized

Health
• Klein sees "nothing wrong" with private health clinics that bill Alberta
  Health *and* charge "facility fees" to patients
• Government may sell shut-down hospitals to private operators
• Hospital in Cardston takes U.S. patients as private patients
• Klein talks of de-insuring services currently covered by Alberta Health

Labour
• Privatization, where appropriate (e.g. mediation, employment standards,
  occupational health, and safety laboratory)
• Information Services privatized or outsourcing of services

Municipal Affairs
• Privatized most registry services 1993
• Privatized Alberta Liquor Control Board 1993-94
• Plans for private sector to manage all aspects of seniors lodges: construc-
  tion, repair, and upgrading
• Plans for a greater private-sector role in planning and property assessment

Public Works, Supply and Services
• Further contracting out of property management services for space, capital
  development, realty, and transportation services
• Outsource a portion of central computer processing

Treasury
• Outsource "responsibility" for accounts payable, payroll, and accounting
  services

*Sources: Alberta, A Better Way — A Plan for Securing Alberta's Future (Edmonton: Government of Al-
berta, 24 February 1994); Edmonton Journal, various issues.*

soning was based on an argument seldom used by the Klein Team in its breakneck pace to remake government. Treasury Branches have "become a treasured part of the province's financial fabric," he said. More candidly, he invited the Liberals to confront the 200,000 Albertans who bank with the Treasury Branches.[29] He could have added that rural Albertans are the Tory electoral base, whose sacred cows should not be gored.

In September 1994, Jim Dinning floated the idea that the private sector should build and operate new schools and hospitals. This idea was not well-received by the education and health care sectors and, at the time of writing, it was unclear whether this was just a trial balloon.

Also not likely to be privatized are most of the functions of the old Alberta Oil Sands Technology Research Authority (AOSTRA), which was set up in the mid-1970s to conduct research into more efficient methods of extracting oil from the province's vast supplies of tar sands. AOSTRA's budget had been slashed to less than one-third its early 1980s, oil-boom levels of financing; before the Klein government folded the crown corporation into the Ministry of Energy. It has now become the Oil Sands and Research Division of the ministry. The ministry plans to privatize half of its share in the underground test facility at Fort McMurray, but the research division could hardly be privatized unless the government closed down research and let the oil companies take up the slack. The oil industry does not seem to want to do this. Oil analyst Ian Doig commented that "there's got to be government-directed research."[24] Although the ministry charges license fees for the successful technologies it develops, it subsidizes big oil companies. AOSTRA discovered ways to reduce the cost of processing and upgrading heavy oil and tar sands, the future of the oil industry in Canada.

If Treasury Branches and AOSTRA manage to escape Klein's hatchet, it shows that this government is not driven purely by ideology. They respond to rural voters and to the power of big oil.

Alternative Forms of Privatization

Is privatization a good thing? In what circumstances should it be done? Is there a core area of public service that is done best through public sector delivery? By what process should privatization plans be reviewed before proceeding? We have seen that "privatization" is a zebra of many stripes. Are there better models of privatization that, instead of discarding public employees as just so much rubbish, enable them to provide better services to the public?

Clearly Klein's privatization policies are models of how not to remake government. There is no coherent plan. Although they must vet major changes through cabinet committees and often caucus, individual ministers seem to have a lot of discretion over privatizing. Some ministers are gung-ho to privatize everything they can; others are more circumspect. Which services are privatized, and how and when, is haphazard. This is no way to proceed.

Privatization can be a good thing. We all know instances where public services are bureaucratic, rigid, and inefficient. But we should not assume that this is always the case. Most teachers, nurses, social workers, and other public servants with whom I have dealt are idealistic professionals, highly-motivated to do a good job. In Ralph Klein's Alberta they are hamstrung by budget cuts that spread them too thin and run them ragged.

But good workers are often stuck in poorly-structured work organizations that do not use their talents efficiently and to full advantage. This is the case in the private sector as well. It is possible, indeed necessary, to design better work situations in the public sector. It is not useful to oppose all change because one objects to the way the Klein government is doing it. But public-sector workers and the general public should be brought in on the changes. Lightening announcements by administrative fiat that avoids legislative debate is no way to do this. It is, however, the Klein way. It shows little concern for the turmoil in employees' lives and for public-service users. It does not produce the best results.

The first thing to do is set up a planning process for each case of privatization. In March 1994, the Liberals tabled a bill that proposed such a process for assessment.[31] They asked questions such as: can the private sector do this better, what are the costs and benefits, how would it be implemented? The Liberal bill proposed that privatization documents be tabled or published in *Alberta Gazette*. This is not enough. Legislative approval should be required. Instead of dealing with the intent of the Liberal bill, the Tories dismissed it as bureaucratic.

Are there progressive forms of privatization? Yes. It is not useful to hold on to every status quo. The first thing to do is identify core areas of public services that must be kept in public service delivery. Privatization should be confined to non-core areas. My preference in these areas is to explore delivery by the "social economy" rather than the private sector. Two forms I want to discuss are nonprofit agencies and for-profit, worker-co-operatives.

Nonprofit delivery of social services have been with us from time immemorial. Catholic Social Services in Alberta, one of the largest nongovernment providers of a wide range of services, from immigrant counselling to child protection, carries on the age-old tradition of church-based social services. The Children's Aid Society in Ontario, an organization I worked for briefly in the early 1970s, is a secular and highly respected nonprofit agency in the child protection field. Contracting out government services to such organizations may be good if the environment for high-quality services is supported. The key elements here are adequate financing and provincial enforcement of high professional standards. Both are missing in Ralph Klein's Alberta.

Rather than asking how to improve social services at affordable costs, the government's goal in contracting out is deficit-driven. In contrast to many other areas of privatization, it is the government, not individual citizens, who pay for the services. When government looks for the lowest bidder, who is likely to win? The contractor which pays the lowest and has the least scruple about professional standards and case-loads. If this means that social service workers are paid less and unions broken, so be it. In such a climate, unscrupulous for-profit businesses are likely to win out over those nonprofit agencies with boards filled by idealistic people.

In the provision of social services in Ralph Klein's Alberta, some professional workers have been laid off. Those remaining are burdened by case-loads so high that clients are often treated in assembly-line fashion.

A second kind of privatization, and one I favour, is worker-owned co-operatives. In the mid-1980s, the Québec government proposed that the Société des Alcools du Québec (SAQ), Québec's equivalent to the ALCB, be privatized. The form of privatization was interesting. They proposed that each of the 360 stores be run as worker co-operatives and that the wholesaling operation act as a second-tier co-operative to keep the system coherent and integrated. Unfortunately the union, a local of the CSN, rejected this proposal, seeing it as an attempt to break up the bargaining unit. This was a radical idea for unions then and the SAQ was not privatized.

A similar situation arose in British Columbia in 1987 when the Vander Zalm government decided to privatize road and bridge maintenance for neoliberal goals.[32] Vander Zalm sounded a different note by indicating that the government would "provide incentives to encourage employee ownership." The British Columbia Government Employees Union surprised Vander Zalm by taking him up on the offer. They set up a team of senior managers and proposed to buy the whole road maintenance service and run it as a nonprofit corporation. The government said it was not politically acceptable to have the service contracted to one corporation. In the end eight employee-owned companies received about a third of BC's maintenance contracts. Workers in some of these companies are still represented by their former union.

In Québec, the CSN union central have changed their minds since the mid-1980s and made themselves ready for privatization. They work closely with an independent consulting agency, the Groupe de Consultation, that develops plans in conjunction with union members who want to organize worker-owned businesses. In the late 1980s, nine worker-owned co-operatives were established including five ambulance services, encompassing about one-third of the service in Québec.[33]

Conclusion

Klein's Tories have haphazardly overturned all public services at break-neck speed. Privatization has been a favourite way to reinvent government. The stated purposes are to deliver public services more effectively at lower cost and to create opportunities for private businesses. But there is no plan. The Klein government's trademark is to shoot from the hip and call what they hit the target. Instead of plan, consult, and then implement, it's "fire, aim, ready." The danger is that a patchwork of services will result and that some Albertans in need will fall between the cracks. As well, the opportunities for corruption are great. Instead of establishing free enterprises, the Klein government has set up protected sectors of privatized sector delivery that are politically dependent on government to stay in business (see chapter nine).

If privatization were simply a way to find the best means to deliver public services, it might be a creative process. Pre-existing practice is not sacred. But for the Klein government, privatization is a smokescreen for a fiscal, ideological and even corrupt agenda. As Brendan Martin argues about privatization:

> For all the rhetoric, the aim of public sector reform within the neoliberal agenda has not been to improve the quality of public services. It has been to cheapen them, to open up new markets to transnational companies and to redirect public finance from social services.[34]

The Klein government has taken out large chunks of funding at the same time it turned public services over to private operators who often charge fees. The effect is to reduce the quality of services and to leave lower-income Albertans out in the cold.

The ethic of the private sector, to maximize profits, is not always appropriate to the delivery of public services. Old-fashioned as it may sound, we should not discard the ethic of "public service." There is often a conflict between the demands of the privatization businesses for high profits and the need for universal coverage for all citizens at the lowest prices. The best way to resolve such conflicts is often public ownership or public delivery of services.[35]

Albertans have never had strong democratic traditions, usually opting for one-party dominance and seeing dissent as disloyalty. If privatizations are carried out, there is need for more regulation and public accountability, not less. To make sure the public interest is served, a more robust democratic culture needs to emerge.

Notes

1. This chapter has benefitted from discussions with Trevor Harrison, Gurston Dacks, Les Kennedy, Mike Percy, Jack Quarter, Rich Vivone, and Allan Warrack. Thanks are extended to Peter Puplampu for research.
2. *Alberta Hansard*, 28 March 1994, 892.
3. For example, in the late 1980s, British industry strongly criticized Thatcher's government for neglecting infrastructure investment. See W. Keegan, *The Spectre of Capitalism* (London: Vintage, 1993), 106. To pay for his military buildup and tax reductions for the well-to-do, Reagan's economic policies kept the U.S. dollar artificially high and hurt the competitive position of one American industry after another. See R. Kuttner, *The End of Laissez-Faire* (New York: Knopf, 1991), 82 ff.
4. British Columbia in the 1980s under the Social Credit ran a close second.
5. *Calgary Sun*, 1 February 1994, 3.
6. A. Finkel, *The Social Credit Phenomenon in Alberta* (Toronto: University of Toronto Press, 1989), 44-6.
7. J. Richards and L. Pratt, *Prairie Capitalism* (Toronto: McClelland and Stewart, 1979), 216.
8. M. Hammer and J. Champy, *Reengineering the Corporation: A Manifesto for Business Revolution* (New York: Harper Business, 1993). The authors began to popularize these ideas in 1987.
9. *Edmonton Journal*, 13 May 1995, C2.
10. R. Douglas, *Unfinished Business* (Auckland, N. Z.: Random House, 1993).
11. D. Osborne and T. Gaebler, *Reinventing Government. How the Entrepreneurial Spirit is Transforming the Public Sector* (New York: Plume, 1992).
12. D. Wanagas, "The Principal Problem." In A. Nikiforuk, S. Pratt, and D. Wanagas, eds., *Running on Empty* (Edmonton: NeWest Press, 1987), 214.

13. *Edmonton Journal*, 22 December 1994, A1. Government losses continued to mount. By 1994, Alberta taxpayers had lost $257 million on the Swan Hills waste treatment plant. See chapter sixteen by J. McInnis and I. Urquhart.

14. In the debates on Bill 12 to privatize the ALCB, Len Bracko, Percy Wickman, and Mike Percy all led off with comments of support for the concept. See *Alberta Hansard*, 9 November 1993, 1405-06.

15. See M. Lisac, *The Klein Revolution* (Edmonton: NeWest Press, 1995) chapter 8.

16. *Alberta Hansard*, 15 March 1994.

17. M. Pirie, *Privatisation* (Aldershot: Wildwood House, 1988), 21.

18. Osborne and Gaebler, *Reinventing Government*, 45.

19. Pirie, *Privatisation*.

20. Bill 10, the Alberta Registries Act was introduced in October 1993 and went through first and second readings, but was withdrawn before third reading. Some parts of the Bill 10 were included in Bill 41, passed a year later.

21. Alberta, Registry, Information and Licensing Services. *Agent's Product Catalogue*, Schedule "A,"1 February 1995.

22. Revenues from motor vehicles and land titles were $202 million in 1992-3, $208 million in 1993-4, and $206 million in 1994-5. *Alberta Public Accounts 1992-3; 1993-4; Second Quarter Budget Projections Update 1994.*

23. The *Calgary Sun*, 19 July 1994, 22.

24. *Alberta Hansard*, 28 March 1994, 892.

25. Alberta Liquor Control Board, *A New Era in Liquor Administration* (St. Albert: ALCB, December 1994).

26. G. Laxer, D. Green, T. Harrison and D. Neu, *Out of Control. Paying the Price for Privatising Alberta's Liquor Control Board* (Ottawa: Canadian Centre for Policy Alternatives, 1994). As one of the authors, I have quoted freely from the report.

27. *Edmonton Journal*, 30 April 1994, C1.

28. Alberta Law Reform Institute, *Enforcement of Money Judgments*, Vol. 1, Report No. 61, March 1991, 72.

29. *Alberta Report*, 26 April 1993, 20.

30. *Alberta Report*, 27 December 1993, 13.

31. Bill 205, *Alberta Hansard*, 9 March 1994, 214ff.

32. J. Quarter, *Crossing the Line. Unionized Employee Ownership and Investment Funds*. Manuscript, quoted with the permission of the author. This section also benefitted from discussion with Jack Quarter.

33. Ibid.

34. B. Martin, *In the Public Interest?* (London: Zed Books, 1993), 14.

35. W. Hutton, column in *The Guardian Weekly*, 18 December 1994, 13.

Chapter Nine

MAKING THE TRAINS RUN ON TIME: CORPORATISM IN ALBERTA[1]

Trevor Harrison

> Mussolini put together a partnership, just as we're talking here,
> between the government ... and big business.
>
> Opposition Liberal MLA Nick Taylor, October, 1994.[2]

Much of the public's continued love affair with the Klein government, two years into office, is attributable to a belief that it is making government not only more efficient, but also more open and accountable to the people. Beliefs once in place are not easily shaken. Nonetheless, the 1994 fall sitting of the legislature saw doubt enter the minds of at least some Albertans.

The source of this doubt was two bills: Bill 41, the Government Organization Act, and Bill 57, the Delegated Organization Act. Introduced with little fanfare, the bills soon aroused both the Opposition Liberals and the public whose response to most government measures until then had been largely muted. In their finest hour since the 1993 election, the Liberals denounced the bills as both an abdication of responsibility and a grab for more power. Legislative speeches, newspaper columns, and radio talk-shows resounded with such words as "corporatism" and even "fascism." It was not just idle talk. Some Albertans had become genuinely afraid of the Klein Tories' manner of governance.

This chapter examines the concept of corporatism, showing that, in many ways, it is an apt description of how State-civil relations are today structured in Alberta. In contrast to the still prevailing myth, government in Alberta is even less open and accountable today than it was prior to the 1993 election. The roots of this corporatist turn are examined, as are the forms of power and control increasingly employed by the Klein administration. The controversy surrounding Bills 41 and 57 is described. Finally, some of the implications for Albertans posed by a corporatist form of government are examined.

What is Corporatism?

Corporatism is an ambiguous term. Sometimes it is defined as an ideology, sometimes as a political style, sometimes as an aspect of particular political cultures. Adding to this confusion is corporatism's historical association with various fascist regimes. But, while fascist regimes are necessarily corporatist, not all corporatist regimes are necessarily fascist. For example, Scandinavian countries have been social democratic and largely corporatist, in one way or another. So what is corporatism?

Briefly, corporatism refers to a distinctive system of organizing functional interests and influencing public policy. (Alternative systems include pluralism, syndicalism, or communism.) Corporatism involves the incorporation into society of "members," whether defined as individuals, families, firms, or various groups, through a "limited number of singular, ... noncompetitive, hierarchically ordered, and functionally differentiated" associations.[3] Such associations may arise "naturally," with significant grass-roots input (termed societal corporatism); or be State-created (State corporatism). Social democratic corporatist States, such as Sweden in the past, tend to revolve around tripartite arrangements between the State, labour, and capital. Liberal democratic States, such as the United States and Canada, and extreme right-wing corporatist regimes, such as Mussolini's Italy, Franco's Spain, and Salazar's Portugal, tend to revolve around a State-business partnership although, in the latter instances, the Catholic church also played an important role.[4]

As I will show, governance in Alberta today may reasonably be described as right-wing and corporatist, although certainly not without "popular" support. Forms of governance, however, do not emerge all at once. The Klein government's corporatism can only be understood in the context of Alberta's unique political heritage.

The Roots of Klein Corporatism

Several traditions within Alberta politics made possible the Klein form of governance. One tradition is that of one-party rule, revolving around a strong party leader. Only four parties have ever governed Alberta: the Liberals (1905-1921); the United Farmers (1921-1935); Social Credit (1935-1971); and the Conservatives (since 1971). The effect of this tradition — what political scientist C. B. Macpherson referred to as a quasi-party system[5] — has been to prevent the development of a sufficient number of strong, independent political sites within which a pluralist system of democracy can thrive.

A second tradition within Alberta's political culture, coincident with the first, is that of conformity. For all their rhetoric of individualism, captured in images of lone cowboys tending herds, most Albertans when faced with a crisis are more comfortable with being one of the cattle. This tendency to conformity is fuelled by an illusion, long-cultivated by the province's political and economic elites, of a general interest. Throughout much of the province's history, Albertans have heeded the call that they must pull together against various outside threats, whether Bay Street industrialists and bankers during the 1930s, the communists after World War Two, or the Trudeau Liberals after 1968. This perceived need to defend Alberta's general interest has stifled internal dissent and squelched such questions as whose interests are really being served.

A third allied tradition is that of deference to authorities. Not all authorities, mind you. Academics and unionists have always been suspect. By contrast, Alberta's business and financial elites and, to an extent, government technocrats can do no wrong. This deference to authority was expressed no better than in 1935 when William Aberhart urged Albertans to vote Social Credit. They didn't need to understand how Social Credit worked, said Aberhart, anymore than they had to understand how electricity worked in order to have light. They just had to push the button, leaving the rest to experts. So it would also be with Social Credit, he said.[6]

One important side effect of this deference is that Alberta's elites, whether in business or the public managerial class, also have come to view their near monopoly of power as a kind of natural gift. When things go wrong, the typical response of Alberta's elites is to call for more power. With just a little more power, they are sure that — at last! — they could set Alberta right.

Despite these flaws, the province for much of its history has possessed a recognizable civic culture. Its survival was helped by the continued presence of small businesses, including family farms, and relatively late urbanization compared with most other Canadian provinces.

The boundary between State and civil society also was preserved during the early days of Social Credit by that party's largely anti-statist ideology. Certainly, the line moved on economic matters, such as when Aberhart's administration issued "script" and created the Treasury Branches, but it did not blur. This gradually began to change, however, under Aberhart's successor, Ernest Manning. Under Manning, Social Credit grew more reluctant to intervene in the economy — the creation of the Alberta Gas Trunk Line

Company (later Nova Corporation) in 1954 being a notable exception. At the same time, the party became more willing to blur State-civil relations regarding moral questions. Social Credit's last years in power saw an increasingly evangelical Christian stamp put on conservative appeals to the patriarchal family, conformity, sobriety, and sexual restraint.[7]

Unlike Social Credit, Lougheed's Conservatives held strong views on how the government should use its political leverage to shape Alberta's economic future, but were more laissez-faire on social issues. The Tory's election in 1971 augured the beginning of a phase of "province building" that swept all the western provinces, in one fashion or another, throughout the 1970s, bringing particular success to Alberta. Key to Alberta's success was a fortuitous rise in world oil prices during the 1970s, and an even closer relationship between government and business than had existed under Social Credit.[8]

Unfortunately, when the recessions hit in the 1980s, the government — and Alberta taxpayers — were left holding the bag. The Tory's pals in the business community were only too glad to accept government seed money and financial backing during the good times. Now they quickly denounced what they termed the provincial government's interference and mismanagement. The growing list of failing government enterprises and a rising provincial debt made easy these accusations.

If the increased power of the oil interests and the blurring of government-business relations in general during the Lougheed/Getty administrations began to erase the lines between the State and civil society, these years also, albeit indirectly, made it possible in another way for the later emergence of a right-wing corporatist government. For the government's small "l" liberal inclinations also opened up space for a more inclusive and tolerant society — the beginnings for what conceivably might have evolved into a genuinely pluralistic society and political system had they been given time to find root. Unfortunately, Alberta's experiment in civic pluralism was shallow and still in its infancy when the recession hit in 1985-86.[9] In the midst of this crisis, Albertans did what came natural to them: They circled wagons against the enemy. As in the past, many Albertans vented their anger against Ottawa and "the east" (Québec and Ontario). By now, however, there also were new "enemies," this time within Alberta's borders. For the first time in its history, the source of Alberta's cohesion began to draw upon internal distinctions between "real Albertans" and a kind of pariah class that first encompassed politicians, then civil servants, but would later spread also to include welfare clients, unionists, the unemployed, immigrants, gays, and other assorted "special interests."

Alberta's traditions of one-party rule, conformity, and a slavish deference to the prescriptions proffered by business leaders and technocrats underpinned the manner in which debate about the deficit and debt crisis
unfolded in the 1993 election. Heeding the mantra of the market, Albertan's decided en masse that the crisis of the debt and deficit called for the
ship of State to make a 180 degree turn. Anyone thrown from the deck and
unable to swim had only themselves to blame. After all, the collective fate of
Alberta was at stake.

Forms of Power and Control Under Corporatism

Power and control in corporatist regimes take several forms exercised
at different levels. At the societal level, control over members is exercised
through indoctrination, coercive sanctions, and/or the withdrawal of services, such as licenses, certifications, etc. that threaten members' economic
security. At the associational level, control over intermediate bodies is exercised through co-responsibility for decisions, the devolution of policy implementation, and the threatened withdrawal of associational monopoly.[10]

Of course, these forms of control are not restricted to corporatist regimes. For example, selective government control of information is an old
practice everywhere. But Alberta always has taken it a step further than
most provincial governments. Alberta and Nova Scotia are the only provinces in Canada to never have a freedom of information act. One is now
scheduled to come into effect in 1995, but the amount of government information available to the public is actually becoming more restricted.

In the past, a lot of government information came from separate departments, as well as the Alberta Bureau of Statistics. But the latter was
closed in 1994, and the amount of information being collected or made
easily accessible to the public by individual departments is shrinking. As
with so many government services, access to information also has become
contingent upon an applicant's ability and willingness to pay.[11]

Since coming to power, the Klein government also has moved to limit
the manner in which information is presented and conclusions drawn.
These attempts have been particularly evident in the government's stage-
managed efforts at public consultation. As McInnis and Urquhart relate in
chapter sixteen, Klein had previously learned the symbolic value of holding
public hearings during his tenure as Environment minister. Between 1993
and the beginning of 1995, the Klein government held a series of public forums throughout the province on such things as health, education, and
criminal justice. On the surface, these forums seemed legitimate attempts

at obtaining public input. In fact, the forums were tightly controlled, with guests, presenters, and team leaders carefully selected. Just enough "dissenters" were always invited so as to give an appearance of balance, but never enough to derail the government's pre-set agenda.

The key to the government's success in manipulating the political process is Klein himself. Undoubtedly, he is the most adept politician in Canada today. As a former news reporter, he knows "poli-optics" better than any politician around. Every couple of months, Klein appears on a radio talk-show ("the Klein Hotline") where he massages voters' concerns and in general reactivates his "he listens, he cares" image that the Tories cultivated with voters in 1993.

But even Klein can sometimes be too obvious in his efforts to manipulate information. In January 1995, he went on private television to talk to Albertans about his government's plans for the next year. Nothing wrong with this. Except that he did it using public funds — $115,000 — to pay for the broadcast. Particularly galling was the fact that the government was offered free broadcast time on CBC, but turned it down because CBC guidelines would have required the broadcaster to also give equal time to the Opposition Liberal leader, Grant Mitchell. (The Klein government subsequently refused to pay out of public funds for Mitchell's response.)[12] Still, the incident is unlikely to do long-term damage to Klein or his government.

Alberta also has a long history of holding workers economically threatened either through the "discipline of the market" or through threats to services. Alberta's unstable economy historically has relied upon a steady stream of cheap, transient labour. Its cheapness is ensured by laws that make it very difficult to unionize workers — Alberta has by far the lowest unionization rate in Canada[13] — and relatively high unemployment. During boom times, workers flock into Alberta to obtain jobs. During hard times, the lack of jobs and low provincial benefits encourage many of the unemployed to leave the province. Even despite this migration, however, Alberta traditionally has had high unemployment rates, a desirable situation in the eyes of many Alberta government officials and their business supporters. In the early 1980s, the then Labour Minister Ernie Isley remarked that he hoped Alberta would never again see full employment because it increased employers' wage costs.

The Klein government increased the use of economic coercion. Supports to people on welfare, particularly to the single unemployed, have been reduced to below subsistence levels (see chapter twenty-one). The government's threats to economic security have not ended, however, with the unemployed. The Klein government's economic reign of terror has particularly hit workers in the public sector. The daily threat of privatization hangs over their heads like a guillotine, with life and death decisions often seemingly made by ministerial whim (see Gordon Laxer's review of the ALCB's privatization, chapter eight). Yet most public sector workers also feel that they cannot talk about what is happening for fear of losing their jobs even sooner. This fear is based in reality. In January 1994, the minister of social services, Mike Cardinal, issued a warning that social workers who spoke against government policies would be fired.[14] The perception that other ministers have unspoken gag orders has sufficiently silenced workers in other departments or government-funded institutions.[15]

The Klein government's economic threats have not ended with the unemployed or civil servants. Even professionals — normally thought to be somewhat safe from political interference — are under threat. The chief means of increasing control over these other societal groups is by threats to restrict licensing or security of contract. For example, despite occasional denials, the Tories continue to float the idea of making teaching licenses renewable every five years. Such threats cast a wide shadow. Will other professional groups, or even various small business operators, eventually find their economic survival dependent upon subservience to the government?

It is the Klein government's control over intermediate associations, however, that has broken new ground in eroding the separation of State and civil society in Alberta, and has thus earned it the corporatist label. Masked by the rhetoric of "the market," the Klein government is turning over fiduciary responsibility for everything to do with economic development in Alberta, or that simply makes a profit, to the private sector. Today, economic development is directed by the Alberta Economic Development Authority. The Authority is made up of fifty private businesspeople, almost entirely men. Although the authority's titular head is Murray Smith, minister without portfolio for economic development, real power resides with Art Smith, an influential Calgary businessman.[16] Privatization of the Tourism Education Council, renamed the Alberta Tourism Partnership, has also recently been implemented.

While the Klein government is turning over real power and authority over economic matters to the private sector, it is pursuing a very different tack in the areas of social program expenditures. Certainly, the government has made much of its plans to delegate co-responsibility for decisions and outcomes to various boards, whether in health, education, or social services, or to local communities. Much of this sounds good — in theory. There is clearly a demand by many people for more local decision-making. At the very least, the provision of services might regain a human touch. Looked at more closely, however, the government's delegation of decision-making is very limited. Much of the Klein government's restructuring appears to be aimed rather more at creating an illusion of increasing local autonomy while deflecting criticism and actually expanding political control through the creation of provincially-appointed regional boards.

Moves by the Klein government to create charter schools provide one example of its apparent efforts at eliminating intermediate bodies that it does not directly control. A central argument of those who favour charter schools seems to be that such schools would be able to hire teachers from outside of the Alberta Teachers' Association — in effect, breaking up the ATA monopoly (see chapter thirteen). The government's apparent antipathy towards autonomous, "naturally" formed associations, such as the ATA, while creating new intermediate associations, such as regional boards in education, health, and social services, is reminiscent of State corporatist practices elsewhere.

These State-created boards will not have real power. The government has made it clear that it will maintain its fiscal hammer. But give the Klein government credit. It learned from its predecessor that the kitchen sometimes gets pretty hot, so it is restructuring government so as to avoid ever getting burned. The mafia launders money through banks in places like the Cayman Islands. The Klein government is laundering its social responsibilities through a complicated network of boards and private agencies.

Some evidence of the real intentions behind restructuring was provided by Social Service's Minister Mike Cardinal in the fall of 1994. Following that department's announcement that children's services would be turned over to the "nonprofit" sector[17], Cardinal later suggested that the province would no longer be ultimately responsible for what happened to children; that, if anything happened to them while in care, it would be the sole responsibility of the delegated organization.[18] Embarrassed department officials quickly issued a statement saying that Cardinal had been misunderstood. Still, the minister's comments seem to point to the direction that he, and perhaps much of the government, would like to take: More power, less responsibility — the dream of every hormonally-charged adolescent.

In short, since its election in June 1993, the Klein government has taken various steps that appear to spread the tentacles of State control deeper into the heart of Alberta's civil society. One result of this intrusion has been the emergence of an almost palpable sense of fear and anxiety among people throughout Alberta. In the fall of 1994, these fears reached new heights with the introduction of Bills 41 and 57.

Making the Trains Run On Time: Bills 41 and 57

As the fall 1994 sitting began, few could have imagined the firestorm that would soon rage around the government's proposed legislation. Certainly, the government itself was unprepared for the controversy. Opposition to the Klein government until then had been largely muted. Moreover, the Liberal opposition was in the process of selecting a new leader to succeed Laurence Decore who had resigned several months earlier. Nonetheless, the session was one of the most controversial in recent Alberta political history, marked by heated legislative debate.

At the heart of the controversy were two particular bills: Bill 41, the Government Organization Act, and Bill 57 the Delegated Administration Act. The bills were introduced by Premier Klein and subsequently defended at every turn by House Leader Stockwell Day as simply "housekeeping" bills that would streamline government operations and make them more efficient.

From the beginning, however, the government was on the defensive. Led by interim leader Betty Hewes and former leader Nick Taylor, the Liberals launched a spirited attack against the bills. Chief among the Liberal's contentions were that the bills gave almost unlimited power to executive council and individual ministers, thereby skirting the legislature. For example, under Bill 41, ministers would be able to create programs and services, change regulations, make loans, sell public property, or transfer programs and services to the private sector which in turn could set fees — all without legislative approval. The Liberals justifiably denounced Bill 41 as "government by regulation as opposed to legislation," "a massive derogation of power from the Legislative Assembly," and a threat "to parliamentary democracy."[19]

Similarly, the Liberals contended that Bill 57 avoided legislative scrutiny and seemed to allow for the privatization of any and all government services at ministerial whim and without accountability. Like Bill 41, Bill 57 seemed to open the door to unlimited "user fees" for services previously covered by the State. Both bills seemed ripe with potential for patronage and kickbacks. Perhaps more fundamentally, both also seemed to involve a substantial diminution of legislative authority. In the days that followed the bills' introduction, the word "fascism" increasingly crept into *Hansard*. In this atmosphere, Nick Taylor spoke on October 31:

> You have to put your mind back to Italy in the 1920s ... Mussolini put together a partnership, just as we're talking here, be-

tween the government, or elected officials, of the day and big business ... what happened very soon is that the lions of industry and the captains of industry soon started telling the politicians, "Well, it's all right to go through this election in four years every time, but we don't want to be dealing with a separate set of politicians ..." Well, my friend Benito had a very simple solution to it. He did away with elections ... I'm not saying that this government would call what they're putting in fascism, but they're on the long, slippery road of trying to make the trains run on time, and this has to concern all of us a bit.[20]

The government's response to these accusations was silence. The almost bovine supineness normally the preserve of Tory backbenchers spilled over as well into the government's front bench.[21]

The press was not silent, however. In a rare case of united opposition to the government, Alberta's two moderately small "l" liberal papers, the *Edmonton Journal* and *Calgary Herald*, and even the right-wing tabloid, the *Edmonton Sun*, denounced the bills. An *Edmonton Journal* editorial commented that:

It's impossible to guess what they'll do next. It wouldn't be surprising if they locked the doors of the assembly, retired to a pub for the duration of the term, and leased the entire operation to Government "R" Us Inc. of Omaha.[22]

As point-man for the legislation, Stockwell Day at first attempted to ridicule the Liberal's accusations as extremist.[23] Realizing that he was losing the public relations war, Day later accepted a challenge to publicly debate the bills with interim Liberal leader Betty Hewes on a radio talk-show broadcast throughout the province. It was not a successful strategy. Overwhelmingly, the callers denounced the legislation, stating their concerns that Alberta was slipping towards a dictatorship.[24] Another talk-show on CBC radio, held around the same period, reflected similar anxiety from Albertans, with not one caller coming out in support of Bill 57. Finally, Day wrote a long guest column to the *Edmonton Journal* in which he once more attempted to defend Bill 57 as simply enabling legislation.[25] His response won few converts. Public concern over the bills remained high.

Echoing Taylor's now-famous speech to the legislature, Liberal MLA Duco Van Binsbergen on November 7 hit the Tories with another historical allusion, this time to Nazi Germany:

> I would like to refer to an expression that I have heard con-
> stantly in connection with Bills 41 and 57, and that is that it is
> only housekeeping and its is only enabling legislation ... that
> word "enabling" reverberated in my head. I did a little digging
> into the past ... I found that reference to enabling legislation
> before, and I refer the members back to March 23, 1933, when
> under the force of Chancellor Adolf Hitler the enabling Act
> was passed by the German Reichstag, and it gave the German
> government absolute power for four years ...[26]

The allusion was clearly overdrawn, and perhaps distracted from a more serious consideration of the Klein government's corporatist methods. Nonetheless, the Tories had had enough. On November 8, Day announced that Bill
57 was being dropped from the fall legislative agenda. Blaming the withdrawal on "a very public misinformation campaign" launched by the Liberals, Day nonetheless conceded that there had been public concern.

It was a rare defeat for the government, although some wondered if
the defeat was more symbolic than real. Bill 41, which had been the source
of much of the Liberal's anger, had been passed, once again using closure.
The *Edmonton Journal* quoted a government insider as stating: "They don't
need 57, if they've got 41. It's got everything in it. They can already do
what's in 57 through regulation."[27]

In any case, the government at first seemed committed to reintroduc-
ing Bill 57 at the next spring session. In January 1995, it sent out a discussion paper, meant to address "a number of inaccuracies" about parts of the
bill, to a select number of groups in the province.[28] Stockwell Day continued to insist that Bill 57 was a key part of government legislation. Its passage
seemed inevitable.

Then, suddenly, on February 13, 1995, following the throne speech to
open the spring session of the legislature, Klein announced that Bill 57 was
being withdrawn. "[Y]ou will probably not see Bill 57 reach the light of
day," he said. "There are too many problems with it. What I'm hearing is
that this bill goes far too far."[29]

What Klein, always the astute politician, was actually saying was that the
Tories were continuing to receive too much flak over the bill. Presumably,
there are better — that is, less accountable — ways to skin government services. Bill 57, a bill that would have allowed the privatization of everything at
once, was gone, but there is no reason to believe that piecemeal privatization will not continue. The day after Bill 57's withdrawal, Day announced
that its absence would not halt the delegation of administrative authority

for government operations, for example, the setting up of a self-regulating body for the real estate industry.[30]

Bills 41 and 57 fit within the form of corporatist government being en-acted by the Klein Tories: less accountable, more diffuse, yet more powerful than ever, while also opening up new avenues for profit by the govern-ment's business associates. But the Klein government's corporatist turn also has a broader impact for Albertans regarding the notion of citizenship.

Corporatism and the Reconstructed Individual

As Gordon Laxer persuasively argues elsewhere in this book (chapter eight), the goal of neoliberalism is to turn citizens into merely clients and consumers. This aspect of neoliberalism is alive and well within the Klein administration. Check out the government's business plan.[31] The notion of citizenship is entirely absent from the document. Instead, Albertans are de-scribed as either clients or consumers. Similarly, the Klein government's throne speech of February 1995 repeatedly refers to Albertans not as citi-zens but as "customers."

The difference between citizens and consumers/customers is impor-tant. Citizenship involves a notion of universal rights irrespective of one's place in the market, and of collective/community decision-making. By con-trast, consumers/customers involves a notion of individual rights that are commensurate with the size of one's purchasing power. Citizens are equals; consumers in the market-place are not.

In a similar fashion, corporatism also restricts "the 'number of citizens' and their 'sphere of interests'."[32] But corporatism goes one step further in then reincorporating these atomized masses in ways that cannot be socially disruptive or effectively challenge the dominant elite. As such, corporatism is a useful adjunct for conservatives who still believe that the notion of soci-ety is more than merely an abstraction and who fear the anarchy that com-plete liberal/libertarian notions would bring.

Few members of the Klein government presumably have thought this through in any systematic fashion. As Laxer notes, the Klein government is not a collection of deep thinkers and planners. Few of its members perhaps have even heard of corporatism. Nonetheless, the mode of political practice being voiced and enacted by the Klein government is State corporatist in nature, providing the Tory party and its business supporters the perfect so-lution to problems of maintaining social control in a highly volatile re-source-based economy. Klein's right-wing corporatism binds Albertans through a series of government-created or sanctioned organizations and associations to the State, "freeing" them to act as consumers, but otherwise isolating them and restricting their full participation as citizens, a participation that might eventually challenge the manner in which Alberta's political-economy is organized. The sites within which "unacceptable" ideas can be nourished shrinks, closed off by fear, dependency, and the shadow of the ever present State.

Conclusion

Alberta is not a fascist State. It is, however, a right-wing corporatist State. Such a State is ultimately not compatible with a thriving democracy. Albertans have never fully understood that democracy means nothing if it is not a dialogue between genuine equals. Neither have they comprehended the hard work democracy entails or the constant vigilance it requires. At best, they have construed it to mean the right to vote every few years; at worst, a call for majoritarian rule. Perhaps, in the coming days of the Klein administration, they will discover its meaning. If they do, they may be able to stop the train before it arrives.

Notes

1. I want to thank Gordon Laxer for comments made on previous drafts of this chapter.
2. *Alberta Hansard*, 31 October 1994, 2678.
3. P. C. Schmitter, "Still the century of corporatism?" In P. C. Schmitter and G. Lehmbruck, eds., *Trends Toward Corporatist Intermediation. Contemporary Political Sociology*, Vol. I (Beverly Hills: Sage Publications, 1979); and P. C. Schmitter, "Corporatism." In J. Krieger, ed., *The Oxford Companion to Politics of the World* (Oxford: Oxford University Press, 1993).
4. Catholic corporatism, in its classical form, was especially concerned with economic justice, less with choices made in the political realm. During the 1920s and 1930s, however, the Catholic church frequently took a political stance, often forming tacit alliances with fascist leaderships to combat "atheistic" communism. See R. A. Webster, *The Cross and the Fasces: Christian Democracy and Fascism in Italy* (Stanford: Stanford University Press, 1960).
5. C. B. Macpherson, *Democracy in Alberta: Social Credit and the Party System* (Toronto: University of Toronto Press, 1953).
6. Story is related in C. Caldarola, "The Social Credit in Alberta, 1935-1971," p. 39. In C. Caldarola, ed., *Society and Politics in Alberta* (Toronto: Methuen Publications, 1979).
7. See A. Finkel's, *The Social Credit Phenomenon in Alberta* (Toronto: University of Toronto Press, 1989).

8. See J. Richards and L. Pratt, *Prairie Capitalism: Power and Influence in the New West* (Toronto: McClelland and Stewart Ltd., 1979).

9. "[T]he origins of state corporatism lie in the rapid, highly visible demise of nascent pluralism" (P. A Schmitter, "Still the century of corporatism," 23).

10. Schmitter, "Corporatism," 197.

11. See M. Lisac's column in the *Edmonton Journal*, 14 January 1995, A6.

12. *Edmonton Journal*, 11 January 1995, A5; and 25 January 1995, A3.

13. H. Krahn and G. Lowe, *Work, Industry, and Canadian Society* (Scarborough: Nelson Canada, 1993), 247. Alberta's low unionization rate appears related to its labour laws. In most jurisdictions, if 51 percent of workers at a site sign cards, this is sufficient to allow for unionization. In Alberta, however, signing the cards only ensures the holding of a certification vote. In the interim between signing the card and voting, management is able to pressure workers in ways, including firing, that prejudice the vote's eventual outcome.

14. *Edmonton Journal*, 5 January 1994, A5.

15. See S. Das' column in the *Edmonton Journal*, 15 May 1995, A6.

16. A list of members on the Authority's economic council appears in the *Edmonton Journal*, 15 December 1994, B9; see also the *Edmonton Journal*, 1 February 1995, A7.

17. The term "nonprofit" is misleading. The salaries of private social service managers can be quite lucrative but rather than being termed "profit" are disguised under administrative expenses.

18. *Calgary Herald*, 1 Dec., 1994, A3.

19. *Alberta Hansard*, 24 October 1994, 2506, 2509.

20. *Alberta Hansard*, 31 October 1994, 2678; also *Alberta Hansard*, 24 October 1994, 2511.

21. M. Lisak's column in the *Edmonton Journal*, 3 November 1994, A14.

22. *Edmonton Journal*, 4 November 1994, A18.

23. *Alberta Hansard*, 31 October 1994, 2689-2692.

24. See S. Feschuk's article in the *Globe and Mail*, 5 November 1994, A1 and A2; also, the *Edmonton Journal*, 5 November 1994, A7.

25. *Edmonton Journal*, 16 November 1994, A13.

26. *Alberta Hansard*, 7 November 1994, 2894. Van Binsbergen's basic description of the Enabling Act — the "Law for Removing the Distress of People and Reich" — is accurate. See W. L. Shirer, *The Rise and Fall of the Third Reich: A History of Nazi Germany* (New York: Simon and Schuster, 1960), 198.

27. *Edmonton Journal*, 9 November 1994, A7.

28. Alberta, *Delegated Administrative Organizations: A "Third Option"* (Edmonton: Government of Alberta, January 1995).

29. *Edmonton Journal*, 14 February 1995, A7.

30. *Edmonton Journal*, 15 February 1995, A6.

31. Alberta, *A Better Way* (Edmonton: Government of Alberta, February 1994).

32. Schmitter, "Still the century of corporatism," 16.

ECONOMICS

Chapter Ten

ONE-TRACK (THINKING) TOWARDS DEFICIT REDUCTION[1]

Melville L. McMillan and Allan A. Warrack

A New Way to Pay Old Debts.
Title of play by 17th-century playwright Phillip Massinger.[2]

Ralph Klein became premier of Alberta in December 1992. Almost immediately, the severity of the province's fiscal difficulties emerged to become the focus of attention with a January budget revision announcing an extraordinarily large and unexpectedly high deficit and the Auditor General's Annual Report for 1991-92 announcing an unprecedented level of provincial debt. The concerns raised were reinforced by a sequence of three reports; one from the Institute of Chartered Accountants of Alberta,[3] a second from the province's own Alberta Financial Review Commission[4] and the third by ourselves.[5] The Commission implored the urgency of deficit elimination, found that budget monitoring and reporting was inadequate, and noted that the Heritage Fund gave Albertans a false sense of security. McMillan and Warrack agreed with deficit elimination objectives and proposed that the magnitude of the problem was so great that a balanced approach of expenditure cuts and concurrent revenue increases was necessary to rid Alberta quickly of its fiscal difficulties.

The provincial government's response came in its May 1993 budget. It outlined a plan to eliminate the deficit within four years by cutting expenditures twenty percent without increasing taxes. Mr. Klein took this budget to the voters in the June election which his provincial Progressive Conservative party won. Interestingly, the two parties which won seats, the provincial Conservatives and Liberals, both campaigned for deficit reduction through expenditure cuts. The Klein government affirmed its commitment to its deficit elimination plan in a post-election September 1993 budget update and followed through in its February 1994 budget which stayed the course on the planned deep expenditure reductions, increased revenues somewhat through higher fees and charges but without tax increases, and introduced privatization initiatives.

Public concerns about deficits and government debt are national and heightened by their magnitude at the federal level and by their ubiquity and magnitudes across the provinces. Consequently, there is extensive policy and political debate everywhere in Canada. The uniqueness of the Klein government's plan to eliminate the deficit through expenditure cuts alone has caused much attention to be focused on Alberta. Much of that attention, especially from the business community and business press, has been very positive. While there is much to say on behalf of the province's initiatives, the potential of the Klein government's approach may be overstated.

Our concern with Alberta's fiscal situation led us to investigate the problems and explore solutions in our earlier study.[6] We update and extend that analysis here from the clearer perspective available as of January 1995. Examining the current realities and policy options, we find them surprisingly and regrettably similar to those of 1993. Indeed, the situation defined by the current fiscal circumstances and the present provincial deficit elimination plan only reinforces our earlier position. The fiscal problems of the province are greater than is generally acknowledged and, we believe, are so large that they cannot be solved successfully by expenditure reductions alone because provincial services would be reduced to extraordinarily (and unacceptably) low levels. We expect that in the absence of exceptional improvement in natural resource revenues, a long term and sustainable solution to the difficulties imposed by the structural deficit and the stock of debt will require some increase in taxes. Fortunately, because of the high tax capacity and low tax effort, Albertans can increase provincial taxes somewhat in order to preserve reasonable services and still enjoy lower provincial taxes than residents of other provinces. Consequently, we predict, and would recommend, that ultimately a balanced or two-track approach will be taken to righting Alberta's fiscal situation: that is, a policy combining expenditure reduction with some increase in tax revenue.

The arguments and evidence bringing us to these conclusions are outlined below. Initially, the revenue and expenditure history of the province since 1970 is reviewed to illustrate how the current problems developed. Following that, we first outline the province's deficit elimination plan and its implications and then we consider the revenue options of the province. The scope of the Alberta Heritage Savings Trust Fund (AHSTF) to soften the deficit/debt burden is analyzed. We then define the new fiscal realities and options. The chapter ends with a brief conclusion.

Where We Were, Where We Are, and How We Got Here

This section of the paper reviews the recent history of Alberta's provincial public finances with the aim of providing context for assessing our current fiscal predicament. We rely upon the Financial Management Series (FMS) provided by Statistics Canada. These data permit us to compare Alberta's fiscal position with that of other provinces through time using data that adjusts for differences in provincial accounting practices to ensure comparability. The adjustments incorporated into the FMS data provide a comprehensive picture of provincial government finances in Canada. The limitation of this comparability is that we are restricted to using data that ends with estimates for the fiscal year 1993-94, the most recent FMS available. Fortunately, these data clearly highlight the sources of Alberta's current fiscal problems, the dramatic changes which occurred, and the difficult choices being made.

Revenue History. The Alberta government's revenue history post 1970 is summarized in Figure 10.1. This graph and subsequent ones show the data in per capita real (1986) dollars so as to avoid the complications of population and price changes. For the purposes of comparison the average per capita real provincial revenue for all provinces is also given.

Alberta's provincial government per capita real revenues were $2,274 in 1970, a level slightly higher than the all-province average. The impact of the energy boom and bust clearly stand out. From 1974 to 1986 Alberta's per capita real revenues far exceed those of other provinces because of surging energy revenues. The rise in Alberta's resource revenues is also depicted in Figure 10.1. Between 1978 and 1981, natural resource revenues actually accounted for more than 50 percent of the province's total revenues. However, with the collapse of energy prices in 1986, resource revenues fell to less than 25 percent of provincial government revenues. Alberta's per capita real provincial revenues declined relative to the all province average and actually fell below the average in 1993-94: $4,171 for Alberta vsersus $4,245 for the provincial average. Having had the benefit of significant resource revenues, Alberta's nonresource revenues have been consistently below provincial average revenues and have been reflected largely in lower taxes in Alberta.

"Rainy Days" and the Alberta Heritage Savings Trust Fund

Surging energy revenues allowed the provincial government to save some of that revenue in the Alberta Heritage Savings Trust Fund (AHSTF). The AHSTF was established in 1976 and contributions were

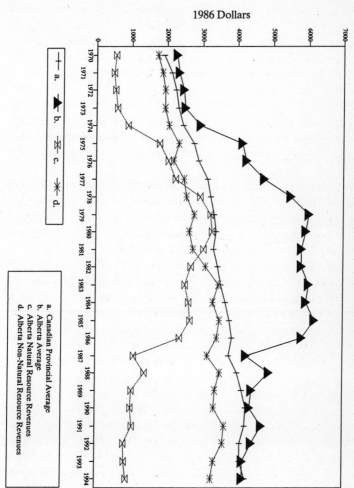

Figure 10.1: Provincial Real Per
Capita Revenues (1969-70 to 1993-94)

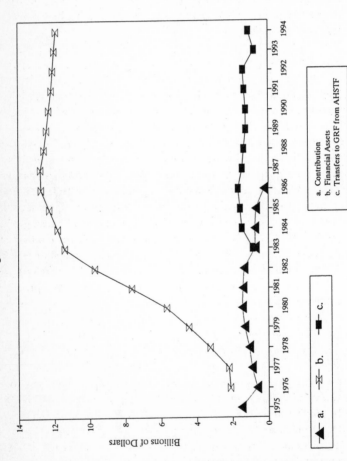

Figure 10.2: Alberta Heritage
Savings Trust Fund

a. Contribution
b. Financial Assets
c. Transfers to GRF from AHSTF

made to it between 1976 and 1986. With contributions and investment income, the book value of financial assets of the fund grew to exceed $12 billion by 1985 and has since stabilized at about that level: $11.9 billion in 1993-94.[7] In 1987, the provincial government ceased to earmark any energy revenues for the AHSTF and since 1983 all interest income from the fund has been allocated to the General Revenue Fund. Figure 10.2 clearly illustrates the demise of the fund as a savings account. Also, in real terms, the AHSTF is now only 72 percent of its value in 1986, the last year a contribution was made to it.

Expenditure History

Real expenditures per capita in Alberta have consistently exceeded the average of other provinces. The magnitude of this expenditure difference is shown in Figure 10.3 by the top line for Alberta and the lower line for all provinces. Since 1970, real expenditures per capita have risen from $1907 to $4840 per capita for all provinces and from $2,334 to $4,842 per capita in Alberta. While the increase in real per capita expenditures has been relatively steady over time for all provinces, the pattern for Alberta has been far more erratic. Expenditures ratcheted up in Alberta in 1975 (for 1975-79), again for the 1980-82 period and then again to a much higher level during 1983-87. Since 1988, expenditures in Alberta have been moving down towards the Canadian average, reaching it in 1994. Alberta is no longer the high-expenditure province. Notice too that, while expenditure declined, the reduction in real expenditures per capita in time and amount lagged significantly behind revenue declines thus creating the deficit problem that is discussed later.

Expenditure Adjustments: Expenditures on the Resource Base

Our Figure 10.3 likely exaggerates the magnitude of the difference in provincial public services provided in Alberta relative to other provinces. The large provincially-owned resource base in Alberta costs something to manage and those costs are included in expenditures. While they enable the province to earn substantial resource revenues, those outlays themselves do not enhance services to Alberta residents. Our data show that in 1991-92, for example, Alberta spent $441 more per person in the expenditure category "resource conservation and industrial development" than other provinces: $706 versus $265 in 1986 dollars. In order to adjust the expenditures for this extraordinary cost to Alberta, the difference between Alberta and the all-province average of resource conservation and industrial development costs are subtracted from the Alberta estimate of real per capita ex-

140

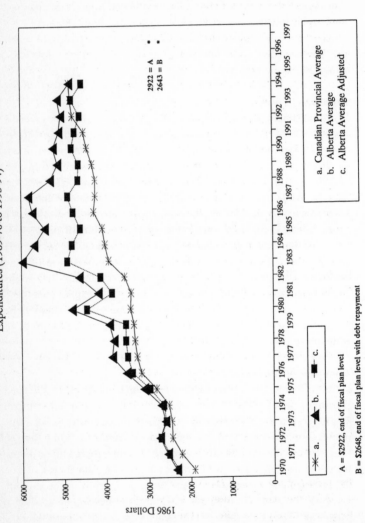

FIGURE 10.3: Provincial Real Per Capita
Expenditures (1969-70 to 1993-94)

a. Canadian Provincial Average
b. Alberta Average
c. Alberta Average Adjusted

A = $2922, end of fiscal plan level

B = $2648, end of fiscal plan level with debt repayment

2922 = A
2643 = B

penditures. This adjustment yields an estimate of what Alberta's expenditures would have been had it only the all-province average in the expenditure category resource conservation and industrial development. This revised estimate, although arguably imperfect, better reflects the actual expenditures for services benefiting Albertans directly, and so is a figure more comparable to expenditures in other provinces.

The levels of expenditure excluding extra resource management costs are shown by the middle line in Figure 10.3. The difference between Alberta and the average is considerably reduced. In fact, per capita expenditures in Alberta *fell below* the Canadian provincial average in 1991-92: $4,593 versus $4,758 and have remained below since then. That is, since 1991-92 Alberta spent *less* per capita than the average of the Canadian provinces for provincial government services. In 1993-94, Alberta spent $307 less per capita (i.e., 6.3 percent less) than the average of the provinces.

Some may quibble over comparing per capita expenditures in Alberta with the all-province average. That is, does what occurs elsewhere matter? Our position is that the all-province averages are relevant reference points. Albertans and their politicians have been and continue to be fond of comparing Alberta's taxes and (now less so) services to those in other provinces. We simply continue in that context while attempting to provide a somewhat broader and more complete and exact basis. The Alberta numbers have fluctuated greatly over the past twenty-five years. Hence, it is helpful to refer to developments in the other provinces where provincial fiscal situations have been much more stable. It is also relevant to consider the choices that have been made in provinces that have not had the fiscal advantages of (still, though now less) large natural resource revenues. It is also a mistake to believe that the expenditure levels in other provinces are inflated relative to those in Alberta by larger debt servicing costs. As shown below, the rapid growth of provincial debt in Alberta has resulted in per capita debt service charges in Alberta equalling the average for the other provinces since 1989-90. Hence, there was no need for adding an adjustment on that account. On the expenditure side of the budget, Alberta paralleled closely the average Canadian province when the Klein government took over.

Provincial Expenditures and Local Government

A further consideration when comparing expenditures across provinces is that local government activities and funding varies among the provinces. In the calendar year 1992 (the latest data available), national consolidated provincial and local expenditures per person in 1992 dollars were $7,005. Correcting for the difference in resource management and industrial development costs between Alberta and the average province ($431), comparable expenditures in Alberta were $7,197, 2.7 percent greater. In comparison to the two other "have" provinces, Ontario and B.C., Alberta's expenditures were 4.4 percent and 12.2 percent larger, respectively, in 1992.[8]

Deficits and Debt

In recent years expenditures have surpassed revenues in Alberta with the persistent deficits accumulating into a growing stock of debt. Figure 10.4 depicts Alberta's deficit record from the 1970s to the present. There were modest deficits in Alberta from 1970 to 1973. From then until 1987, the provincial public sector ran a surplus. In 1987, the Alberta government incurred an extraordinarily large deficit, $1,561 (1986 dollars) per capita, and since then, smaller but still relatively large deficits have continued. Alberta is not unique in running deficits as the fiscal position has not been that good in other provinces either. On average, provincial governments have been in a deficit position every year since 1970 except 1979.

Provincial debt in Alberta has grown at a dramatic pace. The speed is evident from Figure 10.5. Provincial government General Revenue Fund and Capital Fund debt went from almost zero in 1986 to $18.5 billion (or $7,100 per person) in 1994. Debt servicing has grown lock-step with the growth of debt (Figure 10.6). Before 1982 debt servicing in real per capita terms was consistently less than $200 per capita (Figure 10.4). By 1988 it had risen to slightly less than $400 in real per capita terms; by 1990 it exceeded $500, and by 1994 it exceeded $600. Debt servicing is now the third largest expenditure item, exceeded only by health and education (and marginally greater than social services). As a result of recent large deficits, Alberta's per capita debt and debt servicing costs rose to equal the all-province average by 1990 and have kept abreast of the average since then. It is only in the two years after 1994-95 that the planned deficits will be first small and then zero.

What's Left: Debt versus the Alberta Heritage Fund

The size of Alberta's gross and net debt can be calculated several ways. Figure 10.5 showed the combined un-matured debt of the General Revenue Fund and the Capital Fund. The province also has financial liabilities in other accounts. In response to criticism from the Auditor General and the Alberta Finance Review Committee, the provincial government modified its reporting of provincial liabilities so as to better reveal the financial status

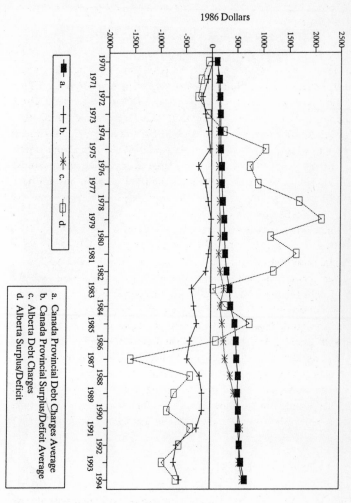

1986 Dollars

FIGURE 10.4: Provincial Per Capita
Real Deficit & Debt Servicing Costs

- ■ a.
- + b.
- ✳ c.
- ⊟ d.

a. Canada Provincial Debt Charges Average
b. Canada Provincial Surplus/Deficit Average
c. Alberta Debt Charges
d. Alberta Surplus/Deficit

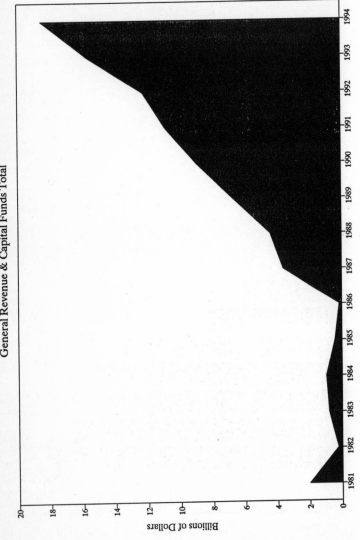

FIGURE 10.5: Provincial Unmatured Debt:
General Revenue & Capital Funds Total

145

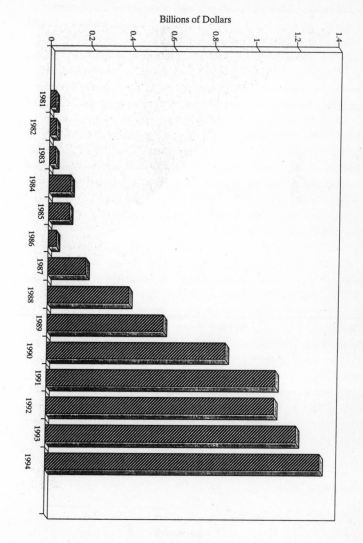

FIGURE 10.6: Provincial Debt Servicing
Cost: General Revenue Fund

Billions of Dollars

of the provincial government. As a result, the total un-matured debt for 1992 was shown to be $17.4 billion and is forecast to be $22.5 billion, or $8,630 per capita, as of March 31, 1994. These figures still exclude the un-funded pension liabilities ($5.1 billion) and other actual and potential liabilities. Including such items brings the total debt and liabilities to $32 billion, according to 1994 Budget documents.

Net debt is the gross debt less the value of financial assets held by the province. The AHST Fund is the major source of such assets but there is some debate about the value and/or availability of those assets. For example, the Auditor General estimated the funds available from the AHSTF at $8 billion as of March 31, 1992[9]: considerably less than the $12 billion attributed to the Fund by the provincial government. Professor G. Mumey of the University of Alberta has undertaken independent reviews of the realizable market value of the assets held in the Fund. His latest analysis estimates those assets at $8.5 billion. The major sources of the difference between his estimate and the province's $11.9 billion figure come from obligations of the province itself that are owed to the Fund and discounting of poorly secured loans to Crown corporations.[10]

The net debt of the province is influenced significantly by which estimate of the AHSTF assets is used. Focusing only on the un-matured debt of $22.5 billion, the provincial figure results in an obligation of $10.6 billion ($22.5-$11.9) or $4,069 per capita. Employing the more conservative estimate of the realizable market value of AHSTF assets, the net debt comes to $14 billion ($22.5-$8.5) or $5,374 per capita.

Albertans are fortunate but can take only modest comfort from the existence of the assets in the AHSTF. The Fund is a significant reserve and earnings on it contribute to the general revenues of the province. However, the Fund is not growing while the provincial debt is still expanding. Furthermore, as Mumey indicates, the AHSTF is increasingly becoming the provincial government's bank account as it comes to account for a larger share of the province's liquid funds. Hence, less of the AHSTF assets would be available to apply to the provincial debt should such a move be made.

The Options and the Choice

Ralph Klein faced major fiscal problems immediately upon becoming leader of the Alberta Progressive Conservative party and premier of the province in the fall of 1992. In January 1993, the provincial treasurer released a Budget Update for the 1992-93 fiscal year which raised the forecast operating deficit from $2.3 billion to almost $2.8 billion or $1,100 per per-

son. Not only was this the seventh successive deficit but the largest in a sequence of (almost steadily) growing deficits since 1987-88. Although real
per capita expenditures by the provincial government had been declining
steadily since 1986-87 (except for 1992-93, the year just preceding the latest
provincial election), that reduction had not matched the dramatic drop in
the provincial government's natural resource revenues and the moderate
loss of other revenues due to the early 1990s recession. That these deficits
were accumulating into a large debt was emphasized by the Annual Report
of the Auditor General[11], released early in 1993, which placed the province's un-matured debt as of March 31, 1992 at $17.4 billion. These sober-
ing data on deficits and debt followed public concerns already heightened
by the magnitude of federal deficits and debt. Thus, the provincial government, and the new premier, faced an extraordinarily large deficit and a
growing debt with limited prospects of either coming under control soon
with existing policies.

Debt can only be controlled by first tackling the deficit. The deficit can
be eliminated by reducing expenditures, increasing revenues, or a combination of the two. We discuss the two distinct options in turn.

Expenditure Control

In its 1992 Budget, the Alberta government had proposed a plan to
deal with the structural deficit. The plan introduced a downward "fiscal
correction" to provincial government expenditure. In effect, the plan was
to hold nominal expenditures constant at 1992-93 levels over the next four
years, i.e., until 1996-97, by which time revenues were predicted to increase
sufficiently to balance the budget. That plan was rejected by the Klein government which, in its pre-election budget of May 6, 1993, announced its
plan to balance the provincial budget by 1996-97 through a 20 percent reduction in program expenditures.

The Klein government's Balanced Budget Plan was reaffirmed and re-
fined somewhat (with new deficit figures) in the Alberta Treasury's September 1993 Budget Update. The essence of that plan (under which the
government is still operating) and some of the fiscal implications are reported in Table 1. Over the period of the plan, revenue is projected to grow
by 8.3 percent from its $11.47 billion level in 1992-93 to $12.425 billion in
1996-97. However, expenditure reduction is the focus of the attack on the
deficit. By 1996-97, program expenditures (i.e., those providing goods and
services to Alberta residents) are scheduled to fall to $10.195 billion from
the 1992-93 level of $13.028 billion: a 21.7 percent decline.

Population growth and price changes effect the impact that these ex-

TABLE 10.1

Government of Alberta Balanced Budget Plan and Fiscal Implications
(millions of dollars unless otherwise indicated)

	1992-93	1993-94	1994-95	1995-96	1996-97	Percentage Change 1992 to 1996
Revenue[a]	11,470	11,462	11,725	12,065	12,425	8.3
Program Expenditures[a]	13,028	12,021	11,385	10,790	10,195	-21.7
Population[b] (thousands)	2,529	2,568	2,605	2,640	2,674	5.7
Expenditures per Capita	5,152	4,681	4,371	4,087	3,813	-26.0
Price Index[c] (1986=100)	128.1	130.4	127.1	128.8	130.5	1.9
Real Expenditures per Capita (1986$)	4,022	3,590	3,423	3,173	2,922	-27.4
Operating Deficit[a]	2,777	1,959	1,310	455	(510)	-
Consolidated Deficit[a]	3,409	2,444	1,790	755	(220)	-
Unmatured Debt[a]	20,181	22,967	24,700	25,450	25,250	25.1
Gross Debt[a]	29,068	32,075	34,101	35,053	35,026	20.5

Notes: a. From Budget '93 Update, Alberta Treasury, September 1993.
         b. Statistics Canada.
         c. Consumer Price Index adjusted for 1994-95 and projected.

penditure reductions will have upon Albertans. Using Statistics Canada projections of the Alberta population, the per capita expenditure in 1996-97 is expected to be $3,813: 26 percent below that in 1992-93. Rising prices might also erode the value of expenditures even though inflation has slowed. However, as part of its cost reducing efforts, the provincial government cut public sector employee compensation by five percent in its 1994 budget. Not all of this cut translated into cost reduction because part was realized by unpaid days off: i.e., reduced service. Reasonable assumptions about the impact of this on the cost of government services lead to a 3.4 percentage point drop in the price index (using the CPI) in 1994-95. Inflation is expected to restore the index to 130.5 by 1996-97. Employing these price adjustments, real expenditures per capita in 1986 dollars fall from $4,022 in 1992-93 to $2,922 in 1996-97: i.e., by 27.4 percent.

The Klein government's 20 percent cut in program expenditures is expected to translate into a 27.4 percent cut in services to Albertans. This is a very significant reduction in two ways. First, it follows upon a 15 percent real decline in per capita spending that has already been imposed since the mid-1980s. That reduction, although insufficient in itself, indicates the degree of the earlier expenditure control efforts which brought us from an exceptionally high level of per capita services to an average level (although Albertans still benefit from living off the depreciation of a large, high quality stock of public infrastructure). The further 27.4 percent reduction is significant also because it will move Albertans from an about average level of provincial services to well below average level. Although changes are occurring elsewhere, it is reasonable to expect that a 27.4 percent cut will result in provincial services significantly below those elsewhere in the country. In 1993-94, no province spent less than 90 percent of the per capita all-province average.

Recent developments portend the possible extent of Alberta's deviation from other provinces. During the spring of 1995, six provinces projected balanced budgets for 1995-96 (British Columbia, Manitoba, New Brunswick, Newfoundland, Prince Edward Island, and Saskatchewan). Analysis of these provincial budget figures indicates that per-capita program spending in each of these provinces will exceed the (resource conservation and industrial development adjusted) level planned for Alberta when it balances its budget. Alberta's expenditure will be between 9 and 18 percent less. These are remarkable differences, especially when recognizing the much greater fiscal capacity of Alberta and the fact that all of these six provinces, except British Columbia, are among the "have-not" provinces in the sense that they receive equalization payments from the federal government. It needs also to be remembered that Alberta's planned expenditure cuts only balance the budget and do not begin to generate the revenue to pay down the debt. Continuing the present approach to accomplish debt reduction also would require even further significant expenditure cuts.

Over the course of the Balanced Budget Plan, the operating deficit declines from $2.777 billion in 1992-93 to zero; actually a small surplus ($0.51 billion) is projected for 1996-97. Similar success is expected with the consolidated account. While reducing the deficit to zero, the debt continues to grow (by $5 to $6 billion). The un-matured debt increases 25.1 percent to $25.25 billion and the gross debt (including pension and other liabilities) by 20.5 percent to $35 billion.

The prospect of repaying this debt opens for discussion an unpleasant and largely unmentioned topic. To reduce the accumulated debt will require the provincial government to raise additional revenues or cut expenditures even further. Keeping with the spirit of the deficit elimination strategy, we contemplate the effects of repaying the debt by further expenditure reductions. Assuming a level of un-matured debt ($24.15 billion) and interest rates (about 6.3 percent) consistent with the 1994 provincial budget, repayment of the debt over fifteen years would require an additional outlay of almost one billion dollars annually. Reducing expenditures again to realize this amount would result in real per capita expenditures falling to $2,648 (versus $2,922 in 1996-97); B rather than A in figure 10.3. Repaying the debt under these assumptions implies a 34.2 percent reduction in per capita expenditures and service. If the debt were to be amortized over twenty years, the decline would be 31.6 percent (but for a longer time) and if over ten years the necessary decline would be 40 percent.[12]

Eliminating the deficit according to the Klein government's Balanced Budget Plan is imposing a substantial reduction in services to Alberta residents. Eventually, the decline will be about 27 percent per capita from the 1992-93 level (which was approximately the all-province average). Eliminating the deficit is only part of the necessary program. Utilizing the same approach to pay down the provincial debt would require a further cut in expenditures and services. A cutback of 33 percent in total is quite reasonable to project. Cutbacks of this magnitude would certainly leave Alberta, one of Canada's wealthiest provinces, with the lowest level of provincial government services. Although the Alberta government is well along in its deficit reduction program and its efforts appear to have retained considerable popular support thus far, will Albertans wish to pursue to the end this single track route to deficit control and debt reduction?

Revenue Options

Reducing expenditures is the logical first step towards controlling the deficit, but raising revenues is the other lever and it is one which affords Alberta considerable leeway. The major sources of provincial revenue are shown in Table 10.2 for 1993-94, the initial year of the deficit elimination program. Again, these data are on an FMS accounting basis and so are comparable among provinces. Note too that these data include the various provincial levies imposed to support health care finances. The per capita dollar amounts are interesting. Per capita taxes borne by firms and individuals are low in Alberta; at $2,195 in 1993-94, they are $1,200 less than the all prov-

TABLE 10.2				
Provincial Taxes and Revenues, 1993-94				
	Percent of Provincial Revenues		Per Capita Revenue	
	All Prov.	Alberta	All Prov.	Alberta
Taxes				
Personal Income	26.4	19.7	$1460	$1073
Corporate Income	2.8	4.7	156	255
General Sales	13.1	0	725	0
Motive Fuels	3.8	3.6	210	196
Alcohol & Tobacco	1.7	2.2	93	121
Real Property	3.7	1.7	204	95
Health Insurance Levies	6.7	6.3	370	341
Other Taxes	3.2	2.1	178	113
Total Taxes				
(a) % of Revenue	61.4	40.3		
(b) $ per capita			3396	2195
Other Revenue				
Natural Resource	3.6	21.1	199	1150
Return on Investments	9.8	19.0	539	1036
Federal Transfers	18.9	15.2	1045	825
Other	6.2	4.4	344	237
Total Revenue	100.0	100.0	5523	5443

Source: Perry, David B., "Fiscal Figures," *Canadian Tax Journal*, Vol. 42, No. 3, 1994, pp. 966-77.

ince average. On the other hand, natural resource revenues and returns on investments are much greater in Alberta. Together, at $2,186 per person, they are almost three times the all province average. Despite these large amounts, total revenue per capita in Alberta actually fell below the provincial average in 1993-94: $5,443 versus $5,523. As indicated in Figure 1, this below-average position is a first in recent history. Normally, natural resource revenues have kept provincial per capita total revenues in Alberta well above the all-province average and allowed well-below-average taxes. For example, in 1991-92, per capita revenue was $904 above the all province average while per capita taxes were $1,000 less. Although Alberta has become an average province in terms of total revenue, it continues to raise only 40 percent of its revenue from taxation while other provinces rely upon taxation for over 60 percent.

The potential to raise additional revenue through taxation depends very much upon how much Alberta currently taxes its existing tax base. Does Al-

TABLE 10.3				
Provincial Tax Capacity and Effort for Selected Taxes, 1990-91				
	Per Capita Tax Revenue			
Tax	All Province Average	Alberta at Alberta Tax Rates	Alberta at National Average Tax Rate	Alberta Tax Capacity[a]	Alberta Tax Effort[a]
Personal Income	$1386	$1131	$1421	1.03	0.796
Business Income	229	327	376	1.64	0.871
Business Capital	69	15	120	1.73	0.127
Sales Taxes	710	10	881	1.24	0.011
Motive Fuels	173	158	235	1.35	0.673
Alcohol & Tobacco	214	276	230	1.07	1.203
Real Property (provincial & local)	900	968	1068	1.19	0.907
Total	3681	2885	4331		
All Revenues Subject to Equalization	4703	4878	6405		
Alberta Overall Tax Capacity and Tax Effort (all provincial and local revenues)				1.33	0.750

Source: Canada Department of Finance, *Provincial Fiscal Equalization, Seventh Estimate*, February, 1992.

Note: a.   These are not the official Equalization Program indices of capacity and effort which are confidential but are approximate values estimated from available data.

berta have under-utilized tax capacity? Information about major taxes are reported in Table 10.3. Since these data come from a different data source they are not strictly comparable to those in Table 10.2. That the data are for 1990-91 is not a concern. The relative figures change only slowly from year to year and, at best, the data could be updated by only one year at this time. Also note that business income taxes do not correspond exactly to the corporate income tax; the business capital tax is included as are local property taxes (the major source of local tax revenue). The collection reported here accounts for about 85 percent of consolidated provincial-local tax revenues and are the major taxes and revenues entering the fiscal equalization formula for determining grants to "have not" provinces. Again we compare the per person tax revenue raised in Alberta with the all-province average and, again, Albertans are found to pay less tax than the average province resident; $2,885 versus $3,681 per capita for the tax sources reported.

The third column shows the tax per person that would have been generated in Alberta if the Canadian average tax rates were applied to Alberta's 1990-91 tax bases. At the average rates, Alberta would have generated more revenue from all tax bases shown except for alcohol and tobacco. Provincial average rates would have raised $4,331 per capita rather than the $2,885 that was actually collected. The absence of a provincial sales tax accounts for only 60 percent of the $1,446 difference.

Not only are Alberta's tax rates lower but the size of the Alberta tax base is greater than that of the average province. In each case, Alberta's per capita tax base exceeds the average over all provinces for the items of Table 10.3: i.e., the fiscal capacity index exceeds 1.0. In fact, over the 37 provincial revenue sources that enter equalization calculations, Alberta is below average in very few (revenue from mineral resources other than coal, water power, and sales of beer). Over the 37 revenue sources, Alberta's fiscal capacity is 33 percent greater than the all-province average. Only slightly more than half of the above-average fiscal capacity is due to oil and gas resource revenues. Only Ontario and British Columbia also have fiscal capacity measures exceeding one, about 1.10 and 1.08 respectively.

Alberta does not impose as heavy a tax burden as the average province. The measure of tax effort — the ratio of what is raised to what could be raised at Canadian average provincial tax rates — shows Alberta is at 75 percent of the all-province average. For only one of the major taxes shown (that on alcohol and tobacco) is the Alberta effort above average. In fact, if more recent data were available, they would likely show that Alberta's tax effort has declined relatively because many provinces have raised taxes somewhat as well as reduced expenditures in their efforts to reduce provincial deficits while Alberta has shunned tax increases. Thus, one of the avenues for addressing the deficit is to consider tax increases.

Figure 10.7 shows the additional tax revenues that could be generated from simply imposing taxes at the 1990-91 all province average rates in Alberta on Alberta's 1990-91 tax bases. For all but taxes on alcohol and tobacco, more revenue would be realized. Even without a provincial sales tax, over $600 per capita could be raised, or approximately $1.5 billion, in additional tax revenue. The striking option is a provincial sales tax which does not exist in Alberta. At the average rate, which is an effective rate of 7.83 percent, which is less than Ontario's 8.92 percent effective rate, $871 per capita or about $2.2 billion would be raised.[13]

Thus, looking simply from the revenue side only, a relatively moderate level of sales tax could have handled the structural component of the deficit while leaving other Alberta taxes at their existing, generally below aver-

154

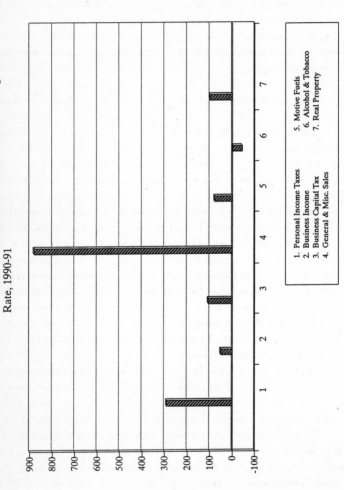

Figure 10.7: Additional Per Capita Revenue from Major Tax Sources if Alberta Taxed at the Provincial Average Rate, 1990-91

1. Personal Income Taxes
2. Business Income
3. Business Capital Tax
4. General & Misc. Sales
5. Motive Fuels
6. Alcohol & Tobacco
7. Real Property

age, level. Alternatively, even without a provincial sales tax, there is room in the existing level of Alberta taxes to go some considerable distance towards deficit reduction. Hence, consideration of tax possibilities did and still does present feasible options that enhance fiscal flexibility by opening up a wide range of alternatives. These options should not be ignored due to a fixation with only one side of the ledger. Indeed, unless there is a substantial recovery of natural resource revenues, it seems likely, given the magnitude of expenditure and service reduction otherwise necessary and the low taxes in Alberta, that Albertans will reconsider tax alternatives before the deficit and debt issue is fully resolved.

What About the Heritage Savings Trust Fund?

Should the Fund be retained or liquidated? A recent paper has concluded that the economic impact of the Fund has been limited and that economic development is insufficient reason to retain the fund.[14] The current role of the Fund, by direct allocations and indirectly as a source of provincial general revenues, is simply to finance ordinary government expenditures. Notably, investment income from the AHSTF supplements provincial general revenues by about a billion dollars annually. Orderly liquidation of the Fund and retiring debt with the proceeds would reduce debt servicing requirements while also lowering available revenue. Initially, one would expect that the net debt position of the province would remain unchanged. However, partial liquidation has in effect already happened inasmuch as Fund assets increasingly have been held as very close substitutes for cash; the Alberta government holds little other cash.[15] That is, the province has come to rely upon a part of the Fund as its chequing account. This means that, if considering possible AHSTF disinvestment, less money would be available to pay down debt unless the province supplemented its liquid reserves with other sources. Mumey suggests that about $2 billion less would be available because that amount of the Fund is now being utilized as the province's cash reserve.

While the actual fiscal position of the province is affected little by the presence or liquidation of the AHSTF, its continued existence may obscure the underlying reality of Alberta's current fiscal position. A survey of Chartered Accountants in Alberta revealed that 75 percent supported orderly liquidation of the Fund.[16] The reality is that the province is a net debtor and focusing on the assets of the AHSTF causes some people to neglect the fact these assets have been more than offset by liabilities incurred elsewhere by the provincial government. Moreover, Canadians outside the province are misled into perceiving that the province has a nest egg or "rainy day" fund, instead of the reality that the province is a net debtor and is still struggling to eliminate its structural deficit and resultant increasing debt.

Policy Options in the Evolving Fiscal Circumstances

The evidence clearly suggests that Alberta had a structural deficit of at least $2 billion, (for realistic energy price and economic growth projections), as it entered the Klein "fiscal renovation" period in 1993. This structural deficit combined with accumulating debt servicing requirements of the growing stock of debt implied, with no change in expenditures nor revenues, an increasing structural deficit through time. Clearly this option was not sustainable. Rising debt and debt servicing requirements would have soon brought a lowering of the province's debt rating and even greater debt servicing costs. This dynamic implied ever accelerating debt and debt servicing in the absence of expenditure reductions and/or revenue increases to eliminate or reduce the deficit.

Moreover, ongoing structural factors made a "do nothing" policy response even more unrealistic after 1992-93, and they continue to exert pressure for fiscal adjustment. For example, an aging population puts further upward pressure on health care expenditures while the share of producing taxpayers declines. On the revenue side about 20 percent of provincial government revenues arises from nonrenewable resources. Declining light crude production and constant real prices for oil mean falling revenue from this source that may or may not be offset by higher revenues from natural gas sales. Payments from the Government of Canada make up approximately 15 percent of provincial government revenues and the evidence is clear that the federal government is off-loading its financial responsibilities for shared cost programs on to the provinces, especially the "have" provinces. Income from the AHSTF is 7.3 percent of provincial operating revenues in 1994-95[17] (down from 8.7 percent in 1991-93) but in the absence of capital infusions the fund cannot sustain its absolute or relative level of investment income, especially as inflation erodes its purchasing power. In total, over 40 percent of the forecast revenue base of the province in 1994-95 is likely to decline further in real value over the coming years. Without major corrective measures, this possibility could only further exacerbate the existing structural deficit.

Scarcely half of the structural deficit is being deleted by the 1993-94 and (especially) 1994-95 Alberta government expenditure reductions and fee increases.[18] While cyclical buoyancy of resource revenues may mask this deficit temporarily, the hard reality remains. Looking ahead, it is essential to address the challenges and choices of today's fiscal circumstances beginning in 1995. Deficit reduction to date has been substantial and reflects major policy and political effort by the provincial government but the action taken and planned is inadequate to address the full scope of the problem. Consideration of future options must be in the context of the fiscal realities identified in the foregoing analysis.

Fiscal Realities for Alberta in 1995

The realities enumerated below calculate Alberta's new fiscal position. Many of the magnitudes are smaller, and the situation has much improved over that which might have prevailed, but the fiscal difficulties continue to be foreboding. Despite the initiatives, efforts and sacrifices of the last two years, many of the 1995 realities are discouragingly similar to those of 1993.

- Reality #1. *Debt:* Alberta is a net debtor with net debt equal to at least $11 billion and growing. The assets of the AHSTF are less than half of Alberta's tax-supported gross debt; investment income consequently is much less than debt servicing requirements. Moreover, the value of the Heritage Fund is shrinking gradually whilst debt servicing costs are increasing and have become the third-largest and fastest-growing expenditure item. If recent interest rate and exchange changes sustain, the impact will be even worse.

- Reality #2. *Deficit:* Although reduced, a structural deficit remains. However, a firm plan, based on expenditure reductions, is in place to reduce the deficit to zero by 1996-97. For 1994-95, the planned deficit of $1.55 billion or $600 per capita ($2,100 per family) amounts to approximately 12.3 percent of expenditures and 13.6 percent of revenue. However, primarily because of unexpected revenues of $680 million, the second quarter budget forecast projects a much smaller deficit for 1994-95 ($655 million).[19] Half the revenue gains came from improved natural resource revenues and one-quarter from unplanned increases in lottery income. Although the province is already cautious about the resource revenue increases, one cannot be too confident that these increases will continue.

- Reality #3. *Revenues:* The likelihood of a declining real value of over 40 percent of the provincial government's revenue base (natural resource revenue, investment income and federal transfers) means that revenue erosion is likely to place continuing pressure on budget balancing in the absence of fiscal reforms by the provincial government involving either expenditure reduction or revenue (tax) increases or both.

- Reality #4. *Expenditures*: The evidence shows that in terms of expenditures on goods and services (excluding those on resource conservation and industrial development) Alberta fell below the all-province average in 1991-92. The 1994-95 levels are even lower. That is, Albertans now receive a below-average level of services from their provincial government and further deterioration is ahead. Alone, the expenditure cuts necessary to balance the budget and then to begin to pay off the accumulated debt would necessitate an additional reduction in the order of 15-20 percent beyond the 15 percent decline that is expected to be realized in the first two years of the deficit elimination program. Cuts of a magnitude at least as large as those realized to date will be more difficult to achieve and to accept.

- Reality #5. *Tax Effort:* The evidence on provincial government revenue sources reveals that all Alberta's major tax bases exceed the provincial average while tax effort in the province is significantly below the national average not only because there is no provincial sales tax but also due to lower tax effort on most tax bases.

- Reality #6. *Heritage Fund*: The AHSTF is a shrinking financial factor in Alberta's fiscal picture. Depending on which estimate of value is used, it offsets one-third to one-half of Alberta's debt. In contrast with 1993, the provincial government has indicated a willingness to consider orderly liquidation. A Legislative Committee has been formed to assess the future of the Fund.

A Two-Tracked Approach to Deficit and Debt Elimination

We have noted that the province's structural deficit can be eliminated and movement towards pay-down of the stock of debt can be accomplished by provincial government expenditure reductions, revenue increases, or some combination of the two. Thus far, the province has followed a single track approach: i.e., deficit reduction through expenditure cuts alone. To us the evidence is compelling that a more comprehensive approach involving the following elements is essential if we are to rid Alberta of the deficit and begin to repay what are still increasing levels of debt.

1. Expenditure Reduction Alone Is Unlikely to be Enough. Although up to now it has been "politically correct" to focus solely on expenditure reduction, it must be borne in mind that once Alberta's expenditures are adjusted for extra expenditures on account of its resource base, per capita spending in real terms on programs has been below the all province aver-

age since 1991-92. Reducing program expenditures by at least another billion below their current nominal level over the next two years to just balance the budget implies a 27.4 percent cut in expenditures and services to Albertans. By a considerable margin, no province now experiences such a low level of expenditure and service. Alberta, one of the three wealthiest provinces in Canada, would certainly be at the bottom in provincial services. Services in education, health care, and social services would reflect this fiscal reality. Additional cuts to enable debt repayment could easily imply provincial services reduced to two-thirds of the average across provinces. Such reductions would only exacerbate the disparities between Alberta and other provinces.

2. Two Sources of Revenue Increases and Still Below-Average Taxes. The current structural deficit should be tackled by a combination of expenditure reductions and revenue increases. On the revenue side, two options are possible. For example, either (i) increase taxes to the national average rates on all non-sales tax bases but not impose a provincial sales tax (making the Alberta tax effort 90 percent of the average), or (ii) introduce a provincial sales tax and hold tax effort constant on the existing taxes. A sales tax of 5 percent imposed on personal consumption expenditures, or a higher rate for a narrower tax base, would yield about $1.6 billion.[20] The alternative, that of increasing (non-sales tax) tax effort in the province to the all province average would raise a similar amount. While subsequent provincial budget measures may have reduced some of the disparity in tax effort, these are unlikely to have changed it substantially nor the revenue implications of moving to the all province average.

3. A Balanced Approach to Deficit Reduction. If the above revenue initiatives were taken and combined with expenditure cuts already imposed, the remainder of the structural deficit would be cleared. The expenditure cuts would have preceded major new tax initiatives. Although taxes would be increased somewhat, Albertans would continue to enjoy a considerable tax advantage over residents of other provinces. Albertans may prefer some other division between expenditure cuts and tax increases, but we expect that some form of a combined approach will be required to meet Albertans' expectations of provincial government services and still eliminate the deficit and begin to pay the debt. That is, without unexpectedly buoyant natural resource revenues, the long-run sustainable solution to the province's fiscal problems will require the combination of reduced expenditures and tax increases.

4. Liquidate the AHSTF to Reduce Provincial Debt? To ensure that Albertans recognize the fiscal realities necessitating the above actions, it may

be necessary to repeal the AHSTF Act and instead legislate an Alberta debt retirement Act. The Fund assets can be liquidated efficiently over time. An implication of liquidating the AHSTF is that revenues from it would not be available to support the operating budget and specifically contribute towards meeting debt servicing costs. The remaining Alberta debt servicing costs would be funded out of general revenues. The province has the capacity to carry this debt load if the source of debt growth, the structural deficit, is eliminated.

5. Strategy for Eliminating Alberta's Debt. Our accumulated debt exceeded the Heritage Fund by about the end of 1991; now Fund monies can pay off only about 25-30 percent of the debt. Thus a strategy beyond the AHSTF is needed for the future. Expenditure cuts and tax increases could be used to retire the debt in an even and regular pattern. Due to public ownership of highly-valued resources, a unique supplemental strategy is available to Alberta that reduces the size and so eases the burden of the regular payments. Resource markets and revenues are inherently cyclical. Net of the Heritage Fund and after deficit elimination, the debt would be sustainable; hence Alberta could afford to reduce the magnitude of its annual repayments and wait for future "spikes" in resource revenue cycles (from oil, natural gas, forestry, coal, tar sands) to provide revenue for irregular but large lump sum payments. With conservative budgetary forecasts and expectations, such revenue windfalls are likely to be available from time to time. Such a strategy demands a commitment to reserve such windfalls for debt reduction.

Conclusion

During 1994, Premier Klein often spoke of the progress that was being made towards reducing Alberta's deficit. He frequently seemed to claim that the worst was past for the province. His very optimistic perspective culminated at the end of the year when he spoke of looking ahead to 1995 to potential personal income tax cuts and wage increases for civil servants.[21] In our opinion, the premier's view is unduly rosy and downplays, if not neglects, the fiscal realities. Even if realized, the premier's year-end projections might only amount to teasing concessions made primarily for the benefit of political rhetoric. The evidence we advance in this paper indicates that the province is now only halfway towards solving its fiscal problems and that Albertans can only expect considerably more of what they have already received from the Klein government: i.e., further expenditure cuts and further reduced services if it continues on this one-track approach to deficit and debt reduction. As they continue, the expenditure cuts become more onerous and move Alberta into a less and less enviable position: perhaps to an "Alberta disadvantage." Consequently, we argue that a balanced approach that blends expenditure cuts with tax revenue increases is necessary to resolve the province's fiscal problems.

Notes

1. This article previously appeared under the title, "Alberta's Fiscal Update: One-Track (Thinking) Towards Deficit Reduction." In *Information Bulletin* #28 (Edmonton: The Western Centre for Economic Research, February 1995).
2. E. M. Beck, Barlett's Familiar Quotations (Toronto: Little, Brown and Company, 1980), 263.
3. Institute of Chartered Accountants of Alberta (ICAA), "Facing Fiscal Facts II," January 1993. See also the Institute's report, "Staying the Fiscal Course," February 1994.
4. Alberta Financial Review Commission, "A Report to Albertans," March 1993.
5. M. McMillan and A. Warrack, "Alberta's Fiscal Situation: Identifying the Problem, Looking for Solutions." In *Information Bulletin* #14 (Edmonton: Western Centre for Economic Research, April 1993).
6. Ibid.
7. Alberta Treasury, *Alberta Heritage Trust Fund Annual Report 1993-94.*
8. Some might think that the State and local spending of our American neighbours would provide a good example. International comparisons are fraught with difficulties and a really reliable comparison would be a major study but we observe that the average level of State and local expenditures in the United States in 1992 was $5,353 (U.S. dollars). This amount would be equivalent to the Canadian average of $7005 (Canadian dollars) at an exchange rate of $0.76, well above recent rates which would imply a greater average in the U.S. That is, at reasonable rates of exchange, the level of per capita total spending of subnational governments in Canada and the United States appear comparable (not larger in Canada). While U.S. state and local governments spend less on debt servicing (4 percent versus 11 percent), they also spend very much less on health and hospitals (6 percent versus 22 percent).
9. Auditor General, *Public Accounts 1991-92* (Edmonton: Alberta Treasury, January 1993).
10. The provincial government sought advice from a group of investment dealers regarding the value of the AHSTF. For those elements of the Fund that they were directed to consider, they concluded in general that those assets were highly marketable and liquid (see Nesbitt Burns/RBC Dominion/Scotia McLeod/Wood Gundy, *Alberta Heritage Savings Trust Fund Assessment of Market Value,* December 1994). However, six assets (with a cost-based value of $939 million) were excluded from their consideration. Some of the debate about the

market value of the Fund relates to these excluded assets. In fact, the province has since written-down one of these assets (the Lloydminster Upgrader).

11. Auditor General, *Public Accounts 1991-92.*

12. If interest rates are higher than the 6.3 percent implied and used for these calculations, the required expenditure cut becomes larger. For example, if the rate were 8.0 percent (which is less than the 9.0 percent paid by the province over the past three years), the resulting real per capita program expenditure, amortized over fifteen years, would drop to $2571; that is, a cut of 36.1 percent from the 1992-93 level.

13. Utilization of the 1990-91 data is expected to underestimate the revenue that could be generated today from the same policies.

14. A. Warrack, "Alberta Heritage Fund: Regional Economic Development Assessment," Paper presented to the Western Regional Science Association, Tucson, Arizona, February 1994.

15. G. Mumey, "The Alberta Heritage Fund in 1994."In *Information Bulletin* #26 (Edmonton: Western Centre for Economic Research, November 1994), 10.

16. ICAA, "Facing Fiscal Facts II."

17. Alberta Treasury, *Alberta Heritage Savings Trust Fund Quarterly Report,* December 1994.

18. Increases in fees and charges have contributed quite modestly towards deficit reduction. From the latest budget estimates, total revenues from premiums, fees, and licences in 1994-95 are projected to be $942 million, $156 million over the 1992-93 level. $132 million of this increase is due to higher health insurance premiums. These additional charges are not considered to be tax increases by the government. However, raising an extra $132 million from alternative tax sources, higher fuel taxes for example, would require a 25 percent increase in fuel taxes.

19. Alberta Treasury, *1994 Quarterly Budget Report,* November 1994.

20. The possibility of a sales tax in Alberta seems a little less remote today than it did in 1993. We note that the Alberta Tax Reform Commission, February 1994, supported introducing a sales tax although under rather different circumstances than argued here. The Commission supported a sales tax only after the deficit was eliminated and only then so as to allow personal and corporate income taxes to be reduced.

21. *Edmonton Journal,* 31 December 1994, 1.

Chapter Eleven

THE POLITICS OF DEBT AND DEFICIT IN ALBERTA[1]

David J. Cooper and Dean Neu

> Goodness Gracious! ... The sky is falling down. I must run and tell the king.
>
> Chicken Little.[2]

In Alberta, as elsewhere, deficits and debt are a popular topic. The repackaging of the provincial Conservatives as fiscally responsible helped them retain their grip on power, despite the string of financial scandals that plagued the Getty years.[3] With the reelection of the provincial Conservatives, and with the federal success of the Reform Party, the issue of deficits and debt has become the rallying cry for those intent on restructuring Alberta's social and economic landscape. In April 1993, Premier Klein released a paper, Seizing Opportunity, which outlined the Tories economic strategy. One of that strategy's key features was to balance the budget. The provincial budget statement of that year included a four year fiscal plan to balance the budget, through spending cuts rather than an increase in taxation. The plan was embedded in the Deficit Elimination Act of 1993 and the budget of 1994 tightened the plan.[4]

This conservative rhetoric has been successful in capturing the popular imagination and shaping public debate. Provincial Liberals as well as Conservatives unquestionably accept the "problem" of both the annual deficits and the accumulated debt. Policy options are weighed in terms of their impact on the deficit and the debt. Dissent is reduced to weak statements such as "I agree with deficit reduction BUT ..." The popularity of deficits and debt as a media topic is eclipsed only by the statistically unfounded hype surrounding crime. We argue that the hype over the deficit is about as meaningful as that about crime; changes in reporting measures of the deficit fuel debt phobia and foreclose rational debate about the underlying problems and alternative solutions.

Although it may seem heretical, we ask: "are deficits bad in all circumstances?" We further ask whether Alberta has a deficit problem. Much of the rhetoric surrounding deficits and debt has prejudged the issue. Discussion has been limited to deciding how to eliminate the "apparent" deficit without first deciding whether a problem actually exists, and if there is a problem, its nature and extent. We will show that the 1994 Provincial Accounts do not "tell it like it is," as the message from the provincial treasurer promises on the first page. We dispute important figures in those statements which depict the 1994 deficit at $1.68 billion,[5] and the accumulated net debt at $13.379 billion. The third question we ask is, Who is really paying for the cuts in expenditures? We show that, to the extent that there is a need to deal with the deficit and the debt, the real issue is a political one; how to deal with deficit, who should contribute to the solution, and over what time period.

To answer these fundamentally political questions, we adopt an historical perspective that considers provincial revenues and expenditures for the last ten years.[6] Based on this analysis, we conclude that the rhetoric surrounding deficits/debt is not really about fiscal stewardship, but rather is about fuelling public anxiety. Creating a phobia about deficit and debt facilitates a shifting of the burden of paying for public services away from those that can afford it, to those less able to do so.

Our plea is that we start seriously discussing the extent to which deficits and debt are a major problem for Alberta. Clearly, paying interest on the debt is a significant cash flow problem that cannot be ignored.[7] Large foreign holdings of Albertan government debt in particular undermines the ability of Albertans to control the economy. But we must also ask about the related benefits deriving from government expenditures, and whether they represent assets to the province. We would be surprised if the representation of the deficit and debt in the Provincial Accounts would "fool" the bankers and financial analysts who arrange Alberta's borrowing[8], but the Public Accounts may undermine serious public debate about public finance and policy in Alberta. It seems that the rhetoric of debt and deficit currently serves as a convenient political rationale for restructuring Alberta's social and economic landscape. We fear that we are almost giving away the province's natural resource wealth and failing to provide for the future of our children in the false belief that it is unfair to pass any debt onto future generations. Future generations should bear their fair share of the costs of investments that they will benefit from. In the same way that parents may not mind passing on debts to their children if they also pass on assets that will yield substantial benefits to those children, leaving a debt is not unfair if the current generation provides real assets to the province. And any debt is unlikely even to be a significant burden if the population and the economy keep on growing.

Deficit Phobia

Political pronouncements and media coverage of the deficit/debt are reminiscent of "Chicken Little" of children's story fame who announces that "the sky is falling, the sky is falling" to anyone who might listen. Two questions arise for the Chicken Littles of Alberta. First, are deficits necessarily bad? The second question is whether the public accounts and the pronouncements of the accounting profession have created a false impression that the sky is falling.

The danger of deficits is frequently overstated, as Rosenbluth and Schworm showed in the British Columbian case.[9] Government revenues are likely to vary with the regular ups and downs of economic activity, yet it is unlikely that we would want government expenditures on education, health, or support for communities to fluctuate dramatically, year by year. Of course, for a resource based economy like Alberta's, those fluctuations can be quite extreme. The Klein government has succumbed to the temptation to cut spending to the revenue levels which McMillan and Warrack show (chapter ten), are at their lowest point, in real per capita terms, since 1975.

Keynes, a notable economist whose policy advice was central in getting many countries out of the depression of the 1930s and whose ideas formed the basis of the post war economic boom, offers another reason to be wary of the fiscal Chicken Littles. He showed that an important role of government is to operate counter to economic cycles. Economies tend to be cyclical with periods of growth followed by periods of decline. Expansionary cycles of five-to-ten years followed by similar recessionary cycles are not uncommon. Thus, over the longer-term, there will invariably be periods when government revenues exceed expenditures (surpluses) and periods where the converse is true (deficits). Indeed, in the ten years prior to 1983, Alberta enjoyed large and consistent surpluses.

Recognizing these cycles, good government consists of saving the surpluses from the expansionary cycles to buffer against the "rainy days" that inevitably follow. Good government requires a long-sighted perspective and the discipline to save during boom periods in order to avoid reactionary cutting during the down periods. Such discipline effectively buffers the citizenry against the vagaries of the marketplace, protecting those segments of society that are most vulnerable. A counter cyclical policy by governments helps maintain production and employment in slumps, and stops the economy from overheating in expansionary periods.

The preceding suggests that surpluses and deficits are natural consequences of the business cycle, but what do we mean by surpluses and deficits? We must here address the second question. To what extent do accounting statements like the public accounts represent the situation in the province? There have been numerous commentaries on government accounts by professional accounting bodies like the Institute of Chartered Accountants of Alberta and the Public Sector Accounting and Auditing Committee of the Canadian Institute, as well as the "business executives and financial experts" selected by Alberta's Treasurer in 1993 to review Alberta's financial position and procedures. These experts and accountants are almost invariably financial conservatives who represent or advise business, rather than the poor and less well off. Their attitude is to recognise all possible debts and potential financial obligations, but to ignore assets and revenues that are not reasonably certain. Attitudes to the recognition of revenues and expenditures are inevitably subjective, but the partisan judgments in Alberta have led to massive increases in the reported deficit and debt of the province in the last few years.[10]

For example, recognising loan guarantees and pension obligations for public employees in the public accounts has not actually affected these guarantees, loans, and obligations. They existed whether or not they were included in the financial statements. We suspect that investment bankers and credit rating agencies recognise the realities behind the cosmetic changes to the provincial accounts, and indeed it is rarely mentioned in the media that Alberta continues to enjoy a very high credit rating, second only to British Columbia of the Canadian provinces. But recording about $7.2 billion of pension liabilities and school board's debt in the public accounts, most of which was not included until a year or so ago, certainly makes the debt and deficit issue look more worrying to the average Albertan, and contributes to the paranoia and phobia that reduces our capacity to rationally debate policy options about provincial affairs. And we can expect the fiscal conservatives to discover further liabilities which they will want recognized in the future, for example the likely future costs of cleaning up the Swan Hills toxic waste plant or even some of the rivers affected by pulp mill operations. Each "recognition" will increase the apparent size of the debt, yet these costs exist whether they are recognized or not,[11] and the fiscal conservatives are unlikely to recognize potential revenues and assets with the same vigour.

When governments speak of surpluses and deficits they are basically referring to the difference between the amount of money collected during the year and the amount spent. Accountants refer to this as the cash basis of accounting; however because of the distortions caused by this method, the accrual basis of accounting is used by most nongovernmental organizations. To illustrate the difference between the cash basis and the accrual basis, let's take an individual example. Suppose that your daughter, Robyn, has just graduated from high school and is considering attending university. She has decided that a university education is important for both personal reasons and for future employment prospects. Since her income from part-time employment doesn't cover her expenses, she is forced to borrow in the short-term based on the expectation that once she completes her degree she will be in a better position to repay the loan. After graduating Robyn accepts a position as a representative for a book publisher. One of the requirements of the job is that she have a car. Since she is now accreditation-rich but still cash-poor, Robyn borrows money to purchase the car that will allow her to fulfil her job responsibilities.

Throughout her university years and in her first year of employment, Robyn's expenditures exceeded her income, resulting in deficits for five straight years. Does this mean that she was financially imprudent? Of course not, since investments in education and an automobile were capital expenditures that are expected to yield long-term benefits. Without these investments, Robyn would not have been in a position to accept employment and to be a contributing citizen. Similarly, well managed companies often borrow money when they believe that investing in projects will produce future returns, even if the returns take a long time to materialise. The important issues are the overall return on investment (whether the investment is in plant, roads, education, or a healthy and committed workforce) and having the cash flow to pay the interest on the debt.

These examples indicate the importance of deciding whether expenditures are capital investments expected to yield future benefits or expenditures for day-to-day operations. The accrual basis of accounting recognizes this distinction and capitalizes expenditures having future economic benefit. These expenditures are then depreciated over future periods, thereby matching the costs against the benefits to be received. In Robyn's case, we might argue that the costs of her education will provide life-long benefits and thus a small amount should be depreciated each year. Contrast this to the cash basis of accounting used by governments which treats these expenditures as an expense in the year incurred. Such an approach might suggest that investments in education are inappropriate since deficits result — a rather myopic conclusion when one looks at the longer term!

The problem is actually worse because financial statements do not recognise many important assets, such as the province's natural resources of oil and gas reserves, forests and mountains as well as its assets of an educated and healthy workforce and a well functioning infrastructure of roads, bridges and dams. Increasing the reported size of Alberta's assets reduces the apparent size of the province's net debt. Of course, there are difficult issues around the recognition of public assets, for example, whether they have a market value and whether they offer future public benefits, such as an increase in future economic activity that will yield future tax receipts. But these observations underscore the point that it does not make economic or social sense to construct provincial policies around the inevitably incomplete and subjective public accounts, especially when they have been loaded with liabilities but don't recognise important assets. In note 5 of the Provincial Accounts, $12.9 billion of tangible assets, such as roads and buildings, are listed; but these assets are not actually included in the Accounts. If we did so the net debt would be reduced from $13.4 billion to $0.5 billion! Fixation with deficit and debt is a recipe for long-term disaster.

Do We Have a Deficit Problem?

Our preceding discussion provides some conceptual tools that can be applied to government accounts when attempting to decide whether there is a deficit problem or not. Specifically, we want to be wary of the ways in which accounting techniques influence our calculations of revenue and expenditure. We also have to try to determine whether changes in revenues and expenditures are the consequence of cyclical business factors that will reverse themselves in the near term or whether they are the consequence of permanent structural changes in the Alberta economy.

To assess the influence of accounting techniques on the reported deficit, we adjusted deficit figures for items that should be accrued instead of expended. Specifically, we adjusted reported deficit numbers for the last ten years by removing capital expenditures that had been expended.[12] Also, since intergovernmental loans represent a government asset instead of a period expense, we removed loans that the Albertan government made to school boards in 1993 and 1994 ($84M and $438M respectively).

Making these adjustments is the first step in changing from cash basis to accrual basis financial statements, but it is also necessary to decide on appropriate depreciation rates for these capital assets. Since the majority of these capital expenditures relate to long-lived assets such as buildings, roads, and other infrastructure we decided to assume a depreciation rate based on a twenty-five year useful asset life.

As the figure 11.1 indicates, changing from cash-basis accounting to an accrual-basis accounting drastically changes deficit levels. For example, the 1994 adjusted deficit is $1.17 billion or $435 per capita, compared to the reported $1.68B or $625 per capita — a 30 percent difference.

These relatively straight-forward adjustments indicate how deficit numbers are sensitive to the method of accounting used by the provincial government (indeed all governments). Decisions on whether to capitalize or expense various items of expenditures have a significant influence on the reported level of deficit. By ignoring the longer-term economic value of capital expenditures, the provincial Tories have been able to present the deficit as over 30 percent higher than our adjustments would suggest. And as later sections of the paper argue, these inflated deficit numbers have been used as ammunition to justify decreased social expenditures.

Even after adjusting the reported deficit numbers, it appears that Alberta is still in a deficit position. But is this deficit just the normal consequence of a cyclical economy or is it indicative of permanent structural changes that require adjustment? Stated differently, is the deficit something that will disappear as the Alberta economy rebounds from its current slump or is government action required?

Looking at the previous graph, we can probably argue both perspectives convincingly. Yes, there is significant variability in the deficit/surplus figures, suggesting that the deficit might be the consequence of a cyclical economy. On the other hand, even the adjusted figures suggest that the province has been in a deficit position since 1987. Which viewpoint is correct?

To answer this question, it is necessary to examine government revenues and expenditures more closely. After all, the deficit simply represents the difference between what the government collects (revenues) and what the government spends (operating expenses). The next section considers changes in government revenue and expenditure patterns for the last ten years.

Provincial Revenues and Expenditures

Examining provincial revenues, two facts become immediately apparent. First, oil and gas royalty revenues are an important component of provincial revenues accounting for approximately 25 percent of revenues.

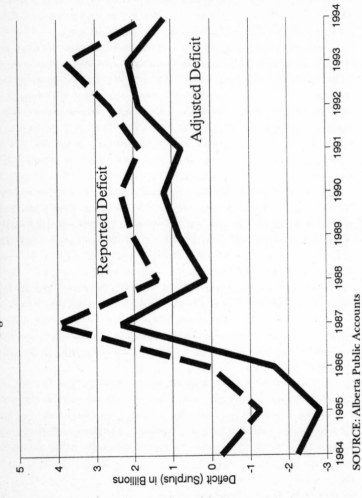

Figure 11.1: Alberta Deficit: 1984-1994

SOURCE: Alberta Public Accounts

Second, the absolute amount of these royalties has decreased substantially from $4.5 billion in 1983 to $2.2 billion in 1993 — a $2.3 billion drop that is larger than the projected 1994 deficit. In 1994, these royalties bounced back somewhat to $2.8 billion.

The taken-for-granted explanation for this decline is that resource prices have declined over this time period resulting in correspondingly lower government revenues. However, this explanation ignores two issues. First, why should Alberta, the owner of the oil and gas reserves, shoulder the full risk of these price changes. The oil and gas companies who drill the wells should share the risks of price changes with the province. Secondly, the oil and gas industry, that special interest group who support the Tories, have successfully lobbied for decreases in royalty rates and other provincial government incentives to the oil and gas industry. Further, the excuse that falling resource prices justify a lower tax contribution by those industries ignores royalty agreements that see government revenues decrease by an amount larger than resource price declines.

Take, for example, the following two graphs (figures 11.2 and 11.3). These graphs plot historical trends in government royalties divided by the market value of oil and gas production (market value is equal to the resource price multiplied by the amount of the resource produced). These two graphs demonstrate that royalty rates as a percentage of the market value of production have fallen steadily over the last fifteen years. Over this same period, total production of oil and gas has increased. Therefore, oil and gas companies are selling increasing amounts of a publicly-owned resource and paying the province less and less for doing so. To add insult to injury, the resource management costs associated with oil and gas production have increased over the last ten years (we suspect partially as a consequence of the increased production levels), resulting in an even lower net benefit from these public resources to the province.

Royalty agreements between the province and resource companies are primarily tied to the market value of oil and gas production, hence the assertion that decreased government revenues are the result of decreased world prices. This ignores the impact however of production incentives and royalty decreases/holidays granted by the government to these companies. For example, natural gas royalty rates were reduced in July 1985 and November 1986, and the province offered an "exploratory gas well incentive program" between 1985 and 1988 that provided a royalty holiday of up to $2 million per well. It has been estimated that the Alberta Royalty Tax Credit provided relief to producers of about $1.7 billion in the period 1987-92. Similar holidays and "incentives" were provided to oil producers in Al-

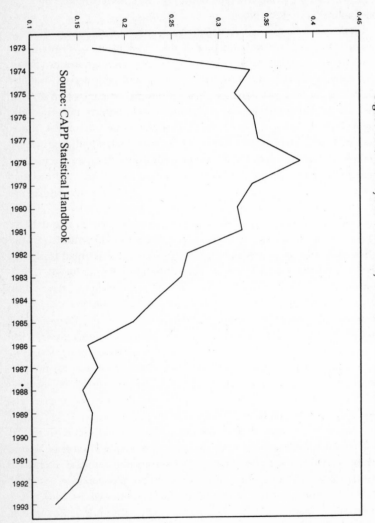

Figure 11.2: Oil Royalties Divided by the Market Value of Production

Source: CAPP Statistical Handbook

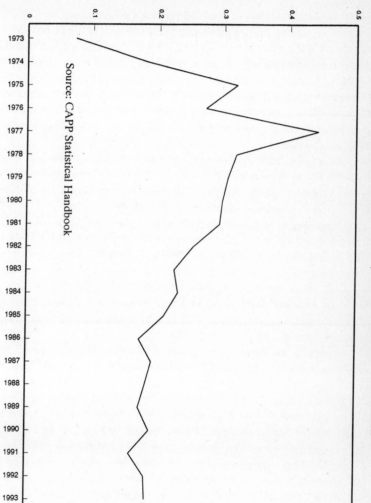

Figure 11.3: Gas Royalties Divided by the Market Value of Production

Source: CAPP Statistical Handbook

berta. It is unsurprising therefore that while resource prices have decreased since 1983, provincial royalty revenues have decreased by an even larger amount.

To illustrate the loss of potential revenues, we calculated an implicit 1983 royalty rate by dividing provincial royalty revenues by the market value of 1983 oil and gas production. As figure 11.4 on the following page shows, when we applied this implicit rate to 1993 production levels the amount of royalty revenues that would have been collected in 1993 if these rates had remained in place would have been $1.16 billion higher than was collected. Interestingly, a $1.16 billion increase in royalty revenues for 1994 would almost offset the $1.17 billion adjusted deficit figure that we calculated in the preceding section.

Our analysis thus suggests that decreased government revenues is a consequence of decreased royalty revenues, but what about expenditures? Are Albertans living beyond their means and receiving excessive levels of social services as government spokespersons are quick to assert?

According to McMillan and Warrack (chapter ten), historical trends indicate that government expenditures net of resource management costs have been declining throughout the 1980s and 1990s. Indeed, according to the authors, Alberta spent less per capita than the average of all Canadian provinces for a comparable set of social services. And the government's own Financial Review Commission acknowledged that the growth in government expenditures from 1986 to 1992 "has been below the combined rate of inflation and population growth."[13]

In sum, our review of historical revenue and expenditure patterns indicates that, contrary to government assertions, our deficit problems may be a revenue problem rather than an expenditure problem. Government policies have encouraged resource companies to sell off more and more of our oil and gas reserves while allowing these companies to contribute less and less for the privilege of doing so. Not only have these policies decreased the gross amount of royalty revenue, they have decreased the net amount by forcing the Alberta government to spend increased amounts on resource management. As our calculations indicate, Alberta's yearly deficit would be minimal if 1993 royalty rates as a percentage of the market value of oil and gas had been maintained at 1983 levels.

Political Ideology or Necessary Cuts?

If Alberta's deficit crisis is easily resolvable, why has the provincial government invested so much effort in convincing us otherwise and why has

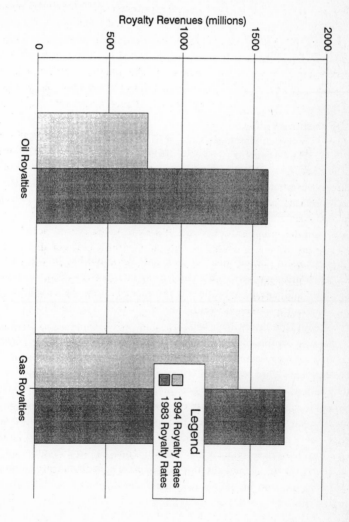

Figure 11.4: 1993 Royalties at 1993 verses 1983 Rates

Table 11.1
Social Assistance Cuts

	No. of People	Estimated per recipient decrease in benefits
STILL RECEIVING BENEFITS:		
Single employables	10,432	$708
Family benefits	47,522	$822
REMOVED FROM SOCIAL ASSISTANCE:		
Single employables	17,154	$5,436
Family benefits	16,846	$12,702

Sources: Government of Alberta, Family & Social Services; *Calgary Herald*, 20 August 1993, A1; and 27 July 1994, A9; and *Alberta Report*, 7 November 1994, 12.

the government slashed spending as it has? We would like to suggest that the deficit crisis has provided a convenient rationale for reorganizing the economic and social landscape. Or put more bluntly, the "Klein revolution" is about transferring wealth from the have-nots to the haves — a reverse Robin Hood story if you will.

To support this conclusion, we provide three examples; these include the financial consequences of social assistance, education, and senior spending cuts. Our contention is that these segments of the population, along with public servants, have been singled out to bear a disproportionate share of the announced spending cuts — that is, the financial impact of the cuts is greater than our adjusted per capita deficit of $435. Compared to other policy options that would impact all Albertans more or less equally (e.g., a sales tax or income tax), or policy options that would require the resource industry to maintain its historical levels of contributions (e.g., royalty revenues), the government has made decisions that target the least able-to-pay and the least able to participate.

Social Assistance Cuts
Social assistance recipients have been a favourite target of the provincial Tories. Statements such as "social assistance corrupts the incentive to

Table 11.2
Senior Assistance Cuts

Income level	No. of Households	Estimated per household decrease in benefits
$0-$10,999	60,766	($366)
$11,000-16,999	52,238	$679
$17,000-24,999	34,247	$968
$25,000+	35,201$	1,464

Sources: Government of Alberta, Senior Benefits documents; Statistics Canada, #93-331 (Ottawa: Statistics Canada, 1993); and the *Calgary Herald*, 9 March 1994, B3; and 30 June 1994, B4.

work" have served as convenient rationalizations to decrease social assistance payments and to arbitrarily remove individuals and families from social assistance.

As Table 11.1 indicates, decreased social assistance payments have had a significant negative impact on the individuals and families affected by these changes.[14] The financial impact of cuts to social assistance greatly exceeds our adjusted per capita deficit amount of $435. In fact, the poor have been forced to sacrifice over $350 million to help balance the books. In keeping with a reverse Robin Hood approach, these financial consequences are extremely regressive in that these individuals and families are the least able to absorb these changes (see also chapter twenty-one).

Senior Assistance Cuts

Although cuts affecting seniors were downplayed compared to the rhetoric surrounding social assistance cuts, changes to accommodation assistance programs and health care premiums had a significant effect on the incomes of seniors. After taking all the changes into consideration, it appears that only the seniors in the lowest income bracket are better off. Senior households with incomes greater than $11,000 will see a decrease in yearly benefits of at least $679 (since benefits are based on household incomes, we have stated changes on a household basis).[15]

Like changes to social assistance, changes to senior's benefits have had

Table 11.3
Education Cuts

	No. of Individuals	Estimated per individual decrease in benefits
University students	51,650	$327
College students	27,030	$126
Kindergarten	40,569	$595

Sources: Statistics Canada,#81-210 & #81-220 (Ottawa: Statistics Canada, 1991-92 and 1993-94); and the *Calgary Herald*, cf 21 October 1994, A1-3.

negative financial consequences for the approximately 180,000 seniors with household incomes above $11,000. They are collectively being "taxed" about $120 million in order to make the deficit look less. While Table 11.2 suggests that the changes are not regressive in the sense that the financial consequences are greater for households with higher incomes, two other factors should be borne in mind. First, regardless of the size of the household, an income of less than $17,000 falls below Statistics Canada Low Income Threshold (i.e., the poverty line). Secondly, these changes are certainly selective in that this implicit tax only applies to Alberta seniors — not to the population at large (see also chapter nineteen).

Education

Changes to kindergarten and postsecondary funding have increased the cost of education for students. While the expected tuition increase for university students is below the adjusted per capita deficit of $435, kindergarten students have seen a $595 decrease in funding. As Table 11.3 indicates, about 119,000 students have been affected by these changes (see also chapters thirteen and fourteen.)

Conclusion

Our starting point in this study was a series of questions regarding deficits and debt that are not often asked by provincial politicians: Are deficits necessarily bad? Do we have a deficit problem? Is this a revenue or expense problem? and What individuals and groups have been forced to bear a disproportionate share? were some of the questions that we tried to answer.

Our analyses argues that deficits are not inherently negative — good government consists of saving the surpluses from expansionary cycles to buffer against the recessionary cycles and deficits that inevitably follow. Further, we have to be wary of deficits that are in large part manufactured by conservative bias of recognizing almost every conceivable liability and ignoring many of the province's assets. In addition, the use of cash-basis accounting methods is inherently short-sighted in that they do not acknowledge the long-term benefits that the province's citizens and corporations receive from capital expenditures. As our analysis indicates, adjusting for these capital expenditures results in a deficit that is 30 percent less than reported by the government.

Additionally, we contend that, if there is a deficit problem, the problem lies with revenues more so than expenditures. Government practices have allowed resource companies to pay less tax at the same time that they are extracting ever-increasing amounts of oil and gas. In contrast, per capita expenditures on social services have declined over the last ten years resulting in per capita expenditures that are below the national average.

Finally, as examples of the political aspect of government budget decisions in Alberta, we highlight that social assistance recipients, seniors ,and students (especially those who would have gone to kindergarten) have borne a disproportionate share of the spending cuts. These cuts reflect a reverse Robin Hood syndrome. Instead of government policies that are progressive and fair — i.e., those that either target individuals/corporations with the ability to pay or target all Albertans equally — government cuts have negatively impacted individuals with the least ability to pay and the least ability to resist. Along with public servants, these individuals have been forced to bear the financial consequences of the government's decision not to levy any "new" individual or corporate taxes.

The rhetoric surrounding deficits and debt seems to have a remarkable staying power. Conservative "think-tanks," conservative politicians, business lobby groups,and the conservative accounting profession constantly bombard us with numbers purporting to show that social service spending must be cut if we are to remain competitive[16] and avert a crisis. But this rhetoric is not impermeable. We must ask impertinent questions such as, Are deficits necessarily bad? Do we have a deficit problem? Does it result from out-of-control expenditures or from tax reductions granted to large corporations? Why are some Albertans being asked to bear an unfair share of the deficit? Indeed, if the Albertan government is willing to break its social contract about the benefits that seniors, students, and welfare recipients can expect from the province, why do we not also debate the possibility of breaking the debt contracts with the bankers in New York and Toronto. The Social Credit government of Alberta renegotiated its debt agreements in 1937. We could consider the costs and benefits of doing so again. We must refuse to be cowed by "economic experts" and government "facts," and to accept that only contracts with Albertans can be broken. By refusing to be mesmerised by incomplete, contestable, and loaded financial statements, to step beyond the figures, we can expose the "sky is falling" ideology of deficits and debt.

Notes

1. We would like to thank Liz Cooper, Lane Daley, Trevor Harrison, and the participants at the Authors' Forum, held at the University of Alberta in January 1995, and the Alternative Perspectives on Accounting workshop at the University of Calgary for helpful comments. They do not necessarily agree with the views expressed herein.
2. C. Szekeres and S. G. Lanes, *A Child's First Book of Nursery Tales* (New York: A Golden Book, 1983), 33.
3. NovAtel, Magcan, and the Principal Group are but three of these scandals.
4. The Deficit Elimination Act set target deficit ceilings of $1.8 billion in 1994-5, $0.8 billion in 1995-56, and a zero deficit in 1996-97. The revised figures are $1.55 billion, $0.497 billion, and a surplus of 212 million in 1996-97. Due to greater than anticipated tax revenues, particularly from oil and gas, an annual surplus is actually likely to be achieved even quicker than planned.
5. In fact, the Public Accounts offer a number of alternative figures, depending on what is included in the calculations. The 1994 deficit as defined consistent with the Deficit Elimination Act is $1.384 billion. What is rarely reported is that the Accounts also show that there is a surplus of $1.77 billion on the delivery of government programs, before expenditures on interest and capital expenditures.
6. Although Kneebone offers a recent history (in *Canadian Public Policy*, June 1994) his analysis is much more general. It only goes to 1993 and unproblematically relies on Statistics Canada data.
7. Unlike the rest of Canada, and contrary to the comments in *Canadian Forum*'s June 1993 discussion on "Demystifying Debt," Alberta's debt and deficit issue is not so much about the level of interest rates. Debt servicing costs are more or less balanced by the income (interest and dividends received) the province earns on its investments, notably in the Heritage Savings Trust Fund.
8. Borrowers are more concerned about a province's ability to pay any debts, perhaps through increasing tax or economic growth. It is worth noting that the credit rating of the province has remained at AA for Standard and Poors since 1987, neither reduced in the Getty years, nor increased since Klein took over.

Further, it is estimated that a change in Alberta's rating will alter the interest rate we would pay on new debt by between one-eighth and one-quarter of a percent.

9. See G. Rosenbluth and W. Schworm, "The Illusion of Provincial Deficit." In W. Magnusson et al., eds., *The New Reality: The Politics of Restraint in British Columbia* (Vancouver: New Star Books, 1984).

10. The partisan nature of accounting treatments is shown by what the accounts do, or do not, make visible. Whereas the pensions of public employees are now included in the public accounts, the obligations of the province to its seniors, the disabled, and to students are not included.

11. There may be progressive reasons to recognise the costs of environmental clean-up in Provincial Accounts, particularly if it draws attention to the costs to Albertans of allowing private corporations to pollute the environment. Yet, the basic point is that potential liabilities are recognised by fiscal conservatives, but many provincial assets, including clean air and water, as well as the general infrastructure of roads, hospitals, schools, and dams, are deemed too difficult or intangible to measure.

12. Let's take the 1994 figures to illustrate our calculations. Total expenditure for 1994 is $14,926 million, from which we deducted the capital expenditures of $692 million and determined a depreciation figure of $27.68 million (one-twenty-fifth of $692 million). That depreciation expense will then be charged as an expense for each of the next twenty-five years. The final figure for expenses is $14,854 billion (14,926-692+620, the depreciation charge brought forward from the previous nine years).

13. Alberta, Financial Review Commission (Edmonton: Government of Alberta, 1993), 15.

14. It is important to note that the social assistance rates used in the following table represent the maximum available benefits: caseworkers have discretion to adjust these rates downward.

15. Of course, senior assistance consists of a variety of programs with assistance based on income, family size, and type of accommodation. The figures have been adjusted to accommodate these complexities.

16. Commentators such as Krugman (see, for example, "Competitiveness: A Dangerous Obsession," *Foreign Affairs* [March 1994]) have observed that the view that national and provincial policies should be based on competitive position ignores the fact that most national and regional production and consumption takes place within the borders of the region. It thus makes only limited sense to base government policy on attempts to make the region "internationally competitive," especially if this is at the expense of those who live in the province. Indeed, as Sten Drugge points out in chapter twelve, the Alberta Tories appeal to "The Alberta Advantage" is unlikely to attract large inflows of international capital into the province.

Chapter Twelve

THE ALBERTA TAX ADVANTAGE: MYTH AND REALITY

Sten Drugge

It is clear that our low tax rates are possible only because of our natural wealth. If energy prices or markets deteriorate, or if expenditures on services cannot be contained, there will be no alternative but to look at a combination of service cuts and tax increases.

Lou Hyndman, Provincial Treasurer, 1984.[1]

In his budget address of May 6, 1993, Alberta Treasurer Jim Dinning introduced his government's "budget-plan" for Alberta.[2] The plan's purpose is to balance the provincial government's budget by fiscal year 1996-97.

The precise details of this budget plan were stated in the legislative assembly February 24, 1994.[3] This budget plan indicated that the large provincial deficits occurring since fiscal year 1986-87 to the present were wholly due to excessive government spending, and not due to deficiencies in provincial tax collections.

On numerous occasions the government has defended this one-sided approach to attacking the deficit problems of the province on the grounds that the current tax regime confers an "Alberta advantage" to the economic performance of the province. This chapter examines the efficacy of this argument.

The Real Sources of the 1992-93 Deficit

The government's assertion that the recent deficits are wholly due to excessive government spending is empirically difficult to defend. Real government expenditures in Alberta in fact have not increased significantly since 1986, and just prior to the large deficit of 1992-93, Alberta's per capita spending was only 2.8 percent above the other nine-province average. If the exceptionally large expenditures on conservation and industrial programs are deducted from Alberta's total expenditures, Alberta's per capita expenditures by 1991-92 fell below the average of the other nine provinces (see McMillan and Warrack, chapter ten).

The real source of the deficits reported since 1986-87 was the collapse of oil prices in that year from $30 to $12 U.S. per barrel, and this resulted in a huge decline in natural resource revenues year-over-year of approximately $3 billion, amounting to a 23 percent decline in overall government revenues in that one year. This revenue decline was accentuated by the implementation of the "Alberta Economic Resurgence Plan" introduced in 1982, which doubled both the tax credit on Crown royalties from 25 percent to 50 percent and the maximum annual allowable credit from $1 million to $2 million. This amounted to a total tax expenditure estimated at $1.6 billion over the period 1982-83 to 1984-85.[4] The reported deficit of 1992-93 (-$3.4 billion), that precipitated the current government expenditure cuts, was caused by this ongoing structural tax deficiency from energy royalty losses, coupled with further losses from personal and corporate income tax revenue, as the national recession struck Alberta in 1992-93. Indeed, government expenditures in fiscal 1992-93 actually declined by 1.5 percent, while revenue fell by 11 percent.

A previous Alberta Treasurer, Dick Johnston, in his 1987 budget address pointed out that prior to the oil price collapse in 1986-87, natural resource revenues were the equivalent to an 18 percent provincial sales tax, reduced to the equivalent of a 6 percent rate after the oil price collapse of 1986-87.[5] Additionally, Treasurer Jim Dinning in his 1993 budget address estimated that should Alberta apply the typical tax regimes existing in the other nine provinces, revenues would have increased by $3 billion in fiscal year 1992-93, virtually balancing the government's operating deficit.[6] These data notwithstanding, the government has defended this deficient tax effort that is producing Alberta's recent deficits, based on the concept of the "Alberta advantage."

The Alberta "Advantage"

This justification for low taxes as an incentive for business investment and personal consumption is never fully documented, seemingly based on an appeal to common sense. For example, in his 1989 budget speech, Treasurer Dick Johnston stated that "Alberta corporations benefited from a competitive tax climate ... our corporate tax structure has encouraged corporations to invest and create jobs." Albertans are proud to live in the only province without a retail sales tax.[7]

> Albertans already pay the lowest personal income taxes in Canada. They do not pay a provincial sales tax. This budget enhances Alberta's already substantial tax advantage. Alberta will continue to be the best place in Canada to live and work.[8]

Along these same lines, the Alberta Tax Reform Commission was established by the Treasurer of Alberta in September 1993 with the goal of making proposals to "put in place a tax system that fosters the economic prosperity and security of Albertans." The Commission's conclusions were that the best tax mix provides the "lowest possible personal and corporate tax rates to improve competitiveness and economic prosperity for individuals."[9]

Alberta Treasurer Jim Dinning's 1995 Budget paper, "Building a Strong Foundation," explicitly uses this concept of the Alberta advantage.[10] However, its evaluative time frame is highly selective (1990-95), a period during which the rest of Canada was experiencing a severe recession, while Alberta's economy was benefiting from improved oil and gas sales. Notably, the terms of reference of the Alberta advantage have been expanded to include investment in human capital. For example, both the role of post-secondary education in producing high labour quality and the relatively better performance of Alberta students in basic reading, math, and writing skills, are also now cited as important by the treasurer.

Taxation and Economic Advantage

Alberta's economic strategy is implicitly based on the premise that low-taxes are a key locational attraction for industry investment, and are a substantial factor in producing high regional consumer spending.

This casual approach to location theory does not robustly accord, however, with generally accepted location models employed by regional analysts. In these models, the two strategic elements are market advantage (in terms of volumes of sales) and unit price advantage, combined with low-cost, high quality inputs, inclusive of low transport costs on products and inputs.

Maximum profits are therefore obtained by simultaneously counterbalancing spatially-determined market revenue advantages and input costs advantages. The government's ad hoc approach to regional location theory stands this well-received location theory on its head, contending that after-tax profits drive the regional economy, ignoring those strategic factors which determine business profitability in the first place.

The second element of the government's policy "model" is somewhat more realistic. Low personal income taxes are assumed to provide a basis for powerful consumer spending in a region. Nonetheless, this simplistic approach also ignores more fundamental factors in consumer expenditure behaviour, such as regional worker productivity and hence, wage and salary levels, wealth levels, and current interest rates.

Tax Advantage and Recent Survey Results

Two very recent small-business surveys have been published by Statistics Canada, indicating the significant factors in their economic success.[11] The results of such a survey are important insofar as Provincial Treasurer Dick Johnston in his budget address of 1987 stated that "small businesses play a key role in the government's diversification strategy."[12] Indeed, a small-business preferential tax exists in the province to give special aid to this industry subgroup.

The findings of these national surveys do not substantiate the low-tax policy position of the Government of Alberta. The Statistics Canada survey covered 1,480 successful small businesses over the period 1984 to 1988, asking them to identify the most important elements in their economic success, as measured by growth in employment, assets and sales. The findings of this survey were consistent with the regional locational model noted above. Input and market demand factors were ranked the highest (skilled management, skilled labour, and marketing ability, combined with market demand or access were the top four elements cited). Contrary to the espoused belief of Alberta government officials, low corporate or business taxes were not mentioned at all in the survey as contributors to business success, although the last-ranked was government assistance, in the form of export, research, and development incentives, and market information.

Data in this survey was also compiled vis-a-vis factors which contributed most to the outstandingly successful firms, as compared to the least of the also "successful." Ranked as the foremost factor in the most successful firms was research and development capacity, access to markets, technological ability, and government assistance, while the "less" successful firms were weak in these areas. Low taxes again were not cited as a significant factor in the economic performance of these most successful of firms.

The concept of low regional tax rates as a source of economic advantage appears simply to be based on armchair empiricism related to an ideological vision of economic realities. The fundamental sources of business advantage are the key locational demand and supply variables specifically cited in micro-economic terms in the national survey.

The Alberta Advantage: Comparisons of Economic Advantage

A further test of the government of Alberta's contention that low tax effort provides a basis for superior economic performance can be undertaken by inter-provincial comparisons of key economic measures of performance.

In particular, the low corporate tax rates that have prevailed in the province for decades should have been expected to produce high rates of real investment in business, plant, machinery, and equipment, while the long-term presence of low personal income taxes and the absence of a provincial sales tax would be expected to produce relatively high rates of increase in real consumer expenditures over time. While these specific elements of performance are key in evaluating the advantages to the private business and consumption sectors in the province, other performance measures are also extremely useful. For example, relative bankruptcy rates, unemployment rates, public sector debt growth, and overall real economic growth performance in the province also are vital measures of comparative performance.

Table 12.1 provides longer-term data over the period 1981 to 1993, indicating Alberta's relative economic performance, as measured by these economic indicators, compared to that of the neighbouring provinces of British Columbia and Saskatchewan, as well as Ontario and Canada as a whole. The extended period (1981-93) is carefully selected to allow the presence of a low tax regime to have significant positive economic effects, if such exist. This period allows the analyst to ascertain Alberta's relative economic performance during a period covering two national recessions, and two energy price shocks to the province's energy industries. Given the Alberta "advantage" as related to the low taxation which prevailed during this entire period, the expectation would be that the province's relative economic performance would have been superior to the national and other provincial averages.

Table 12.1 clearly indicates Alberta's deficient economic performance (for the period 1981-93) in average rate of change in two key tax-related elements: real business investment performance was -3.0 percent per annum, compared to Ontario's at 7 percent, and the overall average rate of change in Canada of 2.9 percent.

Table 12.1
Measures of Alberta's Economic Performance Compared To British
Columbia, Saskatchewan, Ontario and Canada, 1981-1993

	Alberta	Canada	B.C	Sask.	Ontario
Average Annual Real Economic Growth Rate	0.6	2.54	2.9	0.5	3.5
Average Annual Unemployment Rate	8.3	9.6	10.7	7.3	7.9
Average Bankruptcy Ratio*	1.50	.87	1.24	.72	.72
Average Annual Real Growth Rate, Retail Sales	0.3	0.7	1.3	-1.2	0.8
Average Annual Real Growth Rate, Business Investment	-3.0	2.9	1.4	1.6	7.1
Average Annual Growth Rate, Gross Debt	33.0	28.6	47.1	30.8	22.0

*Measured as the ratio of the relative size of the province's economy to the national economy (12% in Alberta's case), divided into Alberta's percentage of all Canadian bankruptcies (18%), given a bankruptcy ratio in Alberta of 1.53 over the period 1981-1993.

Sources: Statistics Canada, *Canadian Economic Observer: Historical Statistical Supplement, 1992-93* (Ottawa: Statistics Canada, 1993), Table 12.2, 103; Table 12.5, 106; Table 44; Table 12.10, 110; Table 12.13, 114; Statistics Canada, *Provincial Economic Accounts: Annual Estimate, 1988-92* (Ottawa: Statistics Canada, 1994), Analytic Table, xivi-livi; and Statistics Canada, *Public Sector Assets and Liabilities: Historical Overview* (Ottawa: Statistics Canada, 1994), Table 1.11, 49-50.

Secondly, the effect of low personal income taxes and the lack of provincial sales tax does not provide Alberta with a performance superiority in average annual growth rates in real retail sales (0.3 percent) compared to British Columbia's average growth rate of 1.3 percent, or the national growth rate of 0.7 percent.

Low business taxes would be expected to provide a successful business climate in the province, but the data in Table 12.1 indicates that Alberta's bankruptcy rate was 53 percent larger than its relative economic size compared to the national economy. Alberta's public sector gross debt grew much faster than the federal government's over this period at 33 percent per annum, compared to 28.6 percent, and was only exceeded by British Columbia's rate (47 percent) in this sample. As an omnibus measure of performance, the province's average real growth rate from 1981 to 1993 (0.6 percent) was also deficient compared to the national average of 2.5 percent. (Although not noted in Table 12.1, Alberta's real income per person fell from first to third among the ten provinces over this period.) Only the provincial unemployment performance measure appears reasonable, when compared to the national average rate.

The conclusion to be drawn from this data is that Alberta's relative economic performance over the medium term has been deficient, low taxes notwithstanding. The deficient economic performance prevailing over this period was undoubtedly caused by the fundamental factors that drive Alberta's regional economy. These fundamentals are the unit prices and volumes of crude oil, natural gas, and agricultural sales. Alberta's deficient performance over the period 1981 to 1993 stemmed from the two oil price shocks of 1982 and 1986, excess volumes of natural gas supplies in North America during the 1980s, and significant price declines in agricultural products during this period. The province's low tax effort simply could not begin to compensate for these negative fundamentals affecting Alberta's regional economic performance.

More directly, the causal relationship between low taxes and the Alberta advantage is exactly the reverse of the government's ad hoc model: Alberta's economic advantage is based upon revenue-rich oil and gas production, and this has allowed the low-tax regime that exists in the province.

Mistargeting the Deficit Source: Economic Implications

The continued mistargeting of the real sources of the most recent deficits onto public expenditure levels, while ignoring obvious revenue deficiencies will have serious social and economic implications for the

province. In strategic terms, the current Alberta budget plan can be seen as
an attempt to reduce human capital investment in the province, in order to
sustain private consumption levels.

Prior to the expenditure reductions now underway, Alberta's per capita
expenditures in health care ranked third among the provinces, fifth in family welfare, and seventh in per capita expenditure on education. If expenditure cuts in these three programs occur up to 1997 (as outlined in the 1994
budget address), per capita spending in Alberta on health and welfare will
be reduced to eighth rank, and education per capita expenditures will lead
Alberta to be tied for ninth rank with a number of other provinces. Moreover, these rank estimates for 1997 are based on the optimistic assumption
that no other provincial government will increase its expenditures to 1997
in these categories. (For example, British Columbia and Saskatchewan in
their budget-balancing efforts to 1997, have both proposed increases in expenditures in health and education.)

This reduced investment in human capital negatively affects precisely
those factors such as the quality of labour and management noted as the
key sources of economic success in the small business surveys cited above.
These expenditure reductions must therefore raise serious questions about
the underlying logic of the government's policies.

The government's rigid adherence to the politically expedient but fal-
lacious concept of the low-tax advantage requires, in the face of ongoing
deficits, that large reductions be made in health care, public and post-secondary education, and social welfare spending. It should be obvious that
this defense of a false concept of economic advantage can lead to serious
impairment and damage to the real factors of economic advantage in the
form of a healthy, well-trained management and labour force. The premier
of the province has stated that historically no jurisdiction has ever taxed its
way to prosperity; but if taxes are wisely spent on human resource development, taxing ourselves is the key to economic prosperity in the context of
the global economy. Indeed, if low taxation is such an economically successful strategy, why haven't all the other provinces followed suit, even Prince
Edward Island, thereby becoming the economic powerhouse of Canada?

The Current Economic Outlook

Can the government of Alberta balance its budget in fiscal year 1997 by
this unilateral approach, based solely on expenditure reductions? A balanced budget does not depend on the size or rapidity of public sector expenditure reductions, as the government contends, but more

fundamentally relates to the price and output performance of Alberta's key energy and agricultural industries in the critical period leading up to 1997.

It is noteworthy that during the fiscal period 1993 to 1994, the government of Alberta was able to reduce its budgetary deficit below target and produce a surplus of $105 million because of windfall oil and gas royalty increases, and unexpected gains in corporate income tax revenues. But what if this situation is quickly reversed by unexpected declines in oil and gas prices equivalent to the unexpected increases that occurred in 1993-94? This possibility represents the Alberta "disadvantage" and ominously indicates, given the government's budget balancing strategy, that no matter how severe revenue reductions may be in the future, government expenditures on health, education, and welfare must fall by equal amounts in order to balance the province's budget. This strategy cannot be the basis for an effective, realistic public policy.

If oil prices seriously decline in the fiscal period to 1997, as natural gas prices already have, current government expenditure cuts to balance the budget can be viewed as a rapid re-deployment of deck chairs on an economic Titanic. The worst-case scenario is that oil and gas prices simultaneously decline through 1997, producing contractional forces on Alberta's regional economy from the energy export sector, combined with the budget-planned contractionary fiscal policy in the public sector. Indeed, Treasurer Jim Dinning has stated that if natural gas prices do not reverse their current decline from the $1.80 per thousand cubic foot price factored into the 1994-95 budget (the current February 1995 price is $1.39 per thousand cubic feet), the province's entire budget-balancing time frame may have to be prolonged beyond 1997.[13]

The most serious consequence of this imbalanced approach is related to the inherent instability of Alberta's regional economy and the resulting violent instability in public sector budget balances. In the short or even medium term, provincial policy can do little to change the industrial structure of the province. Of critical policy importance is the need for a new portfolio of selected tax sources to simultaneously drive a stable tax wedge between the province's unstable economy and its Treasury, and to bring a more balanced closure on current deficits without doing serious damage to Alberta's real economic advantages.

Conclusion

A current overview of Alberta public finances poses an interesting case study of missed opportunities and wishful thinking. Since the major factor in producing Alberta's deficits was the collapse of oil prices in 1986-87, why didn't the government of the day publicly acknowledge the very serious loss of government revenue out of the energy sector that had occurred through no fault of its own?

At the time, budget-balancing would have required unpopular out-of-pocket tax increases for Albertans, since the energy sector was no longer able to pay the previous levels of taxes on behalf of Albertans. Later, the government feared a political backlash to increased taxation, given that it had successfully squandered hundreds of millions of dollars in failed industrial ventures such as Magcan, Gainer's, and NovAtel. Finally, administrations between 1987 and 1993 had consistently stated that the province's budget would be balanced, but were unable to do so, even though real expenditures did not increase over this period. Having continually failed to deliver on this promise, the government fell back on its other major promise that a sales tax (or other income-based tax increases) would not be imposed on the province.

Having promised no significant tax increases and no provincial sales tax, the low tax regime existing in the province required some modest intellectual justification; thus the concept of the "Alberta tax advantage" was coined. This low-tax, no sales tax posture has succeeded, however, in poisoning the policy well. As a result, both the current administration and — conceivably — future ones may fail to undertake the correct targeting of the province's revenue-generated deficit problems, thus producing further reductions in human capital investment that are of serious consequence to the real economic competitiveness of a modern industrial society. Simultaneously, this adamant refusal to restructure the deficient Alberta tax system delays balancing the province's budget, while sustaining the destabilizing forces that have so seriously affected Alberta's public sector budget balances in the past.

Notes

1. Alberta Treasury, *Budget Speech*. Presented by Lou Hyndman (Edmonton: Alberta Treasury, 27 March 1984).
2. Alberta Treasury, *Budget '93: A Financial Plan For Alberta*. Presented by Jim Dinning (Edmonton: Alberta Treasury, 6 May 1993).
3. Alberta Treasury, *Budget '94: Securing Alberta's Future*. Presented by Jim Dinning (Edmonton: Alberta Treasury, 24 February 1994).
4. Alberta Treasury, *Budget Speech*. Presented by Lou Hyndman (Edmonton: Alberta Treasury, 27 March 1984), 9 and 23.

5. Alberta Treasury, *Budget Address, 1987*. Presented by Dick Johnston (Edmonton: Alberta Treasury, 20 March 1987, 20.

6. Alberta Treasury, *Budget '93: A Financial Plan For Alberta*. Presented by Jim Dinning (Edmonton: Alberta Treasury, 6 May 1993), 12.

7. Alberta Treasury, *Budget Address, 1989*. Presented by Dick Johnston (Edmonton: Alberta Treasury, 8 June 1989), 21.

8. Alberta Treasury, *Budget Address, 1992*. Presented by Dick Johnston (Edmonton: Alberta Treasury, 13 April 1992), 13.

9. Alberta Financial Review Commission, Report to Albertans (Edmonton: AFRC, March 1993).

10. Alberta Treasury, *Budget '95: Building a Strong Foundation*. Presented by Jim Dinning (Edmonton: Alberta Treasury, 21 February 1995), 117-130.

11. J. Baldwin, M. Rafiquzzaman, and W. Chandler, "A Profile of Growing Small Firms," In *Canadian Economic Observer Monthly* (Feature article) (February 1994), 3.13.16. See also J. Baldwin, M. Rafiquzzaman, and W. Chandler, "Innovation: The Key to Success in Small Firms," In *Canadian Economic Observer Monthly* (Feature article) (August 1994), 3.1 -3.14.

12. Alberta Treasury, *Budget Address, 1987*, 20.

13. *Edmonton Journal*, 20 November 1994, 1.

SECTORS

Chapter Thirteen

RESTRUCTURING FROM THE RIGHT: SCHOOL REFORM IN ALBERTA[1]

Heather-jane Robertson and Maude Barlow

"Meeting the needs of Alberta students is the highest priority for this government — that's what Albertans told us during our consultation — to make Albertans' priorities government's priorities. Our kids come first."

Halvar Jonson, Alberta minister of education.[2]

Indeed they do. First to feel the effects of the Alberta government's all-out assault on the deficit. In his three-year plan to eliminate Alberta's $2.4 billion deficit by 1997, Premier Klein put small children at the head of the line to feel the full force of his spending cuts.

Assuring parents that "preparing children for formal learning can be attained with less time in the classroom," the government cut funding to kindergarten by 50 percent, while graciously allowing individual schools to decide whether to halve the hours of kindergarten instruction, or to bill parents to make up the shortfall. Recognizing that these same small children also need daycare, subsidies for this program were also cut by 20 percent.[3] Taxpayers seemed to agree that they had been unwisely subsidizing too many government-dependent five year olds who needed incentives to stand on their own two tiny feet. While the minister justified the "kindergarten clawback" on budgetary grounds, "user-pay" education was in fact just one of many ideological reforms on their way.

This ideology begins with getting rid of government. In the "new" Alberta, there will be sixty school boards rather than 141. Many of their regular functions, including setting mill rates, appointing superintendents, and determining spending have been appropriated by the provincial government; the rest are to be delegated to individual schools and "parent councils." The minister broadly hinted that communities may no longer need to bother electing trustees, as their only remaining function will be to advise government.[4] This unanticipated raid on school board authority was seen by some as perverse, given the prevailing rhetoric about local autonomy. But as the government had planned, public attention focused on funding, not on the transfer of power.

Reforms proposed in the "Business Plan" of Alberta Education which would have equally great effects received even less attention.[5] The "Plan" decreed that all schools were to adopt "school-based management." Standardized achievement testing would be increased; reporting on results would be "increased and improved." Sixty-six community schools which provided services for families of at-risk students would lose their funding. Teachers would be placed on a province-wide payscale; their salaries cut by a minimum of 5 percent. Teacher certification would be reviewed. The government promised to "involve business in the delivery of career and technology studies," "increase the use of technology to deliver education," provide "incentives to schools for student achievement," "privatize some services" of the Ministry, and introduce "joint selection of superintendents" with the few remaining school boards. The political centrepiece of the Klein reforms appeared in two phrases: "provide more choice and more parental involvement" and "pilot charter schools."

Government rhetoric notwithstanding, the bulk of these reforms were neither pedagogical nor fiscal, but ideological and political, consistent with ultra-conservative beliefs about the role of government, the role of the private sector and a deregulated marketplace. As with the rest of the Klein agenda, deficit-mongering enabled the government to couch its extremism in the language of fiscal responsibility. As the *Edmonton Journal* put it:

> There is a blind assumption, untested by fact or reality, that government can do nothing well. Everything that was once in public hands, maintained as a public trust for the public interest, must be turned over to private hands ... much of what the government proposes has nothing to do with finances and everything to do with ideology.[6]

But Klein was not playing to the likes of the press. A more important audience was beginning to take notice. Politicians of all persuasions began viewing Alberta as a "political petri dish," and public opinion seemed to indicate that nothing toxic to political self-interest was breeding. If anything, it appeared that Canadians' resistance to applied neoconservatism had been overestimated.

There has been resistance, of course, but those who protested that the education cuts amounted to child abuse were dismissed "with the worst expletive this ideology knows — they're 'special interest groups' so they must be ignored." Public-sector critics were treated with particular contempt, as the government saw public employees as the "inferior, even evil" enemy of the private sector.[7] The Alberta Teachers' Association (ATA) drew its share of government hostility, and the credibility of its opposition was cleverly undermined by including teacher paycuts in the reform package, making it easier for the government to claim that the ATA was driven by selfish motives.

Countering the positioning of the initiatives as bitter but necessary medicine would not be easy. School boards were preoccupied by the prospect of their own demise. The number and complexity of the intertwined educational effects of the reforms left teachers debating which issues to fight. The public was unlikely to follow long explanations about how the reforms would transform the institution of public education, not just how schools operated. Other organizations and unions might be sympathetic, but they were fully occupied fighting severe cuts to their own service areas.

Yet a plan was formulated; the ATA swiftly launched a half-million dollar public information campaign and commissioned a public opinion poll. The union made some political mileage with the findings: seventy-two percent thought the government had been spending "the right amount" or "too little" on education; half preferred to see taxes increased rather than 239 million dollars cut.[8] Suddenly there were rumblings that the ATA had become too militant and too powerful. Private members bills attempted to split the organization into a "professional" body and a "union" body. Another sought to withdraw ATA's entitlement to automatic membership and union dues. If the ATA really cared about education, the premier taunted, why didn't it volunteer pay cuts of 5 percent to help out? ATA president Bauni Mackay agreed, but only in exchange for guarantees on class size and a 300-day moratorium to allow for public discussion of education reform. The ATA also asked Premier Klein for a commitment to maintain publicly-funded schools open to all children, to prohibit tuition fees in public schools, and to ensure that all teachers in publicly-funded schools would be certified professionals. The premier refused.[9]

Parent Power!

Premier Klein and Minister Jonson claimed that the "Business Plan" represented populist will, as expressed at the invitational consultations

known as the Premier's Roundtables on Education. Yet the power grab of
Board functions, and the consolidation of authority at the provincial level
seemed to contradict the spirit of the Roundtables, which had been convened under the theme of "greater local autonomy." In response, the government claimed that the principle of "local autonomy" would be upheld
by empowering parents. The fact that those losing power were democrati-
cally elected, while those gaining power represented only themselves has
not been of particular public concern, which comes as little surprise in an
antigovernment climate.

"Parent control" is the rallying cry of restructure-from-the-right advocates, and a doctrine of the ideology of populism. "Parents have the ultimate authority over education ... but we have surrendered that to
government," says influential Alberta education critic Joe Freedman.[10] But
it is not just populists who see potential in breaking the hold of "the system." According to some, "parent and teacher" -run schools are models of
co-operation that are "finding enthusiastic support from one sector with a
particularly sharp eye on public schools — the business community." "We
don't have the luxury of solitudes any more, or the luxury of enemies," says
Gordon Cressy, president of The Learning Partnership, an organization devoted to creating closer ties between schools and the private sector.[11]

The question of the appropriate role of parents is not the exclusive
concern of the far right or business lobbies. "Reaching out" to parents is a
philosophy preached (if only intermittently practised) by schools everywhere. When parent involvement is low, the school is usually blamed for being unfriendly, condescending, or secretive. *Maclean's* suggests that parent
activism is a response to the incompetency of schools:

> Employing a vocabulary of so-called "edubabble" about "child-
> centred learning" and "the primacy of self-esteem," parents
> feel that the educational establishment has closed ranks, ex-
> cluding outsiders from the debate. In the process, they say, edu-
> cators have camouflaged their own failure to ensure that
> children learn the basics.[12]

There appears to be enough blame to spread around. Parents are sometimes
scapegoated as disinterested, but just as many are disinclined to become involved with the school. Some parents believe that what happens at school is
the school's business; but more seem to be unable to find the time or energy
to be active in the life of the school. With the average two-parent family putting in a seventy-five hour workweek (according to Statistics Canada), drop-

ping in on class during the school day is out of the question. Whatever the appropriate role of parents under ideal circumstances, day-to-day realities shape the parent-school relationship more than the philosophy of the school.

In a December 1994 document outlining the "roles and responsibilities" of various groups, Alberta Education presented a menu of options for local school councils.[13] While they must exist for every school, each has the power — after it has been "selected" — to determine whether it will play a minimal and token role, or whether it will take advantage of the new prerogatives it has been granted. The activist school council "can be involved" in "... determining the school's overall mission, philosophy, policies, rules, and objectives; ... deciding what types of programs to offer; ... extracurricular activities; ... establishing methods of reporting student achievement results to parents and the public; ... decid[ing] what types of school staff to select, and the criteria for selection; and to contribute to decisions" about selecting the principal.

Powers not taken up by the parent council will default to the principal and staff. The council's chair, vice-chair, and the majority of its members must be the parents or guardians of registered students; "at least" one teacher, secondary student, and "community" representative make up the other voting members. While parent representatives are to be elected by parents present at an annual meeting, no minimum participation rate has been established, and no voting procedures are prescribed. Only following their election are councillors to "... identify the areas in which they intend to have primary or contributory roles in decision-making." The council alone decides if it will be minimalist or activist; the dynamics of micropolitics will determine whether it is effective, frustrated, or merely deeply divided.

It does not require a conspiracy theorist to recognize how easily a council might be hi-jacked. Every school that takes "parent participation" seriously knows that its most active parents are not necessarily representative of the parent body. This is clear even when parents play a small role in the school decisions; it becomes a major equity issue when individual schools control program, staffing, and budget decisions. There is a significant danger of disenfranchising those families who feel that the school is not responding to their needs. Parent councils will attract the most confident, vocal, and persuasive — read middle-class — parents whose life experiences and priorities may not be the same as those of the less-privileged members of the school community. The opportunities for a narrow group sharing a particular religious, political, or pedagogical persuasion to seize control are abundant.

In theory, everyone wants parents involved. In practice, there are many problems to be worked out, as new possibilities for school-based chaos are presented when the inexperienced struggle over the undefined. Without a coherent plan, "empowering parents" is not just a downloading of decision-making, it is the downloading of the tensions created by a system in which expectations exceed resources, and in which pedagogical and political directives are in conflict.

Adding inter-school competition to this situation can only make things worse, even for a parent council that is functioning well. With schools vying for students, decisions must be tempered by whether they will attract more students next year: each decision will be measured by its marketing potential. How can the cost of building a wheelchair-friendly play structure compete with a proposal to update the physics lab?

Such choices are not currently determined by individual schools, but by school boards and ministries obliged to make decisions in favour of balance and equity. In the past, it has not been considered wise to leave choices such as whether to set up a "sheltered" classroom for emotionally disturbed children to the whims of school or parent politics. Many systems have created "specialized schools," particularly at the high school level, because school boards can ensure the overall balance in the system: schools emphasizing the fine arts can be a complement to schools specializing in science and technology. However, if no one is obliged to consider system balance, passionate parents need consider only their own short-term interests.

The Alberta government has come down clearly on the question of whom schools should serve, and concluded that only parents are the legitimate "clients" of schools. Yet the institution of public education answers this question differently, reflecting the principle that in a democracy, education serves and protects society by balancing the particular needs of the individual with the need for common experience, knowledge, and collective values. Schools have had no "clients" or "customers" of special merit; the elderly and the young, parents and non-parents have an equally-vested interest in the success of education for all. Sharing the funding of public education through general taxation reinforces this principle. Decision-making by elected bodies removed from the intensity of self interest attempts to ensure that the public interest is the basis for decision-making. When we abandon this principle in favour of "parent power," we abandon the contract between schools and society, and between one generation and the next.

Albertans for Quality Education

"Parent Power" is a key tenet of populist education reformers, but it is not their only article of faith, nor is this movement unique to Alberta. Across Canada and the United States, organizations claiming to be grass-roots citizen's groups have mobilized to advance populist right-wing educational reforms. Most have close ties with the religious right.[14]

"Parents, businessmen, and educators" founded "Albertans for Quality Education" (AQE) in 1993 because "the quality of education in Alberta has declined to unacceptably low levels," according to their promotional materials.[15] The AQE's newsletter alerts parents to the causes of this decline: one issue includes a critique of multi-age classes (split grades), continuous learning, child-centred education, and the insufficient time devoted to "pure science" in the elementary grades. One correspondent rails against "progressive" education, and the "disturbing trend ... that children must be treated as individual and unique human beings."[16] However, the greatest amount of print is devoted to school violence, drug and alcohol use, and the values children are learning at school. A feature article warns that a video on AIDS is being shown to high school students. Abstinence is not always getting top billing in discussions of safe sex, readers are warned; prostitution and even homosexuality allegedly had been discussed during sex education classes! William Gairdner's books, (*The War Against the Family* and *Public Schools and the War Against the Family*), are favourably reviewed and recommended to AQE members. Nearly every article concludes with the same message: parents must reclaim their ownership of schools; "choice" will restore consumer power to its rightful place.[17]

AQE moved from the margins of educational debate to centre stage through the Roundtable process. Although it admitted to representing only 325 members, AQE was invited to four meetings, twice the number of the Calgary Separate Board.[18] Their advice did not fall on deaf ears: AQE's Roundtable brief is a virtual template for Alberta Education's "Business Plan."[19]

AQE's brief affirmed the need for "quality education," but argued that as spending had no effect on quality, cuts to the education budget could be used to achieve provincial deficit reduction. Money could be saved by reducing the number of teachers and administrators (and their salaries), and by reducing funding for nonessential programs and subjects. Each school must be free to decide how deeply to cut, AQE contends, thus enabling "the education priorities for the populist" to emerge. Language arts, mathematics, and science make AQE's "more essential" list, and so does guidance counselling, so long as it is "career-related" and supportive of "family values." English as a Second Language (ESL) appears last on their "essentials" list, but only if it is "funded by Federal Departments responsible for Immigration or [by] local immigrant communities."

On the AQE's "less essential" list are the "second half" of kindergarten, instruction in second languages, and before and after school care programs. AQE identifies "hot lunch programs" as the least essential program, although they suggest that lunches might still be provided to the children of those on social assistance, but only if costs were deducted from parents' welfare cheques.

AQE's brief commended the government's apparent intentions for education reform, but it decried insufficient curricular respect paid to the role of the business sector: "Students should understand the role that innovation plays in spawning new entrepreneurial businesses as well as entrepreneurial efforts within the larger corporations and institutions that generate wealth and/or provide products and services to Albertans." Food for thought in lieu of a hot lunch.

AQE's brief also deals with educational equity. Their first concern is the unfair advantage of students with special needs: "Our compassionate society can degenerate into a coercive society where more and more of those best able to articulate their special needs gain access to a greater than average share of educational resources." Surely equity can get out of hand:

> Parents ... may feel that their children have fewer resources because they are subsidizing learning disabled children and this is inequitable. They might feel that the parents of learning disabled children should fund the incremental costs above the average per student cost or raise the funds through charitable donations. The same perceived inequities could apply to the teaching of French, ESL, behaviourally handicapped children, children from broken homes,[sic] native children, and other groups.

The solution, according to AQE, is to limit how much is spent on any one student. "Funding requirements in excess of these limits would then be obtained from user fees, charitable donations, or other fund-raising methods." Begging, the quintessential entrepreneurial activity, is never out of place.

A second inequity is the "preferential treatment" enjoyed by public education; the solution is to undertake "a careful review ... of the public schools' commitment to satisfy their customers as a precondition to the continuance of their virtual monopoly over education." AQE also recommends "that any deliverer of education, whether private, public, or homeschooling, if proven to meet acceptable standards, should be properly funded by Alberta Education."

Other AQE recommendations include funding based on instructional hours, so that field trips and professional development days would reduce a school's budget. Increasing pupil-teacher ratios would cut costs and encourage "direct instruction." Moving to provincial collection and distribution of taxation would benefit rural areas, and keep costs under control. Implementing user fees for kindergarten would help, too. Introducing a "merit pay" system would cut the salaries of those teachers "producing only average results" so that excellent teachers could receive "quality enhancement incentives."

Both teacher excellence and student development are clearly quantifiable, and thus AQE urges the expanded use and school-by-school reporting of standardized tests. These quality-control measures would guide parents as consumers, and remind schools just why they are in business. The bottom line of AQE's brief is that education can improve only through competition, and schools can compete only when parents have the right to exercise private choice with public dollars. For AQE, no alternative compares with the promise of "schools of choice."

Schools of Choice

Albertans for Quality Education did not get everything they asked for in the first round of education reform, but in addition to cutting teacher salaries and increasing standardized testing, AQE got its heart's desire: increased parent control and the first Charter Schools in Canada.

On November 22, 1994, the Alberta government released the details of its plans for Charter schools.[20] It describes charter schools as "autonomous public schools which would provide innovative or enhanced means of delivering education to improve student learning." It allows such schools to "specialize" by defining "the characteristics of students for whom the school is established."

Plans for governance, including the "selection" of board members, must be included in proposals; in return the charter school receives "autonomy," i.e., while it must comply with provincial regulations (or whatever remains of them), there is no obligation to follow elected school board policies. Indeed, school boards are entirely redundant; while schools may receive their charter from boards, they may also apply directly to the minister.

Superficially, the proposals deal with the "problem" of equity by explicitly prohibiting charter schools from denying access based on race, gender, national origin, ethnicity, socio-economic background, or religion "to any student for whom the program is designed." The caveat, of course, creatively provides the filtering device at the heart of all charter schools. Not only is "ability" missing from the prohibited grounds of discrimination, it appears that a charter school could quite openly "design" its program for high-achieving students, and reject any whose performance was not up to this level. While religious affiliation could not be touted openly, apparently it would be fine to develop a program "designed" for students of parents who appreciate "traditional" ways, "family values," respect for authority, and individual responsibility. While a mixed-sex charter school could exclude neither boys nor girls, a school "designed" for girls would be unlikely to be forced to reject applications from boys. With no requirement to provide transportation, charter schools established in wealthy suburbs would be unlikely to be overwhelmed with applications bearing inner-city addresses.

The best laid plans, however, cannot prevent the odd "undesirable" child from registering. This problem is nicely finessed by empowering each charter board to "develop and implement a student code of conduct, [and] a discipline, suspension, and expulsion policy." Unlike the public system, which bears some responsibility for the next placement of an expelled student, charter schools need only recruit a more pliant candidate.

While charter schools are not to be allowed to charge tuition fees, parents can be charged for supplies — which could, at least in theory, add up if a personal computer were to be deemed an essential "supply." Since they are not obliged to provide transportation, parents must also bear these hidden tuition costs. Charter schools will have access to "comparable" levels of instructional dollars, but they are not prohibited from fundraising or from attracting a corporate partner.

Financial restraint again proves to be a handy tool to leverage more fundamental reforms: while the draft handbook specifies that teachers must be "certificated," they need not be members of the ATA, which in turn means they need not be paid according to provincial payscales or receive any other negotiated benefits. The qualifications, working conditions, and duties of "other staff" are entirely at the discretion of each school's board.

It's a winning combination, according to Albertan John Mason, who intends to set up a charter school. "We're not interested in having academically challenged kids. And we're not going to have behaviour problems. We're taking the cream of the crop."[21] The government's political friends have been more than appreciative. As Gary Duthler, head of the Association of Independent Schools and Colleges, said, it isn't just the new money: "In terms of the political situation we're miles ahead. ... Now I feel like I'm on a surfboard, on this huge wave, and it's a lot more fun."

To many parents, on the left and the right, charter schools have considerable appeal. No parental anxiety is left unmined by school-choice advocates: drugs, demons, diversity, and deportment are equally susceptible to resolution for "the chosen." Certainly, a parent could sign up for such a school without any particularly unfriendly intent towards other children, their communities, or public education. How can the collective choices of loving parents undermine our common well-being? The answer to this question requires a careful deconstruction of the underlying ideology of charter schools and all schools of choice.

First and foremost, the battle over "school choice" is about ideology, not education. Under the pretence of improving test scores or greater parent involvement, big business, and the religious right are attempting to hijack public education. For some, public education of any kind is inconsistent with "parents' rights"; for others it is inconsistent with reaping the rewards of privilege; for a few it is inconsistent with the unbridled right to profit from children. Ordinary parents, however, are more likely just to go with the flow of populism, a movement which at its best represents a solidarity of common interest; at its worst, however, "populism has had significant undercurrents of anti-intellectualism, puritanism, xenophobia, and religious fundamentalism."[22]

"Schools of choice" come in many incarnations, from for-profit chains of private schools to church-basement collectives, but all share several explicit characteristics. They are as disengaged as possible from any central authority, and vested with as much decision-making as possible at the school level, with parent-run boards wielding more authority than most public school boards. They compete openly with other schools for enrolment, and their funding is tied to the number of students they can attract.

"Schools of choice" also share a number of implicit characteristics. First, to be financially successful, they must obey and profit from the rules of the marketplace, which means maintaining and increasing market share. Thus, some schools and students can gain, but only that which others lose; the fate of the "losers" is merely good news for those on top. Fundamental to this philosophy is a sense of entitlement, and a conviction that the "elect," from an economic, intellectual, or religious standpoint, have the right to disengage the future of their children from the future of other people's children.

Secondly, "schools of choice" set out to be homogeneous. Whether its "clientele" is to be sorted by socio-economic level, religious values, or academic proficiency, each school builds a filtering device into its purposes. As John Chubb, one of the most vocal American proponents of school choice explains, the problem with public schools is diversity — "they must take whoever walks in the door."[23]

Thirdly, proponents of "schools of choice" view teachers as the agents of educational folly, either hoodwinked by the philosophy of "feel-good" education or beaten into submission by their unions. They will be "freed" of this burden by schools of choice where parents will rule by moral conviction rather than regulation, and where populist wisdom will replace professional judgement.

"Schools of choice" may well succeed because they pit self-interest against the collective good, and it is not only in Alberta that the collective is coming up short. There will be two categories of victims if public schools are dismantled in favour of choice: some of us and all of us. The "some" will be those who already have the least cultural capital, political clout, and recourse against those who would leave them behind.

That all of us will be victims may be less obvious, but no less true. For if the quality of education all children receive ceases to matter to each of us, we have acceded to the self-concern democracy attempts to restrain. If we believe in equity and justice, we will structure our schools one way. If we believe that our children are entitled to succeed on the backs of others, we will structure them differently.

One or two charter schools will not bring public education to its knees, but they will divert dollars and attention from improving all schools to enhancing a few. And because of the apparent injustice of only some children "benefitting" from choice, the public may well conclude that all our schools should be put in the hands of parents and "partners." It will not be long before taxpayers who are not parents resist funding something over which they have no influence. Corporations will "spend" education dollars not on taxes for the support of the many, but on "partnerships" for the benefit of a few. As funds for all schools decline, some parents will demand the right to top off tax-funded tuition fees, or to insist that some programs are more crucial to the economy than others and thus deserve more public investment.

And while these problems cause dissonance in our still quasi-public school system, the chorus of harmonization will be heard in the background. Canadians will watch as American businesses underwrite "boutique" schools, for which the capital investment will be worth its weight in tax credits. The middle classes, frantic to leave crumbling public schools, will find the tuition to get into the "best" school. Those without ambition or hope or resources will simply "choose" the remains that are left.

It will be said that the problem in Canada is that we didn't go far enough. "Charter schools" may have been a typically Canadian compromise, it will be argued, but their fundamental anarchy is too confusing and unwieldy. The solution will be the utter deregulation of public education, an acquiescence to the imperatives of the marketplace.

Conclusion

It is not surprising that "the Alberta Experiment," as it has come to be known, should have taken on education. Premier Klein, his mentors, and his allies are ahead of most of the public in realizing that everything about schools is political. No matter is of more central importance to a democracy than what its children are taught, and which of them will be encouraged to learn it well. The premier found that education was a vulnerable target, ripe for takeover and weakly defended. Those who wish the experiment not be repeated in other parts of the country would do well to pay attention. "The Alberta Experiment" proves that what is deplorable is not necessarily unlikely.

Notes

1. This chapter is adapted from M. Barlow and H.-j. Robertson, *Class Warfare: The Assault on Canada's Schools* (Toronto: Key Porter Books, 1994).
2. Alberta Government, "Press Release," 18 January 1994.
3. *ATA News*, 25 January 1994.
4. *Western Report*, 14 February 1994, 6-11.
5. Alberta Education, *Meeting the Challenge: Three-year Business Plan* (Edmonton: Government of Alberta, 1994).
6. Editorial in the *Edmonton Journal*, 11 February 1994, A14.
7. Ibid.
8. P. Marck article in the *Edmonton Journal*, 11 February 1994, A7.
9. *ATA News*, 23 February 1994.
10. J. Freedman, "Proposal for an Alternative Model School." Society for Advancing Educational Research, February 1994.
11. V. Dwyer article in *Maclean's*, 14 March 1994, pp. 44-49.
12. Ibid.

13. Alberta Education, *Roles and Responsibilities in Education: A Position Paper* (Edmonton: Government of Alberta, December 1994).

14. National Education Association, *The People's Cause: Mobilizing for Public Education* (Washington, D.C. : NEA, 1994).

15. *AQE News and Views*, 1/1 (September 1993).

16. Colin Penman's article in *AQE News and Views* (January 1994).

17. *AQE News and Views*, 1/1 (September 1993).

18. A. Taylor, "How do they get away with this stuff?: The context of Educational Restructuring in Alberta." Paper presented at the CSAA, Learned Societies Conference, Calgary, Alberta, June 1994.

19. D. Levson et al., "Presentation to Government of Alberta Education Round Table," *AQE* (5 November 1993).

20. Alberta Education, *Charter Schools Handbook* (Draft) (Edmonton: Government of Alberta, 1995).

21. J. Lewington's article in *The Globe and Mail*, 7 April 1994, C1.

22. G. Stevenson, "Class and class politics in Alberta." In L. Pratt, ed., *Socialism and Democracy in Alberta: Essays in honour of Grant Notley* (Edmonton: NeWest Press, 1986), 210.

23. J. Kozol, "Whittle's Raid on Public Education." False Choices, a special edition of *Rethinking Schools*, 1992.

Chapter Fourteen

CLEARCUTTING IN THE GROVES OF ACADEME

Jim Marino

Education is our hope for the future.
Alberta's Throne Speech, February 14, 1995.[1]

In the silly movie *Monty Python and the Holy Grail*, there is a scene in which King Arthur meets the Black Knight. In the ensuing duel Arthur hacks off the knight's arms and legs. After each cut he expects his opponent to surrender, but the knight, or what's left of him, refuses to yield. In the end, the head and torso, in gruesome idiocy, continue the challenge, "Have at you! I'll bite your legs!" While the Klein government delivered cut after cut to colleges, institutes, and universities, board chairs, presidents, administrators, deans, and faculty celebrated the losses with cries of "Excelsior!" and misty-eyed acceptance of the new challenge, promising excellence and better learning and greater research, even as they thrashed about, trying to find their feet. As a result, the public has a wrong impression of how well advanced education in the province is handling the cuts.

The Reward for Doing More With Less is Still Less

Reductions were already in place before the Klein government got the axe sharpened and stumbled on the New Zealand clear-cutting model of fiscal reform, in which all departments are hit, and hit fast, without preferential considerations. The money to be saved by cutting in post-secondary education (PSE) is not as great as in health and K-12 education because it is not as big a part of the public expenditure to start with; not as many people are served by PSE as in health, education, or municipalities, and, most importantly, the costs of PSE have decreased over the past decade, and were already in decline before Klein.

It was hard for the post-secondary sector to accept that the Getty government had been spendthrift in advanced education given their history of provincial grants. Of the major areas of public expenditure — health, education, social services, and advanced education — only the last had decreased in the decade ending in 1993. Advanced education spending declined from 10 percent to 9 percent of provincial expenditures, while health and social services actually increased by 10 and 5 percentage points respectively. Enrolments had grown by 55 percent, 93 percent in the public colleges, and 49 percent in the universities, while real operating grants per full-time equivalent student had dropped by nearly 25 percent from 1981 to 1991. At the same time that other provincial governments increased their support for post-secondary education by an average of 6.8 percent, with a high of nearly 11 percent in Ontario, Alberta's spending grew by less than a third of the national average; its 2.3 percent growth was the *lowest* in the country.

Getty's policies resulted in hiring freezes, below cost-of-living salary settlements, reduced or zero capital development, and, by 1992, layoffs, especially among support staff. These changes were characteristic of advanced education under Getty, in fact. A typical example was Medicine Hat College closing its music conservatory as a fully-funded unit taught by full-time faculty. Similar retrenchment occurred in the music divisions of Keyano College and Grande Prairie Regional College. Academic staff at the universities were laid off or terminated, sometimes by incentives for early retirement; support staff were laid off by the score.

Because it was clear that the incoming Klein government was going to outdo Getty in making cuts, some institutional boards expanded their search for ways to reduce operating costs. Boards of governors in Alberta "adopted the problem" of reducing the provincial deficit instead of fulfilling their role as fiduciaries and opposing the Klein cuts. The University of Calgary, for example, announced a plan in January 1993 to reduce its budget for teaching units by 17 percent, and by 20 percent in all others, over the next five years. Similar moves were taken at other campuses. In February 1991, President Paul Davenport of the University of Alberta called for the layoff or termination of twenty-five academic staff and over 200 support staff. The coming Klein reductions in grants would be a matter of degree, not kind; post-secondary institutions had already absorbed significant reductions in their operating and capital grants during the Getty years.

At the universities, real salaries were 2 percent lower in 1992 than they were a decade earlier. Salaries for assistant professors at the University of Calgary had fallen from 5th in the country, to 24th. Capital development was restricted: government's matching grants for capital projects were discontinued. In general, the capital budgets were in poor enough shape that in Fiscal Years (FY) 1991 and 1992 the government allowed boards to transfer part of the operating grant to capital, not for new construction, but to repair crumbling buildings.

The "excesses" of the Getty years were nonetheless a major issue in the Tory leadership campaign and the subsequent provincial election. In PSE, the expansion of programs in the Lougheed years was, by implication, evidence that institutions had become bloated at the oil-boom trough and were now to shed their fiscal excess and educate their students with no decrease in quality but at lower costs to government.

During the late days of the Getty government, in December 1992, then Minister of Advanced Education, John Gogo, received a report from a group called The Strategic Options Task Force[2], but known generally as the "secret committee" because its membership was not announced until soon before reporting its plan, *For All Our Futures: Strategies for the Future of Post-secondary Education in Alberta*, which introduced many of the principles later found in the draft White Paper issued by Jack Ady, Klein's Minister of Advanced Education and Career Development (AECD). Much of the language of the Strategic Options paper referred obliquely to then-popular features of Total Quality Management: outcome-based performance indicators, deregulation, and performance management at all levels. The paper presented the rhetorical mix of "strategies," "choices," and "options" that are the hallmarks of independent reports solicited by government which attempt to disguise their allegiance to the host who has invited them to the political *stammtisch*.

The report gave three "options": degree granting for selected colleges; reduced operating grant "dependency"; and increased shared degrees (on the basis of the first two years of a degree taught at colleges and completion at university). The paper suggested wide public consultation on PSE and its funding. Market-driven models and the language of Total Quality Management especially seem to have a grip on the Klein agenda for public services.

The Advanced Education Advantage

Before looking at the dangers in current policy toward advanced education in Alberta, we must ask: what does the public have to lose in Alberta's system of higher learning? We have two technical institutes, the Northern and Southern Alberta Institutes of Technology (NAIT and SAIT), providing training in job-related skills tied very closely to the provincial labour market. The institutes developed work experience programs putting students in the workplace as part of their training. This education is practical and applied. Because of the distribution of population in Alberta, we have an advantage. The political pull between the poles of Calgary and Edmonton has resulted in a duplication that gave Albertans the advantage of two such institutes. As in the building of two identical Jubilee Auditoriums in Edmonton and Calgary, some political decisions to balance north and south worked out to the taxpayers' advantage because they overcame problems created by the two major cities so far apart but equal in population.

The public college in Alberta is an institution with a mosaic of missions. In a country that has no tradition of large numbers of privately-endowed liberal arts colleges, the role of providing an academic preparation falls to a few publicly funded schools. The system of public colleges in the province does much more than provide degree credit preparation for those whose circumstances do not permit entry into first year university. More importantly, these schools are closely tied to their communities, serving their regions with high-quality certificate and diploma programs available to students living at home.

Alberta's four universities also have a special role. It is one of the peculiarities of modern attitudes that the role of universities is the least understood of any part of advanced education. Teaching and research seem remote from the daily lives of other taxpayers. Of course, the Universities of Alberta and Calgary provide a multitude of services including technical training and diploma programs. They also provide many skills needed in the general market even if these skills seem to be incidental to the more obvious task of acquiring knowledge of a particular academic subject. Biology majors, engineering, and business students, classics scholars — all learn the importance of accurate research, of communications, of the usefulness of technology in their fields. They expect and receive the latest viewpoints in their disciplines, along with the most recent information. But these are ancillary to what all students at university must learn. They are being trained to recognize the important and vital ideas in the subject, to evaluate and support or reject ideas on the basis of their critical judgment. At the graduate level, students are encouraged to find new avenues to advance knowledge and to create new ways of seeing the subject, new ways to judge what is important and what is not. If the faculty who are facilitating the students in their learning are not themselves scholars abreast of their fields, then the students are receiving second-hand knowledge. That particular student need is one of the reasons for the emphasis on research.

Another important feature of most university research distinguishes it from industrial research. The campus is one of the very few venues in Canada for what is called "pure" or, pejoratively, "curiosity-driven" research that does not depend upon the production of a process or product which is immediately applicable to an industrial market. (Conversely, that done solely for the marketplace is called "gizmo" research.) Probably what most distinguishes pure research is that results are freely shared. There is room for patents and licensing, but the whole idea of this form of free inquiry is its independence from market demands, which, in turn, allows the researcher to collaborate in collegial rather than entrepreneurial competition. At best, such research is also free to be unorthodox and to produce meaningfully negative results without penalty. If there is no place in a society for free inquiry, that society will be second-rate in the education of its young and in its contribution to the world of ideas. No substitute can be found in private profit enterprise for this uniquely university function.

Not that the people of Alberta don't profit, in money as well as prestige, from university research. According to the provincial government's latest figures, the two major research universities bring Alberta $140 million of outside money annually.

The University of Lethbridge ranks as one of the best small research universities, providing an excellent program of undergraduate teaching comparable to small private universities in the United States. The students benefit from a research-interested faculty, which ensures that they are being taught by informed and engaged professors. Lethbridge's location provides a geographic balance, giving access to a full university program for students in the south.

Athabasca University serves as the centre of what some consider the future for all of PSE–delivery of courses off-campus. Nowhere in Canada is there a comparable distance university. Its research role lies in the development of new technologies with which to reach students at home or work across Canada.

Once the province built and staffed a good PSE system, it is foolishly destructive to neglect it. The decay comes very swiftly. Let's make the "brain drain" specific by a simple case in point: last year, it was possible to attend an international Shakespeare conference and have one of the renowned acknowledge the University of Alberta on your name tag by recognizing that your English department was home to Linda Woodbridge who did that excellent work on women in the Renaissance. It is no small thing to hear Alberta's name recognized at a meeting in Tokyo, or Cambridge, or anywhere in the scholarly world. It is, in part, what Albertans have paid for; it does well for our graduates and, because recognition attracts grants, it counts in dollars. This year, Professor Woodbridge is gone, one of many excellent scholars who are forced to leave our universities to pursue research and teaching (she received the university teaching award last year) in more supportive environments. The University of Calgary's board of governors' vice chair, Alice Thomas, recently complained, "We are losing a lot of good people." It's significant for the future of the university that the number of assistant professors there has gone from 254 to 186 in two years.[3]

The Klein Campaign to Cut in a New Direction

The Klein government believed or, at least, publicly erected the notion that its election sweep (44 percent of those voting) was not the result of a well-funded campaign and a leadership race which ousted Tories the voters might see as Getty-era big spenders. They insisted their election was a mandate to eliminate the deficit by cutting or privatizing tax-supported services. Soon after the June 1993 election, a budget round-table discussed grant reductions in the public sector.

In PSE this neoconservative swing brought an early promise of even more drastic cuts to operating grants than were endured under Getty. On November 23, 1993, Klein called for "reduction in public sector compensation," which was really a call for a 5 percent rollback in salaries and benefits. Ady had already written, as early as October, to boards and staff associations at the campuses, asking them to consider "compensation reduction strategies" and, in January 1994, the expected announcement came that PSE staff were ordered to take a voluntary 5 percent reduction in compensation or a rollback would be legislated. Salary reduction only makes it more difficult to hire and retain excellent teachers in a very competitive global market.

The second and, by far, the most consequential grant reduction scheme required that each government department submit three-year business plans to cabinet in February 1994, along with their 1994-1995 budgets. On January 17, 1994, Ady announced that post-secondary grants would be cut over three years, beginning in 1994, by 11 percent, 7 percent, and 3 percent. The 5 percent rollback would be part of the first-year reduction, putting pressure on boards and staffs to settle and posing questions about free collective bargaining. This tactic of threatening legislation overriding contracts was one the government would use again.

The minister also announced that institutional operating and capital grants would be combined; a new funding formula, based on outcomes, would be in place by 1996; centres of specialization would be established "to realize economies of scale and eliminate duplication"; new capital development was frozen for three years; and tuition policy would not change until 1995. He also established an "Access Fund" with $47 million to be dispensed over the next three years by a public board to any post-secondary institutions, including publicly-supported private colleges, on a competitive basis giving preference to proposals for nontraditional delivery of services. The Fund was to create ten thousand new student spaces.

Two institutions were singled out for special treatment. Athabasca University was to take grant reductions of 11 percent, 7 percent, and 13 percent percent (ten percentage points more than the others), because of its "low graduation rate." This extra reduction is odd, given the way the government emphasizes distance education as one answer to access problems.

In 1993, a plan for restructuring PSE began a year of wide consultation entitled Adult Learning: Access through Innovation. Background documents were circulated to stakeholders, and thirteen open regional hearings took place in September and October. The dominant themes for discussion were four terms that would live in near-alliterative fame: accessibility, affordability, accountability, and responsiveness.

The results of these hearings was an invitational round, called the Advanced Education Budget Round Table, in Calgary on November 19 and 20. Participants were asked to consider a Workbook which presented options with a distinct bias toward a market-based model of PSE. This meeting, attended by invitees of the department, had the atmosphere of a large seminar wherein the academic participants — students, faculty, administrators, support staff — were instructed in the "realities" of labour market demand and supply-side economics by such companies and business organizations as United Food, TransAlta Corp, the Alberta Restaurant Association, Canadian Manufacturers, Northern Telecom, and the Alberta Chamber of Commerce. After two days of discussion by what the department referred to as "stakeholders" the draft White Paper Access Through Innovation: An Agenda for Change appeared in March.

Following the first draft came, in May, a second round of invited consultation, this time in Calgary and Edmonton. The invitees discussed and responded to the options presented in the draft White Paper, which they were told would lead to modifications in the final policy document. Some of the options reappearing had already been rejected by the participants in the November discussion. It was difficult for the participants to have much faith that their recommendations would have any result.

Further contributing to a growing doubt about the sincerity of the government's consultation process was the fact that by the time of the May round-table the minister had already announced a deal with the Canadian Imperial Bank of Commerce to provide a new funding program for student loans that would establish an "income-sensitive" repayment plan. Loan limits were raised, and the bank given incentives to prevent students from failing to repay their debts. (Previously, when a student defaulted, the banks just called on the government guarantees.)

While the academic "stakeholders" waited and watched through the turbulent summer of 1994, as the press was full of protest and horror stories in health and education, not much of substance moved from Advanced Education and Career Development. Staffs and boards of governors, with a few feisty exceptions, quietly negotiated a mosaic of days without pay, days off without pay, benefit reductions, and salary rollbacks amounting to the demanded 5 percent. A few boards dismissed staff to reduce compensation instead of lowering salaries. At SAIT, about 200 staff were dismissed. At NAIT, the staff refused to ratify a settlement, then had the final proposal of their own team thrust back upon them by the arbitrator. At Grande Prairie Regional College, the nonacademic staff absorbed a 5 percent cut, but the faculty balked and the administration agreed. Keyano College also did not agree to cut salaries. The government did not penalize these colleges because the grants were not affected. The only effect was internal: Grande Prairie faces a considerable deficit over the next two years even though faculty later accepted a compensation reduction; Keyano College has a lesser deficit problem.

White Paper Cuts

The final version of the White Paper, *New Directions for Adult Learning in Alberta*, was released on October 20, 1994. Here, at last, was the agenda for PSE in the province for the next decade. There are no direct changes to institutional roles, and there is little requirement for legislative change (and therefore, little possibility of public debate at that level). Of course, the Access Fund, student loan structure, grants cuts, and changes to tuition limits had already been accomplished before October. The changes all show how the government provokes internal change on campus while claiming that it is respecting the autonomy given by law to institutions.

Tuition: the PSE user fees

The White Paper at least maintained ministerial regulation of tuition fees despite the calls for their complete deregulation made by some participants (both private sector and institutional). Tuition is to rise by a maximum of $215 per year (plus cost of living) until it forms 30 percent of the operating budget of the institution, a limit which cannot be reached until 2000. This rise is likely to produce annual tuition fees around $3,500 per year by 2000 at the universities, against about $2,200 in 1994-95. The minimum tuition for "foreign students" is to be double the regular tuition rate; institutions may charge more. The paper prefaced this penalty on visa students with banner-waving claims about the academic enrichment and economic contributions these students make.

Because the rises in tuition will be gradual while the grant reductions are all up front, tuition won't make up for reduced grants. Further, if enrolment on the urban campuses falls more than 2 percent, or at rural institutions more than 5 percent, government will deduct a penalty, of $2500 per missing student, from the grants.

Access Fund: the new shell game

The "Access Fund" was to create "the equivalent of 10,000 new student spaces over the next three years,"[4] to grow with recovered savings and to fund future program delivery systems, sponsor new partnerships with employers and promote collaboration among providers and responsiveness to regional need. The committee, chaired by Douglas Cattran, vice-president of Dow Chemical Canada Inc. (the remainder of the committee, with the exception of two students and an MLA, were from business), made the first awards ($1.6 million of the $47 million total) in November 1994. The proposals showed one or both of two characteristics: the sharing of programs between institutions, and a promise of employment of graduates. Two themes emerge here that recur elsewhere in the policy: labour market responsiveness, and blurring of the functional lines among types of institutions. Because future "Access Fund" money is to come from "efficiencies" within the PSE system, the Fund is really only a way of redirecting grant money.

Applied degrees: the new work permit

Legislation passed in the spring 1995 session permits public colleges and institutes to offer "applied degrees" as a demonstration project. The degrees, not intended as preparation for postgraduate study, combine six semesters of formal instruction with accredited work experience of at least two semesters. The primary purpose of the degrees is "to prepare Albertans for work." For funding, institutions have to compete for assistance from the "Access Fund," or find the money themselves. Such programs have been approved for Mount Royal College, SAIT, and Grande Prairie Regional College. Alberta College of Art has received approval to grant its own degrees.

Transfer: smoothing moves

A committee of senior academic officers at universities and colleges has informally recommended a common first year that will permit credit transfer into the second year of university. These proposals can make transfers easier for students but there is concern that emphasis on academic degrees will cause a neglect of the community and regional responsiveness of regional colleges.

Rationalization: what politics created, politics can destroy

A province with four universities, two of them placed away from the most populous centres, and with a large network of public colleges would appear to need to beware of overlap of programs. The catch-phrase, "centres of specialization," became popular amongst educators and then politicians in the nineties. In the AECD documents it indicated the need to concentrate programs at particular campuses. A faculty of Law and one of Medicine at both the Universities of Alberta and Calgary are often cited as examples. The Department hasn't said how centres of specialization are to be created. The government may not legislate or otherwise internally interfere, but merely use fiscal pressure to force reductions. The most obvious example is agriculture programs, where pressure to consolidate is put on Fairview College, Lakeland College, Olds College, and Lethbridge Community College.

Performance indicators: education according to the bean counters

Einstein once said, "Not everything that counts, can be counted; and not everything that can be counted, counts." Nonetheless, from the office of the Auditor General, to Alberta Treasury, to Advanced Education and Career Development, to the institutions, flows a desire to count outputs by key performance indicators. They will somehow be linked to grants by 1996. Nothing specific has been announced; there is a lot of talk. Government established the key performance indicators and reports based on them are set for publication in spring of 1996. How they will inform a new funding formula is still unclear.

The Minister's Forum on Adult Learning: is anybody listening?

The Klein government loves what it calls consultation. Sometimes they bring together public service providers and clients and dilute this with invitations to the heads of the larger Alberta corporations; sometimes the group is made up of those immediately concerned with a particular service sector, employees and employers who have publicly expressed concern about cuts, and sometimes they meet privately with a small group of advisors all of whom agree with the free-market, privatizing, and expenditure-cutting program of the PC caucus. Klein likes these consultations so much that departments are establishing quasi-permanent "forums," for example, the annual Minister's Forum on Adult Learning. It seems likely that this will become another layer of unelected, nonresponsible politically acceptable advisors, whose job will be to turn away wrath from the elected minister.

Collective bargaining: dinner with Damocles

For faculty organizations, the most alarming section of the White Paper reads:

> Many post-secondary collective agreements place inappropriate barriers to termination of employment for reasons of fiscal stringency and redundancy. The department expects the boards of the institutions to reexamine and, if necessary, renegotiate their collective agreements by March 1, 1995. The ability of the boards to adjust academic staffing must be increased. The Minister will review each board's progress in renegotiating their agreements.[5]

This announcement attracted international media attention, as it was interpreted to be the "elimination of tenure in Alberta."[6] There are enough barriers to recruitment raised by the cuts to grants without the additional unwarranted reputation of universities without tenure. The facts were quite unremarkable, as the Canadian Association of University Teachers, and the four Alberta university faculty associations were quick to point out: virtually all university contracts elsewhere have such clauses, and, in Alberta, two universities had some of these provisions, and at two, the faculty associations had attempted to negotiate them a year before the White Paper.

Only one college lacked such provisions, and there, the matter soon came under the review of an arbitrator. What faculty spokespersons thought "outrageous" was the minister's demand that agreed-upon contracts be thrown out and new ones written according to government specifications and by a fixed deadline that had nothing to do with the expiration of the contracts. Furthermore, the "negotiations," which would clearly be one-sided would be judged against a secret standard. In the event, all four university boards and faculty associations re-opened their agreements and agreed to clauses governing redundancy and stringency.

This is not to say that there is no threat to tenure. The threat comes not because university boards and faculty are negotiating, but because the impending legislation would most assuredly guarantee management rights to layoff and offer no process, protection, or appeal. There is great misunderstanding outside of campuses about tenure. Because professors are so galvanized by the least shadow on this right, it is easy to assume that it must be at least a guarantee of a job for life. Anyone would fight hard to protect a right to a job for life. That must be why professors get their drawers in a twist over the matter. Except that this explanation is wrong. First of all, tenure is no more a guarantee of a job for life than any other contract is. Professors can be and are fired for a list of specified causes, including incompetence. They are also mandatorily retired at sixty-five, unlike judges, lawyers, clergy, and doctors of medicine. It is nonreplacement that keeps the young from jobs, not tenure. Tenure is a protection that is only granted to those who earn it after a long and demanding probationary period.

So what does tenure guarantee? Protection from dismissal for being unorthodox or unpopular in one's views on the discipline, a protection that can easily be abused, especially in times of fiscal restraint. It is too easy to get rid of the noisome and the politically unpopular and say it was done for financial reasons, if the right is not jealously guarded by legally binding contracts. Maybe those who are not familiar with the need for free inquiry and academic freedom cannot understand the zeal of a professor in fighting for that freedom, but there are too many cases in history where the good-will of university governors was the only guarantee of academic freedom and where public or political relations proved more important. The Supreme Court of Canada has defended the need for tenure in universities.[7] No academic should feel at ease with a government department as the only protector of freedom of scholarship.

University Research: the black hole in the White Paper

Absent from New Directions is any clear policy from the government on university research; a promise is made that it will be reviewed. In late January 1995, Dr. Gilles Cloutier was appointed to make recommendations to the minister for a policy framework for university research. The minister said research distinguishes universities from other institutions. Dr. Cloutier, a past president of the Alberta Research Council and former rector of the University of Montreal, said the minister had placed no preconditions upon his work.

For all that, the universities are, or should be, wary that a market-driven, count-the-gizmos analysis of research will be imposed. While free inquiry may be the distinguishing characteristic of university research, when research is spoken of by the Klein government, it is almost exclusively in market terms. And when university research is defended by university faculty as equal in importance to teaching, it is perforce defended on the grounds of its economic importance and not on the basis of its real worth as the creation and sharing of new knowledge.

New funding formula: reshuffling the deck

In 1996, post-secondary institutions will begin to be funded according to a new funding formula. Part of this funding formula derives from the performance indicators that will be accepted for the system, but government statements about the connections between indicators and money have ranged from "the relationship will not be fine-wired" to "of course they will have an impact." The minister has engaged Dr. Bernard Sheehan, Associate Vice President, Computers and Communications at the University of British Columbia, to develop the funding formula. Some stakeholder groups (but not all) have been asked for their responses to a new funding formula; however, the main call for response will come after Dr. Sheehan releases his report. The formula will reflect neoconservative assumptions that if some loss looks good, total loss must be better — a kind of fiscal anorexia.

Conclusion

The Klein government has begun a series of changes that will take some time to work their way through the system. But some things are indisputable. Education will become more expensive for students, and indebtedness of graduates will rise. Most of the changes curtail or impinge upon the autonomy of institutions; most campuses are being infused with a market model with the student as consumer (and will the customer always be right?) and the attractiveness of Alberta institutions as places to work is being eroded. Albertans have long believed in adult education; Alberta has the highest participation rate in Canada. Klein has propagated the myth that funds can be reduced without danger to the quality of the system. Boards and administrations have not challenged this assertion. As institutions become more threadbare, and as student costs rise, can Albertans study, learn, and contribute their ideas as they have in the past?

Someday, the first term of the Klein government will be seen as the time when the politicians most directed the running of the colleges, institutes, and universities in Alberta. When Klein, while insisting on less government, manipulated programs, degrees, funding, recruitment and retention of staff, student populations, and even the missions of universities, colleges, and institutes; when the *mish-mash* of entrenched management practices and newly reimported management styles which promised so much and delivered so little change in the North American way of doing business was welcomed into the academy with pomp and ceremony and awarded a degree *honoris causa*. At the same time, there's no doubt that the hurly-burly of the marketplace will have replaced whatever is left of reflection and rational thought in the academy.

Notes

1. *Edmonton Journal*, 14 February 1995, A7.
2. Chairing the committee was Professor Stephen Murgatroyd, then dean of the Faculty of Administrative Studies at Athabasca University, who has published extensively on Total Quality Management in business and in education. He and another member of the committee, John Ballheim, president of DeVry Institute in Calgary, were much listened-to by the department in the development of Alberta's PSE plans.
3. *Calgary Herald*, 10 February 1995, B2. A report to the governors says that the University of Calgary is losing twenty-two teaching staff per year to retirements and, without replacements because of cuts, will lose 133 by 1997 (Annual Academic Personnel Report, reported in The University of Calgary *Gauntlet*, 16 February 1995, 1).
4. *New Directions*, 8.
5. *New Directions*, 15.
6. An article in the *Toronto Globe and Mail* headlined, "O, to have a job that lasts forever" (19 March 1994). The Advanced Education Supplement of *The Times* (London) and *Atlantic Monthly* in the U.S. also contacted Alberta faculty.
7. McKinney vs. University of Guelph. 1990 76 DLR (4th), 545.

Chapter Fifteen

CHIPPING AWAY AT MEDICARE: "ROME WASN'T SACKED IN A DAY"

Simon Renouf

> We're becoming the battleground because we're probably go-
> ing through the most phenomenal and significant restructur-
> ing of health care."
>
> Ralph Klein, April 1995.[1]

Health care *has* become a battleground in Alberta, but the "restructuring" has been neither planned nor beneficial. Rather, it has engendered confusion, anxiety, and fear among Albertans. In particular, restructuring has created the fear that the Klein government is bent on abandoning the Canadian system of medicare in favour of the discredited American system of health care administration and funding. These fears came to a head in the spring of 1995 as a result of numerous comments made by Ralph Klein and Health Minister Shirley McClellan,[2] sparking an almost surreal scene in the legislature as Opposition Liberal MLA's sang the Star-Bangled Banner to the embarrassed government, while Alberta Treasurer Jim Dinning meekly waved a Canadian flag.[3]

Of course, similar fears have arisen among people in other areas touched by the Klein government. However, no single government initiative shows more the ideological base of the so-called "Klein revolution" — and the dangers it presents — than its approach to health care. This chapter explores health care in Alberta under the Klein government: what has happened and why, and what it may mean for Canadian health care in general.

Two-Tiered or Not Two-Tiered: That is the Question

By 1995, Ralph Klein and his Health Minister Shirley McClellan were so confident of their health care agenda that they were prepared to speak openly about a two-tiered health system. At its annual convention on April 1, 1995, the ruling Progressive Conservative Party adopted a resolution calling for the province to allow "excess" hospital capacity created by budget cuts and hospital closures to be sold to private companies offering health care to U.S. or other foreign patients. The support was not unanimous. One Conservative delegate denounced the proposal as a first step in killing universal medicare. "It's a way to ... undermine and destroy the fundamental basis of medicare in this nation," said Richard Plain, a Tory delegate and health care economist.[4] But a majority of Tory delegates supported the resolution. It seemed wholly consistent with the Klein revolution. Earlier, a prominent Edmonton surgeon had proposed opening a private hospital, and in 1994, Klein had met with three Calgary doctors who wanted to set up a private facility.[5]

The initial suggestion of limiting private health care to "foreign" patients did not last long. A few days after the Tory convention Ralph Klein was telling reporters "Albertans ... simply want to say 'look, I want to get into this hospital quicker.' Maybe there's an opportunity for that person to get in quicker and have the operation done, just as that person might say 'I am going to take my own money and go to the Mayo Clinic or go to the Houston Medical Centre or go to a facility in the United States'." Klein told reporters that such a system "perhaps could be construed as a two-tiered system."[6]

Perhaps sensing the hostile public response to his "two-tier" remarks, Klein tried to modify the message. On his monthly "Talk to the Premier" radio show on April 8, 1995, Klein said "I'm not talking about a two-tiered system ... I'm talking about what is essential and what is not essential."[7]

But the genie could not be easily put back into the bottle. The Alberta Medical Association, which speaks for most Alberta physicians, applauded the notion of two-tiered health care. A.M.A. President Dr. Fred Moriarty was quoted as endorsing "preferential" access for patients willing to pay and told reporters that the medical association was working with the Klein government to develop a new approach to private medicine. The medical association also maintained that doctors working in the private system should also be able to work in the public system and get paid by medicare.[8] A day later, a former medical association head told a reporter that he could see nothing wrong with a doctor using public hospitals to serve private patients who pay for their own care.[9]

Health as a Target

Why has the Klein government singled out health care for attack? On balance, there are many sound reasons not to attack health care: Canadians (including most Albertans) are proud of a system which has, with considerable success, combined American style high-tech medicine with a publicly-funded and publicly-administered system for delivering hospital and medical services. In theory, there would be little advantage to a government attack on this popular system. Further, interests in support of the status quo — health professionals, apparently powerful health care worker unions, and locally based hospital boards — appeared at the advent of the Klein era able to present a strong and concerted opposition to significant cuts in health care funding. But Alberta's Tories have never been supporters of medicare. Moreover, pre-Klein, the provincial government's expenditure on the "health" portion of its budget totalled 4.13 billion dollars, about 30 percent of the government's annual expenditures.[10] When the debt and deficit became the focus of Alberta politics during the 1993 provincial election, and when the decision was made to balance the provincial budget without generating new revenues from corporations and raising the taxes of the well-to-do, health became an obvious target for budget cuts.

But the Klein government's attack on medicare goes far beyond spending reductions. The ultimate objective, as the government itself has proclaimed, is the replacement of a publicly-administered, universal, and comprehensive system for the provision of medical and hospital services with a private insurance system.

The origins of this attack are not recent, and no one should have been surprised by the fierce attack on medicare implemented by Alberta's Klein government. The government's "Starting Points" document released in December 1993 set out a blue print for the direction of Alberta's component of the Canadian medicare system:

> Given the need to reduce health funding, it is imperative that new ways be developed to fund services. This should include consumers paying for those services determined to be nonessential. True consumer health insurance must become a reality, but alternative methods of paying for nonessential services should be provided. Again, consumer choice must be respected. At the same time, health regions must work to limit their costs by reducing unnecessary overhead. The private sector should be allowed to provide services if the services meet or exceed health standards. Partnerships should be established between health regions to create and operate facilities for mutual benefits, and between pharmaceutical companies and health regions to limit drug costs.[11]

The government's statement put it on a direct course of confrontation with the federal government over the future of medicare. In doing so, the Klein government's position reflected a long tradition of antipathy by conservative governments in the province towards a public health system.

What is Medicare?

Canada's medicare system is based on five widely accepted principles, agreed to by the provinces and enforced through the mechanism of federal legislation through the vehicle of the Canada Health Act. Those principles are universality, portability, public administration, accessibility, and comprehensiveness.[12] The first government in Canada to fully embrace publicly funded and publicly administered medical and hospital insurance was the provincial government of Saskatchewan during the 1960s. The report of the federal Royal Commission on health services in 1964 paved the way for a greater acceptance of publicly-administered health insurance and made recommendations for the administration of private and physician sponsored or approved health insurance plans to be assumed by provincial governments at the cost to provincial and federal taxpayers rather than individuals.[13] While most provinces fund their contribution to medicare from the general corporate and individual tax base, Alberta maintains a form of regressive individual payments labelled, for ideological purposes, as "premiums." Recent increases (effective July 1, 1995) mean that these "premiums" now cost individuals $32 and families $64 *per month.*

Conservative governments across Canada have never been more than reluctant partners in medicare, prepared to accept transfers of federal dollars and tax points, but begrudging the "socialist" undertones of medicare's principles. Although the national medicare system began in the 1960s, the Alberta government long resisted the elimination of extra-billing by physicians. That practice did not end until the 1984 amendments to the Canada Health Act by Parliament. Even after steps were taken to end physician extra-billing, the Alberta government continued (with the assistance of a compliant Conservative federal government) to permit privately-owned clinics to charge both patient fees and medicare charges for the same services. At best, past Alberta governments showed only a lukewarm commitment to the Canadian model of medicare.

Also, medicare at its best represented only a partial response to the health care needs of Canadians. "Comprehensiveness" has never been taken literally as a principle for Canada's health delivery system. In most provinces, including Alberta, dental care, pharmaceuticals (including prescribed medicines), nursing homes, and some aspects of physicians' services have been relegated to the private sector from the beginning. Only limited efforts have been made to provide comprehensive health services to native people living off reserves, or to those in isolated communities. Poverty has always been a bar to the provision of basic health needs for Albertans, especially if one includes as basic health needs such things as safe running water, adequate sewage arrangements, access to regular medical and dental care, and prescription medicines.

Still, Canada's medicare system has emerged as one of the best medical insurance systems in the world — certainly far in advance of the inefficient American system (see below). Moreover, medicare stands as one of the linch-pins of Canadian pride and identity, even in Alberta. More than just medicare alone, it is a sense of "Canadian-ness" which is threatened by the Klein government's approach to medicare.

The Triumph of Ideology

That the Klein government's approach to health care delivery represents a triumph of ideology over political pragmatism is demonstrated by the deep unpopularity of the perceived "Americanization" of Alberta's health delivery system. The government does not release the results of its own polling. But a poll commissioned by a group of Alberta health care unions released in late 1993 showed strong underlying support for Canadian model medicare[14]

The poll commissioned by the health care unions showed that nearly 30 percent of those polled approved or strongly approved, of the government's decision to cut 25 percent of the current health care budget. But when it came to the question of fears for the future, between 80 percent and 91 percent of Albertans expressed grave reservations. Health care was regarded as too important to be left to private operators, one service which people expected the government to provide. Even in conservative Alberta, very strong resistance to privatization of health care was demonstrated. It is unlikely that the government's own polls showed different results. Nonetheless, the government continued for primarily ideological and immediate political reasons to attack medicare.

Further polling conducted by the University of Alberta's population research laboratory between February and April 1995 confirmed that a large majority of Albertans were concerned about the direction of health care in Alberta. Sixty-nine percent of respondents agreed or strongly agreed with the statement "budget cuts will reduce the quality of health care in Alberta over the next few years." Over 54 percent of respondents agreed or strongly agreed with the statement "increasing reliance on private, for profit health services will reduce the quality of health care in Alberta." Over 64 percent of respondents agreed or strongly agreed with the statement "changes happening to health care in Alberta are creating two health care systems: one for the rich and one for the rest of the people."[15]

Three Objectives

The Klein government's approach to medicare has pursued three objectives: First a downsizing and reorganization of hospital services; secondly a reduction of compensation levels for remaining health care workers; and thirdly, efforts aimed at creating new opportunities for the private sector in health care delivery and insurance. All have proceeded in an overlapping fashion, but they also can be seen as meeting short-, medium-, and long-term goals.

Downsizing
The first objective was largely implemented by the spring of 1995. In January 1994, the Klein government announced that Alberta's 140 traditional hospital and health unit boards would be replaced by seventeen regional health boards. In fact, this was never the target, much less something which was achieved. The government never intended to eliminate all hospital boards, only regional boards. There are still many independent hospitals and groups of hospitals that continue to wrangle with the seventeen regional health authorities over control. But, rhetoric aside, there was a very real shake up in hospital organization from 1994 to 1995 and many hospital workers (from building cleaners to nurses to senior executives) lost their jobs. For example, half of the acute care beds in operation in March 1989 in the Edmonton region had been closed by July 1, 1995 (3,237 beds to 1,616 beds).[16]

But those cuts do not affect Edmonton alone. The cuts to the Edmonton region affected many, perhaps most, Albertans. Alberta's Health Services Funding Advisory Committee (HSFAC) published a study in May 1995 which indicated that only 65.2 percent of the hospitalizations occurring in the Edmonton region applied to residents who live in the region of service. In other words, nearly 35 percent of the hospital stays in the Edmonton region were by persons who do not live in the Edmonton region. Cutting the number of active treatment hospital beds in the Edmonton region in half between 1989 and 1995 necessarily had a significant impact on most of the province.[17] Cuts in active treatment beds were also imposed in Calgary, and in most rural health regions.[18]

Central to an understanding of the Klein government's approach to health care is recognition that it has not resulted from any planning process related to health care needs. At the outset of the Klein government's mandate, significant health problems existed, including an over-supply of physicians (at least to the extent that physicians are compensated through the medicare system), an aging population, and a serious lack of integration in both planning and delivery of acute care, long-term care, and community health programs. These real life issues have been largely overlooked or masked by the Klein government's ideologically-based approach to health care.

The restructuring initiative did not engage in any real questioning of the goals or mission of the heath care system, or consideration of how to structure the system in order to meet those goals in an efficient and positive fashion. On the contrary, health care was seen as a large consumer of government expenditures, and "restructuring" was simply a means to the government's end of reducing the amount of that expenditure.

Compensation Reduction

It would be a fundamental error to think that the Alberta health care system was in a state of equilibrium during the 1980s and early 1990s. An appearance of equilibrium exists only in contrast to the extraordinary turmoil of the Klein era. In reality, Alberta's health care system has been riven since the very inception of medicare by conflict: struggles over the distribution of financial resources, struggles for control of health decision making, and struggles between competing ideologies and economic interests. Many Albertans were overlooked by the expanded system of health care. Important public health decisions took a back seat to high tech medicine.

A notable feature of the Alberta health care industry in the 1980s was the open debate about the cost of labour in publicly administered health enterprises. In real terms, the cost of labour in the health care system rose dramatically in the 1980s, with health care wages rising at rates faster than average incomes, and outstripping inflation over the decade. Wages for health care workers were led by unionized nurses whose wages more than doubled between 1980 and 1984. These gains did not come without struggle, exemplified by province-wide strikes of unionized nurses in 1980, 1982, and 1988. Health care unions fought to increase pay levels which, in real terms, had been very low for their predominantly female membership. Compensation increases in the 1980s were neither unjustified nor the product of a lax and free-spending provincial government. Primarily, they reflected pressures to redress long-standing pay inequities. But there was not, in Alberta, in the 1980s a political consensus that health care workers'

wages should rise. On the contrary, despite the pressures to address historically low levels of compensation for female public sector workers, the provincial government and its agencies actively opposed the adjustment in
health care workers' wages each step of the way.

A key element of the Klein government's approach to compensation
was to develop a mechanism whereby reduced levels of funding would be
implemented without encountering strong response from unionized health
care workers. Unlike attempts during the 1980s of earlier conservative provincial governments, the Klein government did not, in 1993 or 1994, involve itself, except in a very limited fashion, in collective bargaining with
health care unions. Rather than embarking on a direct attack on wages
(other than the limited and essentially symbolic 5 percent cut campaign)
the government sought to impose collective bargaining concessions
through the implementation of across-the-board spending cuts. Recognizing that most health care operating expenditures go to wages, the Klein
government approach of simply restricting the flow of funds to health institutions necessarily led to cuts in the wage bill either through direct, negotiated concessions or through staff reductions, lay offs, contracting out, and
privatization as health employers scrambled to offer former levels of services with substantially reduced revenues. Health care unions were largely
unprepared for the decentralized nature of decisions which resulted from
this policy, and have, even into 1995, been slow to analyze and respond to
the Klein government's strategy.

The principal measure was a direct reduction in the health budget of
more than 17 percent from 1993 to 1996. The direct effects of these cuts
were closures and downgrading of major hospitals in both Edmonton and
Calgary, and lay offs of anywhere between 5,000 and 10,000 health care
workers.[19] For many people both inside and outside the health care system,
the Klein government's proposal in the fall of 1993 to seek a voluntary 5
percent pay reduction for all public sector workers was an essential ingredient in the "restructuring" of the health care system. This was not the case.
The "5 percent campaign" was not integrated with any proposal to restructure or downgrade the health care system, or even of funding cuts in the
health system. Employers and employer organizations in the health care
sector sought to achieve much larger cuts in compensation, and with a few
exceptions they were successful in doing so during 1994. However, the "5
percent campaign" worked for the Klein government as much of the public
— and indeed many health care workers — accepted as legitimate a small
cut in public-sector salaries as a temporary measure to address the province's deficit. Health unions facing employer demands for much deeper

cuts found their bargaining positions severely undermined by the broad acceptance of 5 percent, even though 5 percent was seldom offered to workers in the health sector. Health care workers were, in many cases, convinced by Klein's public relations pitch that a painless 5 percent pay cut was all that the government was seeking. Perceived opposition to 5 percent on the part of health union leadership undermined the credibility of unions both at the bargaining table and in the public arena. For many health care workers larger compensation cuts, job losses, de-skilling, and work intensification did not appear to be related to the government's health cut campaign. The government was largely able to characterize these effects as local management decisions far removed from the government's own health plan.

New Private-Sector Opportunities

The Klein government's claim to have addressed fundamental planning issues was weakest with respect to the definition of medically required services. Early in the Klein government's mandate, health care round tables were convened at various locations around Alberta. One of the stated purposes of these round tables was to assist the government in defining "core services" to be provided by the health care system.

In March 1994, after reviewing the process for developing "core services" in other jurisdictions including Oregon, New Zealand, British Columbia and Saskatchewan, Alberta Health released a background paper containing a draft framework for core services in Alberta with the purpose of defining core services for the health system. Yet the draft "inventory" of core services was so vague as to be meaningless. For example, eight "purposes" of health care were listed including, "To prevent disease and injury" and "To provide primary health services."

By March 1995, Alberta Health had abandoned the quest to define core services. Instead, the Alberta government was publicly pressing the Federal Minister of Health, Diane Marleau and Prime Minister Chrétien to define basic health services. The only explanation for this turnaround is that during the one-to-two years that Alberta Health reviewed and studied the question of core services, the government came to the conclusion that it was not politically wise for it to be the party that defined "core" or "basic" health service.

Alberta Health

For over a year and a half — from the time of the health care round tables to the spring of 1995 — the Alberta government hesitated with respect to exactly what would be regarded as "core" services. This in turn, deferred the question of what areas private insurance companies would be permitted to enter. Deferral demonstrated the lack of any significant economic argument in favour of private insurance. If the government is unable to describe in general terms those areas that would be available for private insurance, it is impossible to pinpoint any economic benefits that would be said to result from this. The move towards private insurance is purely ideological.

Not accidentally, the suggestion by the Klein government that the federal government should define basis or core health services has been seconded, at the federal level, by Klein's ideological ally, the Reform Party (see chapter four). In a speech delivered in Saskatoon in April 1995, Reform leader Preston Manning argued that a key to deficit elimination in Canada is major change to the Canada Health Act, and specifically suggested that " the first item on the agenda should be a discussion of how best to divide essential health care services to Canadians into 'core services' and 'non-core services'."

Manning asserted that "core services" would be those which have guaranteed federal and provincial funding "up to some minimal national standard." Non-core services (that is, everything not defined as a "core service") would be the preserve of private insurance.[20]

Neither Manning nor the Klein government have tackled openly the main economic weakness of their approach: opening the field of medical and hospital services to private insurance companies would reduce the efficiency of the Canadian health delivery system, and hugely increase administrative overhead. There are two substantial reasons why this would be the case. First, a reduction in the number of services, or the range of services, provided by medicare could not result in a decrease in the administrative structures currently in place at both the federal and provincial levels in Canada. Indeed, one of the keys to both Klein's and Manning's two-tier approach to health care is to permit physicians to operate both inside the publicly administered system and in the private market at the same time. Under a partially privatized "core services" system, most physicians would find it in their interest to remain part of the medicare system, even if they elected to engage in some privately-financed or privately-insured services. Therefore, there would be no reduction in administrative overhead for the public system. There would simply be an added private insurance system, as in the United States. A recent study by KPMG Management Consulting comparing labour costs in Canada and the United States found, for example, that "medical insurance premiums in the United States cost nearly eight times what Canadian employers pay toward health care in Canada."[21]

Secondly, one of the additional economic advantages of the Canadian medicare system over the American system is the absence of duplication by a number of private insurance companies. Neither the Reform Party nor Klein's Alberta Tories has acknowledged the economic advantage of the current publicly administered system in Canada. They do not wish to address this question as they cannot argue with the logic that ten or twenty insurance companies entering the medical services field, each with a national network of claims, sales, collection, and administrative services, could not possibly add to the overall efficiency of medical delivery. Such a move could only create a huge (private-sector) insurance bureaucracy at an enormous cost to those Canadians able to pay (or negotiate the payment of) private insurance premiums.

No one could persuasively argue that such a system could be cheaper. So instead Reform and the Klein government simply ignore the cost to Canadians of implementing expanded private medical insurance, and focus on the "savings" that would result from reduced government expenditure. Neither the Klein government nor Reform want to debate health care costs including private insurance, because they know that only the really committed ideologues in their camps would favour paying more for a private sector system than for a public sector one. Yet their proposal is ultimately more costly.

In promoting private insurance for health care, the provincial government has failed to address the fact — largely because the opposition has not been effective in raising this question — that the "American" model of multiple payers is less economically efficient than the "single payer" Canadian model. Nonetheless, some observers have noted the ideological thrust of the government's position. In June 1995, a former Alberta health minister (and Klein's leading opponent in the 1992 Tory leadership race [see chapter two]) Nancy Betkowski, warned of a move to a "more Americanized system" of health care in Alberta, stating, "The Federal Minister is right to be concerned if we are starting to break our system down into those who can pay for more and those who can't."[22]

Health Care and Economic Health

There are other economic reasons to avoid the American model. Canada's health system consumes significantly less (as a percent of Gross Domestic Product [GDP]) than does the United States system — 9.7 percent versus 14 percent[23] — even without taking into account the enormous social costs associated with severe inequalities that are a hallmark of the U.S. system (thirty-five million people in the U.S. are uninsured and infant mortality rates in some inner cities approach third-world standards). Yet technologically our systems are very similar. Medical, nursing, and hospital practices in Canada are strongly influenced by United States developments. The most striking difference between Canadian and U.S. models is not in program delivery, but in funding and administration. Canada's "single payer," publicly-administered system for providing medical and hospital care is more efficient than the U.S. patchwork of private insurers, private hospitals, and complex payment systems.

Moreover, this increased efficiency has a significant impact on each country's GDP. If even half of Canada's advantage in proportion of GDP comes from the efficiency of a single payer public administration, the corollary is that a drive to replace that public administration with a U.S.-style insurance system would add literally billions of dollars in nonproductive drag to Canada's economy without any compensatory benefit.

Some statistics serve to put this difference in perspective. As Federal Health Minister Diane Marleau recently reported[24] Canada spends only 1.1 percent of our GDP on health care administration, or about $272 (Canadian) per person per year. The United States spends about two and one-half times as much, about $615 (U.S.) per person per year. Marleau's figures generate the following conclusion: moving Canada's health administration costs to the U.S. model could be expected to cost the Canadian economy more than $13 billion more each year. The economic impact of a move to private insurance would be disastrous for Canada.

Moving beyond the fallacy of private insurance, the "core services" concept does not address the real cost problems with the Canadian health care system. For example, the de-insurance model fails to address in any way the costs associated with the Canadian government's extension of patent privileges for multinational drug companies. Similarly, the de-insurance model has completely failed to address the costs associated with the fee-for-service model for the compensation of physicians. Indeed de-insurance would probably exaggerate the effects of a fee-for-service compensation system.

The 1993 "Starting Points" document released by Alberta Health contained a recommendation "that a true consumer health insurance plan be implemented to provide for basic health services."

The government's document continued:

> Defining basic health services will provide every Albertan with access to quality, publicly funded care. However health services deemed *non-essential* will still be made widely available, but will require partial or full payment by the consumer.
>
> To meet this requirement a health insurance program with a set deductible amount must be implemented (e.g., consumers

pay for non-essential health services to a certain dollar limit and
then insurance pays the outstanding amount).

Insurance premiums must be made by all adult Albertans
including seniors. (Emphasis in the original.)

Given the inevitable controversy that would flow from attempting to define
"non-essential" services, it is not surprising that the province sought to transfer this responsibility to the federal government in March 1995. Thus far, the
federal government has refused to accept this burden. However, here also
there is little room for optimism. The federal budget of February 1995, announcing a gradual elimination of federal cash transfer payments in the field
of health care, and the conversion of remaining transfer payments to a
"block" funding approach, together with statements from Prime Minister
Chrétien indicating a reduced commitment to medicare, have combined to
send a strong signal to Alberta that the "green light" is on for the Klein government's attack on medicare.

By January 1995, there were approximately fifteen private health clinics
in Alberta that were permitted by the provincial government to charge both
a "facility fee" to patients and the standard medicare fee for physicians'
services. All other provinces, and the federal government, took the position
that allowing double-dipping by these clinics contravened both the principles of universality and public funding of the medicare compromise, and
infringed the province's contractual obligations under the Canada Health
Act. Federal Health Minister Diane Marleau took what sounded like a hard
line, threatening Alberta with a reduction in transfer payments should Alberta not eliminate the double-dipping by private clinics. However, by setting a deadline of October 15, 1995, Marleau also cushioned the threat.
Moreover, the subsequent announcement of block funding and reduced
federal transfers effectively removed any real leverage the federal government had in blocking Alberta's initiatives.

Alternatives

There are positive steps which can be taken to address Canadians' concerns about the cost of their health delivery system without dismantling publicly-administered health insurance, and without engaging in restructuring to
the point of destruction. A coalition of Alberta health unions provided the
provincial government with an alternative set of recommendations for true
economies and effective service in the health care system in March 1994.
Some of these recommendations included the creation of true community

health centres, a strengthened role for public health, an enhanced focus on disease and injury prevention in the health system, the promotion of access to alternative (non-physician) providers of health services, the reduction of professional influence in drug purchasing decisions, and a more intelligent use of the current inventory of skills available to the Alberta government. While the government claims that reorganization has meant a move to community health centres, in fact the institutions labelled as community health centres were merely downgraded active treatment hospitals. The unions recommended more sweeping changes. Citing the example of Edmonton's Boyle-McCauley Health Centre, which serves approximately 5,500 clients in Edmonton's inner city, the unions pointed out that the cost of building the centre was recovered in the first year of operation in saved hospital utilization costs.

The government's funding cutbacks have generally reduced accessibility of public health services such as pre-natal clinics, well baby clinics, and public school health programs. The unions recommended that, instead, these programs should be bolstered to achieve long term health care savings.

The unions further endorsed the promotion of alternative providers to health care, noting that the system "gate keeper" for most services in the health industry is the most expensive participant, the physician. The unions stated:

> By placing the community health care centre as the hub of all medical services activity, and equalizing the partnership role between all professions in the industry, substantial savings and efficiency gains can be made. It is estimated that if efficiency were to be the primary factor under consideration, up to 30 percent of current general practice doctors could be replaced by nursing practitioners.[25]

Addressing professional influence in drug purchasing decisions, the unions noted a "lack of incentive or knowledge" with respect to opportunities for generic alternatives to commercial pharmaceuticals. The unions went on to note that "there are many things the provincial government can do to encourage the use of less expensive generic alternatives. The first is to actively lobby the federal government to reverse drug patent legislation that permits companies to hold a twenty-year monopoly on the production of brand name pharmaceuticals." The unions also called for provincial legislation requiring physicians to prescribe a generic alternative when available.[26]

There is no evidence that the Klein government implemented any of these recommendations, or has even addressed them in a formal way. The recommendations did not support the government's overwhelming drive towards private insurance, and as well came from a source (health care unions) to which Alberta conservative governments have never been sympathetic.

Conclusion

The job of delivering high quality health care to all Albertans has never been done in a fully satisfactory fashion. The problem that Alberta faced at the outset of the Klein government was not too much spending on health care. The problem was that even in wealthy Alberta, the revenues collected by the provincial government and passed on to health agencies fell short of what was essential to do the job of delivering high quality health care to all Albertans. The Klein government's solution — to make the job smaller; to say that we can get away with doing less for a growing and aging population — simply failed to address the health needs of the province, compounded structural weaknesses in the health delivery system, and engendered a flight of skilled labour that will not easily be remedied.

In other words, there was no room for complacency about the quality of the health care system, or the level of health care in general in Alberta at the start of the Klein regime. The health system was not then — and is not now — ideally structured or organized. Every dollar has not been wisely spent. But the job is not getting smaller, it is getting larger. Alberta needs more nurses and more physiotherapists, more dental hygienists and more gerontologists, and more health care attendants — not fewer — as the province's population ages. The questions that remain for the future are the degree of permanent damage caused by the Klein revolution, and the size of the task of repairing the damage when the revolution ends.

Notes

1. *Edmonton Journal,* 7 April 1995, A1.
2. *Edmonton Journal,* 5 April 1995, A1.
3. *Edmonton Journal,* 7 April 1995, A7.
4. *Edmonton Journal,* 2 April 1995, A1.
5. Ibid.
6. *Edmonton Journal,* 5 April 1995, A1.

7. *Edmonton Journal*, 9 April 1995, A6.

8. *Edmonton Journal*, 6 April 1995, A1.

9. *Edmonton Journal*, 7 April 1995, A7.

10. *Edmonton Journal*, 11 May 1995, A7.

11. Alberta Health Planning Secretariat, *Starting Points*, December 1993.

12. H. Northcott, "Health Status and Health Care in Canada: Contemporary Issues." In B.S. Bolaria, ed., *Social Issues and Contradictions in Canadian Society*, 2nd Edition (Toronto: Harcourt Brace Canada, 1995), 208.

13. M. Jackman, "The Regulation of Private Health Care Under the Canada Health Act and the Canadian Charter," *Constitutional Forum*,Volume 6, No. 2 (1995), 54-60.

14. Viewpoints Research, *Alberta Health Care Study*, 16 November 1993 (unpublished).

15. G. S. Lowe, "Summary of 1995 Albert Survey Findings on Attitudes Towards Changes in Health Care," prepared for the United Nurses of Alberta, 19 June 1995.

16. *Edmonton Journal*, 30 June 1995, A1.

17. *Health Services Funding Advisory Committee Newsletter*, May 1995, 5.

18. Calgary hospitals serve a significant number of out of region patients (approximately 16 percent of all hospitalizations); the impact of cuts to other regions is not as significant as that in Edmonton.

19. The precise number is elusive. Alberta Health reported a drop in health workforce employment of 7,264 individuals between March 31, 1993 and March 31, 1994. The same period saw a drop of 2,498 "full time equivalent" positions in health units, acute care and auxiliary hospitals, and nursing homes (*Health Workforce in Alberta*, 1994 [Edmonton: Alberta Health, January 1995]). Employment reductions for 1994 and 1995-96 can be expected to be in at least the same range, but were not published at the time of writing.

20. Notes for an Address by Preston Manning to the Saskatoon Club, Saskatoon, Saskatchewan, 6 April 1995.

21. *Globe and Mail*, 16 May 1995, B-8.

22. *Edmonton Sun*, 1 June 1995, 27.

23. *Edmonton Journal*, 10 April 1995, A3. See also Health Canada, Policy and Consultation Branch, *National Health Expenditures in Canada, 1975-1993* (Ottawa: Health Canada, June 1994).

24. Speaking Notes for the Minister of Health, The Honourable Diane Marleau, Fifth National Home Care Conference, Edmonton, 29 May 1995.

25. Health Care Unions of Alberta, *Turning Points: Recommendations Leading to True Economies and Effective Service in Alberta's New Health Care System* (Edmonton: Health Care Unions of Alberta, March 1994), 6.

26. Ibid.

Chapter Sixteen

PROTECTING MOTHER EARTH OR BUSINESS?: ENVIRONMENTAL POLITICS IN ALBERTA

John McInnis and Ian Urquhart

You can't put a price on the environment ... In the protection of the environment, making Alberta a world leader in the environment, it has to be an unlimited budget. We must protect Mother Earth.

Deputy Premier Ken Kowalski, September 23, 1994.[1]

Applause, indifference, anger — how should people who treasure Alberta's natural heritage react to this declaration that no expense should be spared to protect Mother Earth? To innocent ears, Ken Kowalski's comments suggest that Alberta's environment is in good, caring hands. Nothing could be further from the truth. Kowalski's sugary assurances camouflaged a more ominous portrait. Scarred by the Klein revolution, Alberta is now a land where environment ministers bless property owners who strip their lands of trees to feed the insatiable appetite of British Columbia's timber industry. Government, under the spell of the high priests of privatization, talks of letting companies regulate themselves. The public, it is contended, should trust business to be a better steward of environmental protection than government. The public is asked to ignore the chequered environmental reputations of some of the companies who may be entrusted with this responsibility. For the environment, Klein's revolution is one where the protection of Mother Earth finishes a distant second to the protection of business.

Swan Hills: Propping Up Business — Let Us Count the Ways

The controversy surrounding the Swan Hills hazardous waste treatment centre is a spectacular, costly example of how pampering business enjoys pride of place in Alberta. In the past, the Swan Hills Special Waste Treatment Centre was hailed as a "breakthrough" and described as "the most comprehensive treatment facility ever constructed in Canada or the United States."[2] Now, Albertans see that the real "breakthrough" at Swan Hills has been on behalf of the petroleum industry, the company which runs the treatment plant, and local politicians.

In February 1995, the Klein government, at the request of the operator of Swan Hills, opened the doors to the importation of hazardous waste from other provinces. Environmentalists were horrified. They had attacked this change in Alberta's "no import" policy from several different directions. They argued that allowing imports betrayed the government's commitment that Swan Hills would only be used to treat Alberta waste. They warned that the province would become a dumping ground for out-of-province wastes. They insisted that less-expensive waste elimination technologies made Swan Hills obsolete and that greater emphasis must be placed upon reducing the amount of hazardous waste produced by industry.

These arguments fell on deaf ears because they refused to grant legitimacy to the government's view of how the political economy of Alberta should be organized. According to this view, hazardous waste destruction — a laudable environmental objective — must be compromised by the fear of inconveniencing Alberta business. The province's petroleum industry, one of the largest generators of hazardous waste in the province, is excused from using Swan Hills. In 1992, the government had approved a quadrupling of the incineration capacity of Swan Hills — an expansion which assumed that petroleum wastes would be shipped to the plant. In 1993, government regulations excused oil and gas industry waste from the definition of hazardous waste. Since petroleum industry waste was not defined as hazardous it did not have to be sent to Swan Hills for treatment.

The decision to exempt petroleum industry waste from Swan Hills is not the only way in which the government corrupted this environmental initiative in order to appease business. The financing arrangements for Swan Hills are scandalous. They socialize the costs of environmental protection — all of the financial risks of environmental protection are borne by the taxpayers. Bovar, the province's private sector partner in this joint venture, is guaranteed a positive rate of return, even when the facility loses money. This was underlined in the 1993-94 financial report of Swan Hills. The plant lost $18.8 million. This operating loss was borne solely by the province despite its status as the minority partner in the joint venture. The province also paid Bovar $4.9 million (the guaranteed rate of return), bringing the province's total 1993-94 payments to $23.7 million. Small wonder critics condemned Swan Hills as a "sweetheart deal" for Bovar.

By 1994, Albertans had poured $257 million in subsidies, infrastructure, and services into Swan Hills.[3] Realizing the plant had become a financial bottomless pit, the Klein government announced on July 27, 1995 that it would buy its way out of the cost-plus agreement with Bovar. Under the terms of the buyout, Bovar would receive an additional one-time cash payment of $147.5 million to relieve the province of any further financial liability for operating losses, bringing total government losses to more than $400 million. While final details remain under negotiation, the signed letter of agreement provides that Bovar will assume ownership of the government's 40 percent share in the plant.[4]

The Legacy Klein Helped Build

Unfortunately, the Swan Hills story is typical. Alberta governments, whether headed by a Lougheed, a Getty, or a Klein, have never been very friendly to the environment. Several barometers show this. First, during the Lougheed and Getty administrations the prominence of the environment minister within the provincial cabinet dropped sharply.[5] Second, cuts to public spending — a hallmark of Klein's revolution — are nothing new when it comes to the environment. During the 1980s, the environment suffered the most, relatively speaking, as the provincial government practised a mild version of spending restraint which kept program spending increases well below the annual provincial inflation rate. While real spending (discounting for inflation) in social services and health rose by 53 percent and 34 percent respectively during the 1980s, real spending on the environmental function fell by a staggering 92 percent.[6]

The marginal importance of environmental protection to Alberta's governors is illustrated also by the history of the Environment Council of Alberta (ECA). In November 1994, Ty Lund, Alberta's Environmental Protection Minister announced the imminent death of the ECA. He would introduce legislation in the spring of 1995 repealing the Environmental Council of Alberta Act. For the province's environmental community, the death of the ECA preceded Lund's announcement by years. Since the 1970s, the authority of the ECA was sapped by successive administrations.

Politicians ignored recommendations that threatened development or important political constituencies — such as the ECA's opposition to the Oldman River Dam or to government-subsidized pulp mills which would pollute the province's waterways. Jim Henderson, the province's first environment minister, captured the essence of the ECA's marginal role in resource decision-making: "[T]he Tories found they couldn't take the heat that went with having an independent conservation authority ... so they castrated it and made it a kind of listening board for the minister."[7] Lund's announcement simply transferred the ECA from the land of the living dead to a more permanent internment.

Ralph Klein's journey to the premier's office began with his election in 1989 and his appointment to the high profile, if politically weak, environment ministry. He happened upon the post at a time when public concern about the environment was growing to unprecedented levels. The Chernobyl nuclear accident, global warming, ozone depletion, all helped propel environmental concerns to the upper strata of public opinion polls. In the aftermath of the criminal Exxon Valdez oil spill, the environment became the single most important issue in North America. In Alberta, provincial issues also fuelled environmental awareness. The Oldman River Dam controversy in the south, and pulp and paper mill megaprojects in the north stimulated environmental group formation and intense debate over environmental issues.

Klein's early rhetoric and actions teased provincial environmentalists. Some thought he would challenge the sorry legacy he inherited. He seemed to have packed the populist intuitions he used so well as Calgary's mayor into his suitcase when he journeyed north to join Premier Getty's cabinet. Opponents of the Alberta-Pacific pulp mill, shunned by Klein's predecessor, were welcomed by the new minister. He took steps to increase their access to the environmental impact assessment of this project. To a degree, this gesture revealed Klein's appreciation of the political advantages which could be realized through the magic of the "multi-stakeholder consultation." He established extensive public consultations to help draft the Alberta Environmental Protection and Enhancement Act. The Act, primarily a consolidation of existing legislation, increased substantially the penalties for serious environmental infractions and was often cited as evidence of Klein's commitment to environmental protection. The public also was consulted about economic instruments for waste reduction, a provincial clean air strategy, environmental impact assessments, and amending the Water Resources Act, among other issues.

For some, Klein's enthusiasm for public consultation as environment minister is a sign of shrewd political calculation. Well-managed public consultation processes defuse explosive issues and contain criticisms of government policies. As we argue later, this view of the symbolic nature of public consultation finds its strongest support in the tack Klein has steered since becoming premier, a tack which stresses the government's deregulatory intentions.

According to another view, however, Environment Minister Klein did not fit the robes of the shrewd master of political manipulation particularly well. Instead, his enthusiasm for consultation was bred from populist tendencies. He believed that any sign of public support was a vital, powerful political resource. Naiveté about the essence of political power may be found in the statements made by Rod Love, Klein's executive assistant and alter-ego (see chapter two), about the impact public consultation would have upon the environmental protection and enhancement legislation. Pointing to a stack of letters from Albertans demanding a tough regulatory profile Love concluded that: "We now know we can be as tough or as harsh as we want and nobody is going to stand up and say, 'Hey, what are you doing to Alberta business'."[8]

Events soon underlined for both Klein and Love that the real power in provincial politics was not wielded by letter-writing Albertans. Real power rested with the corporations that inhabit the vital sectors of the province's political economy (such as energy, construction, and forestry). This message was hammered home by the government's reaction to the environmental assessment of the Alberta-Pacific pulp mill project. Klein believed that the government should accept whatever recommendations were made by the joint federal-provincial environmental assessment review panel. "It would be political folly," he said, "not to abide by the recommendations."[9]

When the Review Board recommended withholding provincial approval for the pulp mill project the proponents of the project and their allies in the Getty cabinet and caucus lobbied the premier to circumvent the Review Board's recommendations. While Klein was attending an environmental conference in Vancouver the pulp mill defenders struck a deal with Premier Getty. The deal called for Alberta-Pacific to incorporate a slight process modification into its mill. In return, the pulp mill would not receive a further environmental review. This effectively guaranteed that the megaproject would proceed.

Klein was understandably livid about his exclusion from such an important meeting regarding an issue which was central to Klein's environmental credentials. Here was his opportunity to put into action his brave words about standing up to the premier in defence of the environment.[10] How-

ever, after a private meeting with the premier, Klein became contrite and
went along with the deal. Other than his sense that public opinion supported his position, Klein held few cards in this dispute. On the other side
of the table sat the premier, economic development ministers, one of the
world's most powerful multinationals, and the rank and file of the Progressive Conservative party. Klein folded. It was perhaps on this day that, by putting the environmental agenda aside, Ralph Klein "earned his spurs" in the
eyes of his Progressive Conservative colleagues.[11]

More of Same: Environmental Protection's Business Plan

Labour Minister Stockwell Day, one of the influential ministers in the
Klein government, has characterized the revolutionary potential of the government's agenda as "a total restructuring of what government is doing,
how much of it and why."[12] For the environment, the new orthodoxy inspired first the creation of the Department of Environmental Protection, a
merger of most of the components of the Departments of Environment and
Forestry, Lands, and Wildlife and parts of the Department of Recreation
and Parks. From the environmental protection perspective, this amalgamation had merit. It eliminated some of the departmental fragmentation that
may frustrate natural resource management. This fragmentation was criticized sharply during the Alberta-Pacific environmental impact assessment.
During this assessment the environmental consequences of forest management were never considered. Forestry, Lands, and Wildlife jealously
guarded all aspects of the forests and the environmental consequences of
logging were kept beyond the scope of Environment's assessment.[13]

Any advantages this amalgamation might deliver depends, however,
upon ensuring that the new department has sufficient financial resources
to carry out its mandate. This would require giving environment more, not
less, money. This course of action is rejected soundly in the three year
"business plan" drafted by Environmental Protection for the 1994-95/1996-
97 period. Meeting the government's deficit reduction target is near the
top of the list of goals outlined in the department's business plan. By 1996-
97, this plan calls for a 25.3 percent cut in departmental spending from actual 1992-93 levels.

For the environment, the business plan's significance rests as well upon
the signal it sent about the Klein government's view of who should be entrusted to protect the environment. The business plan endorses market-based
environmentalism. This approach presumes that market incentives and privatizing public goods offer more effective environmental safeguards than

regulations. The business plan calls upon the department to "privatize and outsource" and to "deregulate and streamline the regulatory process."

With this attack on the government's regulatory role, the ultimate symbolism of earlier rounds of public consultation with Albertans becomes strikingly apparent. When the government was nearly finished allocating virtually all of the northern boreal forest to the pulp and paper industry, the minister of Forestry, Lands, and Wildlife commissioned a study of the public comments expressed during open houses and public meetings held during early 1989. Throughout northern Alberta, the idea of deregulation was a heresy. Public commentary was dotted with concerns about whether Alberta had enough forestry and wildlife officers to police the spectacular growth of the forest products sector. More staff would be needed to ensure that industry complied with forestry and wildlife regulations.[14] Furthermore, when Klein invited Albertans to tell him about their thoughts on an environmental vision statement any interest in deregulation was noticeably absent from the thousands of replies he received. Instead of deregulation, Albertans demanded tougher laws and the political will and departmental capability needed to enforce those laws. "Albertans are looking for a determined and disciplined government," reported Alberta Environment, "one not 'afraid' to enforce strict laws, to see that strong measures are taken to protect their environment."[15]

This public outlook clashes sharply with the traditional approach to environmental protection in this province. The Alberta tradition in regards to environmental regulation is one of dialogue and negotiation with industry. This has contributed to confusion over environmental standards. Few Albertans realize that there are no provincial safety standards for many hazardous pollutants. Individual licence limits are negotiated for each plant. The "standards" which result are those set by the technical limitations of the existing or proposed plant technology — the "best practicable technology" in the words of the government. In some cases, particularly in the petroleum and petrochemical industries, pollution emission levels are high.

If Albertans were not enthusiastic about following the deregulatory path, industry left little doubt that it favours some combination of self- and de-regulation. Just before leaving the environment portfolio in October 1994, Brian Evans noted that the forest industry was interested in exploring the possibility of establishing self-regulatory relationships in "all of the responsibilities that the forest industry has — including reforestation, including the appropriate amount of cutting on the basis of sustainable forest yield ..."[16] For the forest industry, this interest springs in part from the additional operating costs changing environmental standards have had upon their operations. For example, the Daishowa-Marubeni International pulp mill at Peace River complained about being forced to change its pulp mill design to meet new pulp mill standards introduced by officials of the environment ministry. Companies have also objected to the ongoing expense of the monitoring and data collection demanded by government regulators. Many forest companies feel that their expenditures on expensive monitoring and data collection systems is a waste of company resources.

Industry's interest in deregulation certainly falls upon receptive ears in the person of Ty Lund, Evans' replacement in the Environmental Protection portfolio. Lund used his ministerial debut in the legislature to stress that "... I intend to look after the environment. I am committed to the government's goals of deregulation and intend to streamline and make the department more efficient."[17] This public policy preference and its implications for Environmental Protection were underlined emphatically in *Alberta Government Deregulation: Back to Basics*, a report released in November 1994 by the Progressive Conservative Caucus Task Force on Deregulation (see chapter eight). Many activities in Environmental Protection have been or are being placed under the deregulatory microscope. The regulations and/or procedures of four Acts are on this list as are timber management, foreign land ownership, and restricted development area regulations.[18] Water resource and integrated resource planning are also being investigated "to address stakeholder concerns."[19]

Should Albertans be concerned about these developments? The caucus task force offers soothing words that deregulation will not threaten environmental protection since it will only affect "out of date" rules: "Deregulation of this outdated legislation will have little affect on Albertans, but will make the total body of legislation that is in effect easier to access and to administrate [sic]."[20]

We remain sceptical. Government statements offer little when it comes to identifying the yardsticks for evaluating the worth of provincial regulations. What exactly are "stakeholder concerns" and how complementary are they to the department's environmental protection mandate? The regulatory review criteria identified by the Task Force — "necessary, efficient, and effective" — are notoriously malleable. We have little doubt that in the hands of Klein and his ministers these terms will become synonymous with making life easier for Alberta business, with scant regard for the environmental consequences.

The consultation process regarding the Task Force report virtually guarantees this result. Only business was regarded as a stakeholder in respect to government regulation. Therefore, only representatives of the province's business community were asked to respond to the report of the caucus task force. The idea that environment is a public good and something in which all Albertans hold a stake is subversive to the Klein government.

Public Participation as Symbolic, Manipulative Politics

One of the striking features of the Klein revolution in Alberta is the increasing extent to which public participation in the province has become symbolic and manipulative. The commitment to deregulating environmental protection generally illustrates the corruption of public consultation in the province. The decision to study the issue of deregulation through the vehicle of a Progressive Conservative caucus task force rather than an independent panel or an all-party legislative committee was further confirmation of this. Consultation is not offered to parties and members of the public who might not share the government's enthusiasm for this policy option.

A similar approach to public consultation characterizes other policy areas as well. For example, and most importantly, the budgetary direction taken by the Klein government has come from the Alberta Financial Review Commission, a blue ribbon panel of experts drawn overwhelmingly from the fields of business and accountancy. There were no alternative voices.

We strongly suspect that this same symbolic type of consultation will be prominent in the legacy of the Alberta Forest Conservation Strategy (AFCS). There is considerable irony in the fact that the AFCS was established after virtually the entire Green Area of the province was reserved for timber production. The strategy calls for a multi-stakeholder review of forest policy and legislation. Its lineage may be traced to the United States where it was developed to try to resolve the spotted owl controversy in the Pacific Northwest. Its core is a fascinating hybrid concept — "ecosystem management" — an ideal which purports to combine magically the key demand of the environmental movement for ecosystem protection with the need of industry and government to manage resources. As the offspring of the ambiguous, if not deceptive, concept of sustainable development, ecosystem management offers a certain level of security and safety. Why should we worry, after all, if the ecosystem is being managed?

The AFCS, like other forays into ecosystem management, depends upon a multi-stakeholder consultation process to generate land use planning and management decisions. Elsewhere, this approach has reduced conflict by reducing the autonomy of indigenous communities and the integrity of environmentally sensitive areas. It has promoted the myth that shared use of the forest is equitable and has ignored the fact that nature's carrying capacity cannot meet the demands placed upon it by consensus politics. Ecosystem management may place too high a value upon human knowledge and technology. Timber harvesting too often is allowed to proceed, only to discover later inadequacies in the inventory and monitoring systems used to calculate the sustainable allowable cut. It assumes that industry and government can manage the environment in ways that mimic, but are superior to natural processes. It assumes that industry has the skill, finance, and patience to create "natural disturbance regimes." So far the only known result is an emphasis on "management flexibility" and a desire for larger clearcuts. It remains to be seen whether the AFCS initiative will produce a consensus. The bold promise of the ecosystem management concept has proven elusive in practice. The AFCS is expected to report in the fall of 1995.

Bill 41: Another Step to Take Care of the Business Environment

Perhaps the development of greatest long-term concern on the environmental front was the passage of the Alberta Government Organization Act (Bill 41) in the fall 1994 session of the Alberta legislature. The legislation enables the government to make administrative changes to departmental organization without debating the matter in the legislature. It repeals a series of Acts pertaining to the organization of departments, gives cabinet the authority to change the names and composition of departments, and gives ministers the opportunity to modify their responsibilities by administrative decree. Government MLAs, such as Jocelyn Burgener of Calgary-Currie, freely acknowledged that Bill 41 was intended to allow the government to delegate responsibilities to private sector agencies. In legislative debate Burgener noted that "there are a number of provisions that allow for delegation, and quite frankly that is the way that the government wants to move on this issue: to establish the framework and develop the appropriate responsibilities."[21] (For a fuller discussion of Bill 41, see chapter nine.)

As Arlene Kwasniak, staff counsel for the Environmental Law Centre, notes this concentration of authority in ministerial hands raises several unsettling possibilities. Section 14(3) of the Act reads: "A Minister may sell, lease or otherwise dispose of any estate or interest in land under his administration and any personal property acquired by him under this section." It replaces a narrower provision of the Environment Act in which the minister was specifically prohibited from selling public lands. Given the prior existence of a provision in the Public Lands Act allowing government sales of public land at fair market value, Kwasniak worries that section 14(3) allows the minister to sell public lands privately and below fair market value.[22] Moreover, this section may allow ministers to evade other stricter statutory provisions governing the disposition of less than entire interests in the public lands of Alberta. These interests include grazing and land leases and may include the interests conveyed in forest management agreements.

Another provision of the Act, section 9(1), also is disturbing. It gives ministers the authority to "delegate any power, duty or function conferred or imposed on him by the Act or any other Act or regulation to any person." In Kwasniak's opinion, this "enormous delegation power" creates the potential for transferring "just about anything except the right to make regulations" to the private sector. The minister of Environmental Protection's power to overturn the rulings of the Environmental Appeal Board, for example, could be turned over to a company or association.[23]

The broad deregulatory potential contained in the Government Organization Act raises the spectre that the government may increase the opportunities for Alberta industries to conduct their own environmental monitoring. To some extent, this principle of self-monitoring is already a well-established, if controversial, practice in the province's environmental regulatory regime. In the pulp and paper sector, for example, companies are already responsible for monitoring the pollution contained in mill effluent and for supplying the government with that information.

Albertans must be sceptical of self-monitoring. In Alberta, this approach has failed both to protect the environment and to punish polluters adequately. The decade-long struggle waged by Grande Prairie area residents against Procter and Gamble's Grande Prairie pulp mill supports this conclusion.[24] In 1984, ranchers and other members of this northwestern Alberta community gathered to discuss their concerns about the impact which the pulp mill's pollution was having upon the local environment. Downstream of the point where Procter and Gamble discharged pulp mill effluent into the Wapiti river, the waters reeked. The river changed colour, turning dark brown after swallowing the mill's pollution. Ranchers complained that their livestock refused to drink from the tainted waters and speculated that the mill's pollution was somehow linked to the number of aborted calves in their herds. Bob Cameron, a Grande Prairie area sawmill owner and environmentalist, and the South Peace Environmental Association spearheaded efforts to force government to bring Procter and Gamble to court. Cameron, angered by the government's refusal to charge the company with violating the terms of its licences, laid charges of his own against

Procter and Gamble. Although his charges were thrown out of court, Cameron's initiative forced the government to act. The Attorney General's department laid 167 charges of its own against the company for violating the province's Clean Water Act. Subsequently, Procter and Gamble pleaded guilty to 43 charges and was fined $140,000 — the largest fine ever levied for a pollution offense in Alberta.

For the government, this result, as well as fines levied against Daishowa, demonstrated that self-monitoring does not compromise environmental protection. A closer examination of the Grande Prairie case suggests, however, a somewhat different conclusion. In some situations, self-monitoring actually will weaken a government's ability to convict polluters. In regards to Procter and Gamble, the company could not show that it had used proper laboratory procedures when it carried out its monitoring tests, a shortcoming government officials apparently missed. Consequently, the evidence gathered by Procter and Gamble's self-monitoring was of questionable value in the courts and nearly three-quarters of the charges against the company were dropped. Instead of punishing Procter and Gamble for polluting the environment, the government had to settle for punishing the company for not proving that proper laboratory procedures were followed when the toxicity of the mill's effluent was tested. To add insult to environmental injury, the government and the company issued a joint statement saying that there was no evidence that any environmental damage had been done to the Wapiti River.

Conclusion

Under the Klein government, the emaciation of environmental protection continues apace. Looking to the future, we are not optimistic that a change in this attitude is likely. First, Premier Klein seems likely to bask in the praise which his cost-cutting approach to deficit reduction has won him in boardrooms across Canada. Secondly, the provincial political scene does not seem likely to produce an alternative government in the next term that will offer the political and financial commitments environmental protection needs. The Liberals flirt with the same fiscal policy mix as the governing Conservatives while the New Democrats, devastated in the last provincial election, are virtually invisible.

These two tendencies are reinforced by the prevailing norms in the province's political culture. Resource exploitation, not preservation, retains a powerful appeal in the politically powerful rural areas of Alberta, areas which in northern Alberta have grown impatient with their lack of participation in previous provincial economic booms. In this type of political environment, the public's genuine interest in environmental protection is not intense enough to move the government off its chosen path. Barring an environmental disaster, it will be difficult to generate the intensity of public opinion needed to raise the profile of environmental protection issues.

One of the most discouraging features of the environmental policy pattern emerging in Alberta is its uncritical acceptance of the assumption that strict environmental regulations and enforcement are the enemies of economic growth. This, after all, is the thinking behind the embrace of deregulation generally. Regulations, by definition, hurt business; they always damage our economic prospects. If we want economic growth, so the conventional argument goes, the regulatory burden borne by business must be reduced.

An alternative view, one that conceptualizes stringent environmental regulatory regimes as catalysts for improving industrial competitiveness, must be introduced and championed in provincial political debate. This alternative is not the product of wild-eyed "radical" environmentalists, but is articulated instead by Michael Porter, the Harvard Business School expert on economic competitiveness. Tough environmental regulations stimulate innovations which often enhance competitiveness. Among Western industrialized nations, Porter found that Germany and Japan, countries with the strictest environmental laws, out-performed the United States in terms of economic productivity and GNP growth rate. A regulatory environment aiming at outcomes, rather than methods, often leads to an innovation in pollution control technology which "not only pollutes less but lowers costs or improves quality."[25]

Sweden offers another good example of the economic benefits which can be stimulated by tough environmental regulations. Much of the technology now employed to reduce the amounts of harmful chemical compounds produced by pulp and paper mills originated in Sweden. This is not an accident. The Swedish government told the pulp and paper industry in the late 1980s that they had to eliminate these compounds by the turn of the century. The industry responded by developing new, cleaner technologies. Now Sweden exports these technologies to world markets.

There is a further reason for tightening Alberta's environmental regulatory regime. World markets increasingly demand products which are produced in an environmentally sustainable manner. International institutions such as the Forest Stewardship Council, the United Nations Commission on Sustainable Development, and the European Union are working to establish such standards for forest products. Ensuring that industry adopts environmentally sustainable practices will become increasingly important to the global competitiveness of Alberta business.

A tougher environmental protection regime, therefore, must not be viewed as a noose around the neck of economic growth. From our point of view, Albertans must demand that government set higher, not lower, environmental standards and ensure that they are enforced. This is the only option which will lead the province down the path of long-term environmental and economic sustainability.

Notes

1. *Edmonton Journal*, 23 September 1994, A18.
2. B. G. Rabe, "Beyond the Nimby Syndrome in Hazardous Waste Facility Siting: The Albertan Breakthrough and the Prospects For Cooperation in Canada and the United States," *Governance: An International Journal of Policy and Administration*, Vol. 4(2) (April 1991), 193.
3. Applications Management Consulting Ltd., "The Importation of Hazardous Waste: A Review of Public Policy Issues," (June 1994), 6.
4. Government of Alberta, "Government to Exit Special Waste Treatment Business," News Release, 27 July 1995. See also, letter of intent signed by Monty L. Davis, president and CEO of Bovar Inc., and Environment Minister Ty Lund dated 21 July 1995.
5. D. Thomas, *Edmonton Journal*, 4 October 1989, A4.
6. A. Tupper, L. Pratt, and I. Urquhart, "The Role of Government," in A. Tupper and R. Gibbins, ed., *Government and Politics in Alberta*, (Edmonton: University of Alberta Press, 1992), 49-50.
7. *Edmonton Journal*, 4 October 1989, A4.
8. S. McKeen, *Edmonton Journal*, 9 February 1990, A7.
9. B. Laghi, *Edmonton Journal*, 24 December 1989, E1.
10. *Alberta Hansard*, 7 June 1989, 105.
11. For a more detailed account of the environmental politics surrounding the Alberta-Pacific project see L. Pratt and I. Urquhart, *The Last Great Forest: Japanese Multinationals and Alberta's Northern Forests* (Edmonton: NeWest Press, 1994).
12. G. Koch, "The World According to Ralph," *The New Pacific*, no. 10 (spring 1994), 16.
13. In 1990, the government's Expert Panel on Forest Management recommended a less extensive merger between elements of Forestry, Lands, and Wildlife and Recreation and Parks.
14. Concord Scientific Corporation, *Report on Public Information Meetings on Forest Development in Northern Alberta* (Concord Scientific Corporation: October 1989). The Expert Panel on Forest Management also recommended that more forestry

and wildlife management personnel must be hired if the government's stewardship role was to be performed adequately.

15. Alberta Environment, *Thanks from Alberta's Environment*, (no date), 22.
16. I. Urquhart, *Edmonton Journal*, 2 November 1994, A17.
17. *Alberta Hansard*, 24 October 1994, 2504.
18. Alberta, *Alberta Government Deregulation: Back to Basics*, (Edmonton: Government
    of Alberta, November 1994). The four Acts are the Water Resources Act, the
    Public Lands Act, the Wildlife Act, and the Provincial Parks Act.
19. Ibid., 21.
20. Government Reorganization Secretariat, *Facts About Deregulation*, (Edmonton:
    Government of Alberta, November 1994), 3.
21. *Alberta Hansard*, 26 October 1994, 2619.
22. A. Kwasniak, "The Alberta Government Organization Act," *Environment Network
    News*, forthcoming.
23. Letter to the I. Urquhart, 3 November 1994.
24. In 1992, Procter and Gamble sold its forest products assets, including the
    Grande Prairie mill, to Weyerhaeuser.
25. M. E. Porter, "America's green strategy," *Scientific American*, Vol. 264, no. 4
    (April 1991), 168.

Chapter Seventeen

CULTURE AND THE STATE IN ALBERTA, 1971-1995

George Melnyk

> "In the spring of 1994 the government changed more of its be-
> liefs and operations than at any time since the Conservatives
> had won their first election in 1971."
>
> Political journalist Mark Lisac[1]

On May 26, 1994, the *Calgary Herald* published a cartoon titled "No Funding for 'Risqué' Art Says Government Minister" in which a character from
the "Purity Panel," looking at an abstract painting — sweat streaming from
his face — exclaims in a horrified voice, "Is that a breast?!!"

The cartoon satirized the censorship ideas being floated by the Klein
government as it tried to bring culture under its hard-nosed, cut and slash
agenda the way it had health, education, and the civil service. The result was a
rift between the Klein government and the arts community over censorship, a
signal that relations between culture and the State were changing in Alberta.
But the censorship issue, which became prominent in 1994, had already
started in the last years of the Getty government when the then Minister of
Culture and Multiculturalism, Diane Mirosh, had been involved in gay-bash-
ing over some lesbian art at the Banff Centre, and which the arts community
in both Edmonton and Calgary had resisted vociferously with rallies and public actions. The government retreated but the battle lines had been drawn.

The message appeared that the arts community would suffer economic
penalties if it did not create material that met vaguely defined "community
standards," a phrase generally taken to mean the values promoted by rural
Christian fundamentalists. It harked back to the Social Credit era's view of
State support of the arts which presupposed compliant mainstream expression from artists. During the 1960s, for example, there was much consternation and legislative attack on literary work deemed antisocial which some
professors had published at the University of Alberta.

During the Lougheed era (1971 to 1984) the State's view of the role of culture in expanding Alberta was quite different from that of its penurious Social Credit predecessor and from its equally tight-fisted Klein successor. This article seeks to trace cultural policy in Alberta from the Social Credit period through the Lougheed and Getty administrations to the current situation under Klein. The emphasis will be on the growth fostered under Lougheed in the 1970s, the consolidation and stagnation of the 1980s under Getty, and the threats to culture under Klein in the 1990s. It will point out both the continuity of cultural policy through three decades and the evolution of a new reality determined by economic and political forces associated with the rise of the Reform Party and its reactionary ideology in Alberta.

Culture Under Ernest Manning

In 1946, Premier Manning's Social Credit government passed the Cultural Development Act, which saw the official birth of cultural policy in Alberta. Under the Act, the province became an actor in the cultural arena. The Act simply allowed for the establishment of boards:

> whose function shall be the encouragement, co-ordination, expansion and development of different aspects of the cultural life of the Province, and in particular, library facilities in both urban and rural districts, music, art, drama, handicrafts and physical recreation.[2]

It went on to establish a co-ordinator of cultural activities whose job it was " to supervise and co-ordinate the activities of the boards and report to the Minister."[3]

Most of the cultural activity that the Social Credit government was involved in was educational such as the Banff School of Fine Arts or the funding of libraries. Popular cultural education was carried out primarily through the extension department of the University of Alberta. Eventually other institutions such as the Jubilee Auditoriums and the Glenbow-Alberta Institute became part of cultural life.

In the 1930s and 1940s, drama on radio station CKUA (part of the University of Alberta and so publicly funded) encouraged indigenous talent. In the 1950s and 1960s local theatrical activity was limited, in most cases amateur, and without any critical mass. It was restricted to the activities of the intelligentsia, which itself was a tiny segment of the population, centred at the university. The Province of Alberta reflected the general state of Canadian Anglophone culture, which did not begin a significant indigenous expansion till the mid-1960s. In 1965 there weren't any trade book publishers in Alberta, but by 1995 there were thirty. What had happened?

Culture Under Peter Lougheed

The State's relationship to culture in Alberta took a quantum leap after the Progressive Conservative victory of Peter Lougheed in 1971. Under Social Credit a small bureaucracy had developed to administer cultural funds, but this bureaucracy did not come into its own until Lougheed's election and the ground-breaking creation of a Department of Culture headed by the enthusiastic personality of Horst Schmid.(The Department was originally titled Culture, Youth, and Recreation.) This was a first for prairie Canada and signalled the new government's interest in creating a distinct, though not important, portfolio for culture. As is the case in all Canadian jurisdictions, ministers of culture do not rank very high in cabinet pecking orders.

The Department of Culture dealt with historic sites, the operation of museums and auditoriums, the literary arts, visual and performing arts, etc. It had a budget in 1973 of $7.8 million.[4] In 1979-80 with the 75th anniversary celebrations of the province the budget had gone up to $25.8 million.[5]

Jack O'Neill was the Deputy Minister of Culture from 1980 to 1993. His appointment spanned three administrations (Lougheed, Getty and Klein) and six ministers (Le Messurier, Anderson, Stevens, Main, Mirosh and Mar). He remembers 1980 as being a year with "a very comfortable budget" because of the 75th anniversary celebrations.[6] That was the year that Mel Hurtig received $4 million for his Canadian Encyclopedia project. O'Neill believes that culture did very well under Lougheed with large sums going to capital expenditures to create such institutions as the Royal Tyrrell Museum of Palaeontology and the Calgary Centre for the Performing Arts.

The 1970s were a time of economic boom, of State expansion, of "world-class" aspirations, of a dynamic regional bourgeoisie full of itself and wanting to put some cultural frosting on its economic cake. This nouveau riche urban elite felt comfortable with cultural activity as an adjutant to its new arriviste status.[7] This was quite a change from the rural Social Credit culture of the 1950s. Not surprisingly Jeannie Lougheed, the premier's wife became a key player in cultural development in the province. "She felt it was necessary for the quality of life," O'Neill comments.[8] Mrs. Lougheed was rewarded later on for her cultural advocacy by an appointment to the board of the Canada Council when Mulroney was in power.

One of the main cultural initiatives in the Lougheed years was the establishment of various foundations to fund the arts. The first was The Alberta Art Foundation established in 1972 to purchase Alberta art with a grant of $50,000. By 1985 it was receiving over $1 million, practically all of it from lottery income.[9] After the Art Foundation came the Performing Arts Foundation, the Historical Resources Foundation, the Literary Arts Foundation, as well as noncultural foundations such as the Wild Rose Foundation and the Sports, Wildlife, and Recreation Foundation, all of whom became dependent on lottery income in the 1980s. Cultural funding rose through the 1970s and into the 1980s, first via general revenues and then through lottery income.

In the Lougheed period the administration of cultural policies and grants was the responsibility of civil servants who practised paternalism, making decisions on artistic merit and suitability as well as fulfilling political objectives. The 1970s saw a major growth in local theatre, the publishing scene, and the visual arts, all of which became established by the 1980s. Just as the economy flourished so did a renaissance in cultural activity. It is not farfetched to see the 1970s as an Alberta version of the times of the de Medicis. Art and culture were in and the State had the money to pay for it.

Culture Under Don Getty

O'Neill describes cultural policy under Lougheed's successor, Don Getty, as one of "benign indifference."[10] The Department was renamed Culture and Multiculturalism and general revenue funding for the arts began to decrease, while the importance of the semi-arms-length foundations increased. For example, the Alberta Foundation for the Literary Arts, one of the last foundations to be established (1984), began with $800,000 and ended in 1991 with $1.3 million, an increase of 60 per cent.[11] In 1981 the Alberta Foundation for the Performing Arts received half a million dollars from the lotteries, while in 1989 it received $2.1 million, an increase of over 300 per cent in less than a decade![12]

The financial gusher that had come on stream was the Western Canada Lottery, which had begun as an insignificant source of revenue for the government in the 1970s but which by the 1980s had become a significant pile of money. For example, in 1976 the Alberta Art Foundation received $70,000 in tax revenues and $16,000 from the Interprovincial lottery while ten years later it received zero income from tax revenues but $1.1 million in lottery monies.[13]

The key to this development was the federal government's agreement in the 1970s to get out of the lottery business and leave it in the hands of the provinces. Clive Padfield, currently the Executive Director of the Alberta Foundation for the Arts and the Director of the Arts and Cultural Industries section of the Department of Community Development, remembers being told by informed civil servants back in 1979 (he was working on a cultural study for the provincial government) that lottery income would be a "minuscule" source of funds.[14] At that time no one imagined that lottery funding would become the *prime* source of government monies for the arts. This is what the Getty era inaugurated.

The Getty decade from 1984 to 1993 was a time of consolidation and transformation. The various free-standing foundations were rolled into one foundation in 1991. The Alberta Foundation for the Arts took over the budgets and programs of the three culture-specific foundations for a total of $15.7 million in lottery funds. This amount had increased to $16.1 million by 1994 and is expected to remain steady until 1997 when the lottery licenses are up for renewal.[15]

The Ministry of Culture and Multiculturalism went through a gradual reduction in budget and staff as the Getty government began to consolidate government functions in order to trim costs. Under Lougheed there had been only two ministers of culture, Schmid and LeMessurier, in a thirteen-year period, while under Getty there were four ministers in less than ten years. Culture as a department was losing its status in a time of economic restraint and a downturn in revenues. Rising lottery income was still outside the main government estimates, much to the chagrin of the provincial auditor. Lottery income was viewed as a vast slush-fund that did not need legislative debate or approval. It was not until 1995 that this situation was to change. By that point lottery income was in the billions and could no longer be treated as an adjunct to government finances.

In the 1980s the foundations took over the burden of direct grant funding to the arts because it was an easy source of revenue to move around and allocate. But this meant the Department of Culture and Multiculturalism saw its relevance downgraded and it was eventually placed on the chopping block under Klein. Another Getty funding change for the arts was a further twist on gambling — the use of casinos and bingos to fund arts organizations that had charitable tax status. Volunteer members of many of these nonprofit organizations got used to working casinos to earn money for their cultural activities. In short, the Lougheed world of State intervention and support for the arts was replaced by the Getty view that the arts could be funded through a secondary income source — State-supported gambling. The implications for the arts in Alberta of this fundamental change were not debated. It was accepted by the arts community because it was first viewed as a new source of funding to supplement tax dollars for the arts. As the government's funding for tax-supported cultural activities began to decrease, foundation incomes increased, so there was no great outcry. There was still money around.

Culture under Ralph Klein

The full implications of this retreat from public-funded support for the arts to gambling revenues became apparent under Klein. As a symbolic act of cost-cutting and the creation of a lean and mean cabinet, Ralph Klein amalgamated ministries in 1993. He closed down Culture as a separate entity and rolled it into the Department of Community Development under Gary Mar. (Neither the deputy minister nor the assistant deputy minister are from culture). The Alberta Foundation for the Arts, which Getty had created under his Reform Party-oriented minister of culture, Doug Main, became the sole funder of artists and arts organizations. This final consolidation was sold as a cost-saving administrative reduction. There are currently thirty-three employees of the Arts and Cultural Industries section of Community Development (down from 50 five years ago) and seven employees of the Foundation.[16] The civil servants administer the Cultural Industries Agreement signed with the federal government that has provided $7 million to cultural industries over the past few years and carry out AFA duties, but the paternalistic hands-on experience of the Lougheed years has disappeared. Now cultural industries formulae and peer juries are the key determinants of who gets funding, while the administrative structure of the State is basically used to distribute lottery dollars. "Eighty per cent of the Arts Branch work is now Foundation based," explains Padfield.[17]

What is the profile of culture and the State under Klein? It is both an inheritance of the Getty changes and an initiation of its own, more radical agenda. Denise Roy is the Chair of Arts Administration at Grant MacEwan Community College in Edmonton. She is also the chair of the City of Edmonton Mayor's Task Force on Investment in the Arts. She describes the Klein era as one of "a conservative trend."[18] "If you simply look at the numbers," she explains," it is hard to make the province look bad."[19] The fact that AFA funding is secure at current levels till 1997 reflects this appearance of health. According to the Canadian Council for Business in the Arts, Alberta's per capita funding has fallen from $2.41 in 1990 to $2.28 in 1993.[20] This is still above the national average. However the national average has in-

creased since 1990, while Alberta's has decreased. In real dollars support is
dropping. But Roy feels that funding cuts are not where the real story lies.

The continuing discourse on so-called "community standards" is an expression of censorship and this creates a climate of uncertainty and fear.
She calls it "ideological hysteria."[21] Apparently the government is discussing whether upcoming AFA grant contracts will contain a clause stating the
recipient agrees to return the funds should they be convicted of a criminal
act in the course of completing the project. For some MLAs even this kind
of pressure is not enough; they want something tougher. Another aspect of
culture under Klein is the emphasis on gambling income as the lifeblood of
the arts whether from lotteries or from casinos. Culture is viewed as a non-
essential State activity, indicating that government has only a "soft" relationship to the issue, not a hard one. The final result of such an approach is
that government could use lottery funds for more important purposes, such
as health and education, with culture left to the marketplace.

In looking over the Klein agenda for Alberta, one can readily see that
cultural policy reflects the general thrust of the government. There are a
number of facets to this agenda that have already appeared in other sectors
and from which culture is not exempt, though it has not been as hard-hit as
other areas. These facets are privatization, centralization, censorship, lottery-based funding, no arms-length principle, and homophobia.

Privatization

The major privatization initiative by the Klein government in the cultural area, broadly defined, was the privatization of ACCESS, the province's
education and entertainment television station, and CKUA, Alberta's provincial radio station since the 1920s. ACCESS was sold in 1994 to a Toronto-
based communication company called Canadian Learning Television. The
province committed itself to producing $43 million worth of programming
over the next five years — a nice deal for the buyer. CKUA was a radio station that no private entrepreneur wanted so it was allowed to become a lis-
tener-supported nonprofit foundation. Based on the privatization principle
the province has divested itself of its stake in the media and turned to private stations for its major communication needs. The *Calgary Herald* called
the ACCESS sale "a potential disadvantage for Alberta."[22]

As the government seeks to expand the private sector and reduce
the public sector, there are a number of cultural institutions that could
be sold if a private buyer were available. The major auditoriums in Edmonton and Calgary are a possibility, as well as smaller venues. One
doubts, however, that the Royal Tyrrell Museum of Palaeontology or the

Provincial Museum would go up for sale. Since so much of cultural activity is produced by nonprofit organizations, and private individuals, there is little leeway for privatization.

Centralization

The Alberta Foundation for the Arts with $16 million in lottery funding is the bedrock of State support to the arts in Alberta. Individual artists, arts organizations and performing arts societies are dependent on its programs. It is administered by a board of directors chaired by Jock Osler of Calgary, a former journalist, public relations expert, and one-time press secretary to Conservative Prime Minister, Joe Clark.

The board is composed of ten members from across the province, some of whom have served on the boards of foundations that were rolled in AFA. A great deal of power is concentrated in this organization and this concentration is similar to the centralization of education and health by Klein. With such a small board, dealing with such a breadth of cultural activity from writers to dancers to painters to theatre groups, the innate responsiveness to various artistic constituencies offered by the former foundations has been lost in exchange for the big picture and a harmonization of programs.

The amalgamation represented by AFA was a Getty government initiative that Klein adopted for himself. Its centralized structure meant that the board was a solitary and convenient target for influence whenever the Klein government, which made the appointments, wanted to make its impact felt in the arts. The first area in which it tried to do so was censorship.

Censorship

When Jock Osler was asked about "Community Standards" as a policy that required the payback of government funding if any recipient was convicted of a obscenity charge, he replied in his best public relations manner:

> I feel most profoundly that it is not the role of the Foundation to be a censor. While I could accommodate some notion of recourse or redress in the event of a conviction under the laws of the country, I would not put myself or the Foundation or any Albertan, ahead of the law. Freedom of expression is a very important component of artistic expression. And artists are already bound to observe the laws of the country just like everyone else.

Alberta has a long and successful tradition of arms-length funding and it is important that tradition continue.[23]

At the same time, Gary Mar, the minister responsible for cultural policy, stated for the record that:

Art that breaks federal laws dealing with obscenity, child por-
nography and promotion of hatred against identifiable minorities is subject to criminal prosecution ... There may be financial
risks as well. Under a recommendation of the Alberta Foundation for the Arts, artists and arts organizations convicted under
federal obscenity laws will have to repay any provincial funding
used to create or present illegal work. I support striking a balance between allowing artistic freedom of expression and the
public concern over funding of illegal and obscene work ...[24]

What seems to have happened is that the reference to the courts was a
way to sidestep the pressure from Tory backbenchers for direct censorship
and was Gary Mar's way of applying censorship indirectly. In 1994 an open
letter was sent to Gary Mar by the Ukrainian arts community in Alberta ex-
pressing "alarm" over the community standards issue.[25] While denying he
was an advocate of censorship, the minister replied that, "Financial assistance to artists has always had some string attached."[26]

The threat of having to pay back grant funding after the fact is a serious problem for nonprofit cultural organizations that usually have neither
money left over at the end of the year nor a significant line of credit with
banks. Moreover, cultural workers, who are among the poorest paid in Canada, have no reserves with which to return funds already spent. The implication of such a condition for accepting grants is comparable to libel chill
in journalism. It makes people afraid and fear is a necessary component of
repression.

So far nothing serious has happened. When Brad Fraser's *Poor Super
Man* was staged in Edmonton in 1994, this sexually-explicit play was not
charged under the Criminal Code, but that clause was not yet in place in
the AFA contract. If it had been the theatre may have decided to pass on it
because of the potential risk involved.

The issue of censorship in Alberta under Klein took a major leap forward in 1994 when Tory MLA Victor Doerksen called for the removal of No-
bel Laureate John Steinbeck's *Of Mice and Men*, from school shelves. The
writing and library communities responded vociferously, making Freedom

to Read a major cultural issue. In fact, AFA's Jock Osler appeared at the February 27, 1995, Second Annual Steinbeck Freedom to Read reading in Calgary and spoke once again of his opposition to censorship. Technically, he was right that the courts, not AFA, would impose censorship, but he never mentioned why the concept of a payback provision had to be instituted at this juncture when the foundations had operated well without it in the past and such provisions did not exist in funding agencies like the Canada Council. (The model for the proposed clause was the American National Endowment for the Arts).

The atmosphere of censorship that has come to the fore in cultural policy in Alberta was acknowledged when twelve Tory MLAs, including five ministers of the crown, voted against a motion that the legislature recognize Freedom to Read Week in 1995.[27] In spite of Gary Mar's manoeuvres, cultural repression remains part of the Klein government's agenda.

Lottery-based arts funding

It is clear that the arts in Alberta are now being funded by gambling revenues, which have become a significant source of revenue for the State in Alberta under Klein. Once considered "soft" money, gambling revenue generated by video lottery terminals and lottery ticket sales has become a core income source. This trend had developed under Getty and is now complete under Klein.

The implications for culture are serious for several reasons. First, lottery funding is based on five-year licences which are provided to beneficiaries like AFA and which come up for renewal in 1997. Ruth Smillie of Catalyst Theatre in Edmonton, while speaking at an "economics of censorship" forum in Calgary in 1995, expressed a genuine fear that the Klein government would work to marginalize and criminalize the arts community so that it would have an excuse to cut off funding in 1997.[28]

It is worth examining what is happening to provincial funding. In the case of Catalyst Theatre, which is a socially-active company, the Canada Council provided $35,000 in 1989/90, while AFA's predecessor APFA provided $50,000.[29] A few years later AFA provided only $37,000.[30] In most cases of theatre companies provincial funding is in the range of 10 to 15 percent of gross income. This means that provincial funding is important but not essential to survival.

The small percentage of lottery funding currently going to culture (about 2.5 percent) is not a significant part of lottery income. A decade earlier it amounted to 14 percent.[31] This low figure may be the reason why it has not suffered major cutbacks like other sectors. There just isn't much to

take. Some major cultural institutions have been cut sharply. The Glenbow
Museum in Calgary has seen its provincial funding cut by 26 percent in the
past five years.[32] But the Banff Centre has just received a one-time $7 mil-
lion grant for a planned expansion. These funds are to be used to set up
profit-making operations to fund its arts program. The Centre is anticipat-
ing cuts in provincial operating grants of 39 percent by 96-97 ($14 to $8
million).[33] Everyone is now starting to scramble to meet the new reality of
reduced State support. There is even a worry that lottery funding will be
used to support libraries.[34] With over $2 billion rolling into the provincial
treasury from lotteries, there is a concern in the arts community that its
sideshow status may be pre-empted by the big boys — education, health,
etc. With gambling income a pillar of State revenue in the 1990s, the arts
community has had to fight hard to try to keep away for-profit casinos, an
idea floated by Klein, so as to keep its access to this gambling pot. The Lottery Review Committee, instituted by Klein in 1994 to set new goals for lottery funding, has been holding hearings across the province. Considering
the general mood in the province and the atmosphere of cutbacks to essential services, the arts community is justifiably worried that it will be pushed
aside. This is the end result of removing tax dollar support from culture.

The Arms-length principle

In a recent interview, Clive Padfield, Executive Director of AFA, expressed the view that the province of Alberta hasn't had an "arms-length"
tradition.[35] By this he meant that Alberta has never had an arms-length arts
council such as other provinces have or the federal government has in the
Canada Council. The old act of 1946 indicated the Social Credit government
liked to work through appointed boards but it made sure the minister was in
charge. The Alberta legislation establishing foundations like AFA has never
recognized the arms-length principle and has instead given the minister responsible ultimate authority. The foundations were and continue to be
viewed as arms of the government, carrying out the goals it has set for them.

Historically this has produced tension between the boards of the foundations and the ministry, especially when politically sensitive matters have
come up (from policy to grants) and compromises have been effected. The
current payback idea at AFA could be viewed as an example of political interference if one believes in the arms-length principle applying to AFA, but
as normal business if one follows the letter of the Act. In the House of Commons, when some grant is challenged by the opposition, the minister of the
day responsible for the Canada Council usually defends its independence.
In Alberta the government traditionally gets upset.

In an era of privatization, centralization, censorship, and lottery-based funding it is not surprising that the arms-length principle in culture is under constant jeopardy. Whatever happens to the payback idea in the future, it is obvious that the government of Alberta will make the key decisions and the AFA will implement them.

Homophobia

A basic tenet of the Klein government is homophobia.The government's refusal to make sexual orientation a part of Human Rights Legislation leaves it far behind other Canadian jurisdictions. Not surprisingly, the government's homophobic attitude has surfaced in the cultural field.

Three specific incidents come to mind. The first occurred in 1993 when Diane Mirosh, then minister of Culture and Multiculturalism, attacked a display of lesbian art at the Banff Centre. This uproar (and others) eventually led to Ms. Mirosh's removal from Cabinet. (She's back now.) This incident paralleled the refusal of the Tory-dominated legislature to pass a motion congratulating the Alberta-born lesbian (and vegetarian) singer, k.d. lang, for winning a Grammy. This was followed a year later by the government's refusal to support a motion congratulating the gay playwright, Brad Fraser of Edmonton, for his winning of a major Canadian award. This continuing small-mindedness is a good example of why some artists in Alberta feel that the Klein government has defined them as enemies of the State.

The Future of Arts and Culture in Alberta

The most recent Canada Council statistics (1992-93) detailing the economic impact of the arts and culture sector indicates that almost 60,000 Albertans were employed in the cultural sector and that this produced a $1.3 billion GDP.[36] In 1986, the total cultural workforce was about 25,000, far less than it is today.[37] In 1992, Alberta arts festivals grossed $7.6 million with an attendance of 1.2 million of which almost a half were visitors to the province.[38] Thirty Alberta book publishers produced 150 titles with sales income of $20 million.[39] These figures indicate that culture is a thriving business in Alberta and much of the growth has to be attributed to the base established in the Lougheed period with taxpayer funding of the arts.

In 1992/93 the cultural development component of the Department of Community Development's estimates were $18 million, up from $12 million in 1980, but this amount barely covered inflation and Alberta's share of the Cultural Industries Agreement, which is about to end.[40] The retreat

from State-sponsored cultural activity is gradual but evident. The investment the province has made in culture during the past two decades has
generated a high level of creative achievement. In 1994 three of seven Eng-
lish-language categories of the Governor-General's literary awards were won
by Alberta writers. The about-to-expire Cultural Industries Agreement that
was jointly-funded by the federal and provincial governments made an important impact in an area like publishing, which allowed for international
marketing and for the expansion of locally-based cultural industries. All this
seems to be a thing of the past.

The partial funding of the arts through lottery dollars that occurred
under Getty may have temporarily increased direct arts funding. But there
is a real worry that the ideology of the Klein government is antithetical to
State support for the arts and that by 1997 lottery funding will disappear
just as tax-based funding disappeared under Getty.

This is a reversal of the Lougheed legacy and the arts community recognizes that under Klein it may well be viewed as a liability rather than an
asset. The contemporary size of the cultural sector would suggest that it can
not easily be done away with. If the government had not been a major
player in funding culture in Alberta and had left this area to either the private sector or federal funding, current cultural productivity would probably
be less than half what it is today with all the economic spin-offs that entails.

Conclusion

In spite of the Klein government's unease with State funding of culture, culture has achieved a critical mass since 1971 and has established a
powerful presence in Alberta. Culture is now truly Albertan. The Klein government's attempts to label it as antipopulist and un-Albertan will result in
a battle between image and reality, a dialectic whose outcome cannot be
predicted. Should lottery funding be removed from culture in 1997 there is
every likelihood that there will be a significant decrease in the quality and
quantity of cultural activity in the province.

Notes

1. M. Lisac, *The Klein Revolution* (Edmonton: NeWest Press, 1995), 198.
2. *Revised Statutes of Alberta,*1955, 1181.
3. Ibid, 1183.

4. Alberta Treasury, Dept. Public Accounts 1972/3, 400

5. Alberta Treasury, Dept. Public Accounts 1979/80 vol.1, 6.2.

6. Interview with Jack O'Neill, Edmonton, 15 February 1995.

7. J. Richards and L. Pratt, *Prairie Capitalism: Power and Influence in the New West* (Toronto: McClelland and Stewart, 1979), 166.

8. Interview of 15 February 1995.

9. Ibid.

10. Alberta Art Foundation annual reports, 1972 and 1984/85.

11. Annual Reports of the Alberta Foundation for the Literary Arts 1985/96 and 90/91.

12. Annual Reports of the Alberta Foundation for the Performing Arts 1981/82 and 90/91.

13. Annual Reports of the Alberta Art Foundation, 1976/77 and 1985/86.

14. Interview with Clive Padfield, Edmonton, 16 February 1995.

15. Annual reports of the Alberta Foundation for the Arts 1992/93 and 93/94.

16. Padfield interview.

17. Ibid.

18. Interview with Denise Roy, 16 February 1995.

19. Ibid.

20. Ibid.

21. Ibid.

22. *Calgary Herald*, 20 November 1994, A4.

23. *ArtsBridge*, 9, winter 1994, 12.

24. *ArtsBridge*, 9, winter 1994, 2.

25. *Acua Vitae*, October 1994, 7.

26. Ibid, 8.

27. *Calgary Herald*, Wednesday, 1 March 1995, A12.

28. Ruth Smillie, Alberta Theatre Projects panel, 24 February 1995.

29. Figures provided by Denise Roy.

30. AFA Annual Report for 1993/4.

31. Alberta Lottery Review Committee discussion paper, January 1995, 5.

32. *Calgary Herald*, 23 February 1995, D11.

33. *Calgary Herald*, 11 February 1995, B8.

34. *Calgary Herald*, 15 December 95, B4.

35. Padfield interview.

36. Statistics Canada, Culture Statistics Program, Regional Economic Impact of the Arts and Culture Sector Working Document, 6 December 1994, 8

37. Arts and Cultural Industries Branch working document, Ministry of Alberta Community Development, 1994, 4.

38. Ibid. 2

39. *Calgary Herald*, 25 February 1995, A18.

40. Alberta Treasury Department Estimates 1992/93.

PEOPLE

Chapter Eighteen

ROAD KILL: WOMEN IN ALBERTA'S DRIVE TOWARD DEFICIT ELIMINATION[1]

Gurston Dacks, Joyce Green, and Linda Trimble

> *Economy is the bone, politics is the flesh,*
> *watch who they beat and who they eat,*
> *watch who they relieve themselves on,*
> *watch who they own.*
> *The rest is decoration.*[2]

The Klein government's dramatic budget cuts have claimed many victims. However, one of the most striking patterns in this carnage is the large number of women casualties, far out of proportion to the number of women in Alberta society. This chapter will argue that, because of their unpaid and unrecognized labour in the home and community, their economic dependence on government programs, and their concentration in vulnerable "pink collar ghetto" jobs, women have borne the brunt of reductions in health care, social services, and education spending. The chapter will show that women are the primary victims of cuts to programs and services, layoffs and public service wage reductions.

It will argue that the effects of the Klein budgetary revolution on women's economic and social lives dovetail nicely with the government's antifeminist agenda. This is not to suggest that the Klein cabinet has explicitly made policy choices intended to hurt women. However, it has made its policy choices within an ideological framework whose narrow vision of the role of women in society is entirely consistent with the consequences of its economic and social policy decisions. That is, there are no meaningless coincidences.

The consequences of the Klein agenda reflect the convergence of the two ideologies, neoliberalism and neoconservatism, that drive and are fundamental to understanding the Klein revolution. Neoliberalism is an economic ideology that promotes the freest possible market for what is increasingly fluid and transnational capital, seeking minimum government in general and minimum regulation of corporate activity in particular. A central tenet of neoconservatism is a preference for hierarchical and authoritarian social relations. One of its most important expressions is its promotion of patriarchal social organization — the systematic domination by men of social, economic, and political power — and a social and family mythology emanating from and supportive of patriarchy. Neoliberalism and neoconservatism together promote and rationalize a more hierarchical Alberta that features increasing inequalities of wealth and power.

> **"What we're doing in Alberta is disastrous. We're ignoring needs of a large sector of the population and government is presenting this as essential for deficit fighting."**
>
> *Christopher Smith, Edmonton Social Planning Council.*[3]

The Klein government's vision of the ideal family fuses neoliberal and neoconservative goals. With dad at work and mom at home caring for the kids, providing support for the elderly or ailing relatives, and offering her services to school and community free of charge, many government services can be slashed, satisfying the neoliberal ethic, while women are increasingly compelled to play the role to which the neoconservative agenda consigns them.

Dominant features of the policy landscape of Alberta reinforce this pattern. Women are the primary workers in the sectors targeted for staff reductions, and women and children predominantly rely on the services and supports provided by those same sectors. For example, the loss or reduction of many women's jobs forces them to live out the "back to the kitchen" ideology of Alberta Tories. The increasingly desperate financial situation of Alberta's poorer women can be seen in many cases as punishment for (or at least objectional in the context of) their not conforming to the patriarchal family model upon which neoconservatism insists.

Women, Work, and Poverty

This fate could easily befall women elsewhere in Canada because they tend to possess fewer economic, social, and political resources than men and are therefore particularly vulnerable to the type of deficit reduction measures pursued by the Klein government. Women working full time in the Canadian labour force in 1992 earned on average 71.8 percent of what men working full time earned.[4] But the majority of women do not have full-time jobs, and instead rely on casual or part-time work. Women constitute 45 percent of the total Canadian labour force (and 44 percent of the Alberta labour force), but less than half of female members of the labour force (45 percent) work full time all year round. The 1991 census showed that 30 percent of women in the labour force work part-time, and 25 percent are self-employed, in contract positions or perform seasonal labour. Women comprised 70.4 percent of the part-time labour force in 1991. Part time jobs are less well paid, and are rarely accompanied by benefits such as dental care and pension plans. Women who are employed part-time or as casual workers throughout their working lives will likely not have sufficient pension income to live above the poverty line after age sixty-five.

Because of the unequal distribution of work, pay, and the responsibilities many bear as caregivers to their families, increased labour force participation has not ensured women's economic or social independence. Women, especially elderly women and single or divorced mothers, are significantly more likely than men to live in poverty. A minimum wage earner in 1991 fell well below the poverty line, and, notably, women comprised 60.5 percent of minimum wage earners in Canada. In Alberta, full-time work at the minimum wage of $5.00 per hour yields $10,400 per year, $5,109 below the poverty line. Women form the bulk of the working poor and the unemployed poor; 12.4 percent of Alberta families are "lone parent" families, the vast majority of which (89 percent) are headed by women.[5] The 1991 census showed that in Alberta an alarming 68 percent (47,060) of single mothers with children under the age of eighteen live below the poverty line, compared to 42 percent (6,015) father-headed single parent families. Single, widowed and divorced women, together with their dependent children, are particularly vulnerable to poverty. For example, 47 percent of single women over age sixty-five are poor.

The unequal division of labour within the home, where women continue to perform the bulk of the child care and housework, means many women perform the equivalent of two full-time jobs. In Alberta in 1991, 66 percent of the women working for pay had children at home.[6] Women of all ages, employed or unemployed, are more likely than men to nurse the sick at home; take time from paid work to be home for care purposes; provide unrenumerated services in the school and community; and suffer from stress and overwork as a result of their double or triple shifts.

In the 1970s and 1980s, federal and provincial governments began to address the profound social and economic disadvantages faced by women. Most government measures have been symbolic and/or bureaucratic, such as the creation of status of women offices and task forces to study "women's issues" such as wife battering and the feminization of poverty. However, women have benefited from the development of the welfare State. By providing in the public sector services traditionally performed by women in the unpaid private sphere, such as child care, nursing homes for the elderly, and home care for the sick, governments have helped women move into the paid labour force, that is, into the public sphere. Women benefit from the welfare State in two ways; as recipients of services and as employees. While the welfare State is not the solution to women's historic economic disadvantage, government programs in areas such as health care, child care, education, and social services provide a necessary foundation for many women's economic independence.

The Alberta Disadvantage

It is this foundation that the Klein government is attacking. Its budget slashing ignores women's differential position in the labour market and their disproportionate dependence on the government programs and services. Thus, deficit reduction is not gender neutral. Because of women's tenuous economic position and their reliance on the welfare State, the Alberta approach is especially harmful to them.

The Klein government deficit reduction policy has targeted programs crucial to women's social and economic well-being: social services (18.3 percent budget reduction for 1994-97); education (12.4-percent cut in education spending for 1994-1997, and a 50-percent cut to kindergarten funding); health care (17.5-percent cut to hospitals over four years); the public service (workers have been laid off, forced to take wage reductions of 5 percent, and have been encouraged to accept voluntary termination packages). As well, the government has deregulated, privatized, or eliminated many programs and services essential to women. The day care industry has been deregulated, various social services (such as counselling and child welfare) have been extensively privatized, and programs such as subsidies for seniors and single parents have been dropped. These policies have led to greater job loss and job degradation for women than men, increased the demand for women's unpaid labour in the home, schools, and community, and dramatically reduced government support for women and children on social assistance.

Body Counts

Since the Klein cuts began Alberta women have been losing ground in the labour market.[7] For example, from December of 1992, when

Table 18.1
Job Loss among Members of the Alberta Union of Provincial
Employees, by Gender, 1993-94.

	Male	Female
1993	15,928	28,507
1994	14,221	25,668
Job Loss	1,707	2,939
% Job Loss	10.7	10.3

Source: Alberta Union of Public Employees, 1995.

Ralph Klein became premier, and November of 1994, the average monthly unemployment rate for women moved down only one percentage point. For men it dropped nearly five percentage points. During the same period, the average monthly employment-to-population ratio rose only 2 percent for women compared to 5 percent for men. In addition a trend of women becoming more concentrated in part-time employment is beginning to appear. During the two years under consideration, the proportion of women employed full time declined from 40 percent of all those employed full time in the province to 38 percent. Part time employment for men showed almost no change over the two years, remaining steady at about 60,000 men. The number of women working part time steadily rose from 150,000 in December of 1992 to 165,000 in November of 1994.

It is too soon to determine whether these trends represent short-term phenomena or lasting structural changes and to judge definitively how much of them can be attributed to the Klein government's initiatives and how much to other factors. While a longer time frame and more research are required, it is evident that these figures reflect to a significant degree women's job loss and job degradation in the public service and public agencies dependent on government for a large portion of their revenue (school boards, universities, and hospitals). The substantial job loss in the public sector is indicated by Table 18.1.

Table 18.1 shows employment changes among members of the Alberta Union of Provincial Employees, which includes those employed directly by the provincial government or indirectly by public institutions such as hospitals and post-secondary institutions. These figures cover the April 1993 to April 1994 period, which is the most recent twelve-month comparison available. During this time many more female members of AUPE than male members lost their jobs. While on a per capita basis a slightly smaller percentage of the female public service work force (10.3 percent) lost their jobs than did the male work force (10.7 percent), the significantly higher job loss for women reflects the fact that women greatly outnumber men in the provincial public service. Women comprise 66 percent of AUPE members as of May4, 1995, according to AUPE membership data.

The spending cuts have devastated public employment sectors which are dominated by female workers. This is clearly illustrated by health care, as the nursing profession is 98.6 percent female. Cuts to hospital budget have forced layoffs of thousands of nurses. The United Nurses of Alberta estimates that about 10 percent of nurses have lost their jobs as a result of the first round of cuts.[8] For instance, from April 1, 1993 to the end of September 1994, the University of Alberta Hospital laid off 237 nurses (231 women and 6 men), and the cuts continue. For example, in the two-month period April 1, 1995 to June 1, 1995, 2,500 registered nurses are slated to get pink slips in the cities of Edmonton-St. Albert and Calgary alone.

As well, the nursing profession is suffering significant casualization — the process by which full-time nurses become part-time and part-time nurses move to casual status thereby working fewer hours and losing their benefits. According to UNA President Heather Smith, 20 percent of nurses working on any given day are working as casuals. Smith calculates that between 2,000 and 3,000 nurses have been shifted from full time to casual over the past three years.[9]

> **"Casualization is the ultimate exploitation of women who were full time and who continue to work full time, with no benefits."**
>
> *Heather Smith, President of UNA.*[10]

Cuts to hospital budgets affect other workers as well, and these are also disproportionately women; indeed, women make up 79 percent of employees in medical and health occupations.[11] For example, from April 1, 1993 to the end of September 1994, the University of Alberta Hospital laid off: 252 support workers, 68 percent of whom were women; seventy-two licensed practical nurses and nursing aids, 71 percent of whom were women; 70 technical workers, 64 percent of whom were women; 36 professionals (dietitians, social workers, psychologists), 86 percent of whom were women; sixty-nine managers, 68 percent of whom were women; two computer analysts, one man, one woman; and a female clerical worker. Altogether, 78 percent of the 740 jobs lost were held by women.

Cuts to education funding have affected women's employment as well. According to Department of Labour layoff statistics for 1994, 668 education workers (approximately 440 of whom are women) lost their jobs that year.[12] However, data on job loss in this area are misleading for a variety of reasons. First, most school boards offered early retirement incentive packages in 1994 and teachers who accepted these packages are not included in the tally of lay-offs. Secondly, a considerable reduction in teaching staff has been accomplished by reducing teachers' positions from full to part time or from part time to a smaller part-time appointment. Job degradation is not visible in statistics on job loss.

Despite the absence of definitive figures, it is clear that women are disproportionately harmed by shrinking salaries and reductions in teaching hours. In 1992-93, 63 percent of Alberta teachers were women. It seems plausible to infer that two female teachers have suffered lay-offs for every male teacher who has met this fate. At the elementary level, which has been forced to absorb a 50-percent reduction in kindergarten funding on top of the other cuts, female teachers outnumber male teachers by a factor of four to one. Again, women are over-represented in the sector which is hit hardest by the deficit reduction measures.

Back to the Kitchen

The job situation in Alberta has many implications for women. First, because of lay-offs in the public sector, women have been forced to seek employment in the private sector. But private sector jobs usually offer low wages and prestige and much poorer job security and benefits packages. For example, the for-profit "We Care" American health firm operating in Alberta hires registered nurses at two-thirds or less of their former wage, often as licensed practical nurses (LPNs).[13] As the employment statistics cited above show, many women are not finding full-time jobs in either the public or the private sector. Many must work part-time or seek casual or seasonal work.

Secondly, when governments withdraw or reduce services, women in their traditional, private, unseen, and unpaid roles have little choice but to pick up the slack as best they can. The re-privatization of nurturing in Alberta is transferring women's work — such as nursing, child care, and kindergarten teaching — from the visible and paid public sector to the invisible, unregulated, and under or unpaid reaches of the private sectors. For instance, as it cuts school funding, the Alberta government has told Alberta families that they should "volunteer" in the schools to replace the labour of the teachers.[14] Some Alberta women responded to the government's statement by pointing out that they already spend hundreds of hours helping out in the schools and volunteering for school activities.[15] That the government seeks to increase this appropriation of women's unpaid time and labour demonstrates its neo-conservative assumptions that women have flexible schedules and no full-time employment outside the home, and that this type of role is a natural extension of women's primary function as caregiver.

> **"The Klein outfit is ... firing the women, and then try-ing to get them back to work for nothing, and I think this is a disgraceful situation."**
>
> *Male caller from Edmonton to Wild Rose Forum, a popular CBC radio talk-show, 30 March 1995.*

Because of the closure of hospitals and the reduction in available hospital beds, some Albertans are denied admission for conditions that formerly would have led to hospitalization, or are forced to delay hospital procedures, and patients are routinely being sent home early from hospital. Delayed or denied admissions and shorter hospital stays burden those who traditionally provide care in the home — women. The work that paid professionals used to do in hospitals is now being provided by underpaid women working in privatized "home care" programs or by unpaid women in their role as family caregivers.

> **"We are told about a woman told to 'volunteer' twelve hours a day to care for a sick relative in hospital. "**
>
> *Heather Smith, President of UNA.*[16]

The Welfare Toll

As David Cooper and Dean Neu demonstrate in chapter eleven, the Klein government's budget cuts have reduced social service and seniors benefits and restricted eligibility for them. These measures have devastated elderly women and single mothers on welfare. Seniors are disproportionately female, and older women are more likely than older men to live in poverty.[17] Yet the Klein government has eliminated or reduced benefits to seniors with incomes above $10,400 per year. Seniors with incomes over

$17,000 ($25,000 for couples) have lost their property tax credit, their health premiums coverage ($279 per year), and their dental and vision subsidies. Those with incomes in between receive subsidies on a sliding scale. Seniors in subsidized housing face rent increases ranging from 25 percent to 30 percent of their incomes.[18] As well, as of December 1, 1994, annual eye examinations are no longer subsidized by the government. For seniors and others on low or fixed incomes, the cost ($45 to $75), particularly when added to the other burdens they must bear, may prove prohibitive. In such cases, Albertans, a majority of them women, will be denied an important medical service.

Alberta's Family and Social Services Department has reduced its budget by slashing monthly welfare rates. On October 1, 1993, the rate for a single adult supporting one child was decreased to $766.00 per month, a reduction of 9 percent. According to the *Edmonton Journal,* this rate is the lowest in the country.[19] In comparison, Ontario provides a single parent with one child $1,221.00 in social assistance per month. As well, stricter eligibility requirements, along with other factors, cut an estimated 36, 566 recipients of family benefits from the Alberta welfare caseload between March 1993 and September 1994.[20] The provincial government saved $200 million in welfare benefits in 1993-94 and expects to save an additional $160 million in 1994-95. Given that 42 percent of welfare cases are single parents and that women head 89 percent of single parent families, it is clear that a large chunk of these savings has come from single women trying to support their children.

> **"I'm a stay at home mother and I take care of my children. I volunteer at the schools, I take care of elderly people, … so now I'm a good guy. If disaster should strike, though, if my husband should suddenly die or, god forbid, leave me, I'm one man away from poverty … I don't like Alberta any more."**
>
> *Woman caller from Millett to Wild Rose Forum, 30 March 1995.*

According to the Alberta Association of Social Workers, families are "hit on all sides by the cuts: they can no longer pay rent and buy food, children are embarrassed in school at lunchtime because of inadequate/nonexistent food, inadequate clothing, and inability to participate in fee for service school activities."[21] The deepening poverty of Alberta's unemployed poor is shown by the dramatic rise in the numbers of people served by food banks. The Edmonton Food Bank reports a 72 percent increase in the number of clients served from October 1993 to October 1994 and predicts that the numbers will continue to climb as the cuts continue.[22]

> **Sandy Rankin, Edmonton Food Bank co-ordinator, says of the enormous increase in clients: "It's a nightmare. ... This is your neighbour. This is your brother. ... If this is what Ralph Klein thinks is progress and the real Alberta Advantage, we really have a problem."[23]**

Stalling Equality

The government of Alberta has inflicted this pain on Albertans, particularly Alberta women, in the course of acting upon an ideology that this paper has already described as both neoliberal and neoconservative. Many of the policies described in the preceding section reflect the neoliberal agenda of expanding the private sector and shrinking the public sector. Not coincidentally, women and children, disproportionately compared to men, depend on the public sector, women for employment and women and children as clients and claimants of benefits that they require because of their politically weak and economically marginal situation in society. Women and children suffer most when the public sector withers.

The neoconservative ideology of so many members of the Tory caucus leads them to publicly proclaim the virtues of the "traditional" (that is, heterosexual and patriarchal) family. Equally it moves them to condemn the vices of a more heterogeneous and progressive society and the policies, such as pay equity and protection for human rights, needed to support such elements of social diversity as single motherhood.

Indeed, many members of the Tory caucus are vocal antifeminists who embrace a narrow and archaic view of women's roles. Some Tory MLAs are publicly allied with the Alberta Federation of Women United for Families, an interest group that promotes the patriarchal division of labour within the family and actively lobbies against child care, employment equity, and pay equity policies.[24] Many members of the Klein cabinet have celebrated the neoconservative family ideology advocated by the report from the Premier's Council on Alberta Families. The Council's 1993 Report identified the need to increase the ability of a single income to meet family needs.

Women working outside the home are urged by the council to reconsider their level of personal responsibility:

> [S]ome families become two income households by choice rather than necessity. Some argue that this has chipped away at the family foundation by reducing family time and by placing an emphasis on accumulating possessions and material wealth. ...[25]

The Council, through its reports and the government, urge a family model centred around the nuclear, heterosexual family. Such a family should be supported by a single wage earned by the father and the unpaid labour of the mother in the home and community. This vision is at the heart of the so-called "Alberta Advantage," for it helps government exploit the unpaid labour of women in order to reduce the public sector and shrink government spending. The government then can attract business and investment to Alberta by passing along the "saving" to corporations via incentives and tax reductions.

Cabinet minister Dianne Mirosh explained to colleagues in the legislature, "Ninety percent of women still enjoy being at home, raising a family. ... They do want to go back to the home and promote the family unit."[26] Indeed, some members of the Conservative caucus imply, or state outright, that if women were doing their "rightful" jobs as mothers, children would be properly taken care of and the government would be rid of a significant regulatory and financial burden. Two examples illustrate this point. First, in response to a Liberal motion to restore full funding to kindergarten, Barry McFarland (PC, Little Bow) said: "I sometimes have to wonder if perhaps ECS has become a convenience mechanism in substitute for a daycare centre."[27] McFarland is equating ECS with publicly-funded babysitting. Secondly, in the 1993 case of the six-year-old girl raped by her babysitter, cited by Jonathan Murphy (see chapter twenty-one), Alberta Family and Social Services at first refused to pay for counselling for the child. The minister, Mike Cardinal, blamed the child's mother for the problem, asserting that she should have chosen her babysitter more carefully. At the same time, the Klein government refuses to support women in situations of family breakup by getting tough on fathers who fail to pay child support payments; opposition Liberal suggestions for tightening up the maintenance enforcement program have been soundly rejected by the Tories.[28] Indeed, Tory MLA Julius Yankowsky (PC, Beverly-Belmont) characterised single mothers seeking regulatory guarantees for child support payments as "vindictive leech moms," who routinely denied fathers access, and made fathers unattractive to new romantic liaisons by forcing them into penury while the single mothers gaily embarked on a profitable new life supported by these unfortunate men.[29] The Klein government supports nuclear families, not single moms.

The Alberta government has eroded or eliminated the few institutions designed to speak on behalf of women, namely the Women's Secretariat and the quasi-independent Alberta Advisory Council on Women's Issues (AACWI). Shortly after the 1993 election that brought the Klein government to power, Tory MLAs began attacking budget allocations for the Secretariat and Council during question period. Victor Doerksen, Tory MLA for Red Deer-South and self-proclaimed advocate of "family values" asked the minister responsible: "The budget estimate for this particular advisory council is $338,000. Can this money not be spent on different and better priorities?"[30] A few days later Doerksen reiterated his view, saying "I believe these are discretionary expenses."[31] Female MLAs have jumped on the anti-Council bandwagon too. Judy Gordon (PC, Lacombe-Stettler)[32] and Heather Forsyth (PC, Calgary-Fish Creek)[33] told the Minister, Gary Mar, that they and their constituents question the "administrative costs" incurred by these agencies. As a result, the Alberta Advisory Council on Women's Issues, created in 1986 after a fourteen year lobbying effort by Alberta Women's groups, will be eliminated in 1996. In the meantime, its budget has been reduced, and the Klein government has been very slow to fill vacancies on the Council's Board of Directors.[34]

The premier's disregard for women's concerns and needs is evident in his responses to questions asked by female Liberal MLAs about the impact of budget cuts on women. Klein dismisses or deflects questions that refer to women's disproportionate job losses or raise concerns about the effect of program cuts on women.[35] The following excerpt from Question Period[36] illustrates Klein's derisive attitude:

> Muriel Abdurahman (Lib): Mr. Speaker, this government has declared war on women. The cuts to health care, education, and the public service affect women far more than men. As a result of this government's bullying, women are forced to choose between family responsibilities and low-paying jobs, when they can find them. My question is to the Premier. Why are you trying to balance your budget, at the expense of women ...?

> Ralph Klein: Mr. Speaker, I just find this absolutely incredible: attack, war on women. I see a mighty fine woman sitting right

here. [Klein points to one of the female cabinet ministers]. She doesn't look like she's been attacked or brutalized in any way at all. I see one over there too. She looks perfectly healthy to me. There's one over there, and here's one here. Stand up. Stand up. [Klein urges female members of the Tory caucus to rise] I see fine looking, healthy women, strong women, hardworking women, intelligent women. I don't see women under attack.

Muriel Abdurahman: Mr. Speaker, I find the Premier's treatment of women totally disrespectful.

A Different Road for Alberta

The problem with the premier's comments is not merely their disrespect. Rather it is what they reveal about the deeply rooted social philosophy of the government of Alberta that animates or at least tolerates much of the pain that Alberta's women are now suffering at the government's hands. The policies of the Klein government both assume and foster the notion that a woman's full-time focus should be the family. With this model in mind, the government can discount the burdens it places on working women and single mothers when it reduces social programs and cuts public sector employment in ways that disproportionately harm women.

However, the gendered division of labour the government finds natural and desirable holds true for only a fraction of Alberta's women. Because the social philosophy of the government legitimizes the suffering that so many of Alberta's women are now experiencing, this neoconservative, patriarchal myth — and the policies that flow from it — stand urgently in need of a reality check. The articulation and acceptance of a new understanding of gender relations, the family, and public policy in Alberta is essential. At minimum, this new understanding and policy regime should contain the following elements:

- recognition of the wide diversity of families in Alberta and of the inappropriateness of basing policy on the assumption of the male breadwinner.
- a higher minimum wage, since most women are minimum wage earners. At $5.00 per hour, Alberta has the second-lowest provincial minimum wage in Canada.[37]
- pay equity and employment equity regulations.
- training, wage, and child care subsidies for single support mothers.

- levels of social assistance benefits that reflect the true cost of a viable standard of living, particularly for single-parent families.
- the extension of the Widow's Pension program to seniors who are divorced.
- end or reduce the 64 new user fees or user fee increases contained in the 1993 and 1994 Alberta budgets,[38] particularly fees for necessities such as health care services. These fees are a highly regressive form of taxation that especially hurts women because they tend to be least able to pay.
- a fairer income tax regime that reduces the tax burden on those Albertans, disproportionately women, least able to pay.
- more regulation, not less, of day care; banning of "for profit" child care, increased education requirements and wages for day care teachers.
- reinstating kindergarten funding and making money available for optional junior kindergarten.
- improvements to (or total overhaul of) the maintenance enforcement program.

As a matter of policy, Alberta's Tories are systematically expanding the private sphere of social life — the family and the increasingly unregulated market — at the expense of the public sphere. Gone is the role of government as the authoritative voice and agent of a progressive society. This "withering of the State" victimizes Alberta's women and children twice over. First, public policy relegates many of them to live disadvantaged lives. Secondly, the neoliberal discourse denies the harsh realities of their lives. It shifts public attention away from their bruising experiences with such features of contemporary Alberta as its labour conditions, child care options, and social policies, and onto the "Alberta Advantage." The lesson of this chapter is that the Alberta Advantage should stay in the spotlight, not so that we can celebrate it but so that we can understand that the base on which it rests is the exploitation of Alberta's women and children. If Albertans can come to understand this truth about the Alberta Advantage, they will then be able to question the neoliberal, neoconservative myth that underlies it and to replace it with a more humane vision and a more constructive public policy. Achieving these changes, more than eliminating the deficit, is the real challenge facing Albertans.

Conclusion

Any jurisdiction considering leaping to the barricades of the Klein revolution should do so with its eyes open to the reality that women will be the revolution's primary victims. In view of the disadvantages that women still experience in the labour market, and the way in which diminished employment prospects for women trap them in a world that wo neatly complements a social ideology that undervalues women, other provinces should view the Klein fiscal revolution with particular caution and scepticism.

Notes

1. The authors gratefully acknowledge the research assistance of Sheryl McInnes, who compiled statistical information for this paper.
2. M. Piercy, "Circles on the Water," 1982, reproduced in S. Brodribb, *Nothing Matters* (Toronto: Lorimer), 1992.
3. Interview, 27 October 1994.
4. The data cited in this paragraph are from Statistics Canada, 1993 reports on the 1991 Census. Data were complied by Sheryl McInnis.
5. Ibid.
6. Ibid.
7. Due to the Klein government disbanding of the Alberta Bureau of Statistics, the trends in Alberta labour force participation and unemployment are taken from Statistics Canada's monthly Labour Force Survey at quarterly intervals beginning in December 1992 and ending November 1994.
8. Interviews with Linda Sloan, President, and Louise Rogers, Executive Director, Staff Nurses Association, 22 August 1994; and with Heather Smith, President of the United Nurses of Alberta, 3 August 1994.
9. Ibid. At the University of Alberta Hospital, fewer than 25 percent of nurses were casuals in 1990; the figure rose to 37 percent in 1994.
10. Interview, 17 August 1994.
11. *Alberta Hansard,* 18 October 1993, 870.
12. *Alberta Hansard,* 8 March 1995, 441. The Alberta Teachers' Association calculates that 1,452 teachers lost their jobs between 1992 and the beginning of the 1994-95 school year.
13. Heather Smith interview, 3 August 1994.
14. Premier Klein commented, "God forbid, parents may have to volunteer." Quoted in the *Edmonton Journal,* 23 January 1994, A1.
15. *Edmonton Journal,* 26 January 1994, A13.
16. Heather Smith interview, 17 August 1994.
17. Statistics Canada data reveal that in 1990, 47 percent of single women over 65 lived below the poverty line, compared with 33 percent of single men.
18. A. Tanner's article, *Edmonton Journal,* 8 March 1994, B2.
19. *Edmonton Journal,* 23 December 1994, A10.
20. Ibid.
21. Alberta Association of Social Workers, Press Release, 5 October 1994.
22. Editorial in the *Edmonton Journal,* 31 March 1995, A14.
23. Interview, Edmonton Food Bank, 3 November 1994.
24. *Alberta Hansard,* 28 September 1993, 525.

25. Cited in Lois Harder, "Depoliticizing Insurgency: The Politics of the Family in Alberta," (Paper presented at the CPSA Annual Meeting, Calgary, 14 June 1994), 26.

26. *Alberta Hansard*, 3 September 1986, 1429-30.

27. M. Lisac's column, *Edmonton Journal*, 11 April 1995, A8.

28. See *Alberta Hansard*, 1 March 1994, 317-322.

29. See the *Edmonton Journal*, 13 April 1995, A1 and A7. T. Arnold, in the latter story, quotes Yankowsky as complaining that enforcement of Alberta's child support regulations "have made dads unemployable in many cases because of the loss of driving privileges and made them unmarriageable because in many cases they have huge maintenance payments." He then said, "If child support is such a problem, perhaps the courts are awarding (custody) to the wrong person. In no other instance can one get a choice in life and someone else pay for it." Premier Klein subsequently termed the remarks "inappropriate" and on April 25 Yankowsky apologised, albeit equivocally, for being inflammatory while adding he was happy to have contributed to discussion of the issue.

30. *Alberta Hansard*, 28 September 1993, 525.

31. *Alberta Hansard*, 6 October, 1993, 750-51.

32. *Alberta Hansard*, 30 September 1993, 610-11.

33. *Alberta Hansard*, 6 October 1993, 754.

34. *Alberta Hansard*, 16 September 1993, 312-13.

35. *Alberta Hansard*, 7 March 1994, 417-19.

36. *Alberta Hansard*, 7 March 1994, 419.

37. The lowest provincial minimum wage is paid by Prince Edward Island and New-foundland, at $4.75 an hour. Alberta is tied with Manitoba and New Brunswick, at $5.00 per hour. However, the federal government cannot be underbid in this category, coming in at $4.00 per hour. Ontario has the highest provincial mini-mum wage, at $6.70 as of January 1994. It should be noted that most provinces do not set a minimum wage for the under-eighteen crowd, but of the four that do, Alberta has the lowest at $4.50 per hour, and Ontario the highest, at $6.25 per hour. All figures courtesy of Tom Fuller, Alberta Union of Provincial Employees, interview of 28 April 1995.

38. *Edmonton Journal*, 17 February 1995, A6.

Chapter Nineteen

Seniors: The End of a Dream[1]

Fred C. Engelmann

> Seniors have earned a right to live their retirement in dignity
> — Time to stop trying to balance the deficit on the backs of
> those who cannot defend themselves!
>
> An angry senior.[2]

The average Albertan, confronted with complaints about what Klein did to seniors, might shrug and say, "Why should we support those rich people?" Well, they are wrong. The 1991 Census (1990 data), long before Klein's cuts, tells us that 1.6 percent of Alberta seniors had no income, and 56.8 percent had individual annual incomes below $15,000.[3] Only 8.8 percent had individual incomes of $40,000 or more and can thus be considered well off financially. This far from impressive economic status came about only after an increase in the federal income supplement for single seniors and the impact of the Canada Pension Plan. In addition, there were relatively generous provincial policies enacted in the seventies and eighties by the Alberta government, costing, by 1993, $1.1 billion dollars.

Because the Klein government evidently feared seniors as a political force, a decision to cut these expenditures by 17 percent was kept completely secret until the budget of February 24, 1994.[4] One of the secret decisions was to launch a complex benefit program, which, despite misleading positive propaganda, was to help only very low-income seniors by very little and to abolish some and to diminish the rest of the benefits for others. Because many, especially health-related programs were cut separately, only few seniors were actually helped. The interaction of programs was so complex that most seniors were fooled until the decisions had been made public and implemented, and the feared opposing forces were never mobilized. To understand what happened, we have to go back a couple of decades.

History

On the surface, the 1971 election seemed to reflect lop-sided support for Peter Lougheed's winning Progressive Conservatives. The party did not do well, however, in rural Southern Alberta and among seniors. In preparation for the next election (1975) — Lougheed always started this process the day after winning the last election — the Tories sought out means of garnering the support of these reluctant elements. The rural South was relatively easy to win over: all the Tories had to do was dump money into the constituencies. Weaning seniors away from Social Credit, however, required more imagination.

To this end, in 1974, the government commissioned a report on seniors under the auspices of the Department of Health and Social Development. The products were the creation, the following year, of the Senior Citizens Division (later called the Senior Citizens Bureau, then Secretariat),[5] the Provincial Senior Citizens Advisory Council (government-appointed, 1976), and important policy initiatives.

Alberta seniors had not exactly gone empty-handed prior to the creation of these initiatives. The lodge program was started in 1959, followed in 1964 by the Nursing Home Program. Since 1969 seniors enjoyed property tax reduction; since 1972, renters' assistance; since 1973, extended health benefits, some Blue Cross benefits, especially 80 percent coverage for prescription drugs, and a small income supplement if they were entitled to the federal Guaranteed Income Supplement. Except for the latter, these benefits were universal. In addition, in 1972, seniors were relieved from paying health care premiums.

In 1975, the pension supplement (Alberta Assured Income Plan) was increased steeply. A home improvement program was established in 1976, followed in 1978 by a co-ordinated home care program and, in 1979, by increased home improvement grants. The 1982 election campaign brought home heating protection and another home improvement grants program. An income support program for low-income widowed persons aged fifty-five through sixty-four was established in 1983.

During the Lougheed period, renters' grants and homeowners' property tax relief and the income supplement were raised substantially. When Lougheed left office in 1985, Alberta seniors did not enjoy every last benefit available in Canada, but more benefits than those in any other province and, more important, more funds spent, per capita, on these benefits than for any other Canadian seniors. The bulk of the benefits was universal. In sum, "they never had it so good."

Falling oil prices led to some curtailments. In 1990, the home heating plan was dropped. In 1991, there was some reduction in the extended health benefits program (eyeglasses, dental care, and the entitlement to aids to daily living). As quasi-compensation, the Ministry for Seniors was established in 1990 and, in 1991, Premier Getty introduced Bill 1 giving statutory basis to the Seniors Advisory Council for Alberta. To further confuse the image of benefit curtailments, the Seniors Directorate was established in 1990 as part of the Ministry for Seniors. The former spent a considerable amount of money on consultants and a major survey. The minister and the Directorate held major meetings with seniors' representatives and consultation meetings in various areas of the province.

This was the state of affairs when Ralph Klein became premier. He immediately abolished the Ministry for Seniors, leaving only the Advisory Council and its staff who were incorporated into the new Department of Community Development. Joe Forsyth, an assistant deputy minister was put in charge not only of seniors but also of women, human rights, and multiculturalism. Seniors became just another "special interest group."

Klein's "Benefit" Program

During the 1993 campaign, Klein promised that there would be no changes to seniors' programs without consultation.[6] This consultation consisted of exactly one meeting of seniors and others invited by the government, held in Red Deer in September 1993, which was chaired by Marjorie Bowker, a former family court judge who became a well-known author in retirement. The meeting recognized that there had to be some reduction in benefits, but strongly suggested that low-income seniors should be fully protected. Soon after, the bureaucracy of the Department of Community Development — Gary Mar had become the minister — took the lead in working out a benefit scheme under the direction of Assistant Deputy Minister Joe Forsyth.

The resulting bombshell came on February 24, 1994, the Bastille Day of the Klein Revolution, when Provincial Treasurer Jim Dinning, revealed his budget. On that day, the Lougheed dream ended, not only for Alberta's affluent seniors, but — to some extent at least, as became clear in stages — for all Alberta seniors with an individual annual income above $15,000 and for many with income below that. To understand what was to follow, and to trace better the salami tactics employed by the government, excerpts from the budget speech[7] will be helpful:

In the past we have provided extensive programs for all seniors regardless of their ability to pay ... we simply can no longer afford to provide all these services free of charge to all seniors. We asked Alberta seniors: what should the priorities be for your benefit programs? They told us that seniors who can afford it are willing to pay their share. They also said, "Streamline the administration so we don't have to go from one office to another trying to sort out the benefits that we're eligible for," and most of all they said, "Protect the lower-income seniors."

We're taking their advice. Today we are introducing a new co-ordinated grant program for seniors. It's based on six key principles. First, low-income seniors must be protected. Secondly, seniors' benefits and administration must be simplified and moved to a one-window approach to make it easier for seniors to access the support they need. Thirdly, those who can afford to pay for shelter and health care premiums should pay for them. Fourthly, benefit rates should be fair and based on a senior's income, not a means test. Fifthly, any changes and their impact on seniors must be carefully monitored. Last but not least, consultation with seniors must take place so that the program can be made more effective and responsive to their needs.

Dinning announced that the new program, Alberta Seniors Benefit, would bring together five existing programs: the Alberta Assured Income Plan, property tax reductions, renters' grants, extended health benefits, and exemption from health care premiums. The new program was to be income-tested.

It is good to remember that the six principles are: protection of low-income seniors; a one-window approach; those who can afford it shall pay; benefit rates to be based on income, not means; careful monitoring; and consultation.

Because the Alberta Seniors Benefit program affected all seniors and went through a review process, it will receive more attention here than the other programs. It must be mentioned, however, that all programs (until 1994, fifteen in number) experienced cuts that impacted upon many — sometimes all — seniors, no matter how poor. The programs not covered by Alberta Seniors Benefit (ASB) will be dealt with later in this chapter. Finally, we must remember that very many seniors are feeling the cumulative effect of several or many cuts.

The budget speech was about all seniors had to go on. The impact of the benefit program for various income levels was kept secret — only the department staff had tables showing the calculated rates. Even so, the huge budget-day news release of Gary Mar's Department of Community Development[8] had ominous news: 65 percent of seniors would lose benefits (almost 60 percent of Alberta seniors reported 1990 individual annual incomes of less than $15,000) and 45 percent would have to pay health care premiums. The only seniors not subject to health care premiums were single seniors with annual incomes below $17,000 and those who, as couples, had annual incomes below $25,000. There was a ridiculously low phase-in range. Full annual premiums of $368 per person would be collected from singles with incomes over $18,200 and couples over $27,600. Beyond that, there was so little publicity given to the program that only very well-informed seniors were stunned. The rolling together of the income support plan, the property tax reduction, renters' assistance, and extended health benefits, made it easy for the bureaucrats to engage in gobbledygook, some just confusing, some plain dishonest, as the following example shows.[9]

According to the news release, a single homeowner entitled to the full federal Guaranteed Income Supplement, $10,432 (no additional income from any source), would receive an income supplement of $1,150, a cash replacement of $116 for the extended health benefits, a cash replacement of $650 for the property tax reduction, and a health care premium remission of $368 for a total of $2,300. Sure enough, at this income level, the income support had risen by all of $10 a year. However, the extended health benefits had been cut for all those needing both dental care and eyeglasses, since this would almost certainly cost more than $116 annually. The property tax reduction remained about the same, but the health care premium was not a remission at all since before Klein, there had been no premiums for seniors. Some benefit!

Before long, seniors' groups and some greatly aware seniors found or figured out a bit more about the badly misnamed benefit program. Consequently, criticism sprang up from various sources.

It was then that Dinning's sixth principle, consultation, came into play. Suddenly, there was feverish action. The minister of Community Development was sent from town to town and from village to village. He had little to say. Rather than consultation, it was one-way communication from the government. It was reported that at least one group of angry seniors asked him to leave. Government staff members had to take time away from their regular duties to travel to these "consultations." Word spread (though there is no written proof) that subsidized seniors' groups were intimidated. But there was enough noise to persuade Gary Mar, the minister, to appoint a review panel of ten seniors, consisting of three members of the Seniors Advisory Council, three members of the Inter-Agency Council (including Neil Reimer, the knowledgeable and committed president of the Alberta Council on Aging), one senior centre representative and three senior citizens-at-large. The group met from April 22 to May 2, just in time to enable the passing of the legislation before the already set date for the commencement of the benefit program, July 1, 1994.

The Alberta Seniors Benefit Review Panel reported to Gary Mar on May 2.[10] It issued fourteen recommendations, five of which were of basic importance for the program.

The first proposed the transfer of the Extended Health Care Benefits Program to Alberta Health. It was accepted by the government. The second proposed that all shelter benefits (for homeowners and renters) be uniform, at $850. Here, the government persisted with the status quo, $650 for homeowners and $1,200 for renters. The third proposed that health care premiums be replaced by a surtax; it was rejected. The fourth proposed thresholds (beyond which there would be no benefits) be set at $27,000 for single seniors and $35,000 for couples. It also suggested that $1,000 private income for singles and $2,000 for couples be exempt when benefits are calculated and that thresholds be fully indexed to the cost-of-living. The government cleverly seized on these two figures ($1,000 for singles and $2,000 for couples), making them the *threshold* increases, and it rejected the indexing. The fifth (Recommendation Nine) proposed an independent appeal body which the government claimed to have accepted.

The government announced flatly that it had accepted eleven of the fourteen recommendations fully or partially. Of the important ones mentioned above, the government claimed full acceptance of the first and fifth and rejection of the second, third, and fourth. In fact, as shown above, the government also rejected the fifth. Ninety percent of the threshold increase for singles and 80 percent for couples was rejected, and the appeal body, instead of being independent, is headed (as of February 1995) by — believe it or not — Joe Forsyth, the bureaucrat who authored the cuts.[11] The government's claimed score on the Review Panel's recommendations of eleven to three was based mostly on minor items and, like Mark Twain's death, was "grossly exaggerated." Without explanation of where the extra money was coming from, Mar announced that the total spent on seniors remained at $916 million, a 17 percent decrease of the amount spent before Klein.

What does the Alberta Seniors Benefit program mean to Alberta's seniors? Who benefits? Who sacrifices? How large are the benefits? How great are the sacrifices? How do the sacrifices compare with those of Ralph Klein and the members of his cabinet?

The bureaucratic jumble continues to confound many Alberta seniors, particularly those who have not read the fine print carefully and who are not arithmetic wizards. To bring order into this chaos, which many well-informed seniors believe to be intentional, we must deal separately with single homeowners, homeowner couples, single renters, and renting couples.[12]

Single homeowners with incomes (including the ASB) of up to $15,000 receive a greater benefit under the new program than before Klein, if perfectly healthy and living in their own home (maximum increase 3.5 percent). The sacrifice is greatest at income levels between $20,000 and $21,000 at which point they have no ASB and are beginning to pay the health care insurance premium: they have a reduction in benefits of 4.7 percent.

Home-owning couples (again, in perfect health) benefit up to a total income of $24,000. Their largest benefit, 6.7 percent, is at $20,000. Their sacrifice is greatest — 4.3 percent — at $33,000.

Renters, despite their larger shelter benefits, do even more poorly. Healthy single renters benefit up to a total income (including the ASB) of about $14,500. For them, the largest benefit, compared to 1992, amounts to a whopping 2.1 percent. Their greatest sacrifice, at a total income of $20,292, is 7.2 percent, which is the greatest reduction of income through ASB of any group of seniors. It must be remembered that this is the universal sacrifice; it would be greater for seniors not in perfect health.

Renting couples (healthy) benefit up to a total income of about $23,500. Their largest benefit — 5.9 percent — comes at a total income of $21,608. Their largest sacrifice — also 5.9 percent — comes at a total income of $32,350.

Ralph Klein's much touted 5 percent cut is on his gross salary. If his nontaxable income is not affected by the cut, the cut after taxes amounts to a measly 2.9 percent because his marginal tax rate is 42.2 percent (29 percent x 1.455 — Alberta's share). The cuts of seniors receiving benefits are at a marginal tax rate of 24.7 percent (17 percent x 1.455), if they pay tax at all. Thus, they lose between 100 percent and 75.3 percent of the amount of the cut. Seniors have to have a handsome income before they lose less than Klein and his ministers. A drastic change in thresholds would be needed for all seniors' sacrifices to come down to Klein's level. If radical changes are not forthcoming quickly, or unless the whole ASB experience is dropped and 1992 conditions are restored, including no health care premiums, the following change needs to take place at the top. Unless Klein immediately, and retroactively to July 1, 1994, reduces his gross salary by 9.3 percent (6.3 percent if his total income is cut)[13] below its 1992 level, seniors may — legitimately — feel that he has his hands in their pockets. The 9.3 percent (or 6.3 percent) cut before taxes would be the equivalent of the 7.2 percent cut (5.4 percent after taxes) sustained by the healthy single renter who has a total income of $20,292.

It did not take Gary Mar's bureaucracy long to prepare Bill 35, the Seniors Benefit Act. Mar introduced it on May 12, 1994, ten days after the Review Panel's report. He introduced it in the legislature as follows:

> The Bill establishes the new Alberta seniors' program under the Department of Community Development which allows for three different seniors' cash benefits to be combined under one program. It will also give authority for Alberta Health to bill higher income seniors for all or part of their health care insurance premiums.[14]

The Bill was terse. Most of the meat was to be produced by regulations coming from bureaucrats in Community Development.

On May 16, in the second reading debate, Julius Yankowsky — the Liberals' seniors critic until he defected to the Progressive Conservatives after Grant Mitchell became Liberal leader — asked: "Why is this government continuing its attack on the most vulnerable segment of our society?"[15] He called it a regulatory bill. Bette Hewes, who later became Yankowsky's successor as seniors critic, asked why Mar had paid no attention to the seniors on the Review Panel and in his many consultations.[16]

On May 25, closure was invoked. Stockwell Day, the government house leader, defended it by saying: "We would be here all summer, all winter, if we didn't do it."[17] Later that day, Liberal Gene Zwosdesky threatened: "This is a bad Bill and the seniors will see through that, and they'll prove it in the next election."[18] On June 1, Bill 35 received Royal Assent.[19]

The administration of the ASB exceeded the worst apprehensions. Community Development might have expected a great run on the office when seniors were asked to submit, by the end of July 1994, a form demanding highly detailed information about their finances, using their 1993 income tax form. In order to receive benefits, they had to give permission to the Alberta government to check with Revenue Canada on their income information.[20] Because of the complexity of the application form, there was a flood of questions, and staff had to be hired or temporarily transferred from other government departments. Some staff were not well-informed and gave wrong information to seniors, and some seniors misunderstood the application form, which resulted in some seniors being informed that they received more than they should have, and that they must return the difference. Some seniors, needy by definition due to the narrow income band for the benefits, had to wait several months for their first payment.[21]

Klein prides himself on having established the Alberta advantage through the lowest taxes anywhere in Canada. Con Duemler, a highly knowledgeable retired income tax specialist, subjected this claim to close analysis.[22] Duemler found that Alberta seniors with individual incomes between $14,000 and $29,000 do not enjoy the Alberta advantage at all. He, of course, included the payment of health care premiums in his calculations as these are covered by taxes in eight provinces. Even including the sales taxes of other provinces, he found that seniors in Ontario and Manitoba with incomes up to $40,000 in the former and $35,000 in the latter were taxed less than Alberta seniors with identical incomes. He found a "tax hump" peaking at $20,500 at which Alberta's low- and middle-income seniors were most disadvantaged.

Before Paul Martin announced the 1995 federal budget, Klein asserted that, in case of a tax increase, he would rebate the provincial portion to Alberta taxpayers. A year earlier, when Martin abolished the seniors' age credit for incomes above $49,134 and reduced it between $25,921 and $49,134, Klein showed no such concern for Alberta seniors, allowing them to enrich the Alberta treasury.

At this point, let us look at the six principles mentioned in Dinning's Budget Speech. 1) "Protection of low-income seniors." As we have seen, the protection of low-income seniors (they are less protected — or not protected at all — if they have health problems) only reaches up to individual incomes of $15,000. 2) "A one-window approach." The application process has been thoroughly complicated rather than simplified. Seniors now must make two applications for income support, while previously only a federal application was necessary. The provincial application for the shelter support used to be a simple form requiring relatively little information. The billing for the health care premiums is handled by Alberta Health, not by the ASB office in Community Development. In sum, the one-window approach does not exist. 3) "Those who can afford it shall pay." Yes, those who can afford it do pay, but so do many thousands who cannot afford it. 4) "Benefit rates to be based on income, not means." A means test was never seriously considered. It has been used as a red herring. 5) "Careful monitoring." This has consisted of damage control only. 6) "Consultation." Consultation only took place before the program went into effect, and it was mostly one-way, the government doing the talking. There has been none since that time (as of January 1995). In sum, none of the six principles has been fully met and the second principle not at all.

Other Klein Changes

The discussion so far has been centred on the ASB. The Klein Revolution has cut or abolished every other seniors' program.[23] We have discussed the four programs amalgamated in the ASB — there are eleven others.[24]

Alberta Blue Cross. Seniors' co-payment for drugs was increased from 20 percent to 30 percent. For a frail senior needing $100 worth of drugs monthly, this means an extra $120 a year.

Extended Health Benefits Program. Optical reimbursements were diminished, and a number of dental care items, including cleaning, bridges, and crowns, are no longer covered. Poor seniors may have to go without clean teeth and almost certainly with what parts of teeth are left in their mouth (dentures, however, are partially covered).

Long-term care centres. Here, ordinary ward accommodation has been raised by $1,186 a year, to $7,848, leaving a senior on minimum income $215 monthly for everything except room and board and drugs (or reliance on family, if the senior is lucky).

Seniors' Emergency Medic Alert. The program, allowing up to $700, was eliminated.

Seniors' Independent Living Program. These grants (up to $4,000) for lower-income seniors' home repairs, were eliminated.

Self-contained apartments for seniors. Rent in these accommodations for lower-income seniors was at 25 percent of income and increases on April 1, 1995, to 30 percent of income, a 20 percent increase. In addition, the renters' grant of $600 annually for these seniors has been eliminated. This means an annual loss of $1,122 for seniors on minimum income.

Lodge Program. Here, rents have been deregulated. Seniors are to be left with no less than $265 monthly for expenses other than room, board, and laundry. The rental amount is left to municipal boards, some of which have invoked major increases.

Home Care/Community Long-Term Care. Support services, medical, and others, are essential for seniors discharged from hospitals or kept at home to save hospital or institutional costs. Charges for support services used by seniors not receiving the federal income supplement have been raised from $2.00 to $5.00 per hour (maximum monthly charge between $50 and $300 depending on income).

Aids to Daily Living Program. This program includes hearing aids and other important aids and supplies; it is now under review.

Family and Community Support Services. While under municipal control, about 20 percent of the grant funds have been directed to services used by seniors such as senior centres and meals-on-wheels. These funds have now been pooled with other grants to municipalities — seniors having to compete with potholes!

Transportation grants. These are pooled with other grants to municipalities.

We can see from this that the typical senior, once s/he has any kind of a problem, is subjected to a double or even multiple whammy. Increased costs will almost certainly eat up all or more than any increase coming from ASB. An income below $15,000 slightly favours seniors if they are healthy and living in their own home or paying low rent. If these conditions do not prevail, they all lose.

Impact on Seniors

What has the Klein Revolution done to seniors? It has certainly shattered the dream into which Lougheed had, quite sincerely, lulled them. Granted that more had been given to seniors in the seventies than they had demanded, we still come face to face with three claims made either by them or on their behalf. The first is that they built the country and have paid their taxes which should give them economic rights regardless of cost, though many seniors would not make this claim. The second claim is that seniors have the right to live out their lives in independence and dignity. For seniors with individual incomes of up to $30,000, this right is endangered. The third claim is the most serious. It is that seniors have a fixed income and that it should not be tampered with. They have made their plans on the basis of the previous benefits and services, and they cannot get part-time jobs to make ends meet. Therefore, negative changes should have been phased in slowly or grandfathered in, so that those already retired are not disadvantaged. This claim was certainly ignored when the Klein changes took place.

Neil Reimer, president of the Alberta Council on Aging, has come to the conclusion that Albertans, living in the province with the smallest percentage of seniors, just don't care for their seniors. The Manning and Lougheed policies were exceptions. Too many Albertans, oblivious of their own future, just wish seniors would go away — or beyond.

Since seniors with individual incomes of $15,000 to $30,000 constitute about 30 percent of Alberta seniors (in 1990, 58 percent reported individual incomes below $15,000), it is surprising that these claims have not been voiced more strongly since early 1994.[25] The large majority of seniors have to give up some or all amenities and those not living in their own homes or renting cheaply, or those with health care costs now no longer covered, or with increased co-payment charges, have to give up much more, sometimes more than they have.[26] These seniors may well have to lean on their families for support — a situation often injurious to independence and dignity. At present, with many young people unemployed or underemployed, many seniors are helping their children financially — this is becoming impossible for many.

Even more than the younger poor, poor seniors tend to suffer in silence. One has to go out of one's way to get statements of double or multiple whammies.

A woman, aged sixty-five, is suffering from juvenile diabetes with heart complications.[27] Turning sixty-five in April 1994, she was taken off social assistance. She is single and draws a Canada Pension of $1,300 annually. Her Old Age Security benefit plus Guaranteed Income Supplement (OAS/GIS) amounts to about $9,000 annually. This entitles her to an annual ASB of slightly below $1,700. Her monthly income is thus slightly above $1,000. Of this, she pays $434 rent, about $200 for food and in excess of $100 out-of-pocket for drugs and diabetic supplies (four injections and blood tests daily; the latter is subsidized at $360 annually). This leaves a disposable income of no more than $250 (for clothes, phone, cable, transportation, etc.). Because of her status change in 1994, the ASB application form confused her, and she was asked to refund $900. Fortunately, an accountant friend saved her from having to pay it.

A man, seventy-nine years old and very hard of hearing, had to give up his apartment and move into subsidized housing in 1994 ($357 before the 1995 increase of about $20).[28] He is on OAS/GIS, GST credit and ASB only, giving him just about $965 a month. After rent, food and drugs, this leaves him about $350 disposable income. This would be fine, but he owes for his move in 1994 and a utility bill of $600 (his rent and utilities amounted to $750 before his move). He owns a car but cannot use it, as he cannot afford the insurance. Once he gets on an even keel, his first priority will be to replace the broken-down bed on which he sleeps.

A couple are eighty-one and seventy-two years of age.[29] His eyesight is very poor. He also is incontinent and wheel-chair bound. She has been on oxygen for ten years. They are on minimum income except for his Canada Pension of $341 monthly. Their total monthly income is $1,766, and their room rate in a long term care centre will be, as of April 1995, $1,621 per month. This leaves a disposable income of $144 of which they need to spend $40 on laundry (she washes while on oxygen) and $20 each on cable and phone. Their budget is so tight that once she can no longer do the laundry and cut his hair, they will have to give up phone and cable.

Conclusion

Through 1994, most of the protests against seniors' changes were issued by the leadership of the Alberta Council on Aging and a few militant groups. Most demonstrations against the government's policies in any area were pitifully small, although they always had a healthy sprinkling of seniors. The Mar-Forsyth package of confusion and opaque formulas, and the confusion about other cuts, seemed to do the trick. Even Klein remarked several times that he expected more of an outcry.[30]

Nonetheless, things may be changing. Evidently, Klein has been informed that more and more seniors are grumbling, leading him to talk of being more flexible regarding seniors and possibly even raising the threshold of the ASB. Could it be that seniors, instead of being an above-average proportion of Klein's support, have gone below average? Surely Klein knows that seniors' voting participation is at least slightly higher than that of the total population. Perhaps it has taken a while for those on a fixed income to figure out the cumulative effect of the Klein cuts, but the reality may be dawning.

The 91 percent of Alberta seniors who are not particularly well off have been hit hard and some even devastated by the fiscal policies of the Klein revolution. Most seniors are not whiners. Like so many other low-income people, most of those who suffer economically do so in silence. They do not make noises like those rich Albertans who insist on remaining Canada's lowest taxed. Many of those who complain are outraged that the builders of the province and the sufferers of the Great Depression should be singled out for a 17 percent cut — a cut which, while calculable by bureaucrats only, may be higher if we include all the health services used disproportionately by seniors.

We do not know yet whether future consultations with seniors may be less of a sham than those of the recent past. We may or may not know by the next election just how rude the awakening from the dream will have been in the end. It is significant that, of all people, Neil Waugh, the Ralph Klein-Rod Love mouthpiece on the *Edmonton Sun*, warns: "… the grey power revolt could be the thing that halts Phase Two of Klein's small revolution dead in its tracks."[31]

Notes

1. I want to thank all those who helped by making materials available to me and by pointing out important facts. Special mention should go to Christine Lawrence of the Alberta Council of Aging, who strongly and constructively criticized an earlier version. I also owe thanks to Con Duemler who criticized my figures (for which I remain responsible) and to Walter Coombs of the Society for the Retired and Semi-Retired (Edmonton) who directed my attention to Margaret Ross and Carolyn Carlson who in turn helped with case studies. The interpretations are entirely my own and not those of friends or relatives. I bear sole and full responsibility for all that is written here.

2. One of the many comments accompanying the Alberta Council on Aging's ballot returns on Klein's cuts to seniors' programs.

3. The data are slightly skewed downward by those living alone. However, those who live in institutions, whose income tends to be less, were not included. Statistics Canada, *Selected Income Statistics* (Ottawa: Industry, Science and Technology Canada, 1993); and *1991 Census of Canada, Catalogue Nr. 93-331* (Ottawa: Statistics Canada, 1991), 20 percent sample of population not living in collective dwellings.

4. On March 6, 1995, Liberal MLA Bettie Hewes stated in the legislature, and was not contradicted by the government: "This represents in total a further 5 percent cut to seniors on a per capita basis, and that we add to the already rather difficult 17 percent which has been documented for seniors to date" (*Alberta Hansard*, 6 March 1995, 377).

5. For past (and present) agencies and policies, see Seniors Advisory Council for Alberta, *Older Albertans*, June 1993, 108-109.

6. On April 11, 1995, Bettie Hewes quoted in the legislative assembly from a brochure distributed by Premier Klein on May 1, 1993, under the heading "Seniors Control Their Future":

   Seniors will be consulted to ensure all seniors programs reflect the wishes of seniors. 245,000 seniors will continue to receive Basic Health services and Blue Cross; a further 140,000 receive extended benefits. 109,380 seniors will benefit from the Property Tax Reduction program; another 57,000 will be helped by the Renter's Assistance Program (*Alberta Hansard*, 11 April 1995, 1173).

   While Stockwell Day, the government house leader, raised two points of order during the ensuing debate, he did question the veracity of Mrs. Hewes quotations. The brochure was not known to the writer when the body of this chapter was written. Readers are asked to remember the brochure when reading the remainder of the chapter.

7. *Alberta Hansard*, 24 February 1994, 258.

8. Government of Alberta, "Proposing a Fair and Effective Way to Meet the Needs of Seniors," *News Release*, 24 February 1994, 258.

9. Ibid. ("Backgrounder"), 3.

10. *Alberta Seniors Benefit Review Panel Report* (Edmonton: Alberta Community Development, 1994), 6-11, 17-18.

11. In early 1995, a trial balloon was launched. ASB appeals were to go to the body handling welfare appeals, with an additional senior on the board. There seem to have been complaints about this, as no final decision was made by April 1995.

12. The following information is taken from tables prepared on the basis of the formula published in "Optional Worksheet for Estimating Cost Benefits," *Worksheet* (Edmonton: Alberta Community Development, 1994), 13-14.

13. I owe this suggestion to Con Duemler, a retired income tax specialist.

14. *Alberta Hansard,* 12 May 1994, 1911.

15. *Alberta Hansard,* 16 May 1994, 1947.

16. Ibid., 1950.

17. *Alberta Hansard,* 25 May 1994, 2183.

18. Ibid., 2233.

19. *Alberta Hansard,* 1 June 1994, 2397.

20. Application form for the Alberta Seniors Benefit, 2.

21. Glitches in administration were reported by numerous seniors to the Alberta Council on Aging.

22. This information is taken from a lecture by Con Duemler to the Society for the Retired and Semi-Retired, Edmonton, 12 January 1995, and from a graph prepared by the lecturer.

23. For information about programs other than the ASB, see "Update on Alberta Programs for Seniors," (Edmonton: Alberta Community Development, July 1994); and "Alberta's Programs for Seniors: Then and Now" (Edmonton: Alberta Council on Aging, 1994).

24. The basic information for the following is derived from the Alberta Council on Aging.

25. In late 1994, the Alberta Council on Aging distributed a ballot to its members and to senior centres: "Do you support the Klein government's actions with respect to changes to all seniors' programs?" Some of the negative result is probably due to the fact that "complainers" are more likely to return such a ballot. Still, the outcome is significant: of 1,761 ballots returned, 62 (3.6 percent) replied "Yes" while 1,682 (95.5 percent) replied "No." Many seniors added expletives or reasoned strong statements to their votes.

26. There is reason to believe that the cuts hit women harder than men. Women are older, are expected to live longer, have lower incomes, and a higher proportion are receiving the federal income supplement. Seniors Advisory Council for Alberta, *Older Albertans,* 7, 13, 26, and 47.

27. I was referred to her by Margaret Ross of the Society for the Retired and Semi-Retired, Edmonton.

28. The information was supplied by Carolyn Carlson of the Society for the Retired and Semi-Retired, Edmonton.

29. Information from the Alberta Council on Aging.

30. *Edmonton Sun,* 25 January 1995, p. 11

31. Information from the Alberta Council on Aging.

Chapter Twenty

LABOUR IN THE KLEIN REVOLUTION

Jeff Taylor

> You are headed for one of the biggest labour battles that you've
> seen in this province.
> > Carol Anne Dean, AUPE President, November 24, 1993.[1]

> I'm solidly on side with AUPE. [Public-sector] employers are
> reprehensible for demanding wage rollbacks beyond 5 percent.
> > Ralph Klein, Alberta Premier, March 9, 1994.[2]

Workers and their unions are among the major casualties of the Klein government's assault on the public sector. Reductions of up to 30 percent in
the size of the public-sector workforce, a slashing of the wages and salaries
paid to public-sector workers, and the remaking of workplaces have had a
significant impact on this important group of Albertans. Like other aspects
of the Klein program to reduce public expenditure and to "reengineer"
the public sector, however, this effort appears to have been unplanned.
Cuts were announced incrementally and there was no province-wide public-sector wage reduction. Instead, ministries were given varying cuts and
public-sector employers were expected to implement the cuts as they saw
fit. Hence, Albertans were confronted with such ludicrous displays as
Ralph Klein "asking" all public-sector employees to accept a 5 percent
wage cut over three years when the actual cuts that managers were forced
to cope with were as high as 35 percent over that time period. The balance
of the cuts, according to the Klein rhetoric, was to come from administrative savings.

Some people reacted to the fast, furious, and apparently chaotic pace
of the cuts by suggesting that the Tories didn't know what they were doing,
other than cutting and declaring war on the public sector. Others main-

tained that the chaos was a strategy to defuse any potential resistance. Whichever view is correct, it is clear that a piecemeal, laissez-faire, "post-modern" approach is resulting in a radically restructured public service with surprisingly little organized opposition. Why hasn't there been a more effective resistance to the assault? Recent Alberta labour history suggests that it should have been forthcoming. Can we determine, amidst the chaos and debris, how many jobs have been lost? How did unions respond to Klein's request to negotiate wage and salary reductions?

Historical Context[3]

It is commonplace for labour studies and industrial relations practitioners to speak of a post-war industrial relations regime in Canada. According to this view, a compromise between labour and capital emerged from the labour militancy of the latter years of World War II and the immediate post-war period. The federal Industrial Disputes and Investigation Act of 1948, and the various post-war provincial labour codes that resulted from it, established a collective-bargaining framework that recognized the right of workers to form unions and bargain over terms and conditions of employment, banned unfair labour practices, banned strikes during the life of a contract, and recognized a wide range of workplace issues as falling under the management rights clauses that became a feature of post-war collective agreements. In return for periods of stability and a free hand in managing the workplace, employers, with governmental urging, granted workers collective-bargaining rights. Through the long period of economic growth in the fifties, sixties, and early seventies, this system worked reasonably well: as long as employers were making profits, they were willing to share some of the wealth with unionized workers. Furthermore, as the public-sector workforce expanded during this period to administer the welfare State and to play a limited role in managing the economy, public-sector workers organized associations that eventually were granted collective-bargaining rights under federal and provincial labour legislation. Increasingly since the 1970s, however, the post-war regime has been under attack. As profit levels declined and governments suffered fiscal crises in the waning of post-war prosperity, governments were willing to intervene in industrial disputes to legislate workers back to work or to roll back workers' wages.

While this account may accurately describe post-war Canadian industrial relations in general, Alberta is an exception. It is stretching the meaning of the word to suggest that relations between labour and capital in Alberta from the 1940s through the 1970s were a compromise. Alberta's Social Credit government did join other Canadian provinces in passing new private-sector labour legislation during the 1940s, but the Alberta labour code owed more to Ernest Manning's conservative anticommunism than to William Lyon Mackenzie King's corporate liberalism. In the Alberta Labour Act of 1947 and 1948, conciliation and compulsory arbitration were imposed when requested by either party to a dispute; there were steep penalties for violations; and collective agreements were deemed null and void in the case of illegal strikes. Furthermore, there was a provision that union organizing could not take place in a workplace without the employer's permission. The Act was further amended in 1960 to prohibit information picketing outside an employer's premises and to deny certification to any bargaining unit organized using such pickets. Finally, unionized workers were prohibited from taking action to protest the hiring of nonunion workers and from engaging in secondary picketing.

In the public sector, meanwhile, the Civil Service Association (CSA) was formed in the 1940s as a voluntary organization of Alberta civil servants. From the forties through the sixties the CSA enjoyed a cosy, collaborationist relationship with the Social Credit government. In 1968, this relationship changed slightly with a new Public Service Act that declared the CSA the sole bargaining agent of government employees. Nonetheless, the minister of labour retained final authority as to what was negotiable and the Cabinet had the power to impose agreements if they could not be settled through mediation. Nine years later the Public Service Employee Relations Act (1977) removed the Cabinet's final power in disputes between the government and the Alberta Union of Provincial Employees (AUPE, the renamed CSA), but it imposed a system of compulsory and binding arbitration and banned civil service strikes. The net effect of this legal framework in the public and private sectors was to deter labour organization; and, as Alvin Finkel has argued, an absence of labour law might have been more conducive to collective bargaining than legislation that was pro-employer.

Whereas in Canada generally the mid-seventies are said to mark a transition in industrial relations from the consent of the post-war period to a new period of coercion, in Alberta the eighties mark a break with the coercion of the post-war years and a return, in some ways, to the militancy of the World War II and pre-World War II periods. During this decade private- and public-sector Alberta workers engaged in industrial action that challenged the power of business and government.

In the Gainers' strike of 1986, Peter Pocklington, the company owner, attempted to break the union, local 280P of the United Food and Commercial Workers. He had extracted a concessionary agreement from the workers in 1984, with the threat of scabs, and wanted a similar agreement in 1986. But in 1986 the workers were not prepared to accept concessions nor were they prepared to have scabs take their jobs. Their decision to strike was supported by the rest of the Alberta labour movement. Furthermore, police assaults on the picket lines sparked significant community support for the strike, notably from the churches. The eventual settlement froze wages in the short term while saving jobs and the union. It was a modest victory for the workers under the circumstances. Nonetheless, the strike revealed that Alberta labour was still able to express solidarity when fundamental trade-union principles were under attack.

One of the results of the Gainers' strike was pressure on the provincial government to reform the labour laws. Comparing Alberta's laws to Alabama's repressive labour regime, the Alberta Federation of Labour (AFL) organized a "change-the-law" campaign. After two years of hearings and debate the government passed a new Labour Code in June 1988. The result, however, was a more coercive code placing further restrictions on the right to strike, picketing, and certification.

These legislative changes notwithstanding, Alberta was the scene of another militant and significant strike in 1988 when nurses took industrial action. While nurses lost the legal right to strike in 1983, the United Nurses of Alberta (UNA) had continued to maintain a moral right to strike. Refusing to accept an arbitrated settlement, UNA went on illegal strike. Government and hospital managers responded with fines and firings of nurses, but UNA persisted, aided by support from other unions and the community mobilized through the AFL. The strike eventually ended with a negotiated contract.

Against a historical background of repression and coercion, the Alberta labour movement showed by the general support these strikes generated that Alberta workers were prepared to insist on their fundamental rights to bargain collectively and withdraw their labour. Could this labour commitment be sustained in the face of the Klein revolution? Before answering this question, I will attempt to provide some sense of the extent of the job losses resulting from the 1993-94 cuts.

Job Losses[4]

How many jobs have been lost? With the exception of the government service, the cuts have been implemented on a board-by-board, or employer-by-employer basis. For this reason therefore, it is difficult to determine the total number of jobs lost as a result of the cuts, or the broader effects on the rest of the Alberta economy. The worst case scenario was presented by Michael McCracken of Infometrica in January 1994. McCracken calculated that a cut of $2.5 billion in government spending would result in a direct and indirect loss of 40,000 jobs across the economy.[5] Government statements, meanwhile, have been limited to losses in the government service.

In the February 1994 budget, for example, Provincial Treasurer Jim Dinning predicted that about 2,200 government workers would lose their jobs by the end of the 1997 fiscal year. In fact, the cuts have been much deeper. The government's own figures show that between January 1993 and the end of 1994 alone the public service was reduced by about 7,000 positions, including 1,800 through early retirement and 1,300 through attrition. The government also anticipates that a further 1,100 jobs will be lost by March 1997, cutting a total of 8,000 civil-service positions, from 36,000 to 28,000, or 22 percent of Alberta's civil service. While it is difficult to determine absolute numbers, this estimate would appear possible considering that AUPE, which represents not only some workers directly employed by government but others in the broader public service, experienced a membership decline from 38,000 to 28,000 between 1990 and 1994.

Accurate assessments of job losses in the broader public sector are impossible because cuts are ongoing and there are no global numbers. In health care, for example, the majority of the cuts will be made by regional health authorities, newly-established in the fall of 1994. Many jobs, however, have disappeared, and predictions have been made on the basis of the funding cuts that have been announced. When health care cuts of $191 million for the 1993-94 fiscal year were announced, predictions of jobs lost ranged from 1,500 to 2,500. It is estimated that the total number employed in health care in Alberta was about 30,000 before the cuts began. Based on these calculations, the cut of $734 million over the 1993 to 1996 period yields job losses of about 6,000 to 9,400, a workforce reduction of from 20 percent to 30 percent. At the end of 1994 UNA was predicting the loss of 1,800 full-time-equivalent health-care jobs (2,500 real jobs because so many are part-time) in Edmonton alone. Between 1993 and 1997 the University of Alberta hospital in Edmonton, considered a good indicator of what will happen across the health sector, will eliminate about one-third of its nursing staff. While some jobs are eliminated, others are redesigned to save money, intensify work and de-professionalize nurses. For instance, the University of Alberta hospital hired an American consultant in 1994 to redesign work so housekeeping staff could do some nursing functions, thereby replacing more highly-paid nurses with cheaper labour.

Negotiating Concessions

The cuts across the various sectors were announced haphazardly between May 1993 and March 1994. The earliest announcements in the
spring and summer of 1993 focused on health and government services,
particularly welfare. By July 1993 it was known that health care would be cut
that year by $191 million; hence, throughout the summer, employers were
making noises about the wage cuts and layoffs that would be required. Edmonton's Royal Alexandria hospital, for example, in July proposed a 6 percent wage cut or, if that couldn't be achieved, the layoff of 200 workers. By
the end of August the government had conducted its round-table consultations in the health sector. A 5 percent wage cut for workers was one of the
recommendations that emerged. In response, during September and October, Klein "asked" all health-care, municipal, school, university, and government workers to take a 5 percent pay cut. Health-care workers were given
until November 23 to come up with a process for implementing the cuts,
which were "voluntary" and would come into effect at the beginning of
1994. The other sectors had a longer time frame because the compensation
reduction came into effect in the 1994-95 fiscal year.

The implementation of the wage rollback had the effect of fracturing
any potential common bargaining or political strategy on the part of the
various bargaining agents involved in the process. The union resistance to
the Klein cuts was sporadic and local. While it appeared, at times, that a
broad-based and co-ordinated resistance might develop, individual unions
were too busy fighting their own battles and negotiating their own collective
agreements to have energy left to build an effective coalition to challenge
the Klein steamroller. Coalitions did form in the individual sectors, and the
initial reaction to the announcement of wage rollbacks was defiant, but in
the end the government was able to extract what it wanted from public- and
para-public-sector workers with minimal effort. Whether planned or not,
the government was able to take advantage of the labour movement's investment in collective bargaining to derail any co-ordinated fightback: individual unions had to put their energies into collective bargaining to protect
their members' interests. In contrast to other jurisdictions where rollbacks
were legislated, forcing unions to take a political stance against governmental interference in collective bargaining, ultimately meaningless bargaining
took place at dozens of tables across Alberta, consuming the political and
emotional energies of union activists.

Health care showed the most promise of unified resistance, with the
Canadian Union of Public Employees (CUPE), AUPE, and UNA all making

defiant noises. In July 1993, as the depth of the cuts in health became clear, for the first time in its history the Alberta Association of Registered Nurses joined with UNA and the Staff Nurses Association of Alberta to signal concern about the ability of nurses to provide safe patient care. One month later, CUPE and AUPE announced that they were boycotting the government's health round tables; the process was a fraud, they suggested, because the decision to cut had already been made. By October, when it was clear that Klein was demanding a salary rollback as part of the attack on public-sector workers, a health-care coalition had been formed. This coalition of eight unions offered to discuss wage reductions if the government would give them input into the long-term restructuring of health care. Both the unions and the Alberta Healthcare Association, which bargains for hospital management, rejected the request for a voluntary rollback because it interfered with the collective bargaining process. In response, the government agreed to meet with the unions to discuss the overall restructuring of health care.

This coalition was splintered in early December when CUPE, representing 8,500 janitors, clerks, dietitians, and housekeepers, accepted rollbacks amounting to 5 percent in exchange for a ban on contracting out until March 1995. This deal, perceived by some as a breaking of solidarity, angered other unions. Ron Hodgins of the Health Care Employees Union of Alberta (HCEU) said, "I'm shocked and appalled. It's a horrible, horrible settlement. I wouldn't call them traitors, but I would call them very naive." John Malthouse, CUPE negotiator, responded that they did not take the cut because of the demands of Klein, but after on-going negotiations with their cash-strapped employers. It was, in other words, the result of negotiation, not government fiat. Another CUPE leader, meanwhile, suggested that the HCEU wanted to raid CUPE.

Despite this setback, health-care unions continued to pursue tripartite negotiations involving the government and employers. Finally, in December government officials joined hospital administrators and health-care unions at the bargaining table. The unions refused to discuss wage rollbacks until the government and employers addressed several other issues, including severance packages, early retirement, compensation, retraining, and funding for community health programs. The unions, in other words, wanted to discuss terms and conditions of employment other than wages and they wanted some input into the restructuring of health care. Unfortunately and unsurprisingly, the tripartite talks lasted only two days before the employers walked out and the government failed to return to the table.

In November, Klein upped the ante by announcing that the salary budgets for health, education, advanced education, and civil servants were being cut by 5 percent. By December the government was on its way to having health-care workers accept the 5 percent reduction in compensation. The various boards and authorities were then expected to negotiate salary reductions with their employees or impose layoffs. While most health-care support staff (including those represented by CUPE) had accepted the rollback by December, the first few months of 1994 were filled with stories of employers demanding wage rollbacks of 12 percent, 15 percent, 20 percent, and as much as 30 percent at the various health-care bargaining tables. By April, UNA was the only major union that had not agreed to a wage rollback. In August, UNA members at small- and medium-sized hospitals accepted a mediator's recommendation of a 5.8 percent cut and a letter of understanding on severance pay. Heather Smith, president of UNA, conceded that it was not a good settlement but noted that a long list of contract concessions had been removed. Then, in September, UNA members at the teaching hospitals in Edmonton and Calgary accepted a mediator's package that differed little from the settlement at the smaller hospitals.

A similar process took place in education, though given the professional ideology of many of the workers in this sector, there was less likelihood for concerted action. Soon after Klein's November announcement of a 5 percent compensation reduction, an anticuts Quality Education Coalition was formed with representatives from the basic and post-secondary levels, bringing together workers ranging from school caretakers to university professors. The rhetorical response from this group, particularly from the Alberta Teachers Association (ATA), was defiant. Bauni McKay, president of the ATA, called the 5 percent salary rollback a selective tax on public-sector workers, noting that it was equivalent to a 35 percent tax increase based on a teacher's average taxable income. Furthermore, they vowed that they would never accept rollbacks. In February 1994, McKay offered to the government that she would recommend to her members that they accept a 5 percent rollback for one year and then a two-year salary freeze. In return, however, she wanted a 300-day reprieve in school funding cuts in order to give Albertans more say in the cuts, a guarantee to parents that class sizes would not increase, and a guarantee that students would be taught by certified professionals during those 300 days. Klein rejected this proposal, responding that there could be no delays in his budget-cutting agenda. Subsequently, teachers employed by various boards across the province accepted settlements that reduced their compensation by approximately 5 percent in one form or other. The Edmonton public school board, for example, accepted a mediated settlement in April; Calgary teachers narrowly accepted a negotiated agreement in June.

Defiance also ruled in the civil service, at least in the short term. The leadership of AUPE changed in October 1993. Pat Wocknitz, the incumbent president, was challenged by Carol Anne Dean, the organization's secretary-treasurer. Dean, promising to bring a new militant style to the leadership, criticized Wocknitz for being too willing to accept the government's agenda. On winning the presidency Dean vowed to launch a political and educational campaign among her membership and the public at large about the cutbacks. She pledged that she would lead an illegal strike and go to jail in order to resist the cuts if that was what her membership wanted. When Klein made it clear in November 1993 that 5 percent was coming out of the various salary budgets, Dean responded that "You are headed for one of the biggest labour battles that you've ever seen in this province."

On May Day 1994, six months after her election as AUPE president, Dean was asked why the 40,000 AUPE members had yet to react to her call to militancy. Her response was to note that one of her objectives as president was to change public attitudes towards government workers and, to that end, the union had run a series of newspaper advertisements and had sponsored forums on health-care cuts. Furthermore, she noted, AUPE was working with the AFL to build coalitions among groups affected by the cuts. While there was a wide gulf between these actions and the militant rhetoric about illegal strikes, it is clear that Dean faced a mammoth task when she took over the presidency. She inherited a union that operated like a classic business union, with the leadership delivering the goods to the membership on a regular basis. Pat Wocknitz was the last of a series of AUPE and CSA presidents who saw their role as lobbying government for better terms and conditions of employment, not challenging it with the politics of confrontation. It would have been impossible for any leader, no matter how dedicated, to transform instantly such a union.

But this wasn't the only problem Dean faced. As a result of the massive cuts, the union membership was being decimated and, as a result, the dues that supported a service infrastructure were disappearing as well. During 1993 and 1994 a significant portion of the energies of AUPE's leadership was devoted to averting an organizational crisis. During the November 1993 convention Dean warned the membership that AUPE's budget deficit for 1993-94 would be more than $1.7 million. The following July Dean was forced to take action. Having absorbed a membership loss of 8,000 in eighteen months and facing bankruptcy, the leadership asked the membership for a dues increase. While the organization had been streamlined in the nine months since Dean took over, with the departure of 13 employees, it was still forced to borrow money from CUPE using its $1 million trust fund as collateral. But the 331 delegates at a special convention to consider the dues structure were unwilling to accept any increase. An attempt to increase dues from 1 percent to 1.5 percent of salary was rejected, as was an amended increase to 1.25 percent of salary. Rank and file union members, asked about the effectiveness and relevance of the union, suggested that when the crisis of cutbacks came, AUPE was unable to do anything about layoffs and wage rollbacks. It was not possible, in other words, to change quickly a service organization with a passive membership into a political union with a mobilized membership. Nor would a membership with this legacy countenance the necessary dues increase to carry on the fight.

In June of 1994, AUPE members voted 67 percent against a package reducing their salaries by 2.35 percent retroactive to April 1, 1994 and requiring workers to take seven unpaid holidays off per year. The combined effect was a 5 percent cut. AUPE leadership had urged rejection of the deal, noting that there was no guarantee of job security and that low-paid employees could not afford a 5 percent cut. Carol Anne Dean claimed that government workers rejected the Klein agenda by voting the way they did. Klein responded to the rejection by asking AUPE members to reconsider and by reaffirming that the government's compensation budget had been reduced by 5 percent in any event, and the money would be saved either by salary decreases or by layoffs. He said he would "hate to legislate rollbacks."

In the fall of 1994, AUPE accepted an agreement that differed little from the deal that was rejected earlier that year. They voted 68 percent in favour of a three-year deal, including a 5 percent decrease in the first year and no increases during the following two years. Two and three-tenths percent of the rollback was in salary, while the balance of the cut was in the form of seven unpaid holidays. The differences between the deal rejected in June and the one accepted in the fall were that the latter agreement took effect on September 1 rather than April 1 and removed an earlier provision that would have protected from the cut those earning less than $24,000. The new agreement also reinstated the holiday pay after three years. In explaining why her members voted for the deal, Dean said that they were "held to ransom" and that they had little choice, presumably referring to a threat of further layoffs.

Where's the Resistance?

What happened to the union militancy that was seen in the Gainers' and nurses' strikes? In both cases, the broader labour movement rallied to support the striking workers in a show of solidarity that, on the face of it, should have provided a legacy for future challenges. What happened between 1988 and 1994?

In fact, the mobilization of the Alberta labour and progressive movements showed promise at the end of the 1980s and the beginning of the 1990s. When Dave Werlin was elected president of the AFL in 1984, he assembled a progressive staff committed to mobilizing the membership and engaging both in parliamentary and extra-parliamentary opposition to business and government attacks on labour rights. Beginning with the Gainers' strike and continuing through the change-the-law campaign to the nurses' strike, the AFL marshalled the support of labour and community groups. Then, when the Pro-Canada Network was formed to oppose the Canada-United States Free Trade Agreement, and later broadened into the Action Canada Network (ACN) to resist the larger neoconservative agenda of the Mulroney government (NAFTA, deregulation, reduced social spending), the AFL provided the Alberta nerve centre for this national coalition of labour, women's, environmental, and other progressive groups. The ACN (Alberta) was responsible for mobilizing and co-ordinating Alberta's popular response to the Goods and Services Tax (GST). In this campaign the coalition developed a high profile because of the depth of opposition to the tax in the province and the wide range of constituencies (from business groups to communists) that accepted ACN's leadership on the issue. Building on this political energy, in the spring of 1991 the ACN (Alberta) held a provincial assembly in Edmonton with about 135 delegates from the labour, women's, environmental, and other social movements. The assembly endorsed a detailed Action Plan leading up to the next federal election, and it established a provincial structure with representatives from the various coalition partners and with regional committees throughout the province.

A key ingredient of this ongoing political mobilization was the fact that throughout this period the AFL provided human and financial resources to coalition-organizing by assigning a staff person, Lucien Royer, to co-ordinate these activities. The federation thereby signalled its commitment to extra-parliamentary politics and, by implication, communicated its belief that, in Alberta at least, labour could not rely on the New Democratic Party and the parliamentary road for political representation. Royer, the best political organizer in Alberta, triumphed in his job. Beginning with the Gainers' strike, he put together a province-wide database containing information on everyone from the busiest union activist to the citizen who came to one anti-GST demonstration. This information was then used to mobilize people for various actions. Royer put his considerable organizing skills to work planning and co-ordinating a series of actions, from the traditional (demonstrations at the legislature) to the carnivalesque (parades with giant puppets and street theatre), maintaining a momentum of opposition to the "neoconservative" corporate agenda.

The Gainers' and nurses' strikes put Alberta labour in the national industrial relations spotlight and ACN (Alberta's) ongoing mobilizations in the early nineties were the envy of other provincial coalitions. Wasn't everything in place to mount an opposition in 1993-94? Unfortunately, in 1992 the AFL abruptly decided to curtail seriously its support for coalition activities and to reassign Royer to other duties. The executive officers argued that, while it continued to support coalition politics, the federation could no longer afford to commit a staff person to this work. Royer subsequently arranged a leave of absence and went to work for the International Confederation of Free Trade Unions in Brussels. There were three significant results of the AFL's decision. First, Royer was no longer doing coalition organizing. Secondly, coalition work was reduced from a major to a minor federation activity since another federation staff person had responsibility "for liaising with coalition partners" added to an already impossible workload. Thirdly, non-AFL activists in the ACN were upset, and did not understand this withdrawal of labour-movement resources from the most significant progressive political organization in Alberta at the time. These three factors combined to precipitate a decline in ACN (Alberta), to deliver a serious setback to coalition politics in the province, and to stall a momentum of resistance that had been building since the mid-eighties.

Hence, when the Klein cuts came there was no active coalition network in place and the Alberta labour movement apparently was not interested or was not able to recommit the human and financial resources necessary to reactivate the network. To be sure, the AFL continues to be committed rhetorically to coalition politics and has facilitated the organization of a range of coalitions opposed to the Klein agenda. Albertans United for Social Justice in welfare and human services, the Quality Education Coalition in education, and the Health Care Coalition in health were all established during 1993 but, with the exception of a few demonstrations and a series of ongoing meetings in which coalition partners exchange information about individual resistance strategies, a broader assault on the Klein agenda has not been forthcoming. Most recently, a "Common Front" was launched in the

fall of 1994, paralleling ACN (Alberta) in structure in that regional committees are being formed throughout the province. The purpose of the Common Front is to co-ordinate actions against the Klein government by, for
example, targeting government MLAs in their home constituencies. While
significant groups like the AFL, AUPE, UNA, and the ATA are members of
the Common Front, the organization has had little effect on the Klein
steamroller. In the absence of a significant commitment of resources to coalition politics, which builds on the legacy of the 1986 to 1992 years, any
fightback strategy is severely constrained.

Conclusion

Alberta's labour movement, and public-sector unions in particular,
faced a major challenge in resisting the 1993-94 cuts. The province's union
density (proportion of the workforce unionized) is the lowest in the country.[6] The province's labour law discourages organizing and does not allow
public-sector strikes. The New Democratic Party did not have a presence in
the provincial legislature after the 1993 election and the Liberal opposition
essentially agreed with the Tories on the need for public-sector expenditure
reduction. Hence, labour lacked a parliamentary voice in this crucial period. In any case, no one was prepared for the fast, furious, and severe assault on the public sector that transpired. Nonetheless, over the previous
decade the Alberta labour movement *had* built an extra-parliamentary opposition in the face of an historical legacy of conservative coercion and
weak labour-friendly political parties. Future political strategies should begin with a reassessment of that experience.

Notes

1. *Edmonton Journal,* 25 November 1993, A6
2. *Edmonton Journal,* 10 March 1994, A7
3. This section is taken from various sources, including W. Caragata, *Alberta Labour:
   A Heritage Untold* (Toronto: James Lorimer, 1979); L. Panitch and D. Swartz, *The
   Assault on Trade Union Freedoms: From Wage Controls to Social Contract* (Toronto:
   Garamond Press, 1993); A. Finkel, "The Cold War, Alberta Labour, and the Social Credit Regime," in *Labour/Le Travail* 21 (spring, 1988); A. Noel and K. Gard-
   ner, "The Gainers Strike: Capitalist Offensive, Militancy, and the Politics of
   Industrial Relations in Canada," in *Studies in Political Economy* 31 (spring, 1990);
   and R. Coulter, "Alberta Nurses and the 'Illegal' Strike of 1988," in L. Briskin

and P. McDermott, eds., *Women Challenging Unions: Feminism, Democracy and Militancy* (Toronto: University of Toronto Press, 1993).

4. Unless otherwise noted, the information in this section is taken from various issues of the *Edmonton Journal,* 1993 and 1994; numerous union and coalition materials; and the author's personal files.

5. Some evidence for the spread-effects of government cuts can be adduced from recent bankruptcy figures. Across Canada, Alberta experienced the steepest increase in both personal and business bankruptcies during the first quarter of 1995 (27 percent). Especially hard hit was Edmonton, the major site of government cuts, with bankruptcies soaring to 49 percent (*Edmonton Journal,* 3 May 1995, D7).

6. H. Krahn and G. Lowe, *Work, Industry, and Canadian Society* (Scarborough, Ontario: Nelson Canada, 1993), 247.

Chapter Twenty-One

WORKFARE WILL MAKE YOU FREE: IDEOLOGY AND SOCIAL POLICY IN KLEIN'S ALBERTA

Jonathan Murphy

> If they don't take part in the [works] program, unless there is a
> better alternative or good reason why they're not, then people
> should lose their benefits. They will lose their benefits.
> Alberta Social Services Minister Mike Cardinal, April 1993.[1]

Alberta has never been the best place to be poor. Since 1935, the province
has been ruled by conservative governments, and strongly influenced by the
values of Protestant fundamentalism and free market capitalism. Nevertheless, through an interplay between federal initiatives, compassionate Christian elements in the Social Credit movement, and the modernizing project
of the Lougheed government, a provincial social safety net was developed
during the post-war years.

Ralph Klein's election as Tory leader and premier in 1992, and his narrow general election victory the next year, heralded a dramatic departure
from Canadian and even Albertan norms. Welfare recipients in particular
and human services in general became early victims of libertarian ideologues who promoted social and economic policies redolent of the militant right wing of American republicanism.

This chapter traces development of social policy in Alberta and documents the dramatic changes implemented as part of the "Klein revolution."

The Development of Welfare Policy in Post-War Alberta

Between 1935 and 1971, the Social Credit League formed Alberta's
government. The League was an unusual cocktail of Christian fundamentalists, anti big-business crusaders, small town conservatives, futurists, and so-

cial justice advocates, with a healthy sprinkling of anti-Semites and other right-wing extremists. For the most part the coalition was successfully held together during the post-war period by longtime premier Ernest Manning. Manning steered along a relatively moderate conservative path, albeit heavily tinged with Christian moralizing.

Until the late 1960s, Alberta spent a considerably smaller proportion of its budget on social welfare than its neighbours.[2] What help the poor and the distraught did receive was accompanied by a healthy dose of disapproval[3] and frequent grumbling from provincial politicians about the growth of the collectivist welfare State in Canada.[4] Alberta did, however, accept federal assistance for social programs through the 1966 Canada Assistance Plan Act, although it united with others to eliminate clauses establishing minimum standards for welfare benefits.

Towards the end of his tenure as premier, Manning attended to the "human resources" of Alberta.[5] While dismissing those defining "their utopia in collectivistic and socialist terms," he emphasized that "the time has come for humanitarian values and social concern to be registered in a much more explicit and positive way."[6] No doubt he was partly motivated by a fear of communism, but the message was consistent with compassionate Christian aspects of Social Credit. Several innovative programs were initiated, including community development among rural Métis, and a preventive social services program which subsidized local voluntary social service initiatives.

The post-war oil boom dramatically changed Alberta. The small town values of Social Credit conflicted with the needs and mores of a growing urban business class. This new elite was represented by Peter Lougheed's Conservatives, which swept the province in the 1971 election.

While the new government cherished the rhetoric of free market capitalism, it quickly expanded State involvement in the economy. As the interests of Alberta's oil economy collided with those of Ontario, the province became increasingly belligerent in federal-provincial negotiations, and also frequently sided with Québec to neutralize centralist federal initiatives.

Back home, government largesse absorbed most shades of political opinion. Urban liberals were seduced by concert halls, theatres, and modern communications, while rural Alberta was paved with asphalt, hospitals, and seniors' lodges. Government acquired the trappings of nascent statehood, including an airline, oil company, and high-tech industries. Although social policy was never a priority, there was even enough money left over to bring welfare benefits and social services up to the national average.

The glory days were short-lived. In the early 1980s oil prices plunged and the province lurched into economic crisis. Lougheed resigned with impeccable timing, and was replaced by the weak Getty administration. Much of the spending continued, now financed by deficits, but the welfare system was hit by a series of cuts,[7] though even these were soon halted by vocal coalitions of social agencies.[8]

The government seemed frozen in indecision, lacking courage to either cut expenditures or raise revenues. By 1992, Getty's own party elite forced him out of power. The subsequent leadership battle, which narrowed to a two-horse race between Ralph Klein and Nancy Betkowski, caused a sharp split within the Conservative coalition.

While both sides[9] agreed that the burgeoning deficit must be eliminated, Klein built a coalition of supporters financed by Calgary oil money, and dependent for votes on the extensive networks of legislators in rural ridings. On the other hand, Betkowski drew mainly upon more progressive urban support, especially in Edmonton.

Klein's second round victory was certainly a testament to the power of the rural legislators and riding associations, but was wrongly assumed to herald an even more crass pork-barrelling regime. Later events[10] showed a dramatic ideological shift had occurred, in which the urban liberal intellectual leadership and the rural lieutenants had been upstaged by a far right coalition of libertarian conservatives and religious fundamentalists. With support from the Calgary oil barons, ideologues used the province's fiscal problems as an excuse to drastically alter government's role in society.

The New Ideologues

Betkowski's departure from the legislature and the Conservative Party shortly after her defeat cut the last significant link with Lougheed's Alberta. The expansive statist dream had died in the face of declining oil revenues and disastrous attempts to diversify the economy. Betkowski and many of her cohorts jumped to the Alberta Liberal Party, but it fell short in the 1993 election, clearing the stage for the new governing coalition. While economic decisions were left in the hands of Treasurer Jim Dinning and a shadowy group of Calgary businessmen,[11] public explanations of the underlying ideology depended on a heady mix of fundamentalism inspired by American southern baptism ("neoconservatism") and libertarian rhetoric from the Ayn Rand school ("neoliberalism"). Leaders of these two ideological currents in cabinet are Stockwell Day and Steve West respectively.

Christian fundamentalism had long been an important force in Alberta politics, but its importance waned after 1971. Only after the Conservatives lost seats in Edmonton and Calgary in 1986 and 1989 did the deeply religious rural areas regain power.

Stockwell Day soon emerged as leader of the religious right. He grew up in central Canada, but relocated to Alberta and took up the fundamentalist ministry, eventually becoming administrator of a private Christian school, and spokesman for the Alberta Association of Independent Church Schools. His church supporters came out en masse to assure his nomination as Tory candidate in Red Deer. After winning, Day declared, "the whole thing was birthed in prayer,"[12] and promised to speak up for moral issues and less government waste. He scraped in to the legislature in 1986 with 41 percent of the votes, and set out to fulfil his divinely inspired agenda.

Day's public comments identify him with the new American religious-political right wing, whose prescriptive view of Christian ethics justifies the use of political power to force compliance of the whole population. Key elements of this ideology include a moral endorsement of capitalism, "the free enterprise system is clearly outlined in the book of Proverbs,"[13] opposition to welfare based on Biblical exegesis such as, "If any would not work, neither should he eat"[14]; and an effort to 'preserve the family' through attacks upon mothers working outside the home, opposition to birth control education, hostility towards employment equity, and antipathy towards single parent families.

Day opposes improved social assistance on the grounds that there are many jobs available, the problem being an unwillingness to work: "Socialistic thinking has perpetuated an idea that some jobs should be beneath our dignity. If it's minimum wage or if it involves waiting on someone or cleaning up somebody else's mess, that's beneath our dignity."[15]

His rosy view of waitressing extended to justify opposition to employment equity programs for women. Day claimed to know an Edmonton restaurant with "a woman there who's earning just about $60,000 a year as a waitress and really enjoying that."[16] Echoing the retributive approach of the American religious right, he also has called for more young offenders to be tried in adult court and for the establishment of boot camps.[17]

After being appointed chair of the Premier's Council on the family, Day claimed "the percentage of single parent households with children between the ages of 12 and 20 is significantly associated with rates of both violent crime and burglary."[18] He also told of a Statistics Canada study which he said showed, "one in 18 separated women were assaulted compared with one in 56 divorced women and one in 500 married women."

Since his 1992 appointment to cabinet as labour minister, Day has avoided publicizing his more extreme views, though he did weigh in to defend a caucus colleague calling for John Steinbeck's *Of Mice and Men* to be pulled from Alberta schools because of its profanities such as "god-awful" and "god-damn lazy,"[19] and he continued to oppose government funding of abortion.

Steve West cultivates a rugged cowboy image contrasting sharply with Stockwell Day's piety. Indeed his chequered personal history almost derailed his political career. However, his libertarian philosophy effectively complements Day's moral agenda, creating a governing ideology appealing alike to the religious and nonreligious right.

Like Day, West was first elected in 1986, serving one term as a backbencher before becoming parks minister. While other Getty ministers floundered, West quickly downsized and privatized his department. Calling parks too luxurious, in 1990 he cut head office staff by 70 percent and dismantled the branch responsible for planning new parks.[20] Fees for park use were hiked, and management of fifteen parks privatized by 1992.[21]

His appointment as Solicitor General in the latter days of the Getty regime provoked a storm of controversy amid accusations he had abused his first wife,[22] that he had led a vigilante gang in his hometown of Vermilion,[23] that he ate calf testicles as a party trick,[24] and that he had a serious drinking problem which had resulted in a number of confrontations in inner city Edmonton bars.[25]

West weathered the storm and was allowed to keep his position, again implementing an aggressive agenda of cuts, along with harsher treatment of prisoners. He picked up Day's proposals for tougher treatment of young offenders, setting up a work camp in Nordegg in western Alberta,[26] and Ottawa was lobbied to tighten the Young Offenders Act.[27] Departmental staff were ordered to remove colour televisions from young offenders' centres, to be replaced at government expense by "12-inch black and whites."[28] He attempted to reverse a court order requiring the department to pay for juvenile sex offenders' treatment programs,[29] only to be rebuffed by a judge who described his suggestion as "ludicrous."[30]

Inmates' work and good behaviour allowances were cut back, and prisoners double and triple bunked.[31] He suggested parading inmates' work gangs down Highway 2, and intervened unsuccessfully to stop provincial prisoners from voting in the national referendum on the Charlottetown agreement.

After accusations that West had ordered rationing of toilet paper to two squares per person and restricted clean underwear for prisoners, unions warned of rising tensions in institutions. Grande Cache jail guards imposed a week-long lockdown and transferred two dozen prisoners to Edmonton due to fears of a riot.[32]

After less than a year as solicitor general, West was promoted to be minister of municipal affairs after Klein's December 1992 election as Tory leader and premier. Shortly after his appointment, West advised municipalities his department would no longer pay to bury the indigent dead. After doubts were raised about the legality of such a move, he backed off and concentrated on departmental downsizing and eliminating grants to municipalities.

The department's three-year business plan released in early 1994 revealed the overall departmental budget would be reduced from $598 million in 1992/93 to $318 million in 1996/97, departmental staff cut by 47 percent, and all municipal grants were folded into one unconditional block grant, slated to drop in value by over 50 percent in three years.[33]

West gained control of the Family and Community Support Services Program from the Social Services Ministry. The program had been set up by Social Credit to encourage volunteer responses to local social issues, as an alternative to the welfare State. Programs like homemaker services, meals on wheels, boys' and girls' clubs, and seniors' centres were funded in 280 municipalities.

In 1991, a government committee had reviewed the program, finding it invaluable and recommending that funding be increased by 50 percent.[34] While those resources never came, it did get an extra million dollars in 1993 to expand it to the few remaining municipalities not involved, and in November of the same year the program was fingered for added responsibilities in the proposed downloading of child welfare services.

Only sixteen weeks later, it was transferred to municipal affairs and put under Dr. West's knife, where it failed to survive the surgery. It was rolled in with the other municipal grants and municipalities were encouraged to opt out of the legislation and spend the money as they saw fit. Within six months, 111 out of the 280 municipalities had done so.

In a cabinet shuffle after the dismissal of longtime rural lieutenant Peter Trynchy in December 1994, West was moved to the transportation ministry, charged with dismantling the extensive patronage apparatus. Even longtime Conservatives started to become uneasy at West's power and fanaticism.[35] Meanwhile two more right wingers were promoted to cabinet.[36]

Dismantling the Welfare State

Welfare policy in particular and the social services portfolio in general proved a good testing ground for the new ideology. While the new leaders had to build alliances and consolidate power before they could downsize services like health and education,[37] all cabinet factions were happy to see dramatic welfare cuts.

Klein's first cabinet contained the surprise appointment of Mike Cardinal as minister of family and social services. Cardinal was one of only two Aboriginal members of the Tory caucus, and had maintained an extremely low profile during his first three years in the House.

Once promoted to cabinet, however, Cardinal emerged as a clever choice for a government bent on dismantling welfare programs. His own rise to prominence from the poor northern native community of Calling Lake gave his opposition to welfare an authenticity notably absent in most of his colleagues.

After working for eight years in a sawmill, "lost two of my fingers, and gave all my paycheques to my dad,"[38] Cardinal landed a job with Alberta Mortgage and Housing Corporation in 1969, gradually working his way up the bureaucracy, first in career development, then as a consultant for the social services department.[39] He started in politics as a Slave Lake town councillor, and was eventually elected to the legislature in 1989.

Cardinal has a simple analysis of the troubles afflicting many Native communities: "The devastation of the welfare program on the native people in Alberta is nothing to be proud of, and that is why I got into politics, specifically to look at ways of dealing with that issue."[40] "Back before 1955, northern Native communities were completely self-sufficient. The standard of living was low, but people were happy. There was no welfare system, alcoholism was almost unheard of and not a single woman in my community even smoked. Then welfare was introduced into those communities, and within 18 to 20 years people became dependent on welfare — it was devastating."[41]

Few scholars share Cardinal's analysis.[42] Most believe the poverty and consequent dependence upon government assistance of many Aboriginal people results from the overwhelming of traditional culture by the economic, political, and social hegemony of non-Native society. Welfare is only a symptom of powerlessness.

Aboriginal reactions to Cardinal depend upon support for his vision of integrating Aboriginal people. Those who do support his vision are proud of him. John Heavy Shields of Calgary comments that he has "put pride back in Native people. Welfare just took responsibility away."[43] On the other side Joe Blyan of the Buffalo Lake Métis Settlement says, "The government is using him because he's an Indian."[44]

Cardinal surrounded himself with a small group of advisers, most of whom he had known for years. Among them were Don Fleming, a long term civil servant and Cardinal's former boss, who was promoted to Deputy Minister, and Tom Ghostkeeper, a Métis friend who became his adviser on Native issues. Ray Lazanik, a hard-nosed bureaucrat from Ontario, was imported first to oversee the welfare cuts, then charged with privatizing child welfare.

Most controversial of all the members of the inner circle is Bob Scott, the department's media liaison. Ironically Scott's relations with much of the media could scarcely be worse. Scott protects Cardinal from difficult questions, and in return wields an unusual degree of power and a carte blanche to share his harsh views. When a quadriplegic woman was cut off the pension for the severely handicapped, Scott commented, "there are some quadriplegics that may be employable,"[45] while he justified eliminating pension benefits for a blind epileptic on the grounds, "People who are visually impaired are not unemployable. Visually impaired groups would be upset to hear that ... They can take training."[46] As for children on assistance, "Why should we pay for children's vitamin prescriptions when everyone else has to pay for it."[47] When the department was castigated for refusing to pay for counselling for a six-year-old girl who had been repeatedly raped by a baby-sitter, Scott responded, "Is the kid highly traumatized?"[48]

The government was confident enough of popular support for welfare cuts to begin implementing them in April 1993, two months before the election. Publicity for this first round focused mainly upon employment initiatives to get people off assistance, though it also tightened eligibility, eliminated a number of discretionary benefits, and restricted clients' rights.[49]

The works programs offered municipalities and nonprofit agencies six dollar hourly wage subsidies to hire employable recipients who would be forced to participate, in contravention of federal cost-sharing agreements: "If they don't take part in the program, unless there is a better alternative or good reason why they're not, then people should lose their benefits. They will lose their benefits."[50] In practice, many more "lost their benefits" than were placed in jobs. Between March 1993 and August 1994, the adult caseload fell by 54,000 from about 122,000 to 68,000. Only 4,877 of those were placed in jobs.[51] While welfare payments were slashed by $140 million between 1992/93 and 1993/94, the budget for training, work experience, and supplements to earnings rose only $16 million.

Another touted aspect of the reforms was a change to the earnings exemption, the amount recipients can earn before their cheque is reduced. For most low wage recipients, the changes, which allowed people to keep their first $115 of monthly earnings and then 25 percent of anything above that, actually resulted in a net loss from the previous sliding scale. Thus benefits paid to working recipients dropped from $129 million to $107 million between 1992/93 to 1993/94.

The ministry transferred over $50 million to the Career Development Ministry to pay for educational upgrading, no longer available through social services. For people taking high school upgrading, the changes were positive, because more generous living allowances were available, and help was not repayable. On the other hand, anyone taking post-secondary technical training was worse off, as they were cut off assistance and had to take out loans. The government's own estimates showed only a quarter of those cut off social assistance were receiving help through the Career Development Ministry.[52]

Single parents with children were forced to look for work or participate in job training or educational upgrading as soon as their youngest child reached the age of six months. Previously those with children under the age of two were not required to work.

About 2,600 welfare recipients between the ages of sixty and sixty-five now had to claim a reduced Canada Pension Plan immediately, though this meant a permanent 30 percent reduction in their pension. Special food allowances for diabetics and pregnant women were also reduced, and restrictions imposed on dental and drug benefits.[53]

Previous policy guaranteeing families could see an intake worker within two days was abandoned, leaving the destitute without funds for an extended period. Clients would also no longer be entitled to thirty days notice that their benefits are to be terminated, meaning in practice that the department often cuts off recipients by simply failing to send them a cheque at the end of the month. Almost invariably the family then cannot pay rent, is given an eviction notice, and meanwhile has to file an appeal which may not be heard until after they are made homeless. Previously, clients cut off assistance could continue collecting benefits until an appeal was heard.

Most parsimonious of all was the new directive that "clients are only issued benefits other than standard if they request them …"[54] The official policy manual was out of print and unavailable for a number of months, and projects to advise clients of rights and responsibilities were abandoned.

From August 1993, the department slashed payments for school supplies and transportation costs for the children of welfare families. Most schools in the province charge students up to $200 per year for supplies such as use of textbooks. Monthly fees of up to $30 are also charged children to travel to school. From now on, the department would only pay $25 per year for school fees, and $10 per month for transportation. One single mother on assistance responded, "I've told them I'm not going to send them to school. If they want to apprehend them, they can go ahead. That's the only way they're going to get an education."[55]

Caseloads dropped immediately. Though Cardinal initially targeted a reduction of 10,000 cases, which had reached 96,275 by January 1993, the number[56] actually declined by nearly 24,000 between the implementation of this first round of cuts and the second round of cuts in October.

The new cuts were made without even the pretence of being in the interests of recipients. Rather, they were "a move to honour the government's commitment to deficit reduction ... Albertans can no longer afford social service programs which provide welfare recipients with a higher standard of living than that of working Albertans," said Minister of Family and Social Services Mike Cardinal.[57]

His comments pitted working poor Albertans (the $5 minimum wage is lowest in Canada) against welfare recipients. Even before the October reduction, however, single employables received a maximum benefit of only $470 per month, 63 percent of the wage of someone working 35 hours per week at minimum wage. From October 1993, that was cut by 16 percent to $394, just 53 percent of the minimum wage. For single parents, working has also always paid better than staying at home. A single parent working full time at minimum wage with a provincial earnings supplement is $273.75 per month better off than someone who stays at home, without factoring in increased federal benefits paid to working parents.

Benefits declined between seven and 17 percent. Though singles and childless couples were most severely affected, everyone got less. A single parent with one child now had to survive on $766 monthly, a drop of $76. Most discretionary benefits were eliminated, including the costs of utility connection, moving expenses, damage deposits, and telephone installation and operation. After a storm of protest the department did agree to provide a damage deposit to women leaving abusive relationships. Without a deposit it is virtually impossible to rent an accommodation in Alberta.

By October 1994, the welfare caseload was 50,064, down 48 percent from its peak eighteen months earlier. The department made of point of not tracking what had happened to the families whose files had been closed.[58]

Despite the lack of services for sixteen and seventeen-year-olds, a steady trickle of youth arrived at the doorsteps of welfare offices, having fled abuse at home or simply been kicked out. Edmonton youth agencies estimated in 1991 that between two hundred and four hundred youth were homeless, while a Calgary professor interviewed 489 homeless and runaway teenagers in Calgary between April 1992 and November 1993.[59]

Provincial welfare officials in Calgary and Edmonton developed a combined social assistance and child welfare program to help sixteen and seventeen year old youth living independently, providing they attended school, job training, or were working. In January 1992, there were 1,127 youths aged sixteen and seventeen receiving welfare assistance.

In August 1993, Cardinal announced that he would be making it far more difficult for homeless youth to access welfare. Youths applying for assistance at a welfare office were to be refused and sent to a child welfare office for assessment. Only in "exceptional" cases would the child welfare worker recommend assistance. The youth then had to go back to the welfare office and re-apply. Even then they could be refused help.

Social agencies criticized the changes as pushing more youths into crime, prostitution, and homelessness: "The bull's eye for getting assistance has become so narrow and the number of circles around it so much larger, the chance of kids getting help is minuscule," said Irene Kerr, head of the Edmonton Youth Services Association.[60] At the same time, youths who did actually negotiate the obstacles faced a 10 percent cut in help, with a maximum monthly benefit to cover food, shelter, and all other expenses now set at $336.

Consequences

In Mike Cardinal's home community of Calling Lake, Corinne Nipshank and her two children Harley and Karen drowned after the car they were living in went through the ice on a lake as they travelled to an ice fishing hole. The family had been cut off assistance because Nipshank's common-law dropped out of a training program. After the deaths, he was reinstated: "I never asked them for any help today. But they automatically opened the file. They said your living circumstance has changed and we'll be helping you with food and rent and day care."[61] Edmonton's municipal social service department also reported the suicide death of a man who had been denied benefits and could not support his family.[62]

Fears of children from welfare families being turned over to child welfare authorities prompted the child welfare branch to warn that "Children who come to our attention due to S.F.I. (welfare) cutbacks (without lights, permanent address, food) are not necessarily 'endangered' as they can be referred elsewhere to have these needs met."[63]

Thousands of families simply migrated. About five thousand families relocated to British Columbia between September 1993 and August 1994. The influx caused intergovernmental tension and a backlash against welfare recipients in British Columbia. B.C. social services minister Joy McPhail complained, "it's not fair for one province to offload responsibilities on another province,"[64] while Premier Harcourt questioned whether Alberta has a policy to "give people tickets and point on the road map to British Columbia."[65]

Child Welfare Reform

While child welfare budgets were also constrained, the goals of reform were primarily to avoid interference in the sanctity of the family and to implement privatization.

In 1992, a series of tragedies led social services minister John Oldring to appoint the Children's Advocate, Bernd Walter, to head a major inquiry into child welfare services. By the time the 327-page study was released eighteen months later in August 1993, Oldring had been replaced by Cardinal. Walter's report[66] was extremely critical of the department, concluding that, "the system is so bad that no amount of reorganization can salvage it." He detailed cases where children clearly in danger had been left at home with fatal consequences, and reported that child welfare workers felt they could intervene only when "blood is still dripping."[67] He noted requirements that workers be professional social workers had been dropped and that, "Inexperienced workers are routinely required to carry out investigations prior to completion of any training."

Cardinal reacted negatively, suggesting proposed changes were too expensive, and refusing to meet with Walter for several months after the report's release. Meanwhile, the budget for children's services in the Edmonton region was cut by almost a million dollars.[68] A further reduction of $5.3 million in agency contracts throughout the province was part of the October 1993 welfare cuts.[69]

Without ever formally responding to the report, in November 1993 the government unveiled its own plans to keep families together even when abuse had taken place. Parents convicted of physical abuse and neglect could avoid jail by signing a contract with social services and accepting placement of in-home support workers.[70] Support workers, who work for private contractors, are paid only $10 per hour and sent into homes with "no training and little support."[71]

The war of words between the minister and his Children's Advocate heated up, with Walter criticizing the proposal to leave more children in abusive homes: "Aggressive early intervention is part and parcel of good child welfare theory, but the key is: when is in-home support inadequate to protect a child?"[72] His point was underlined the same week. An inquiry into the suicide of an abused nine-year-old boy on the Samson Indian reserve revealed a chronic shortage of services.[73] A few days later, Walter resigned, complaining that, "I gave them ... a world-class blueprint to make a very effective child welfare system and it hasn't been given a moment's notice ... I'm out of the way. I won't be there anymore to point out the dishonesty."[74]

Cardinal tightened discipline in his department, "This is my style of management ... I will continue with this. I will not put up with any of my staff members speaking against policies of the department. And if this continues he will, of course, eventually be fired."[75]

When a six-year-old child was repeatedly raped by her baby-sitter, Cardinal refused to provide counselling to the victim; "Parents have to be more careful and accountable ... no doubt if (the girl's mother) had to do it again, she'd never choose the same baby-sitter."[76] The health department eventually stepped in and offered help. A few months later Cardinal amended legislation so that unlicensed baby-sitters could look after up to six children, instead of three.

Senior staff quit to cash in on opportunities for private contracts. Keith Tredger, manager of program services for north-east Alberta, had set up a government in-home care project in the Bonnyville area. As soon as he left the civil service in January 1994, the government in-home care employees were all laid off and he signed a private contract to deliver their services through his own company. Cardinal defended the untendered contract as only a temporary measure.[77]

In November 1994, the government announced its plan to dismantle the provincial child welfare system.[78] As in health reform, regional authorities would be set up to let contracts and oversee services. Thirteen hundred workers would be out of a job, though many would likely be picked up by agencies.[79] Unions and the former Children's Advocate criticized the plans as providing a cover for further budget cuts.[80]

While the report insisted that "The Government of Alberta will remain ultimately accountable for services managed by local authorities,"[81] Cardinal backed away from that promise in announcing the plan, accepting continued ministerial accountability only "at this time."[82] The provincial ombudsman also warned the new authorities could be outside his mandate to investigate complaints.[83]

Conclusion

There is little doubt that the emphasis on cutting welfare rolls and privatizing services will continue. As of the spring of 1995, the Klein government remained popular. No doubt with an eye to Klein's success, Paul Martin's February 1995 federal budget also adopted a budget-slashing strategy. Cuts to transfer payments for social services, and the promised replacement of the Canada Assistance Plan Act by a new Canadian Social Transfer with few strings attached will bolster Alberta's determination to further dismantle the social safety net.

"Active" income support programs, in which recipients must work or attend training in order to receive benefits, are key to American welfare reforms. Prime Minister Chrétien has also endorsed "workfare" arrangements. In such a receptive environment, Alberta is certain to expand forced training and employment schemes, even though countless studies of American programs have shown that most participants do not go on to secure regular employment, many ending up without any source of income.[84]

Unless social policy advocates can effectively demonstrate the dangers of the Alberta approach, other provinces[85] will feel forced to follow suit in cutting benefits and imposing work requirements. This will lead in turn to a vicious circle of declining services, recreating the depression-era spectre of the poor travelling across the country in search of relief.

Notes

1. *Edmonton Journal*, 16 April 1993, A1.
2. L. Bella, *The Origins of Alberta's Preventive Social Services Program* (Edmonton: University of Alberta Department of Recreational Administration, 1978), 31.
3. Until the mid-1960's, welfare payments were largely the responsibility of the municipalities. In a 1966 speech Edmonton alderman Julia Kiniski complained that welfare families "multiply like flies" and concluded that "we have to be rude to be good." Similar attitudes were expressed regularly by social service ministers after the province took over administration of public welfare (Ibid.,170).
4. Ibid., 44-45.

5. E. C. Manning, *A White Paper on Human Resources Development* (Edmonton: Government of Alberta, 1967).

6. Ibid., p.25.

7. In 1983 welfare shelter allowances were reduced by up to 23 percent. Further reductions in benefits and eligibility restrictions were implemented in 1988.

8. Most effective of the coalitions organized to oppose cuts was the Income Security Action Committee, which was chaired at various times by Brian Bechtel (then of the Edmonton Food Bank), Margaret Duncan (then of the Edmonton Social Planning Council), and Kathy Vandergrift (formerly of Citizens for Public Justice, a Christian social justice group).

9. And indeed the Liberal Party, which replaced the New Democrats as the official opposition.

10. Most notably, the right-wing group engineered the firing of deputy premier and rural general Ken Kowalski in October 1994.

11. M Lisac, *The Klein Revolution* (Edmonton: NeWest Publishers, 1995), chapter nine.

12. *Alberta Sonshine News*, April 1986.

13. Jerry Falwell, quoted in S. S. Hill and D. E. Owen, *The New Religious Political Right in Alberta* (Nashville: Abingdon Press, 1982), 114.

14. II Thessalonians 3:10.

15. *Alberta Hansard*, 23 July 1986, 730.

16. Ibid., 1 May 1990, 945.

17. *Edmonton Journal*, 15 June 1992.

18. *Alberta Hansard*, 3 May 1991, 982.

19. *Edmonton Journal*, 3 March 1994, A7.

20. *Edmonton Journal*, 2 February 1990, B5; and 20 January 1990, A5.

21. *Edmonton Journal*, 25 June 1990, A6; and 25 April 1991, A7.

22. *Edmonton Journal,*, February 28 1992, A7.

23. *Edmonton Journal*, 22 February 1992, A5.

24. *Calgary Herald*, 22 February 1992, A1.

25. *Edmonton Sun*, 6 March 1992, A2.

26. *Edmonton Journal*, 3 September 1992, A7.

27. *Calgary Herald*, 27 May 1992, B1.

28. *Calgary Herald*, 18 September 1992, B4.

29. *Calgary Herald*, 11 June 1992. B1.

30. *Calgary Herald*, 13 June 1992, B1.

31. *Calgary Herald*, 12 November 1992, A11.

32. *Edmonton Journal*, 2 December 1992, A7.

33. Alberta, *A Better Way: A Plan for Securing Alberta's Future* (Edmonton: Government of Alberta, 24 February 1994).

34. "Back to the future: Socred policies too progressive for Ralph's team." In *First Reading*, Volume 12, No. 3 (September/October 1994).

35. "He's doing everything too quickly, too far ahead of the public capacity to accept change. He's like an automaton, a piece of machinery that simply grinds away. West leaves the impression that no-one in government can do the job, that every change must be made right now ... West is too blunt and appears to be ar-

rogant. Albertans have sensed this and it makes them uneasy. 'What on earth is he going to do next'." Al Adair with Frank Dolphin, *Boomer: My Life With Peter, Don, and Ralph* (Edmonton: Polar Bear Publishing, 1994), 107.

36. Butch Fischer of Wainwright was appointed public works minister, while Murray Smith of Calgary became minister without portfolio, responsible for economic development and tourism (see the *Edmonton Journal*, 17 December 1994, A1).

37. In the fall of 1994, deputy premier and rural czar Ken Kowalski was dumped unceremoniously from cabinet after a power struggle, followed less than a month later by Whitecourt M.L.A. and transportation minister Peter Trynchy. Both men had earned a reputation as champions of rural interests and masters of "pork-barrel" politics.

38. Quoted in the *Edmonton Sun*, 2 May 1993, C4.

39. *Edmonton Journal*, 2 October 1993, G1 and G2.

40. *Alberta Hansard*, 26 October 1993, 1043.

41. *Edmonton Sun*, 2 May 1993, C4.

42. There is a vast library of information on this subject by both Aboriginal and non-Aboriginal people. For example: H. Cardinal, *The Rebirth of Canada's Indians* (Edmonton: Hurtig, 1977); and J.R. Miller, *Skyscrapers Hide the Heavens* (Toronto: University of Toronto, 1991).

43. *Calgary Herald*, 12 January 1994, A1.

44. *Edmonton Journal*, 2 October 1993, G1 and G2.

45. *Edmonton Journal*, 22 September 1993, A1.

46. *Edmonton Journal*, 28 August 1993, C1.

47. *Edmonton Journal*, 17 October 1993, B2.

48. *Edmonton Journal*, 5 January 1994, A1.

49. Alberta Family and Social Services, *Supports for Independence Employment Initiatives: Building on Strengths and Focusing on Success*, April 1993.

50. *Edmonton Journal*, 16 April 1993, A1.

51. Alberta Family and Social Services, *Today's Welfare Program*, August 31 1994. Government jobs programs include Alberta Community Employment, Northern Alberta Job Corps, and the Employment Skills Program.

52. *Edmonton Journal*, 4 December 1993, A7; and 18 December 1994, A1 and A5.

53. *Calgary Herald*, 7 May 1993, A6.

54. Quoted in "Welfare reforms have promise, pitfalls." In *First Reading*, Volume 11, No. 2 (May 1993).

55. Bernadette Thompson, quoted in the *Edmonton Journal*, 29 June 1993, B2. After much public and media criticism, school supply allowances were raised a little in February 1994, covering between $50 and $100 depending on the age of the child.

56. A "case" involves a family grouping or an individual recipient of social assistance. The mean average number of adults and children per case is normally around 2.1.

57. Government of Alberta, "News Release," 19 August 1993.

58. *Edmonton Journal*, 27 September 1993, B3.

59. *Calgary Herald*, 22 June 1994, A1.

60. *Edmonton Journal*, 15 February 1994, A8.

61. *Edmonton Journal*, 8 December 1993, A8.

62. Edmonton Community and Family Services, "Recent cuts to social assistance benefits," report to Edmonton city council, 1 March 1994.

63. *Edmonton Journal*, 16 December 1993, B11.

64. *Calgary Herald*, 25 October 1993, A1 .

65. *Edmonton Journal*, 25 November 1993, A9.

66. B. Walter, *In Need of Protection* (Edmonton: Government of Alberta Office of the Children's Advocate, 1993).

67. *Edmonton Journal*, 18 August 1993, A7.

68. *Edmonton Journal*, 13 October 1993, A1.

69. Government of Alberta, "News Release," 19 August 1993.

70. *Calgary Herald*, 9 November 1993, A7.

71. *Edmonton Journal*, 10 November 1993, A7.

72. *Edmonton Journal*, 9 November 1993, A1.

73. *Edmonton Journal*, 13 November 1993, A7.

74. *Edmonton Journal*, 23 November 1993, A1.

75. *Edmonton Journal*, 5 January 1994, A5.

76. *Edmonton Journal*, 5 January 1994, A1.

77. *Edmonton Journal*, 12 May 1994, A7.

78. Alberta Commissioner of Services for Children, *Focus on Children.* November 1994.

79. *Edmonton Journal*, 1 December 1994, A1.

80. *Edmonton Journal*, 2 December 1994, A10.

81. Alberta Commissioner of Services for Children, *Focus on Children.* November 1994, 23.

82. *Calgary Herald*, 1 December 1994, A3.

83. *Calgary Herald*, 9 December 1994, A12.

84. See for example "'Workfare' recipients stay poor." In *New York Newsday*, 25 July 1991; and "Welfare and jobs: Engler's reforms may be less effective than assumed," *Detroit Free Press*, Wednesday 1 March 1995.

85. One of the first actions of Mike Harris' Tories following its election was the cutting of welfare rates (for about 500,000 recipients) by 21-26 percent, effective October 1, 1995 (*Globe and Mail*, 22 July 1995, A1). A while later, that province's new welfare minister suggested that welfare clients might want to move to British Columbia where rates are higher.

A Note on Political Criticism in Alberta Today

Prior to publication, *Trojan Horse* had already ruffled a few feathers of the powers that be in Alberta. The Klein government and the Canadian Association of Petroleum Producers (CAPP), both representing the pinnacle of power in Alberta, made statements that some might interpret as threatening to some of the authors of the book. We quote verbatim from *Alberta Hansard* and from excerpts of a letter by Mr. Gerard J. Protti, then President of CAPP.

Legislative Debates, March 30, 1995 Regarding Chapter Eighteen

Mrs. Judy Gordon (Lacombe-Stettler, Conservative backbencher):

Thank you very much, Mr. Speaker [some applause], what a team.

A stinging U of A political science department paper titled *Road Kill: Women in Alberta's Drive Toward Deficit Elimination* attacks this government as being antifeminist and patriarchal. The paper, written by Gurston Dacks, Joyce Green, and Linda Trimble, starts off with a quotation that reads:

Economy is the bone, politics is the flesh,
watch who they beat and who they eat,
watch who they relieve themselves on,
watch who they own
The rest is decoration.

My first question, Mr. Speaker, is to the minister responsible for women's issues. Mr. minister, considering the subject matter of the research paper, were you ever asked for an interview or invited to comment, providing another side to this political diatribe?

Mr. Gary Mar (minister responsible for women's issues, multiculturalism, etc.):

> Mr. Speaker, I was not asked or interviewed for the purpose of the preparation of this political manifesto.

Mrs. Gordon:

> My supplementary questions, Mr. Speaker, are to the Minister of Advanced Education and Career Development. Mr. Minister, were taxpayer dollars used either directly or indirectly to fund the writing of this overly biased and poorly researched paper?

Ms Karen Leibovici (Edmonton-Meadowlark and Liberal Opposition critic for labour):

> According to whom? [interjections] According to whom?

Mr. Jack Ady (Minister of Advanced Education):

> Mr. Speaker, I have no idea of how that research initiative was funded, whether it was funded externally or internally within the university. I would suggest that any Albertan who has an interest in that should put their concerns to the board of governors of the university.

Mrs. Gordon:

> Could the minister tell us if he will be addressing this issue with the administration and/or the board of governors at the university of Alberta?

Mr. Ady:

> Mr. Speaker, I should also have said that it would be appropriate for interested Albertans to contact the authors of the document and ask them how it was funded. I think that would be fair to do. As far as my intervention: no, I don't intend to do that. I don't think it would be appropriate for the minister to be meddling in the research of the university.

It should be noted that these debates occurred at the precise

time that the province gave the deadline to the universities in
Alberta to water down tenure protection for professors regarding "financial exigency" and "redundancy."

Letter from Mr. Protti Regarding Some of the Contents of Chapter Eleven

Dean Neu and David Cooper published an article in the *Calgary Herald*
on April 11, 1995 entitled "Deceptive Deficit." The article, an abridged version of chapter eleven, "The Politics of Debt and Deficit in Alberta,"
sparked a sharp reply from Mr. Gerard J. Protti, representing the major oil
companies. Parts of his letter are reproduced below. What piqued Mr.
Protti's interest is that Neu and Cooper, established professors of accounting in the business faculties of the University of Calgary and the University
of Alberta, argued that the oil industry was not paying its fair share. They argued that, had Alberta kept the 1983 royalty structure, the province would
have collected more than one billion dollars more in royalties in 1993 than
it did. Their article included a graph showing two lines. One showed oil
production holding just about even from 1983 to 1993 and the other
showed oil royalties plummeting to 40 percent of their previous levels from
1984 to 1986 and remaining pretty level since then. On the basis of the *Calgary Herald* article, the premier newspaper in a city that headquarters Canada's transnational oil companies, the authors received the letter from Mr.
Protti who also forwarded copies to their respective deans, Rodney
Schneck, Dean of the University of Alberta Business Faculty and Mike Ma-
her, Dean of the University of Calgary Faculty of Management.

We reproduce here the first two paragraphs and the last paragraph in
their entirety from Mr. Protti's April 20, 1995 letter to Neu and Cooper:

Dear Sirs:

On behalf of the 190 members of the Canadian Association of
Petroleum Producers, I would like to express our concern with
your article of April 11, 1995 in the Calgary Herald. Our concern does not arise from your views but rather from the clearly
inadequate and illogical research which underpins your opinions. Such poor and, frankly, bizarre analysis can only hurt the
reputation of the two fine institutions at which the two of you
are employed. *By copy of this letter, we recommend to your respective
deans that they have a panel of your peers review your analysis and provide you with their assessment.*

In the following, we provide our comments on your article. Our comments deal first with your analysis of Alberta non-renewable resource revenue and then with your perspective on accounting methodology.

Ten paragraphs of Protti's analysis of these questions follow. The letter concludes:

As academics, I am sure that you will appreciate sound analysis. We urge you to do more in depth research on the petroleum industry in the future before suggesting major changes affecting its survival and the livelihood of many Albertans.

Sincerely,

Gerard J. Protti

President

cc: Rodney Schneck, Dean, U of A Business Faculty
        Mike Maher, Dean, U of C Faculty of Management

The petroleum industry contributes sizeable sums each year to each business faculty.

If the preparation of this book has sparked this sort of reaction prior to publication, the editors are curious to see what further reactions await publication.

G. L. and T. W. H.

THE NEW RESOURCE WARS

Native Struggles Against Multinational Corporations

Al Gedicks

Aboriginal and environmental coalitions fighting against corporate greed and environmental racism is mirrored in hundreds of struggles all over the world, from James Bay, Quebec to the Ecuadorian Amazon Rainforest. This new book documents these struggles and explores the underlying motivations and social forces that propel them. It concludes with a discussion of Native treaty rights and the next stage of the environmental movement.

250 pages, index
Paperback ISBN: 1-551640-00-7 $19.99
Hardcover ISBN: 1-551640-01-5 $48.99

WHEN FREEDOM WAS LOST
The Unemployed, the Agitator, and the State

Lorne Brown

This historical account of the little-known story of the jobless who drifted across the country during the Depression and were drawn into the work camps. Brown's factual and moving history records the desperation, disillusionment, and rebellion of these welfare inmates, and the repressive and shameful way in which they politicians and government authorities tried to keep the situation under control.

Lorne Brown seeks to remedy the dearth of the 30s labour Canadiana with this study of little-known labour camps.
Books in Canada

208 pages, photographs
Paperback ISBN: 0-920057-77-2 $14.99
Hardcover ISBN: 0-920057-75-6 $36.99

BETWEEN LABOR AND CAPITAL

Pat Walker, ed.

Essays on the general topic of class divisions in the U.S., giving both traditional and novel definitions.

337 pages
Paperback ISBN: 0-919618-86-3 $9.99
Hardcover ISBN: 0-919618-87-1 $19.99

FREE TRADE
Neither Free Nor About Trade

Christopher D. Merrett

Canada has been deeply marked by the Free Trade Agreement with the United States and has been brought increasingly under the sway of American trade policy, trade law, and multinational corporations.

The sweeping social and political changes that were initiated and accelerated in North American society as a result of the FTA are the subject of this book. Merrett looks at the mechanisms of Free Trade that are eroding the Nation-State and increasing regional and social disparities in Canada.

300 pages
Paperback ISBN: 1-551640-44-9 $19.99
Hardcover ISBN: 1-551640-45-7 $48.99

HOT MONEY AND THE POLITICS OF DEBT

R.T. Naylor

Introduction by Leonard Silk, former financial editor of the *New York Times*
2nd edition

Naylor discusses the global pool of hot and homeless money... how it is used and abused.
Journal of Economic Literature

As conspiracy theories go, here is one that is truly elegant. It involves everybody.
Washington Post

... a fascinating survey of international finance scams.
Globe and Mail

532 pages, index
Paperback ISBN: 1-895431-94-8 $19.99
Hardcover ISBN: 1-895431-95-6 $48.99

TOWARD A HUMANIST POLITICAL ECONOMY

Phillip Hansen and Harold Chorney

... the themes are relevant for those trying to fathom the post-Reaganite political world of the 1990s.
Canadian Book Review Annual

... their publication in one volume is a welcome addition to both the Canadian political economy literature and the literature on western Canada.
Prairie Forum

224 pages, index
Paperback ISBN:1-895431-22-0 $19.99
Hardcover ISBN:1-895431-23-9 $48.99

MASK OF DEMOCRACY
Labour Rights in Mexico Today

Dan LaBotz

an ILRERF Book

Following scores of interviews with Mexican rank and file workers, labour union officials, women's organizations, lawyers, and human rights activists, Dan LaBotz presents this study of the suppression of workers' rights in Mexico.

... an important offering... it puts the cheerful advocates of open markets and their desire for "economic unity" into moral question... Anybody who has the interest, time or energy to devote to understanding the future of Canadian labour had better read the Mask of Democracy.
Montréal Mirror

223 pages, index
Paperback ISBN: 1-895431-58-1 $19.99
Hardcover ISBN: 1-895431-59-X $38.99

THE CUBAN REVOLUTION
A Critical Perspective

Sam Dolgoff

A historical perspective on Cuba that arrives at new insights into social and political change.

199 pages, index, appendices
Paperback ISBN: 0-919618-35-9 $9.99
Hardcover ISBN: 0-919618-36-7 $19.99

MEXICO
Land and Liberty

Ricardo Flores Magón

As background to the events in Chiapas, here is a seminal collection of essays by the famous theorist and activist Ricardo Flores Magón who influenced the Mexican revolution, particularly the movements of Villa and Zapata.

156 pages, illustrated
Paperback ISBN: 0-919618-30-8 $12.99
Hardcover ISBN: 0-919618-29-4 $29.99